Security and Privacy
in Computer Systems

Security and Privacy
in Computer Systems

LANCE J. HOFFMAN
Department of Electrical Engineering and Computer Sciences
University of California, Berkeley

 Melville Publishing Company
Los Angeles, California

To Kathy, who would rather
read ancient
Aztec than FORTRAN.

 Copyright © 1973, by John Wiley & Sons, Inc.
Published by **Melville Publishing Company**
a Division of John Wiley & Sons, Inc.

All rights reserved. Published simultaneously in Canada.

No part of this book may be reproduced by any means,
nor transmitted, nor translated into a machine language
without the written permission of the publisher.

Library of Congress Cataloging in Publication Data:

Hoffman, Lance J.
 Security and privacy in computer systems.

 (Information sciences series)
 CONTENTS: Franklin, B. A. Surveillance of citizens
stirs debate.—Berkeley, California City Council.
Resolution governing access to police department
records.—Miller, A. R. The national data center and
personal privacy.—[Etc.]

 1. Electronic data processing departments—Security
measures—Addresses, essays, lectures. 2. Privacy,
Right of—Addresses, essays, lectures. I. Title.
HF5548.2.H584   658.4'7   73–6744

 ISBN 0-471-40611-2

Printed in the United States of America

10 9 8 7 6 5 4 3 2 1

PREFACE

This book developed out of a collection of readings used in a one-quarter graduate course on technological methods of security in computer systems. Except for a brief opening look at the civil liberties threats to privacy posed by the computer, the collection is entirely technical, and a good working knowledge of computer programming is assumed. Some knowledge of operating systems is helpful. At Berkeley the course prerequisite is a second course in programming and data structures; completion or concurrent enrollment in an operating systems course is also very desirable.

These readings were assigned as homework in conjunction with the course lectures. The readings should present enough material for approximately 21 hours of lecture material; the remainder of the one-quarter course at Berkeley is devoted to student projects dealing with computer security. As in most readings books, there is similar material covered in some of the selections; I have tried to hold this to an acceptable level.

I would like to thank the organizations and individual authors who permitted these readings to be reproduced for this book. The original source of each article is noted with the article itself. In some cases, previously unpublished material is making its debut in these pages. Dr. Rein Turn provided a very helpful critical review. Mr. David Pessel was especially helpful in some important review and administrative work and also compiled the index. Thanks are due also to Ms. Carol Thompson, who assisted in putting together the collection originally, and to Mr. S. M. Basu, who helped with some of the early technical evaluations of suitability of articles for the collection. Ms. Linsley Dyble cheerfully typed several versions of the editorial material.

It is my hope that this book will help in developing an awareness of the need for measures to protect privacy in computer data
banks and will serve as a vehicle to spread available techniques for
this protection to the computer community. We still have some
time to make sure that computer systems which contain sensitive
personal information are reasonably secure. Many safeguards are
described in the pages that follow. And as Francis Bacon said,
"He that will not apply new remedies must expect new evils,
for time is the greatest innovator."

Berkeley, California   *Lance J. Hoffman*

CONTENTS

Introduction

While methods of protecting confidential data in computer systems are by now well-known, and while new and improved methods are constantly being developed, most computer manufacturers have done very little, if anything, to provide their customers with adequate software or hardware to protect sensitive data from unauthorized disclosure. Citing a "lack of demand" and unknown costs, they currently pass the buck to the harried user, who does not have time to solve these computer system problems—he is having enough trouble solving his own problems.

As a result, most computer systems available today are invitations to disaster; they are like automobiles without seat belts or emergency brakes. Indeed, we are hearing similar arguments against privacy and security controls in computer systems that we heard a few years ago against seat belts—"they are too expensive; nobody uses them; the current system is sufficient."

The fact is that "the current system is not sufficient." While it is true that most areas of computer application do not deal with sensitive personal data, the use of personal data in computer systems is increasing and this use is being accompanied by grossly inadequate safeguards provided by the manufacturers.

We are currently able, by technological means, to effectively destroy the right of privacy. Whether we will choose to prevent this by using technical, legal, and administrative methods to protect privacy is up to the society as a whole. But the technical practitioners who design computer systems and especially those who advise our legislators have a special responsibility. They must have a knowledge of computer security techniques and must be able to communicate to nontechnical people what can and cannot be done with the existing technology.

1

Since the question is more political than technical, and the issue is so important, a book such as this would be seriously remiss if it did not point out some of the civil liberties threats to privacy which have caused increasing concern with the issue of computer data banks. The technical component of solutions in this field is usually only a small part of the solution, and if a technical person confines himself to considering only the technical problems involved, he won't really be solving the problem; he will only be giving the illusion of doing so. For this reason Section I on civil liberties threats is included.

At present, there have been only a few notable invasions of privacy by computer, and in those cases these invasions would have taken place whether or not the files in question had been computerized. However, the scene of Senator Sam Ervin, Jr. of North Carolina holding up a two-inch strip of microfilm containing over 750,000 words (the equivalent of an 11-pound, 1245-page family bible) during a Congressional hearing or the issue of Newsweek which has on its cover a computer system wearing an Uncle Sam hat and equipped with (as peripheral devices) a tapped telephone, a videotape camera, sound recording tapes, microphones, and other snooping devices has heightened public awareness and concern about computer privacy.

We have already started to see some reactions. A data access control plan was required in certain urban information systems funded by the Department of Housing and Urban Development. California law requires an Information Security Officer for each consolidated state data center and continual review of confidentiality policies by the Department of Finance. Criminal justice information system contraints, such as the Project SEARCH administrative regulations and technical guidelines for security and privacy, and the Berkeley, California City Council limitations on the police microfilm information retrieval system (see Section I) are also starting to appear. Codes of ethics have been promulgated by, for example, the New York State Identification and Intelligence System and the Santa Clara County (California) data processing center. These are only a few of the examples that could be cited.

Moreover, more and more federal legislation such as [1]* is being introduced and the handwriting appears to be on the wall, if not this year, then within a few years. We are certainly on our way to some sort of government regulation.

IBM is one of the only computer manufacturers with a clear enough vision of the wall to announce its concern and to fund a significant study of the problems. The other manufacturers have either waved their hands helplessly (lots of talk, but no action) or have kept mum on the topic.

The apprehension among some segments of the public about huge memory banks which contain personal dossiers is well-founded from the technological point of view. At least two firms have already delivered as standard products bulk memories which can store in a small area a one-page dossier on each of the 200 million citizens of the United States and retrieve a piece of information at random in under ten seconds. This is not to say that dossier systems of such scope exist today. In fact, computerized data banks which contain sensitive information on people are not nearly as advanced as the "privacy paranoids" might have us believe. The most sensitive information—character strings of subjective information—has not been put into computer systems for the most part, simply because it has, in the past, been too expensive to store large amounts of text in computer systems. We should not infer, however, that this situation will continue. Precisely because of the technological advances in memories mentioned above, it is becoming economically feasible to store more and more data in relatively fast on-line memories. As the cost of these memories is driven down, more and more textual and subjective information is likely to be stored in computer systems.

There are many applications where this could be a problem. One obvious area is that of law enforcement and criminal justice. With the help of LEAA (Law Enforcement Assistance Administration) funding, many computerized law enforcement systems

---

*References in this section and in the introductory remarks of each subsequent section appear at the end of the book on p. 403.

are emerging, and most of these have very ineffective management controls over who gets what data out of them. Even though
the police claim that only authorized law enforcement agencies
will see sensitive data, the informal law enforcement buddy system mentioned in the National Academy of Sciences Report [2]
ties together a vast network of police officers, district attorneys,
private investigators, detective agencies, and the like. Despite the
guidelines of Project SEARCH [3] or the platitudes issued by
the FBI about the National Crime Information Center [4], this
buddy system will continue to exist with or without computers.
Other areas such as welfare and credit bureaus also are obvious
candidates for large-scale computerization and abuse. Medical
information systems and credit card systems are others where
invasion of privacy could easily take place.

All of the above examples reflect an age-old problem. How
should we resolve the conflict between privacy on the one hand
and data acquisition for better decision making on the other
hand? This is not a black-and-white question, and trade-offs
have to be arrived at. If we want better medical systems, efficient airline reservation systems, faster distribution of welfare
checks, fewer policemen shot when they stop a car, then we
must put some "private" data into computer systems in order
to gain these benefits. It is true that we may increase the risk of
unauthorized disclosure when we put more information into a
system, but the benefits may well be worth the additional risk.
In fact, in many cases, the risk is less in computer systems than
in manual systems. Data are often better protected in these new
systems than in the traditional manual file folders presided over
by flattery-prone clerks working for low wages in large offices.

How, then, can we protect privacy while utilizing our new
machines to the best advantage? The legal controls proposed to
date have already been mentioned. Administrative controls are
dealt with more fully in some other new books which have recently appeared on the topic [5,6]. There is much literature
around on physical security [7] and until this literature is reviewed, one shouldn't even consider what technological controls
to implement. On the other hand, with the institution of adequate physical security and appropriate administrative rules, 90%
of the job is done. Only the last 10% involves technological controls, and that is what most of these readings deal with.

The various techniques which can be used to protect computer programs and data from unauthorized disclosure are by now well-known and have been described in the literature. While research still can be and is carried on in these basic areas, plenty of security techniques exist, ready for use. The articles in Section II do a thorough job of enumerating the available safeguards. However, one of the challenges we still face is that of developing models which will accurately represent the problems and solutions (or threats and countermeasures) involved, and which can be used to test out new techniques for insuring adequate security. Section IV presents several of these models; each of them takes a different approach to the problem. None of them is elegant enough or complete, and development of a new all-encompassing model of secure systems, by synthesizing these or otherwise, remains to be done.

Whether this work should also entail the area of protection, which is not the same as security, is a good question. There has been quite a bit of work done on protection [8,9] which is mainly concerned with the integrity of the computer system and with ensuring that hardware or software does not fail. While these failures lead to security breaches they also lead to failures of the system as a whole and in general I believe this work is more concerned with that problem. Nonetheless, it is not easy to separate protection from security. The topics are clearly inter-woven and are handled as such in this book, in particular in Section VI. The new hardware proposed there and other inno-vative hardware will of course also have to be taken into account in future models of secure systems.

One area which cries out for more work is that of cost meas-urement. We just don't know at this point the costs of various security techniques in terms of CPU overhead, user frustration, administrative inefficiencies, etc. Some initial estimates of the costs of privacy transformations are given in Section III, but even these are merely beginnings; much more experimentation is necessary before we really have a good idea of the costs involved. Moreover, the costs of security systems as a whole have been explored hardly at all. Friedman gives some measures of storage overhead in his paper, and Weissman tells us what actually happened when ADEPT-50 was implemented. Hoffman puts all the overhead-generating code in one place. But nobody has woven all of this together and derived some reasonable cost estimates. Nobody really knows yet what security costs, and that is one of the biggest obstacles to users implementing security measures. Users are afraid of the unknown additional overhead. Determining this overhead is one of the most fertile areas for future research.

We have included Section V on statistical data banks because these types of systems may be implemented by people who do not realize their potential for abuse, and who may not be aware that one can get a dossier from a data bank even though the name and other identifying information about a person are not in the system. Methods of counteracting such threats are presented in the hope that computer scientists can educate the movers behind these "statistical" systems.

Finally, we found it valuable to include a checklist in Section VII so that practitioners could measure their systems against a fairly comprehensive set of guidelines and hopefully find the weak points of their own systems. The many users of OS/360 should also be interested in the description of a more secure modified version of OS/360 which appears there.

Section I
CIVIL LIBERTIES
THREATS

In a recent poll conducted by the American Federation of Information Processing Societies (AFIPS) and TIME Magazine, 53% of a random sample of the public believed that computerized information files might be used to destroy individual freedoms, and 38% believed that computers represent a real threat to people's privacy [10] *. This first section is included to emphasize to the computer science practitioner the fact that the public is concerned about privacy in computer systems.

The first article by Ben A. Franklin highlights the types of data collected by government agencies and fed into computer systems. It should explain to thoughtful computer scientists and others what the furor over data bank privacy is all about and why it has arisen.

A resolution passed by the Berkeley, California City Council which limits and sets guidelines over police record-keeping is included to illustrate steps which can be taken to protect privacy at the local level. This resolution is one of a steadily growing number of policy and legal restrictions on police or "criminal justice" information systems. Some of these include the National Crime Information Center Advisory Policy Board Guidelines, codes of ethics of the New York State Identification and Intelligence System, Santa Clara (California) County's Criminal Justice Information Control system, and the "Model Administrative Regulations for Criminal Offender Record Information" and

*References in the introductory remarks of each section appear at the end of the book on p. 403.

7

"Security and Privacy Considerations in Criminal History Information Systems" issued by Project SEARCH. The Berkeley resolution is unique in that it prohibits information from a specific noncomputerized (microfilm) system from being integrated into any "computerized information exchange system" without prior approval by the City Council of a detailed list of privacy and security safeguards in the computerized system.

In the next article, Professor Arthur Miller of the Harvard Law School lucidly presents the potential threat to privacy which was raised by the proposal several years ago to develop a National Data Bank. Because of the strong arguments presented by Dr. Miller and others, this proposal was buried in a Congressional committee.

A summary of the report of the Project on Computer Databanks of the National Academy of Sciences then sets forth its principal findings and recommendations. The Project concluded that the real issues do not involve the revolutionary capacities for data surveillance that have come into being as a result of computerization; rather, they involve the ways in which computers augment power. Our powerful machines do this at a time when the country has entered a period of fundamental debate over social policies and when the traditional authority of many governmental and private organizations is being questioned. The six priority areas the Project identifies include increased effort on the part of the computer industry and professionals within it to develop technological safeguards which are "available and workable products."

A New York Times editorial on "The Threat to Privacy" of improperly controlled systems concludes this section.

Surveillance of Citizens Stirs Debate

BEN A. FRANKLIN

Washington, Dec. 26—Secretary of Defense Melvin R. Laird's move this week toward curbing military intelligence activities has underlined the gravity with which political leaders in the capital are coming to view the spread of covert intelligence gathering and the permanent storage of such data.

The practice of collecting information on the personal activities of millions of Americans, much of it computerized for quick access by government agencies, has long been under attack here by a handful of critics in Congress led by Senator Sam J. Ervin Jr., Democrat of North Carolina.

That surveillance goes far beyond military surveillance to which Mr. Laird addressed himself, and includes widespread accumulation of similar data by civilian law enforcement agencies. But Mr. Laird was the first leading official of any recent administration to comment on, much less to move to restrain, the growth of such undercover activity.

Mr. Laird disclosed in a memorandum Wednesday that he was placing "urgent priority" on steps to assure that "constitutional rights"—as well as the intelligence needs of "national security"—would henceforth be taken into account in setting the limits of military spying on antiwar and other political activity.

The Secretary was apparently reacting to charges in the last 10 days that Army intelligence agents in Chicago had placed 800 Illinois political figures—including Senator Adlai E. Stevenson 3d, former Gov. Otto Kerner, and Representative Abner J. Mikva—under surveillance to report and assess their stands

SOURCE: The New York Times, Dec. 27, 1970. © 1970, by The New York Times Company. Reprinted by permission.

on issues of interest to military commanders, and that other agents in New York had infiltrated student groups at major universities in the cities.

Mr. Laird announced that, effective Feb. 1, he would insert the civilian authority of the Secretary of Defense directly into the top level of the armed forces intelligence command—taking that perquisite from their respective secretaries.

Senator Ervin and other critics feel that the growth of government surveillance and computerized intelligence gathering on the activities, attitudes, and life histories of millions of Americans seriously threatens constitutionally protected liberties. Proponents say the data collection is justified by the requirement to prevent civil disorders and to properly protect public officials.

The dispute runs deep and portends a struggle. Government agencies do not like to give up the aura of modernity, "involvement" and the expanded activity, budget and personnel that usually accompany an "in-house" computer operation. And they are adding new data-processing equipment at the rate of nearly 500 computer installations a year.

In law enforcement, where computerized personal dossiers are having their greatest growth and controversy, a persuasive argument is being made that the electronic processing of more and more intelligence information on citizen activities serves the cause of justice not only by catching criminals but also by thwarting racial and political confrontations that might lead to violence.

RESISTANCE EXPECTED

"If someone is out there plotting a riot or a bombing," a Federal law enforcement official says, "I think you will agree that it is better for society if we know about it and can act to head it off."

Critics of the Government's development of vast data-bank files expect to try eventually to impose a counterbalancing system of government regulation of computer operations. But the resistance is expected to be strong.

Senator Ervin, chairman of the Subcommittee on Constitutional Rights, is known to be interested in patterning a regulatory system on laws proposed—so far without success—in Britain and Canada. They would endow a special, independent ombudsman-style Government agency with powers to register, perhaps even to license, all data-bank operations, government and private; to demand justification for the records kept, and to enforce a citizen's right to examine and challenge data that could haunt his reputation, his ability to earn a livelihood, his very existence.

Any effort to impose such privacy-protecting controls will be an immense as well as a controversial undertaking.

Counting other kinds of semiautomated records—mechanical card indexes and information on microfilm, for example—the Government, alone, already has various kinds of sensitive information on about 50 million people. The number and variety grows daily.

Unknown to most, for instance, there is now a national computer file in the Transportation Department containing, for police use, the names and offense records of all 2.6 million people in every state who have ever had a driver's license suspended or revoked.

Under a law passed this year, the Justice Department is preparing to computerize and distribute nationally to the police and to prosecutors and courts the names of all persons charged anywhere with drug offenses. A drug user's past record no matter how slight, will become instantly available wherever he goes—by teletyped reports from the computer.

With Federal funds, the states also will be urged soon to pool in a vast permanent central computer file all of their arrest and conviction data on persons involved with the local police or brought to court for any reason.

This system would go far beyond the existing computer data bank of the National Crime Information Center, maintained by the Federal Bureau of Investigation to store and instantly disseminate the names of criminal fugitives and stolen property.

And because it would be a permanent, secret, all-inclusive record of transgressions, even its advocates acknowledge that it contains a threat "to much that has been claimed about the country since its beginnings" concerning the belief that it is possible here to overcome mistakes, to make a new start at life and to redeem disservice to society by good citizenship.

According to Senator Ervin, this frontier tradition in America already is being dangerously eroded by two recent developments.

FOR PLAYING GAMES

One is the remarkable technological advance in merely handling hugh volumes of data. This is a capability of the computer age that, by itself, has encouraged and is used to justify the collection of many new kinds of information about individuals to be stored in expensive "hardware" that otherwise would be underutilized and not "cost-efficient." Several Government spokesmen told an interviewer that they believed their own agencies' acquisition of computers was "for playing games."

Another is that the assassination of President Kennedy in 1963, the outbreak of urban riots in 1967 and 1968, and now the spread of campus violence, "guerrilla warfare" attacks on the police and bombings have done a great deal here to rationalize and make routine a new law-enforcement concept: the keeping of dossiers by police agencies on "persons of interest."

The phrase is an agent's euphemism for "suspects"—those among the law-abiding community as well as among law breakers whose militance in opposition to the war in Vietnam, on Negro grievances or on other matters marks them as possible inciters of violence or harm to officials.

The definition of "persons of interest" used by the United States Secret Service, which has the mission of protecting the President, includes those who might seek merely to "embarrass" the President.

These are persons the observation of whose statements, movement and activities, although often lawful and protected by the Constitution, are believed to be capable—with the vital filing, retrieval and analytic assistance of computers—of giving police and military officials forecasts of civil disturbances or threats against government leaders.

13,200 NAMES RECORDED

To protect the President, example, the Secret Service has begun a computerized intelligence watch on thousands of law abiding but militant critics of national policy. Among other things, the computer can suggest persons for special surveillance in nearly every city in the country when the President travels. Senator Ervin says that he, too, has criticized the President and accordingly may be on the Secret Service list.

The Justice Department's civil disturbance group, organized in 1969, to gauge civil disorder tensions by analyzing intelligence reports, has 13,200 names electronically etched in its computer file of persons ever connected with riots or reported to have urged violence.

Some of this file-keeping activity is accepted even by its critics on a case-by-case basis. A computer file of "malcontents" and the mentally disturbed that actually saves a President from an assassin's bullet, for example, would be hard to question if the data were handled with great privacy and discretion.

But there is no law now to prevent the massive exchange of information from one information system to others.

Many such cross-feeds of data already have occurred or are planned. The Department of Housing and Urban Development, for one, has told Senator Ervin that it is considering meshing its own files of private businessmen and building contractors whose reputations it questions with the 200,000 names in the Justice Department's computerized organized-crime file.

The judgment of one file—perhaps a mistaken judgment—can thus become a pervasive, governmentwide black mark, an indelible decision unknown to its subject and made and distributed without opportunity for redress. It is this prospect that has stirred the sharpest reaction.

The Army has said that its intelligence branch had formerly conducted surveillance of civilian political activity believed to have a bearing on the Army's assignment to suppress any possible civil disorders in as many as 100 cities. Since last June 9, however, the official policy of the Army has been, officials have said, that the service no longer conducts any such surveillance.

PROTECTED AREAS

The Air Force and the Navy, for their part, justify their own separate intelligence gathering among civilian groups on the ground that in a civil disturbance they may have to give "logistical support" to the Army. They may be questioned by Mr. Ervin later.

"Prying into these protected areas of an individual's personality, life, habits, beliefs and legal activities," Senator Ervin has declared, "should be none of the business of government even in a good cause."

"This involves more than the currently popular notion of a so-called right to dissent," the Senator said recently in announcing hearings on Government conduct that he has called a "police-state" infringement of free expressions.

"Our system cannot survive if citizen participation is limited merely to registering a disagreement with official policy. The policies themselves must be the product of the people's views. The protection and encouragement of such participation is a principal purpose of the First Amendment."

He noted that in response to questionnaires, the Civil Service Commission, alone has informed him that it keeps a total of more than 15 million names and index files and personnel dossiers dating back to 1939—10.2 million of them in a "security file" designed to provide "lead information relating to possible questions of suitability involving loyalty and subversive activity."

The "lead information," according to the commission, comes from Congressional and state legislature committee hearings and from newspaper clippings. A proved activist record in these files "without evidence of rehabilitation," Mr. Ervin has been told by Robert E. Hampton, the Civil Service chairman, "renders a demonstrator unfit for public employment under the commission's standards."

A warning against unconstitutional abuses came recently from an important segment of the law-enforcement community. It was included in a 57-page report on the invasion of privacy and Bill of Rights dangers of law-enforcement data banks prepared for the Justice Department's $2.5-million "Project SEARCH."

IRREVOCABLE PREJUDICE SEEN

The project is an experiment in computerizing the police and criminal records of 11 pilot states for national law-enforcement use. SEARCH is an acronym for System for Electronic Analysis and Retrieval of Criminal Histories.

The study was done under the auspices of the California Crime Technical Research Foundation at Sacramento and was headed by Dr. Robert R. J. Gallati, director of the New York identification and intelligence system, which has one of the largest of the existing state criminal-information data banks.

The report insists that only the strictest discretion, control over unauthorized dissemination and right of review of entries by included subjects can save a large interstate criminal-data system from abuses that "might irrevocably prejudice the concept in the eyes of the general public."

The report makes as a fundamental recommendation for any national data system, the requirement favored by Senator Ervin for citizen review of entries. "If a citizen believes that his records are inaccurate or misleadingly incomplete, he should be permitted reasonable opportunities to challenge them," it declares.

LITTLE ENCOURAGEMENT

Insisting, too, on a strict requirement that the criminal data must be purged periodically of the names of persons who have demonstrated that they are not repeat offenders, the report declares that "society ought to encourage the rehabilitation of offenders by ignore (sic) relatively ancient wrongdoing."

The subcommittee has had little encouragement for what promises to be a long and difficult push for reforms against the hostility or indifference of most law-enforcement leaders.

In an interview, for example, a Justice Department official who asked not to be named said that Senator Ervin's drive for regulatory controls over data banks could not be regarded seriously because his proposal would be "unworkable." "Public inspection of our files by those named in them would expose our informants and render them useless, or perhaps dead, and no one is going to make us do that," the official said.

Even while funding the study-group that prepared the privacy report, the Justice Department's $480-million-a-year Law Enforcement Assistance Administration has been spreading millions of dollars in grants for new state and local computer installations at police agencies across the country. They are operating with little semblance of the constitutional precautions urged in the privacy task force report.

One grant of the Administration, for example, gives $18,500 in Federal funds to Oklahoma for a small state-run version of the Army and Justice Department disorder-forecasting surveillance and information system.

Officials of the Administration here have professed surprise that the Oklahoma operation whose surveillance reportedly includes a watch on a "peace candidate" for Congress, Kenneth Kottka, has stirred controversy and inspired a lawsuit by the Oklahoma Civil Liberties Union demanding the destruction of the surveillance data already on file.

The Oklahoma application for the grant, filed with the organization here last June, cites as the proposed targets of surveillance "black student organizations," other activist dissident organizations at colleges, high school," "antiwar draft activities" and "labor disputes, alleged police brutality and other activist-sponsored activities."

Resolution Governing Access to Police Department Records

BERKELEY, CALIFORNIA CITY COUNCIL

ADOPTING POLICY TO GOVERN THE USE AND OPERA-
TION BY THE BERKELEY POLICE DEPARTMENT OF A
MIRACODE INFORMATION RETRIEVAL SYSTEM AND
CREATING THE COMMITTEE ON BPD RECORDS, ACCESS,
PRIVACY AND RETENTION.

BE IT RESOLVED by the Council of the City of Berkeley
as follows:

That there is hereby adopted the following policy to govern
the use and operation by the Berkeley Police Department
(BPD) of a Miracode information retrieval system:

A. *Data Content*
    1.   Data included in the Miracode system shall be
    limited to that:
        (a) Recorded by officers of public agencies di-
            rectly and principally concerned with crime
            prevention, apprehension, adjudication, or
            rehabilitation of offenders; and
        (b) Recorded in satisfaction of public duty di-
            rectly relevant to criminal justice responsi-
            bilities of the agency.
    2.   Without further approval of the Council, the Mira-
    code system shall include only conviction records

Adopted December 15, 1971. Resolution No. 44,825–N.S.

of persons who have been found guilty at trial or who have pled guilty to any of the following offenses:

(a) Arson
(b) Auto Theft
(c) Bombing
(d) Burglary
(e) Felonious Assault
(f) Homicide
(g) Kidnapping
(h) Narcotics
(i) Robbery
(j) Sex Offenses
(k) Weapons Offenses

3. The Miracode system shall exclude unverified data such as that emanating from intelligence sources. The intent here is to prohibit the use and dissemination of data resulting from tips, rumors, second-hand allegations, or information provided by police undercover agents that has not been substantiated by official criminal justice proceedings.

B. *Data Verification; Updating and Correction*

4. In the establishment of the Miracode system, the BPD shall adopt a careful and permanent program of data verification and updating within six (6) months of the date of adoption of this policy by the City Council. This program shall also contain procedures for the correction of inaccuracies or prejudicial omissions. This program shall be subject to the review and approval of the Committee on BPD Records, Access, Privacy, and Retention established hereunder and the final approval of the City Council.

C. *Availability of and Access to Records; Right of Challenge and Redress*

5. An individual or his properly certified agent shall have the right of access to, and the BPD shall make available to the individual or his properly certified agent, the contents of the individual's Miracode record, upon presentation of proper identification or certification. These identification and certification procedures shall be established by the BPD within six (6) months of the date of adoption of this policy by the City Council and shall be subject to the review and approval of the Committee

on BPD Records, Access, Privacy, and Retention established hereunder. These identification and certification procedures shall, after approval, be posted conspicuously at the BPD headquarters.

6. An individual for whom a Miracode record exists shall have the right to challenge the contents thereof, either by demonstrating inaccuracies which shall, if verified, be promptly corrected, or by supplementary information believed by the individual to be necessary in order to make the contents of the record not misleading.

7. Except as otherwise provided herein, access to the contents of the Miracode system will be limited to criminal justice personnel, which is defined to include the following:

    (a) Police forces and departments at all government levels that are responsible for enforcement of general criminal laws. This shall be understood to include highway patrols and similar agencies.

    (b) Prosecutive agencies and departments at all government levels.

    (c) Courts at all government levels with a criminal jurisdiction.

    (d) Correction departments at all government levels, including corrective institutions and probation departments.

    (e) Parole commissions and agencies at all government levels.

    (f) Agencies at all government levels which have as a principal function the collection and provision of criminal justice information.

    Requests from agencies other than these criminal justice agencies to examine the Miracode files will be honored only if such other agency is authorized by law or valid executive directive to do so. The Public Defender has access to criminal history data only for single defendants and only after he appears as attorney of record or is appointed by the Court for that single defendant. Private counsel has access on the same basis as the Public Defender, unless he is a properly certified agent of the individual in a situation not involving litigation.

8. Each agency or individual shall be apprised of the Council policy regarding use of the information and protection of privacy and promising to comply therewith. If the Council policy is not complied with, the BPD shall discontinue criminal history service or the furnishing of any other data from the Miracode system to that agency or individual until the situation has been corrected.

9. The identity of individuals shall not be disclosed on data that is used for research or management analysis.

10. The BPD shall maintain a record of all individuals, certified agents of individuals, individuals and the organization they represent who have been provided access to the Miracode records. Who has obtained access to which records shall also be recorded.

D. *Purging of Records*

11. If an offender is not under correctional supervision and no additions have been made to his Miracode record for a period of time beyond which the likelihood of recidivism is remote, the record shall be purged.

12. If an entry has been ordered sealed or purged by a competent court or executive authority, the record will be purged.

E. *Committee on BPD Records, Access, Privacy and Retention*

13. It is declared to be the policy of the Berkeley City Council that an audit shall be made of the BPD Miracode operations nine (9) months after adoption of this policy by the City Council and every six (6) months thereafter.

14. There is hereby created a standing committee to the Berkeley City Council effective on the date of adoption of this policy by the City Council to be called the Committee on BPD Records, Access, Privacy, and Retention. This Committee will be especially concerned with the area of data security and right of individual privacy. It will have as one of its primary responsibilities the conducting of systematic audits to insure that all provisions of this policy are being complied with. This committee shall consist of a member of the BPD, a City Council member, a civil liberties representative from the Berkeley-Albany Chapter of the ACLU, a member of the general public and a person possessing appropriate expertise in computer science who is not an employee

of the City of Berkeley. There will be no release of funds until the members of the committee have been appointed.

F. *Miscellaneous*

15. All complaints and other allegations of violations regarding the administration or application of this policy shall be brought to the attention of the Berkeley City Council as an agenda item.

16. Nothing included in pages four and five (the introduction) of the LEAA Miracode grant application shall be construed as reflecting official policy of the City of Berkeley, and no provision of the grant contract shall be construed to remove from the Berkeley City Council the power to set police policy on any aspect of police record keeping.

17. Information from the BPD Miracode system shall not be integrated into any computerized information exchange system without prior Council approval. Before any such integration is done, the Council shall obtain and approve a detailed list of technical and administrative safeguards for individual privacy and security which are to be included in the computerized system.

18. The Berkeley City Council may from time to time establish other and further policies and procedures relating to problems of security and privacy and otherwise governing the administration of the Miracode system of the BPD.

The National Data Center
and Personal Privacy

ARTHUR R. MILLER

The modern computer is more than a sophisticated indexing
or adding machine, or a miniaturized library; it is the keystone
for a new communications medium whose capacities and implications we are only beginning to realize. In the foreseeable
future, computer systems will be tied together by television,
satellites, and lasers, and we will move large quantities of
information over vast distances in imperceptible units of time.

The benefits to be derived from the new technology are
many. In one medical center, doctors are already using computers to monitor heart patients in an attempt to isolate the
changes in body chemistry that precede a heart attack. The
search is for an "early warning system" so that treatment is
not delayed until after the heart attack has struck. Elsewhere,
plans are being made to establish a data bank in which vast
amounts of medical information will be accessible through
remote terminals to doctors thousands of miles away. A doctor
will then be able to determine the antidote for various poisons
or get the latest literature on a disease by dialing a telephone
or typing an inquiry on a computer console.

A committee of the Bureau of the Budget has proposed that
the federal government set up a National Data Center to compile statistical information on various facets of our society.
Certainly the computer can help us simplify record-keeping
by assigning everyone a "birth" number that will identify

SOURCE: The Atlantic Monthly, November, 1967. Copyright ©1967,
by the Atlantic Monthly Company, Boston, Mass. Reprinted with
permission.

him for tax returns, banking, education, social security, the draft, and other purposes. This number could also serve as a telephone number, which, when used on modern communication mechanisms, would make it possible to reach its holder directly no matter where he might be.

But such a Data Center poses a grave threat to individual freedom and privacy. With its insatiable appetite for information, its inability to forget anything that has been put into it, a central computer might become the heart of a government surveillance system that would lay bare our finances, our associations, or our mental and physical health to government inquisitors or even to casual observers. Computer technology is moving so rapidly that a sharp line between statistical and intelligence systems is bound to be obliterated. Even the most innocuous of centers could provide the "foot in the door" for the development of an individualized computer-based federal snooping system.

Since a National Data Center would be augmented by numerous subsystems or satellites operated by state and local governments or by private organizations, comprehensive national regulation of computer communications, whether of federal or nonfederal origin, ultimately will become imperative.

Moreover, deliberations should not be conducted in terms of computer capability as it exists today. New computer hardware is constantly being spawned, machine storage capacity and speed are increasing geometrically, and costs are declining. Thus at present we cannot imagine what the dimensions, the sophistication, or the snooping ability of the National Data Center will turn out to be ten or twenty years from now. Nor can we predict what new techniques will be developed to pierce any safeguards that Congress may set up in order to protect people against those who manipulate or falsify information they extract from or put into the center.

Of course, it would be foolish to prohibit the use of data-processing technology to carry out important governmental operations simply because it might be abused. However, it is necessary to fashion an adequate legal structure to protect the public against misuse of information handling.

In the past, privacy has been relatively easy to protect for a number of reasons. Large quantities of information about individuals have not been available. Generally decentralized, uncollected, and uncollated, the available information has been relatively superficial, access to it has been difficult to secure, and most people are unable to interpret it. During the hearings held recently by two of the congressional subcommittees investigating invasions of privacy, however, revelations concerning the widespread use of modern electronic and optical snooping devices shocked us.

In testimony before the House Subcommittee on Invasion of Privacy, Edgar S. Dunn, Jr., a research analyst for Resources for the Future, Incorporated, pointed out that information in the center would not be intelligible to the snooper as are the contents of a manila folder. Computerized data require a machine, a code book, a set of instructions, and a technician in order to be comprehended. Presumably Mr. Dunn's thesis is that if it is difficult or expensive to gain access to and interpret the data in the center, there is little likelihood of anyone's trying to pry; if the snooper's cost for unearthing a unit of dirt increases sufficiently, it will become too expensive for him to try to violate the center's integrity.

Mr. Dunn's logic fails to take into account other factors. First, if all the information gathered about an individual is in one place, the payoff for snooping is sharply enhanced. Thus, although the cost or difficulty of gaining access may be great, the amount of dirt available once access is gained is also great. Second, there is every reason to believe that the art of electronic surveillance will continue to become more efficient and economical. Third, governmental snooping is rarely deterred by cost.

Mr. Dunn also ignores a number of special dangers posed by a computerized National Data Center. Ever since the federal government's entry into the taxation and social welfare spheres, increasing quantities of information have been recorded. Moreover, as recording processes have become mechanized and less cumbersome, there also has been centralization and collation of information. In something akin to Parkinson's Law, the increase in information-handling capacity has created a tendency toward more extensive manipulation and analysis of recorded data, which, in turn, has required the collection of more and more data. The creation of the Data Center with electronic storage and retrieval capacity will accelerate this pattern.

Any increase in the amount of recorded information is certain to increase the risk of errors in reporting and recording and indexing. Information distortion also will be caused by machine malfunctioning. Moreover, people working with the data in Washington or at a distance through remote terminals can misuse the information. As information accumulates, the contents of an individual's computerized dossier will appear more and more impressive and will impart a heightened sense of reliability to the user, which, coupled with the myth of computer infallibility, will make it less likely that the user will try to verify the recorded data. This will be true despite the "softness" or "imprecision" of much of the data. Our success or failure in life ultimately may turn on what other people decide to put into our files and on the programmer's ability, or inability, to evaluate, process, and interrelate information. The great bulk of the information likely to find its way into the center will be gathered and processed by relatively unskilled and unimaginative people who lack discrimination and sensitivity. Furthermore, a computerized file has a certain indelible quality—adversities cannot be overcome simply by the passage of time.

There are further dangers. The very existence of a National Data Center may encourage certain federal officials to engage in questionable surveillance tactics. For example, optical scanners—devices with the capacity to read a variety of type fonts or handwriting at fantastic rates of speed—could be used to monitor our mail. By linking scanners with a computer system, the information drawn in by the scanner would be converted into machine-readable form and transferred into the subject's file in the National Data Center.

Then, with sophisticated programming, the dossiers of all of the surveillance subject's correspondents could be produced at the touch of a button, and an appropriate entry—perhaps "associates with known criminals"—could be added to all of them. As a result, someone who simply exchanges Christmas cards with a person whose mail is being monitored might find himself under surveillance or might be turned down when he applies for a job with the government or requests a government grant or applies for some other governmental benefit. An untested, impersonal, and erroneous computer entry such as "associates with known criminals" has marked him, and he is helpless to rectify the situation. Indeed, it is likely that he would not even be aware that the entry existed.

These tactics, as well as the possibility of coupling wiretapping and computer processing, undoubtedly will be extremely attractive to overzealous law-enforcement officers. Similarly, the ability to transfer into the National Data Center quantities of information maintained in nonfederal files—credit ratings, educational information from schools and universities, local and state tax information, and medical records—will enable governmental snoopers to obtain data that they have no authority to secure on their own.

The compilation of information by unskilled personnel also creates serious problems of accuracy. It is not simply a matter of the truth or falsity of what is recorded. Information can be entirely accurate and sufficient in one context and wholly incomplete and misleading in another. For example, the bare statement of an individual's marital status has entirely different connotations to the selective service, a credit bureau, the Internal Revenue Service, and the social security administration. Consider a computer entry of "divorced" and the different embellishment that would be necessary in each of those contexts to portray an accurate picture of an individual's situation.

The question of context is most graphically illustrated by the unexplained and incomplete arrest record. It is unlikely that a citizen whose file contains an entry "arrested, 6/1/42; convicted felony, 1/6/43; three years, federal penitentiary" would be given federal employment or be accorded the governmental courtesies accorded other citizens. Yet the subject may simply have been a conscientious objector. And what about the entry "arrested, disorderly conduct; sentenced six months Gotham City jail." Without further explanation, who would know that the person involved was a civil rights demonstrator whose conviction was reversed on appeal?

Finally, the risks to privacy created by a National Data Center lie not only in the misuse of the system by those who desire to injure others or who can obtain some personal advantage by doing so. There also is a legitimate concern that government employees in routine clerical positions will have the capacity to inflict damage through negligence, sloppiness, thoughtlessness, or sheer stupidity, by unintentionally rendering a record inaccurate, or losing it, or disseminating its contents to people not authorized to see it.

To ensure freedom from governmental intrusion, Congress must legislate reasonably precise standards regarding the information that can be recorded in the National Data Center. Certain types of information should not be recorded even if it is technically feasible to do so and a legitimate administrative objective exists. For example, it has long been "feasible," and from some vantage points "desirable," to require citizens to carry and display passports when traveling in this country, or to require universal fingerprinting. But we have not done so because these encroachments on our liberties are deemed inconsistent with the philosophical fiber of our society. Likewise, highly personal information, especially medical and psychiatric information, should not be permitted in the center unless human life depends upon recording it.

Legislation sharply limiting the information which federal agencies and officials can extract from private citizens is absolutely essential. To reinforce these limitations, the statute creating the Data Center should prohibit recording any information collected without specific congressional authorization. Until the quality of the center's operations and the nature of its impact on individual privacy can be better perceived, the center's activities should be restricted to the preservation of factual data.

The necessary procedural and technical safeguards seem to fall into two categories: those needed to guarantee the accuracy and integrity of the stored information, and those needed to control its dissemination.

To ensure the accuracy of the center's files, an individual should have an opportunity to correct errors in information concerning him. Perhaps a print-out of his computer file should be sent to him once a year. Admittedly, this process would be expensive; some agencies will argue that the value of certain information will be lost if it is known that the government has it; and there might be squabbles between citizens and the Data Center concerning the accuracy of the file that would entail costly administrative proceedings. Nonetheless, the right of a citizen to be protected against governmental dissemination of misinformation is so important that we must be willing to pay some price to preserve it. Instead of an annual mailing, citizens could be given access to their files on request, perhaps through a network of remote computer terminals situated in government buildings throughout the country. What is necessary is a procedure for periodically determining when data are outmoded or should be removed from the file.

Turning to the question of access, the center's computer hardware and software must be designed to limit access to the information. A medical history given to a government doctor in connection with an application for veteran's benefits should not be available to federal employees not legitimately involved in processing the application. One solution may be to store information according to its sensitivity or its accessibility, or both. Then, governmental officials can be assigned access keys that will let them reach only those portions of the center's files that are relevant to their particular governmental function.

Everyone directing an inquiry to the center or seeking to deposit information in it should be required to identify himself. Finger- or voice-prints ultimately may be the best form of identification. As snooping techniques become more sophisticated, systems may even be needed to counter the possibility of forgery or duplication; perhaps an answer-back system or a combination of finger- and voice-prints will be necessary. In addition, the center should be equipped with protector files to record the identity of inquirers, and these files should be audited to unearth misuse of the system. It probably will also be necessary to audit the programs controlling the manipulation of the files and access to the system to make sure that no one has inserted a secret "door" or a password permitting entry to the data by unauthorized personnel. It is frightening to realize that at present there apparently is no foolproof way to prevent occasional "monitor intrusion" in large data-processing systems. Additional protection against these risks can be achieved by exercising great care in selecting programming personnel.

In the future, sophisticated connections between the center and federal offices throughout the country and between the federal center and numerous state, local, and private centers probably will exist. As a result, information will move into and out of the center over substantial distances by telephone lines or microwave relays. The center's "network" character will require information to be protected against wiretapping and other forms of electronic eavesdropping. Transmission in the clear undoubtedly will have to be proscribed, and data in machine-readable form will have to be scrambled or further encoded so that they can be rendered intelligible only by a decoding process built into the system's authorized terminals. Although it may not be worth the effort or expense to develop completely breakproof codes, sufficient scrambling or coding to make it expensive for an eavesdropper to intercept the center's transmission will be necessary. If information in the center is arranged according to sensitivity or accessibility, the most efficient procedure may be to use codes of different degrees of complexity.

At a minimum, congressional action is necessary to establish the appropriate balance between the needs of the national government in accumulating, processing, and disseminating information and the right of individual privacy. This legislation must be reinforced by statutory civil remedies and penal sanctions.

Testimony before Congress concerning the intrusive activities of the Post Office, the Internal Revenue Service, and the Immigration and Naturalization Service gives us cause to balk at delegating authority over the Data Center to any of the agencies that have a stake in the content of data collected by the government. Some federal personnel are already involved in mail-cover operations, electronic bugging, wiretapping, and other invasions of privacy, and undoubtedly they would try to crack the security of any Data Center that maintains information on an individual basis. Thus it would be folly to leave the center in the hands of any agency whose employees are known to engage in antiprivacy activities. Similarly, the center must be kept away from government officials who are likely to become so entranced with operating sophisticated machinery and manipulating large masses of data that they will not respect an individual's right to privacy.

The conclusion seems inescapable: control over the center must be lodged outside existing channels. A new, completely independent agency, bureau, or office should be established—perhaps as an adjunct to the Census Bureau or the National Archives—to formulate policy under whatever legislative guidelines are enacted to ensure the privacy of all citizens. The organization would operate the center, regulate the nature of the information that can be recorded and stored, ensure its accuracy, and protect the center against breaches of security.

The new agency's ability to avoid becoming a captive of the governmental units using the center would be crucial. Perhaps with proper staffing and well-delineated lines of authority to Congress or the President, the center could achieve the degree of independence needed to protect individuals against governmental or private misuse of information in the center. At the other end of the spectrum, the center cannot become an island unto itself, populated by technocrats whose conduct is shielded by the alleged omniscience of the machines they manage and who are neither responsive nor responsible to anyone.

The proposed agency should be established before the center is planned. To date, there has been virtually no meaningful exchange among scientists, technicians, legal experts, and government people on the implications of the center. The center also might consider supporting some of the planned nonfederal computer networks, such as the Interuniversity Communications Council's (EDUCOM) plan to link the major universities together, using them as models or operating laboratories to test procedures and hardware for the federal center.

To satisfy those who argue for the early establishment of a purely statistical Data Center, it might be possible for the proposed agency to set up a modest center in which information which does not invade privacy could be made available to government officials, educators, and private researchers. Other federal agencies might establish satellite centers that would contain information too sensitive to be recorded in the statistical center during that institution's formative period, although the data in satellites ultimately might be transferred to the national center.

The threat to individual privacy posed by the computer comes from the private sector as well as the proposed federal Data Center. Each year state and local governments, educational institutions, trade associations, and industrial firms establish data centers that collect and store quantities of information about individuals. Because the high cost of computer installation forces many organizations to oper-age on a time-share basis, the nonfederal centers pose a special danger to privacy. Without effective screening and built-in security devices, one participant, accidentally or deliberately, may invade and extract or alter the computer files of another participant. Moreover, because many time-share systems operate over large geographic areas, their transmissions will be vulnerable to tapping or malicious destruction unless they are scrambled or encoded. Right now, a mailing list containing 150 to 170 million names, accompanied by addresses and financial data, is being compiled. The list is so structured that it yields sublists of people in various vocational and avocational categories. Where the necessary information to produce this monster came from and how one gets off the list are mysteries.

Currently there are more than two thousand independent credit bureaus in the United States, many of whose files are being computerized. Eventually, these bureaus will make a network of their computers, creating a ready source of detailed information about an individual's finances. The accuracy of these records will become increasingly crucial; an honest dispute between a consumer and a retailer over a bill may produce an unexplained and unexpungeable "no pay" evaluation in the computer and result in considerable damage to the buyer's credit rating.

In testimony before the House subcommittee, the director of the New York State Identification and Intelligence System described a data bank containing files on "known" criminals that ultimately will contain millions of entries. He expressed a willingness to exchange information with police officials in other states as soon as the state systems could be meshed. If this system is tied into the National Data Center or New York's Bureau of Motor Vehicles or welfare agencies, it would permit someone to direct an inquiry to the computer file of "known" criminals, find an entry under the name of his subject, and rely on that entry to the subject's detriment without attempting to verify its accuracy.

Congress should consider the need for legislation setting standards to be met by nonfederal computer organizations in providing information about private persons and restraining federal officers from access to certain types of information from nonfederal data centers. Nonfederal systems should be required to install some protective devices and procedures. This is not to suggest that Congress should necessarily impose the same controls on nonfederal systems that it may choose to impose on the federal center. But a protector file to record the source of inquiries and modest encoding would probably prevent wide-scale abuse, although security needs vary from system to system. Since security may be facilitated by installing protective devices in the computer hardware itself, the possible need for regulation of certain aspects of computer manufacturing also should be taken into account.

The possibility of regulating transmission between federal and nonfederal centers and the interaction among nonfederal centers also should be considered. The specter of a federal agency, such as the Veterans' Administration, reaching into a citizen's medical file in a data center operated by a network of hospitals to augment the federal center's file is a disturbing one. Regulating the security of the transmissions and imposing sanctions for noncompliance and eavesdropping would preserve individual privacy against governmental snooping and bureaucratic spinelessness or perfidy.

Summary of the
National Academy of Sciences
Databank Report

ALAN F. WESTIN AND ASSOCIATES

The United States has become a records-oriented society. In each major zone of personal and civic life (education, employment, credit, taxation, health, welfare, licensing, law enforcement, etc.), formal, cumulative records are assembled about each of us by hundreds of private and government record-keeping organizations. These personal histories are relied on heavily by the collecting organizations in making many decisions about our rights, benefits, and opportunities, and informal networks for sharing record-information among public and private organizations have become a common feature of organizational life heavily dependent on credentials.

During the past two decades, as most government agencies and private organizations have been computerizing their large-scale files, the American public has become concerned that dangerous changes might be taking place in this record-keeping process. Because of the computer's enormous capacities to record, store, process, and distribute data, at great speeds and in enormous volumes, it is feared that far more personal data might be assembled about the individual than it had been feasible to collect before; that much greater sharing of confidential information might take place among the computerized record holders; and that there might be a lessening of the

SOURCE: Dr. Alan F. Westin. Reprinted by permission of the project director.

individual's ability to know what records have been created about him, and to challenge their accuracy or completeness.

DATABANKS IN A FREE SOCIETY [2] is the report of the first nationwide, factual study of what the use of computers is actually doing to record-keeping processes in the United States, and what the growth of large-scale databanks, both manual and computerized, mean for the citizen's constitutional rights to privacy and due process. It also outlines the kinds of public policy issues about the use of databanks in the 1970's that must be resolved if a proper balance between the individual's civil liberties and society's needs for information is to be achieved.

HOW THE STUDY WAS CONDUCTED

The Project on Computer Data Banks was a three-year research study conducted under the auspices of the Computer Science and Engineering Board of the National Academy of Sciences, under grants of $164,000 from Russell Sage Foundation. The Director of the Project was Dr. Alan F. Westin, Professor of Public Law and Government, Columbia University, and author of the well-known book, Privacy and Freedom, published in 1967. An interdisciplinary staff of seven scholars from the fields of law, computer science, and the social sciences collaborated in the research. The project received continuing guidance not only from the Computer Science and Engineering Board but also a special Advisory Board of 18 prominent figures in public life whose views spanned the full spectrum of opinion on issues of databanks and civil liberties. The final report of the project was written by Dr. Westin and Mr. Michael A. Baker, Assistant Director of the Project and an Instructor in Sociology at Brooklyn College of the City University of New York.

The major sources collected and used by the Project include:

1. Documentary materials on computerized record systems in more than 500 government agencies and private organizations.

2. Detailed on-site staff visits to 55 of the most advanced computerizing organizations, ranging across the most sensitive fields of personal record-keeping.

3. Replies from over 1500 organizations in a national mail survey of developments in computerization and record-keeping among government agencies and private organizations.

4. Extensive interviews with officials from computer companies, software houses, systems consulting firms, industry

associations, civil liberties groups, labor unions, consumer organizations, minority-rights organizations, and professional associations.

5. Legal, legislative, and regulatory-agency materials dealing with databank issues in 25 distinct major fields of personal record-keeping.

6. Materials and interviews on the state of databank developments and regulatory controls in 23 foreign nations, for purposes of comparison with the United States.

HIGHLIGHTS OF THE REPORT

1. A great many commentators have warned that the spread of computers is fundamentally altering the balance between information policies of organizations and individual rights to privacy that marked past eras of record-keeping. Compared to what was done in the manual era, it is said, the new capacities of the computer inevitably lead organizations to collect more detailed and intrusive personal information about individuals; to consolidate confidential information from previously separate files; and to share confidential personal data with government agencies and private organizations that had not received it before. The Project's findings from visits to 55 organizations with highly advanced computer applications is that computerization is not yet having such effects in the overwhelming majority of such organizations. For a combination of technological and organizational reasons, central databank developments are far from being as advanced as many public commentaries have assumed. Organizations have so far failed to achieve the "total" consolidation of their information about individuals which raised civil liberties alarms when such goals were announced in the 1960's by various government agencies or private organizations.

Further, in computerizing their records on individuals, organizations have generally carried over the same policies on data collection and sharing that law and administrative traditions in each field had set in the pre-computer era. Where new law or practices have evolved to protect individual liberties over the past decade, organizations with computerized systems have followed such new policies as fully as those that still use manual files and procedures. Even the most highly computerized organizations continue to rely heavily on manual record-keeping and retain in their paper files the most sensitive personal information they possess.

2.   Another widely held fear is that computerization makes it more difficult for the individual to know what is in the file about him, to have errors corrected, or have the data erased where public policy specifies that certain information about an individual's past should be ignored. The Project's inspection of advanced systems showed that notice to the individual about a record's existence, opportunity to inspect and challenge that record, and policies as to the removal of out-of-date or irrelevant information were not being substantially altered by computerization. Where policies affording individuals rights of due process such as the above had been provided in an organization prior to computerization, those rules are being followed in the new computerized systems as well. Where no such rights were given, the adoption of computers has not made the situation either worse or better. Neither has computerization introduced impersonal decision making in systems where this was not present before, nor forced organizations into greater reliance on "the record" in making decisions about clients, customers, or citizens. Where abuses along these lines were present in computerized systems— raising serious due process questions—they had been carried over from the high-volume "processing" of people in the manual era.

Over and over again, the Project's findings indicate profound public misunderstanding about the effect of computers on large-scale record systems. To some extent, the inflated claims and proposals of organizational managers about the capacities of their computer systems helped to generate what were in fact baseless privacy concerns on the part of the public. In addition, as the Project shows with respect to law enforcement uses and airline-reservations and charge-card systems, many commentators on computers and privacy issues have failed to do adequate research into the actual operations of systems about which they write, and have presented entirely incorrect pictures to the press and public about how these computer systems work. The danger in this, the report points out, is that we may give up the fight in the belief that we have already lost. "If we assume that computer users are already doing things that they are not, we risk surrendering without a fight the border between properly limited and surveillance-oriented computer applications. . .The question of what border control measures should be adopted can hardly be understood and properly considered. . .if the public and opinion leaders assume that the borders have already been obliterated."

3.   Computerization in advanced organizations is producing changes in record-keeping methods that can increase the efficiency with which organizations carry out their basic decision making about

the people they process or serve. Computerization is making it possible for many organizations to maintain more up-to-date and complete records; obtain faster responses to inquiries about a given individual; and make more extensive use of information already in the files. Computers have also made possible dramatic expansion of networks for exchange of data among organizations that have shared data since pre-computer days; and the creation of some large data bases of information about people that would not have been feasible without automation. These changes have been felt already in police information systems, national credit reporting systems, charge card systems, and others.

4.   Looking at technological trends for the remaining years of the 1970's, the Report forecasts that while there will be important continued increases in computer capabilities, no developments are now foreseeable that will alter the technological, organizational, and socio-political considerations that presently frame the databanks and civil liberties issue. Organizations will have more flexible, reliable, and cost-effective computer systems to use in pursuit of their policies, but these will not represent a radical departure from the computer capabilities presently available. The most important development with implications for civil liberties interests will be an increase in the ease with which data can be shared among organizations which have computers, coupled with a reduction in the cost of doing so. This will make it imperative that legal boundaries as to data-sharing are set as clearly as possible.

5.   The Project concluded that the real issue of databanks and civil liberty facing the nation today is not that revolutionary new capacities for data surveillance have come into being as a result of computerization. The real issue is that computers arrived to augment the power of organizations just when the United States entered a period of fundamental debate over social policies and organizational practices, and when the traditional authority of government institutions and private organizations has become the object of wide-spread dissent. Important segments of the population have challenged the goals of major organizations that use personal records to control the rights, benefits, and opportunities of Americans. There is also debate over the criteria that are used to make such judgments (religious, racial, political, cultural, sexual, educational, etc.), and over the procedures by which the decisions are reached, especially those that involve secret proceedings and prevent individuals from having access to their own records. Computers are making the record-keeping of many organizations more efficient precisely at the moment when

trust in many large organizations is low and when major segments of the American population are calling for changes in values that underlie various social programs, for new definitions of personal rights, and for organizational authorities to make their decision making procedures more open to public scrutiny and to the review of specific individuals involved.

6.   Despite the rapid spread of computers, there has been little so far by way of new legislation, judicial rulings, regulatory-agency rules, or other legal remedies defining new rights to privacy and due process in major record systems. The Report stresses that, because of the increased efficiency of record-keeping and the growing intensity of the public's concern, the middle 1970's is the moment when law-makers and the public must confront both long-standing and newly raised civil liberties issues, and evolve a new structure of law and policy to apply principles of privacy and due process to large-scale record-keeping.

7.   The Report identifies six areas of priority for public action, and presents examples of specific policy measures under each of these that ought to be seriously considered by policy makers:

A.   Development of laws to give the individual a right of access and challenge to almost every file in which records about him are kept by city, county, state, or government agencies. At stake here is the possibility that, denied access to records being used for decisions about himself, the citizen is left with "feelings of powerlessness and the conviction that government authority is fundamentally arbitrary."

At the very least, citizens ought to know what record systems exist in government agencies. A Citizen's Guide to Files, published at every appropriate level of government jurisdiction, should "provide the citizen with a thorough, detailed and non-technical directory of the record systems that contain information about him, and the general rules under which it is being held and used." Providing adequate due process protection in government files, the Report suggests, is best achieved by assuming that individuals should be able to see and get a copy of any records used to affect them personally—with the record-keeping agency "bearing the burden of proving that some specific public interest justifies denying access."

B.   Development of explicit laws or rules balancing confidentiality and data-sharing in many sensitive record systems that today do not have clearly defined rules. Among these would be rules governing the provision of information to law enforcement agencies from bank accounts, travel and entertainment card records, airline and hotel reservation systems, etc. The Report predicts that one or two large systems will come to dominate in each of these areas. "This development will make the individual's account record more comprehensive and a very inviting target for investigators of all kinds. With that rise in sensitivity and attractiveness ought to go legislative enactments spelling out retention and destruction policies, confidentiality rules, and procedures for protecting individual rights when outsiders seek to obtain access for what are asserted to be lawful and necessary purposes."

As a case study in how not to build new record systems, the Report discusses some of the major Administration and Congressional proposals for national welfare reform, which generally hinge on the availability of computers for massive data storage and exchange. Several of the welfare system proposals contain "sweeping authorizations for data collection and sharing but almost nothing by way of confidentiality standards and due-process review procedures." The report points out that we may be "creating one of the largest, most sensitive, and highly computerized record systems in the nation's history, without explicit protections for the civil liberties of millions of persons whose lives will be profoundly affected. . ."

C.   Limit the collection of personal information where a proper regard for the citizen's right to privacy suggests that records ought not to be maintained at all by certain organizations, or never furnished for certain uses in the society. Among the examples are the use of arrest-only records in licensing and employment decisions, and the selling to commercial advertising services of names and addresses collected by government under its licensing and regulatory powers, unless the individual specifically consents to such use.

In the case of arrest records, the Report stresses that "a democratic society should not allow arrest records to be collected and circulated nationwide with increasing efficiency without considering directly the actual social impact of their use in the employment and licensing spheres, and without examining the possibility that dissemination beyond law-enforcement agencies represents an official stigmatization of the citizen that ought to be either forbidden by law, or closely regulated."

D.   Increased work by the computer industry and professionals within it on technological safeguards which will make it possible to implement confidentiality policies more effectively than is now feasible. The Report notes that "No 'technological fix' can be applied to the databank problem." Protection of privacy is a matter of social policy, on which "computer professionals are fellow citizens, not experts." But the Project calls for more research, development, and testing efforts to be undertaken by the computer industry to see that the computer's <u>capacities</u> for protection of confidentiality and insurance of proper citizen access are turned into "available and workable products." Law and public pressure, the Report suggests, require that such measures be taken by managers of sensitive record systems when they are computerized, thereby stimulating the "user demand" to provide a practical market for such devices and techniques.

E.   Reconsideration by Congress and the executive branch of the current permissive policies toward use of the social security number in an increasing number of government and private record systems. The Report notes that having such a number is not a prerequisite for linking files within or between organizations, but notes that a common numbering system clearly makes record linkage easier and cheaper. Further, the Project concludes that resolving the critical civil liberties issues in record-keeping "will require that a minimum level of trust be maintained between American citizens and their government. Under these conditions, adopting the social security number as a national identifier or letting its use spread unchecked cannot help but contribute to the public distrust of government."

F.   Experimentation with special information-trust agencies to hold particularly sensitive bodies of personal data. For example, the Report suggests that the handling of both national crime statistics and summary criminal histories ("rap sheets") might be taken away from the Federal Bureau of Investigation and placed in an independent national agency under control of a board that would have public representatives as well as law enforcement officials on it. Such an agency would have to be established "with a clear legislative mandate to be a 'guardian' institution," paying attention to civil liberties interests as well as law enforcement needs.

The Report stressed that the next five years would be a critical period in the reception and control of sensitive personal record systems, especially those managed by computers. More sensitive areas of record-keeping are being entered by many computerizing organizations, many larger on-line (instant access) networks are being brought into operations, and more consolidations of presently scattered records about individuals can be seen as a trend in certain areas, such as criminal justice, credit and financial transactions, and welfare. The Report stresses that unless law makers and organizational managers develop proper safeguards for privacy and due process, and create mechanisms for public scrutiny and review, the record systems they are building could sharpen the already serious debate in American society over the way to apportion rights, benefits, and opportunities in a credential-oriented society, and leave organizational uses of records to control individual futures too far outside the rule of law.

In its closing paragraphs, the Report sums up the databanks and civil liberties problem as follows:

If our empirical findings showed anything, they indicate that man is still in charge of the machines. What is collected, for what purposes, with whom information is shared, and what opportunities individuals have to see and contest records are all matters of policy choice, not technological determinism. Man cannot escape his social or moral responsibilities by murmuring feebly that "the Machine made me do it."

There is also a powerful tendency to romanticize the precomputer era as a time of robust privacy, respect for individuality in organizations, and "face-to-face" relations in decision-making. Such arcadian notions delude us. In every age, limiting the arbitrary use of power, applying broad principles of civil liberty to the troubles and challenges of that time, and using technology to advance the social well-being of the nation represent terribly hard questions of public policy, and always will. We do not help resolve our current dilemmas by thinking that earlier ages had magic answers.

Computers are here to stay. So are large organizations and the need for data. So is the American commitment to civil liberty. Equally real are the social cleavages and cultural reassessments that mark our era. Our task is to see that appropriate safeguards for the individual's rights to privacy, confidentiality, and due process are embedded in every major record system in the nation, particularly the computerizing systems that promise to be the setting for most important organizational uses of information affecting individuals in the coming decades.

The Threat to Privacy

Privacy, said the late Prof. Clinton Rossiter, "is an unbreakable wall of dignity. . .against the entire world." Today, that wall is crumbling. It is being undermined by government snooping and by persistent manipulation through public relations posing as public information. Independence of thought and action is subverted through secret intrusion and subtle indoctrination.

While outright repression always remains the ultimate danger, freedom now faces the more sophisticated threat of electronic surveillance and governmental hucksterism.

"Electronic surveillance," Justice William Brennan Jr. has warned, "destroys all anonymity and all privacy; it makes the government privy to everything. . . ."

The Pentagon has admitted that it has dossiers on 25 million American "personalities." These include persons loosely described as "considered to constitute a threat to security and defense" as well as such public figures as Senator Adlai Stevenson 3d. According to testimony, the data bank, which keeps files on 760,000 organizations and incidents, processes 12,000 requests on an average day. Requests by whom and for what purpose?

Other agencies in the business of keeping tabs on Americans are proliferating. They include the Federal Bureau of Investigation, the Central Intelligence Agency, the Congressional committees dealing with "security," and the Passport Office. An airline has been asked to aid official surveillance by feeding into a computer information on where and in whose company its passengers travel.

Attorneys General, defying the courts, in recent years have stretched their customary privilege of tapping the telephones

SOURCE: The New York Times, March 8, 1971. © 1971, by The New York Times Company. Reprinted by permission.

of potential foreign spies to aim similar surveillance at suspected domestic subversives. Reluctance on the part of Justice Department officials to try to obtain court orders for such purposes—readily granted in any plausible case—is tantamount to admission that these invasions of privacy would be difficult to justify.

Symbolic of the pernicious trend toward secret incursions into privacy and high-powered manipulation of public attitudes is the Pentagon's deep involvement in both activities. The Defense Department's massive data banks have been exposed in the hearings before the Senate Constitutional Rights Subcommittee; its equally massive propaganda machine was portrayed in the Columbia Broadcasting System's documentary, "The Selling of the Pentagon."

Democratic freedoms are in jeopardy when the military simultaneously arrogates to itself the power to act as watchdog over civilians and, under the cover-all of public information, the right to advocate its own views on war and peace. When high-ranking officers—in violation of all military regulations—are allowed to blame domestic dissenters for the failures of American action in Vietnam, the dangers become acute from Army-operated data banks on dissent.

Powerful governmental public relations efforts today try to make war mean "pacification." Opposition to the war thus subtly implies disloyalty. Such manipulations diminish the capacity of individuals to reach political decisions rationally and unafraid.

The Fourth Amendment upholds "the right of the people to be secure in their persons, houses, papers and effects, against unreasonable searches and seizures. . . ." Modern computer technology and public relations techniques, in the hands of powerful government agencies, are capable of extending such searches and seizures into men's minds. When that happens, privacy and freedom are the victims.

Section II
A CRAM COURSE
IN THREATS AND
COUNTERMEASURES

The three articles included in this section will give the reader a good general knowledge of the various types of threats to the security of information in computer systems and of most measures which can be used to counteract or diminish these threats. Usually just a few of the countermeasures will be sufficient since not all the threats will be present. These countermeasures will depend on the installation involved, since there are no "cookbook solutions" to problems of computer security—any actions must be tailored to the needs of a particular system. This choice always involves a trade-off between the level of security we wish to maintain and the resultant inconvenience that we can bear. Many of the solutions discussed in the articles in this section decide this trade-off in favor of greater security; they therefore also involve greater inconvenience than may be acceptable for a given installation; only it can decide what combination of features it will use.

The first article by Charles Beardsley originally appeared in the IEEE Spectrum of January 1972. Beardsley presents for us an excellent survey of possible threats and the physical, administrative, legal, and technological safeguards which can be employed to counteract these threats. All of these safeguards must be considered together, as IBM has stated very well: "The systems design and operations management aspects of a secure data processing installation are almost totally interdependent. Unless operations management maintains physical, procedural, and personal safeguards, the system security will constantly be at risk, no matter how much protection has been programmed in" [11]. Neglecting any of these facets of the system will leave avenues for unauthorized persons to use in compromising security.

Physical security is the first real line of defense for any computer installation. All our technical safeguards will be useless if we do not maintain physical security over the computer system, input-output areas, etc. For this reason we decided to include more on this particular topic—in particular, the excerpt from IBM's fine booklet on data security in a computer environment. Physical security is used to protect against theft or destruction of data as well as against compromise of data and access by unauthorized people. This article contains a good set of points to check in designing a physical security program. For a more detailed treatment of physical security in a computer environment, the reader is referred to [7].

The final paper in this section by Petersen and Turn is a classic—it was the first very good wide-ranging article on the topic and would merit inclusion for historical interest alone. But all of the techniques described there are very applicable today. Their tables of threats and countermeasures are well thought out and have been widely used by many people as guides to protecting their own installation's files.

Is Your Computer Insecure?

CHARLES W. BEARDSLEY

On October 11, 1969, the New York Mets won the World Series. From Wall Street to Washington Heights, exuberant fans tossed paper streamers from high-rise office buildings—a familiar Manhattan ritual on such occasions. In the spontaneous excitement that followed, however, other objects also floated to the street: punched cards, computer printouts, and even strips of magnetic tape. A week later, the management of these firms had only begun to assess the corporate losses that occurred as a consequence of this revelry. For the fortunate, the paper blizzard meant the destruction of only a few duplicate records; for others, the action resulted in the loss of a whole day's transactions, including sensitive and proprietary information. Although these firms undoubtedly provided some form of security indoctrination for their data-processing personnel, such training was obviously inadequate in this instance. All too often, data-processing (DP) employees—or, for that matter, any office personnel—are unaware of the implications of disclosure, loss, or destruction of data. Frequently, such accidents occur as a result of ignorance or naiveté. Because the programs and data files are in machine-readable form, employees will justify their carelessness by maintaining that "nobody can read it anyway."

On a security checklist, the previous incident probably would be best characterized as an example of Murphy's law in action. There are, however, computer-security accidents and crimes that are far more predictable and for which countermeasures exist. In 1969, rioting students at Sir George Williams University

---

SOURCE: IEEE Spectrum, January 1972. Reprinted by permission.

in Montreal destroyed the school's computer center. In 1970, three former Encyclopaedia Britannica computer operators were indicted for the theft of mailing lists valued at $3 million. At the same time, the U.S. Federal Bureau of Investigation arrested an 18-year-old Cincinnati youth who knew the telephone numbers of the processors and was using a remote terminal to tap the lines of a time-sharing firm in Louisville, Ky.

Examples of eavesdropping and fraud can be just as alarming. In 1968, for example, a brokerage firm's vice president was charged with punching special data cards that transferred funds to his accounts. He managed to make off with $250,000 over an eight-year period. In another case, a brokerage employee modified the system to mail dividend checks to his home address. He received checks totaling $18,120 before being caught. Countless other stories have been documented: the touring garden-club matron who took a handful of punched cards from a tray as a souvenir of her visit to a DP center, the explosions at the computer centers of the Universities of Kansas and Wisconsin, the article on "The Technology of Computer Destruction" in the underground newspaper Seed, eavesdropping and theft of geophysical data in the petroleum industry, the frustrated tape librarian who scrawled an obscenity on the computer room wall and then switched labels on all the tape reels. . .

Faced with threats like these, managers of DP centers have started to reevaluate their security options and procedures for hardware and software. One of the first areas to receive their attention was that of unauthorized access and alteration of operating data. Other areas of concern are bombs and natural disasters—the kind of threats that fall in the category of physical security.

FACTS AND FALLACIES

Before evaluating countermeasures, the concerned user should first forget the innumerable horror stories about magnetic erasure and electromagnetic monitoring. Robert H. Courtney, manager of data security and privacy for IBM, serves as a kind of itinerant debunker of the many scare stories and cloak-and-dagger rumors about computer security. According to Courtney, all too many DP novices have visions of bakery trucks laden with antennas and cameras pulling up in front of their computer centers. Industrial espionage exists, but it takes far less sophisticated forms than these "Mission Impossible" fantasies. Courtney likes to point out that discarded paper and punched cards sitting on a loading platform afford a far more rewarding source of sensitive data for those who would beat the trashman to it.

Another security specialist, Joseph J. Wasserman, president of Computer Audit Systems, Inc., describes many of the self-proclaimed security experts who have recently appeared on the scene as "purveyors of snake oil." Like Courtney, Wasserman condemns the scare tactics that prompt DP managers to invest in magnet detectors, bomb shelters, mail-order data scramblers, and elaborate "buffer" zones.

One of the fright fables that Courtney and Wasserman find themselves disproving most frequently is that of damage by magnets in the data-processing center or tape libraries.

The Magnet Myth. Last March, the Wall Street Journal published a story on computer sabotage and fraud that told of a troop of Boy Scouts who, armed with magnets, innocently erased most of a company's computerized records during a plant tour. Bob Courtney brushes off this tale as apocryphal in that even very large magnets cannot damage data at distances in excess of a few centimeters. Except in unusual circumstances, distances of approximately 12 cm between the recording medium and the magnet should provide adequate protection against erasure. Or to put it another way, a magnetic flux density of 200 to 400 gauss (20 to 40 mT) is required at the tape surface for effective erasure. In fact, the 3M Co. claims that a magnetic tape kept only as far as 7 cm from a degausser will not be harmed.

Several letters supporting this evidence appeared in Business Automation last year after the publication of an article that charged that a magnet the size of a quarter could wipe out thousands of reels of magnetic tape. One skeptical reader reported taking a quarter-sized magnet and placing it at distances of 12 and 6 cm from a tape, while rotating the tape in place. There was no change in output until the tape reel was placed on its side and the magnet was moved around the entire surface of the flange. Although this experiment indicated that a small magnet could wipe out tape, it nevertheless showed that a considerable amount of time would be required to destroy thousands of reels.

On the other hand, computer managers should not become as overconfident as the manager of one facility that Bob Courtney visited, where memorandums, posters, and other papers were fastened to the walls with dozens of small magnets. Courtney also cautions against the use of magnetic cabinet latches and flashlights with magnets for holding them against the wall. In short, the threat of erasure by magnetism is neither as dangerous as a few overzealous journalists have led the computer community to believe nor as innocuous as the proponents of magnetic thumbtacks have claimed.

For the manager who insists on guarding against malicious or inadvertent magnetic-tape erasure, there are commercial safeguards such as magnet detectors that can be wired to set off alarms and to lock doors. Such schemes are, however, usually more trouble than they are worth. Switching labels on tape reels can cause almost as much havoc, and in much less time.

The real danger of magnetism occurs during _intentional_ erasure. A faint signal will remain on tape until it is replaced by a new data message. Degaussing does not result in complete erasure. Another important consideration for the security-conscious manager is that, should a magnet maniac gain access to a tape-storage area for a prolonged period, there is no way to tell how much damage has been done, short of reading out the entire library. Most magnets will do a poor job of erasing a tape, but can be a very effective means of introducing errors.

Sloppy storage can often create more problems than magnetism. For example, temperature and humidity extremes cause the metal oxide to flake off a tape. Printthrough of data from one tape layer to another occurs if a tape is wound too tightly. Devices that produce alternating magnet fields, such as transformers, can completely garble a signal.

Electromagnetic Monitoring.   It is technically unfeasible to monitor a central processing unit (CPU) and its related peripherals; however, signals from typewriter terminals and CRT displays are susceptible to intercept. In a CRT display, for example, electron-beam modulation puts out wide-band VHF radiation. For a typewriter terminal, both acoustic and electromagnetic (EM) intercept are possible—although in the case of EM monitoring, there is usually so much RF noise in a typical business installation that EM intercept from more than a meter away is impractical. In any case, sophisticated monitoring ordinarily costs more than bribery. The practical eavesdropper, therefore, would be wise to estimate the value of the data to be monitored before investing in expensive bugs and related hardware.

Here, as with magnets, countermeasures are available, but of questionable value. For example, low-noise terminals eliminate the radiation problem but release ink with an offensive odor that can prove noxious to equipment operators if several consoles are operated in the same room. Radiation shielding is another possible protective measure—not so much as a safeguard against monitoring as a defense against outside interference. When Westinghouse installed a computer center next to Baltimore's Friendship Airport a few years ago, DP personnel discovered that radar was disrupting equipment operation —a problem that was solved by shielding the machine room. Such shielding costs approximately $50 per square meter of combined wall, floor, and ceiling area.

Portable transceivers also have the potential for interfering with system operation. Even low-power transmitters near the equipment may generate field strengths high enough to cause some disruption.

Threats such as radiation monitoring often prompt users to lose sight of less sophisticated dangers. For example, consideration should be given to destroying the ribbon in the printing mechanism, or designing the platen so that impressions cannot be read from it. More elementary than radiation-monitoring devices, "bugs" can be attached directly to a terminal or data communications line. Last year, a firm claiming to provide a security auditing service invaded one company's DP center with scanning equipment that was supposedly capable of detecting hidden transmitters. In truth, the detectors themselves proved to be the transmitters—a fact discovered by the company only after the eavesdropping damage had been done.

So much for the publicized dangers to computer and software security. What are some of the other risks? Joe Wasserman, who was formerly manager of audit development for Bell Telephone Laboratories, pictures security control as a maze (Figure 1). If the system is properly controlled, each of the threats represented by an arrow will be interrupted and negated by applicable control elements. Wasserman places testing controls at the head of his list of control elements. He recommends parallel testing of old and new systems where feasible, or the use of a test deck consisting of fictitious transactions to evaluate system logic. Conversion controls ensure that the data going into a new hardware or software system have been verified and are as complete and error-free as possible. Quality control (QC) requires sampling the accuracy of data both before and after computer processing. A QC unit's major function is to spot data that are obviously unrealistic. Production and machine controls call for reviews of operator interventions, machine halts, and other occurrences indicating unusual conditions. Of course, records of machine performance, preventive maintenance periods, and schedules of operations should be kept up to date. Computer room security deserves mention, if only because so many companies still advocate an open-door

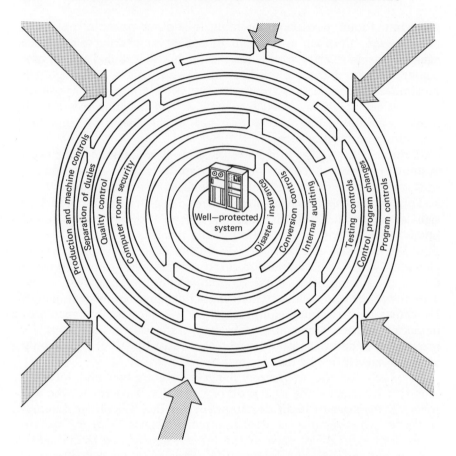

FIGURE 1. The attack arrows have as their objective system destruction. If the system is properly controlled, each of the factors represented by an arrow will be interrupted and negated by applicable control elements. (Courtesy Computer Audit Systems, Inc.)

policy for their computer installations, welcoming visitors and failing to provide even minimum security precautions. Program controls and program change controls can reduce the likelihood of loss from mistakes or unauthorized program changes. An adequate security system should make clear the type of information to be made available to each employee. Separation of duties reduces the possibility of damages from personnel errors because each employee has only a limited role in the entire system's operation. In short, identify the employees who authorize a transaction and produce the input, those who process the data, and those who use the output. Similar controls should cover scheduling, manual and machine operations, and maintenance of programs. Bob Courtney emphasizes that programmers should not have access to the software library, if only to guard against the possibility of malicious damage. Is there enough insurance to avert substantial financial loss in the event of a system disaster? Several insurance companies now offer EDP policies that cover investments in program development, hardware, and stored data.

A somewhat different view of the threats to a DP center is provided by Figure 2—the now-classic configuration of a time-sharing system as conceived by Willis Ware of the Rand Corporation. Figure 2 illustrates a central processor to which are attached computer-based files and a communication network for linking to remote users via a switching center.[1] Consider first the potential threats posed by an unauthorized or malicious user (lower right).

USER IDENTIFICATION AND ACCESS CONTROL

There are three basic ways to identify a terminal user: by something he knows or memorizes, by something he carries, or by a personal physical characteristic.[2] These techniques of access management are aimed at preventing unauthorized users from obtaining services from the system or gaining access to its files.

Passwords. The use of a password or prearranged set of questions requires no special hardware and is the least expensive means of user identification. Prevalent schemes include single or fixed passwords, changeable passwords, random passwords, functional passwords that categorize the user according to his security classification, and "extended handshakes."

In a single- or fixed-password scheme, a typical user sign-on looks something like this:

LOGIN, MAN 2793, ACT 5-172
PASSWORD?
PRIVACY 3
FILE NAME?

Unfortunately, most passwords tend to proliferate like chain letters. People tape passwords to the underside of desk drawers, write them on the last page of their desk calendars, or even tape them to the terminal. Or they will pick passwords that are easily recalled, such as a birthday or anniversary.

One technique to improve the integrity of a password system is to use changeable and random passwords. In one variation of this

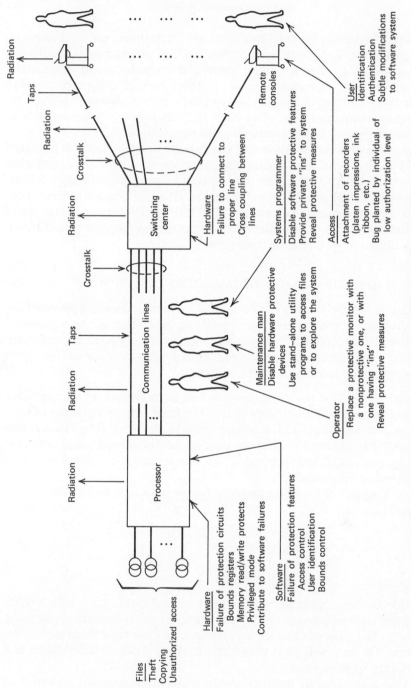

FIGURE 2. Threats to a typical time-sharing system. (Courtesy The Rand Corp.)

scheme, the user receives a stack of cards by registered mail. In addition to a serial number and user number, each card also contains a random number. After signing in, the user takes the random number from the top card, transmits it, and discards the card. The processor compares the number with its own list and permits access if they agree. In installations with strict security controls, each one-time password may be stored in a sealed envelope. One-time passwords, however, are effective only if the transaction rate is slow and the transactions are long. No one would have the time to deal with a user who was out of step in a heavily used administrative system such as IBM's —which has approximately 6000 users on 1300 terminals, and where a rate of half-a-million transactions is typical for a busy Friday. Another disadvantage of one-time passwords is that an intruder can stay on line forever while the authorized user is locked out.

One method of changeable passwords that holds promise supplies the user with a pseudorandom number, which he transforms algebraically. The system then performs the same transformation internally and compares answers. An example of such a transformation is

$$P(x) = \sum_{i=1}^{R} \text{odd digits of } x^{3/2} + \text{hour of the day}$$

The advantage here is that even though a snooper may intercept the argument of the function or the answer transmitted to the computer, he doesn't know the nature of the transformation—so the data are useless.[3]

Also of interest are <u>functional passwords</u> that indicate a user's security classification. In the Generalized Information Retrieval System (GIRS) developed at the University of Western Ontario,[4] three-level protection codes are stored within each user's password. The level 1 code unlocks a specified combination of ten processing functions, level 2 unlocks a combination of ten records within the data file, and level 3 defines the user's security clearance—he can see only those data entries at or below this level.

The Adept-50 time-sharing system, created by the System Development Corp. for the U.S. Department of Defense, makes use of a challenge-response scheme, sometimes called the <u>extended handshake</u>.[5] To gain admittance to the system, a user must first satisfy the Adept LOGIN decision procedure, which is based on user-specified input parameters (Figure 3). The user starts by typing the LOGIN command, his identification code, the terminal identification code, and the current password. Each successful LOGIN throws away the user password; 64 LOGINs are possible before a new set of passwords

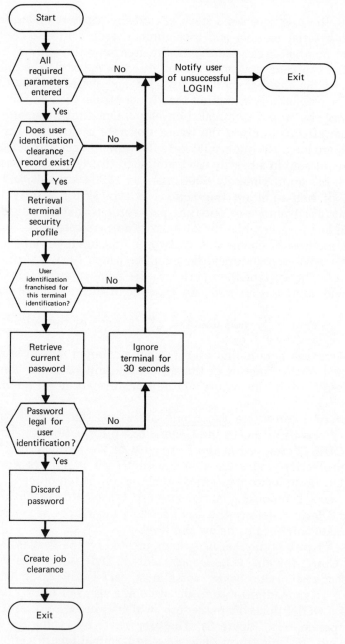

FIGURE 3. The LOGIN decision procedure.

need be established. If a system other than the once-only pass-words is desired, the 64 passwords can be encoded in some algo-rithmic manner, or merely replicated.

A valid user identification provides entry into the SYSLOG file, which creates or updates a system disk file, where each record corre-sponds to an authorized user. If no such record exists, the LOGIN is unsuccessful and system access is denied. If the record is found, LOGIN retrieves the terminal identification code for the keyboard from internal system tables and searches for a match in the terminal identification list for which the user identification code was fran-chised. If the terminal is franchised, then the current password is retrieved from the SYSLOG file for this user identification code and matched against the password entered as a keyboard parameter. Here again, an unsuccessful match is an unsuccessful LOGIN. Furthermore, the terminal will not honor input for 30 seconds (Figure 3), to frustrate high-speed, computer-assisted penetration attempts. If the match is successful, the current password is discarded and LOGIN proceeds to create the job clearance.

Another example of the extended handshake is the access proce-dure of L. J. Hoffman's formulary model.[6] Hoffman argues that most current password schemes prove unsatisfactory because the pass-words are associated with files; that is, information is protected at the file level only. A problem arises when certain information in a file should be available to some but not all authorized users of the file. The file management problems presented and the memory wasted due to duplication of data prevent the creation of large data bases and result in smaller, overlapping data bases. In Hoffman's formulary model, the decision to grant or deny access is made at data-access time rather than at file-creation time.

Blake Greenlee, a project manager specializing in software secu-rity for Citicorp System, Inc., of Cambridge, Mass., recommends voice answerback as a strategy for verifying user identity. For exam-ple, the Rush system, developed by Allen-Babcock Computing, Inc., offers a dial-up and call-back option. Whenever a sensitive file is about to be accessed, the user's identity is confirmed by calling him by telephone and requesting his password. The user can then modify the password if he did not authorize the access.[7]

One problem with password schemes is that they can waste a user's time—particularly in the case of extended handshakes. As pass-word methods become more complex and voice-answerback options are offered, users can expect to spend more and more time just acces-sing the system. Regardless of their effectiveness, passwords can get out of hand, denying access to authorized system users as well as to illegal infiltrators.

Another disadvantage of passwords is that they are printed out on a piece of paper that is probably thrown away. If the system uses a fixed-password scheme, anyone from the cleaning woman to the trashman has the potential to use or sell this information. The greatest vulnerability of passwords, however, lies in the inability of the user to determine if the password has been stolen. This is not true if the user is identified by something he carries, such as a badge or key.

Badges and Keys.   This second means of user identification provides a degree of control not possible with exclusive reliance on intangibles such as an identification number or a password. Because the user must have his key or badge to operate the system, he can recognize and report a loss if it occurs. Another advantage of these devices is that they make the sign-on procedure much easier.

IBM is currently offering a user-identification technique that makes use of an identification card with a magnetic stripe—a scheme similar to that used by the American Banking Assn. for credit cards. The difference is that the IBM ID card need carry only a number and a stripe. If the card is stolen or lost, there is no way of telling whose card it is, or what records the owner has access to. If the card is used after its loss or theft has been reported, the keyboard will lock automatically, and the customer will be notified of a covert penetration attempt.

Physical Characteristics.   Another way of identifying a terminal user is by a personal physical characteristic. This might be his voice, his fingerprints, or—as some of the more fanciful proposals have suggested—the shape of his head or lips. After discarding the latter schemes as impractical, IBM experimented with a speaker-identification system on a 150-terminal time-sharing administrative system between Poughkeepsie and New York City. These tests proved that changes in vocal characteristics are a significant problem. A cold or hay fever attack will frequently cause a computer to reject an authorized user. In effect, such a system requires that the user be in the pink of health. Also, variations in telephone handsets mean that each phone has to be identified.

Another possibility under investigation is that of fingerprint identification. In a system offered by KMS Industries, Inc., of Van Nuys, Calif. (for access to a room only, but presently being redesigned for use with computer terminals), the user first makes a holographic record of his fingerprint, which he inserts into an encoder, where it is recorded. When the user places a fresh fingerprint on a verifier, light from a helium-neon laser passes through the fingerprint, and the modified optical wavefront then passes through the holographic record. If the two wavefronts match, the phases cancel each other, and the user can enter the secure area. The system also offers ID cards that contain holographically scrambled photographs of employees' fingerprints.

Here, too, the possibility of theft or duplication presents disadvantages that may outweigh the benefits of a personal-characteristic identification scheme. Both the human voice and fingerprints can be copied without the user's knowledge. Also, like passwords, these techniques may prove to be more trouble than they are worth. With a voice ID system, a phone must be added to the terminal. There is a loss of operating ease—especially if the computer keeps demanding that the user "say again." Voice ID could easily turn into a variation on the extended-handshake technique. Or, to put it another way, people will probably be just as reluctant to talk to a data terminal as they would to a file cabinet.

CRYPTOGRAPHY

Another area of concern in Figure 2 are the communications links from the central processor to the switching center and from the switching center to the remote terminals. Most commercial computer users fail to realize that digital transmission of information is no more secure than Morse code. Although federal agencies and government contractors have been applying "privacy transformations" for some time—techniques for scrambling or coding the data in user-processor communications or in files—other users have only recently become aware of the threat of infiltration.

Wiretapping and eavesdropping are ordinarily classified as forms of passive infiltration. Active infiltration can pose an even greater threat. Some of the categories of active infiltration include[8]:

- Browsing—the use of legitimate access to the system to obtain unauthorized information.
- Masquerading—posing as a legitimate user after obtaining proper identification by subversive means.
- Trapdoors—software deficiencies that may exist by virtue of the combinatorial aspects of the system control variables.

- Between-lines entry—the penetration of a system when a legitimate user is on a communications channel and his terminal is inactive.
- "Piggyback" entry—selective interception of user-processor communications and the return of a false message to the user.

Sometimes an authorized user can inadvertently gain access to someone else's files. A noisy telephone line, for example, can cause an abort disconnect; that is, the noise forces the data set into an unhooked condition. If an inquiry has already been made, the next person dialing in can receive the first user's data.

One way of combating the vulnerability of data communications lines is by encrypting the signal to be transmitted—either by scrambling the data with a "cryptobox" or by coding the message using traditional cryptographic schemes.

Data Scramblers.   Three commercial firms in the United States and one Swiss company are now marketing enciphering systems that scramble the data bit stream. In this technique, known as end-to-end encryption, a scrambling device is connected to the user's end of the transmission line and a decoding unit is placed at the receiving end.

One method of data scrambling is by addition: using appropriate algebra to combine characters in the message with encoding sequences of characters (the key). For example, the second and fourth bits in a data word could be inverted by summing the incoming clear characters with an encoding character having ones in the second and fourth bits:

Clear text	1	0	1	1	1
Key	0	1	0	1	0
Coded character	1	1	1	0	1

This technique, called the Vernam code after the telegraph engineer who devised the system, may also be thought of as an "exclusive OR" scheme. Unscrambling is performed by summing the scrambled characters with the same encoding character.

Most data scramblers provide a higher degree of security by continuously and randomly changing the encoding character. Such rotating code sequences make use of a pseudorandom sequence generator. When the digital word in the shift register moves one place to the right, a new left-hand bit appears. Some of the bits in the register are wired to modulo-2 adders, connected so that the new left-hand bit is a <u>one</u> if an odd number of one's exists in the inputs to the adders, or a <u>zero</u> if there is an even number of one's. In this way, the word contained in the register changes in an apparently random manner.[9]

Among the scramblers presently offered are the Datocoder by Datotek, Inc., Dallas, Tex.; the Secre/Data by Com/Tech Systems, Inc., Richmond Hill, N.Y.; and the Data Sequestor by Ground Data Corp., Ft. Lauderdale, Fla. Crypto, AG, Zug, Switzerland, also expects to offer a new line of computer coding equipment in the near future.

The $3950 Datocoder, like the other available cryptoboxes, connects between the terminal and the modem. For each file to be enciphered, the user loads the Datocoder by means of a file code consisting of any three ASCII characters typed on the keyboard or by means of internal thumbwheel switches, both of which allow over 4×10^{12} discrete file codes.

Secre/Data offers an automatic cipher synchronization feature that permits an enciphered transmission to be made simultaneously with a local clear copy. Prices range from $700 to $1595—depending on such options as simplex or duplex operation, synchronization, and interface and speed requirements.

The standard Data Sequestor sells for $975 and can be used for synchronous or asynchronous transmission. Ground Data also offers a software program, SEQUEX/1, which performs the same functions as the scrambler and may be called in as an operating subroutine. All of these systems can also be used for encoding data on disk or pack.

Despite the optimism of scrambler manufacturers, some industry representatives remain skeptical about the possibility of a boom in cryptoboxes. Blake Greenlee of Citicorp Systems points out that "Anyone who's read a book on cryptography and knows modern algebra thinks he can design a system. The budding inventor fails to consider that the potential data thief can easily copy the cryptomachine. Because the patent proposals for such devices are made public, the technology is also public. Good crypto design, therefore, relies on changing your encoding variable frequently, rather than attempting to keep the hardware or programs secret.

"Another classic error of crypto designers is to assume that a design is 'unbeatable.' This is not true! All systems not based on a random key can be broken. Also, never depend on a computer program to generate random numbers—everyone knows the algorithms. Instead, use a naturally random process such as radioactive decay."

Greenlee also suggests that anyone with a serious interest in cryptography read David Kahn's The Codebreakers[10] before purchasing or designing a data scrambler.

Other Code Schemes.   Another "additive" type of transformation is the Vigenere cipher, in which a short sequence of characters is repeatedly combined with the characters of the message. Although not suitable for diplomatic or military purposes, it does lend itself to implementation in software. The system essentially consists of an alphabetic table in which the first letters of successive rows have been shifted one or more letters from the previous row:

	A	B	C	D	E	F	G
A	a	b	c	d	e	f	g
B	b	c	d	e	f	g	a
C	c	d	e	f	g	a	b
D	d	e	f	g	a	b	c
E	e	f	g	a	b	c	d
F	f	g	a	b	c	d	e
G	g	a	b	c	d	e	f

A normal alphabet (top row) is used for the plain text, and another alphabet vertically for the key. The key is written above the message, and intersecting rows and columns of the two letters in the table represents the transposition. For example, for the key BAD and the abbreviated table just represented, the message CABBAGE would be encoded as follows:

Key: BADBADB
Plain: CABBAGE
Cipher: daecace

Garrison and Ramamoorthy[3] have evaluated these two techniques —Vernam and Vigenere—on the CDC 6600 (Table I). The first Vernam program, Case 1, uses a periodic key of 60 bits—the standard word length on the 6600—as many times as necessary to cover the text. The second Vernam program, Case 2, uses a nonperiodic key that is as long as the message. Although the latter method, the one-time key, provides better protection, a periodic key requires less storage space. The cost-per-bit figure reflects the time required for encoding/decoding as a percentage of the total CPU time required for the transaction. Although Case 1 is less expensive than Case 2 in terms of processing time, it is less secure. Core requirements for the periodic key technique are minimal; however, the one-time key requires twice as much core as there is information to be stored because the key is as long as the message. The Vigenere method, Case 3, requires more core than the Vernam because a transposition table must be stored whereas only a mathematical algorithm is necessary with Vernam.

TABLE I.   Comparison of Cryptographic Techniques*

Method	Vernam Case 1	Vernam Case 2	Vigenere Case 3
Size of key	Periodic key Variable, 60 bits	One-time key Variable, as long as the message	Variable key 24 bits in length
Additional memory required	Only that required for message	Twice that required for message	Some storage required for table; as many words as letters in text
Difficulty of breaking code	Very good if long, random key is used	Unbreakable in theory unless key is known	Good
Cost per bit for decode/encode (average), percent	1.14×10^{-4}	13.7×10^{-4}	4.373×10^{-4}

*Adapted from Ref. 3.

In addition to evaluating the tradeoffs between memory and the degree of protection required, the prospective cryptographer should also change keys at frequent intervals to discourage trial-and-error code breakers. Other criterions that influence the selection of a class of privacy transformations include the complexity of the code, the effect of transmission errors or processor malfunctioning, and the cost of implementation.[8]

Residue Control.   Residue control refers to the effective erasure of core and other memories after a program has been terminated or transferred to an auxiliary storage device. In the same way that data files can be enciphered, memory can also be scrambled—the ultimate in residue control. If no control is employed, the active threat of browsing becomes serious.[11]

HARDWARE ENFORCEMENT OF SYSTEM-CONTROL PROGRAM INTEGRITY

A user should not be able to get into supervisor state. Hardware protection schemes are one way of protecting the operating system. This control can use storage protect keys of memory bounds registers to provide read and write protection of information in main memory. If this technique is used, core storage is segmented into blocks (pages) identified by an associated hardware protect key (code), which also specifies whether read protection, write protection, or read/write protection is provided for the page. This key—set by a privileged instruction—is compared with a program key when a reference to the page is made by a program or when input/output operations are initiated. Memory bounds registers, consisting of a base address and a limit register, are loaded by the control program when a user program is allotted core storage. The starting address of the allocated core area is loaded into the base address register, and the address of the end of the allocated area is loaded into the limit register. Each core reference is checked against the memory bounds register.[12]

As a result, the matching of codes is performed by system hardware. The system assigns the user his code, which can't be changed even if he successfully "penetrates" the computer because these instructions can be changed only by the operating system. Hardware compartmentization—subdividing memories into sections with different access privileges—is achieved by denying the user instructions that may be executed only by privileged programs such as the operating system. In the case of an unavoidable "crash," the built-in program keeps the memory from being read. These hardware controls also mean a better system for the user in terms of efficiency and reliability.

On IBM Operating Systems 360 and 370, hardware produces two separate instruction sets—one privileged and one that should only be used by the executive program. If any other program tries to execute one of these instructions, an interrupt occurs, which returns control to the operating system.

Microprogrammed hardware checks consist of tests of those hardware elements, such as memory protect registers or decoders, whose failure would not result in an interrupt but could cause sensitive information to be compromised. A microprogram (steps wired into read-only memory) could be executed either on command or cyclically to provide this automatic hardware check capability.[13]

Nevertheless, threats still exist. The circuits for such protections as bounds registers, read-write protect, or privileged mode might fail and permit information to leak to improper destinations (Figure 2, lower left). A large number of hardware failures could contribute to software failures, which, in turn, lead to divulgence.

RINGS OF PROTECTION

A hardware/software system under development by Honeywell, Inc. and the Massachusetts Institute of Technology employs still another variation of compartmentization: rings of protection. In addition to the tree or pyramid structure of conventional data bases, the ring structure is like concentric circles. In this way, segments of the memory containing sensitive information can be placed in a privileged ring together with programs that process, update, and extract this information. A subscriber enters a ring only at a carefully defined point, and once he enters the ring his activity is completely controlled. Various parts of the file have different conditions of access and different levels of privilege. The user must specify all of these, in addition to his name, problem number, account number, and password.

The Multics system, on which this ring concept has been implemented, is a general-purpose, multiple-user, interactive computer system developed at M.I.T.'s Project MAC. In the course of Multics development, MAC researchers discovered that the processor provided only a limited set of access-control mechanisms. A new processor is now being built that implements protection rings almost completely in hardware, whereas the initial version of Multics used software-implemented rings of protection.[14]

Graduate students have always been the best test of system security; in fact, one observer estimates that 90 percent of the people breaking password schemes have been under 25. Students at M.I.T. are no exception. During the early stages of Multics development, one ingenious infiltrator took great delight in daily posting a printout of all user passwords. Multics has, in fact, probably been the object of more penetration attempts than all other time-sharing facilities combined—a dubious distinction, to be sure, but a fact that has alerted Project MAC engineers to "trapdoors" in the system.

SOFTWARE

Another area of vulnerability in Figure 2 is the software. A software failure can cause improper file access, crossing of memory partitions, or improper information routing within the system. Countermeasures include:

- Frequent comparison of the current system-control programs with carefully checked masters, both periodically and after each modification.
- Adequate program testing and software integrity checks, in which precautions are taken to limit the generation and distribution of file print routines, core dumps, trace routines, and other utilities and testing aids.
- Program inventories that include the program name, number, description, and programmer's name.
- Verification of programs on each usage with a check that is independent of the operating system—for example, a checksum.

Software can also be protected by labeling all documentation proprietary or by copyrighting the program. A legal agreement for the protection of proprietary programs is available at no charge from Financial Timesharing Services, Inc., of San Francisco. This firm feels that strict control over proprietary software should _not_ be put into the hands of lawyers in the Patent Office, but rather should be exercised through specific agreements covering a particular software package. In the matter of software, patent lawyers would probably be of little help anyway—only one software patent has ever been issued in the United States, and this was a process patent. That is to say, the program, when combined with a computer, caused a certain process to be performed, but the program by itself failed to meet the criterion of being "an unobvious extension of the state of the art."

One indication of the increasing seriousness of the software ownership problem is the appearance of representatives of the U.S. Justice Department at computer security seminars. A common complaint of these lawyers is that it is practically impossible to prosecute software thieves because most program documentation in unmarked as to ownership or as to who has "the need to know." Unless a thief is found guilty of using this material for embezzlement or fraud, little can be done within the existing legal framework. Even copyrighting a program can be dangerous because such material can be viewed at the Library of Congress. Perhaps the best countermeasure against theft is to have a corporate legal staff deal with each program individually and mark the documentation accordingly. At least this avoids the dilemma of dealing with the employee who pleads, "No one said I couldn't take it."

PHYSICAL SECURITY

Last September, DP personnel at 600 offices of the Metropolitan Life Insurance Co. daily discovered miles of tape strewn over the floors of their computer centers. After service crews from Honeywell failed to find a machine defect that might have caused this tape-spewing, telephone company investigators discovered that three technicians who were on strike against Honeywell were activating the Metropolitan field offices into sending uncontrolled data, which caused the tape backup. Disgruntled employees like these three computer technicians represent just one of many threats to the physical security of an installation.

Fire, flood, earthquakes, power failures, bombs, tornadoes, riots, berserk employees—all these contingencies and more pose physical threats to a computer installation. Although not specifically identified in Figure 2, physical security has now become a matter of considerable concern. The fishbowl concept of a computer center with exterior glass walls is a thing of the past. For $12,000, you can surround your DP center with ultrasonic traps. For another $5,000, a team of consultants will run a physical check on your installation. And for approximately $25,000 the same team promises to plug the leaks in the system.

Although protecting a DP center can be expensive, the loss of the various DP functions such as payroll, production control, or accounts receivable can result in even greater costs. Robert V. Jacobson, president of Bradford Security Systems, Inc., has identified some of these functions whose nonperformance would cause a significant loss to an organization. A 4-hour processing delay, for example, can result in a loss of $3,000 for an organization. After a one-week shutdown, losses can increase to $187,000 as cash flow is delayed, orders and sales are lost, and production efficiency declines. Jacobson further identifies some of the failure modes that can cause delays.

Electric Power Transients, Brownouts, or Blackouts. In 1970, brownouts affected one third of the DP centers in New York City, according to a Computerworld survey. Even a brief change in line voltage can cause undesirable changes in data transfer. Among the countermeasures recommended by Bob Jacobson are dual feeds to combat local power failures, diesel generators as a source of emergency power during blackouts ($300 per kVA), and constant power sources such as flywheel generators for eliminating fluctuations ($800 per kVA). Uninterruptible power sources (UPS) are another means of isolating the system from the power lines.

Air-Conditioning Failure. Redundant hardware, monitors of temperature and humidity, and the location of fresh air intakes are all involved in the design of an environmental control system for a computer installation. Heat and humidity can destroy a tape library far more effectively than can the legendary quarter-sized magnet. Air intakes may ingest sand and other foreign matter or vapors; the DP center at NASA's Mississippi Test Facility was shut down briefly when a skunk wandered past an intake fan.

Fire. The human nose can detect a fire faster than can many artificial sensors. Few employees, however, know how to use a fire extinguisher or how to activate a fire-quenching system. Another potential danger in the event of a fire is damage from water or smoke. A fire at RCA's former Palm Beach Gardens facility corroded $4.5 million worth of computer hardware. In this instance, as in many fires, the danger came not from combustibles but from the products of combustion. Fitted plastic covers for all equipment and storage cabinets can do much to reduce water and smoke damage.

Table II identifies these and other disaster causes in terms of their effect on operations. Temporary interruption refers to a stoppage in work flow not associated with physical damage or loss of data-processing assets; temporary inaccessibility, although similar to a temporary interruption, takes into account the effect of an absence of the DP staff; hardware damage encompasses any damage or breakdown of the computer hardware or supporting hardware; loss of software refers to programs, data files, and supporting documentation—particularly source documents, preprinted forms, and run books; repairable damage describes physical damage that can be repaired in less time than would be required to establish operations at another site; and catastrophic destruction refers to complete destruction of the data center. To analyze a specific DP facility, a company would probably want to expand Table II to include specific disaster causes peculiar to its operation. It may also be helpful to separate the hardware breakdown category into its major elements. A contingency plan may then be drawn up that provides for backup modes of operation.

For the company that has neither the time nor the people to perform a contingency analysis, there are several companies that offer consulting and auditing services—including Bradford Security Systems, Inc., New York, N.Y.; Brandon Applied Systems, Inc., New York, N.Y.; Computer Audit Systems, East Orange, N.J.; Computer Management, Cleveland, Ohio; Data Processing Security, Inc., Hindsdale, Ill.; and DataGuard Systems, Phoenix, Ariz.

Off-site storage of records, more familiarly known as the "Iron Mountain" approach, is another way of safeguarding against the possible destruction of operating programs, shareholder records, payroll

TABLE II. Potential Causes of Disaster and Their Effect on Operations

Potential causes	Temporary Interruption	Temporary Inaccessibility	Hardware Damage	Loss of Software	Repairable Damage	Catastrophic Destruction
Unavailability of key personnel	M		M			
Electric power fluctuations	M		M	M		
Electric power failure	D		M	M		
Air-conditioning failure	M		M			
Communications failure†	D			P		
Sabotage, vandalism	P		M	M	M	M
Strikes, lockouts	P	P			M	
Riot, civil unrest		M			M	M
Evacuation—bomb threat, fire	D	P				
Hardware failure	D		P	M		
Smoke, dirt, dust	M	M	M	M		
Water damage, flooding			M	M	P	M
Operator error	P		M	M		
Fire, explosion	P		M	M	M	M
Procedure errors regarding software				M		
Theft of software				M		
Structural failure			P		D	P

*M = may affect operations; P = probably will affect operations; D = definitely will affect operations. Lesser effects are omitted where obvious.
†Applies to systems with remote terminals.
(Courtesy AMR International, Inc.)

and pension data, and management information system (MIS) data. RCA's corporate management, for example, maintains an Iron Mountain backup vault where tapes are updated monthly. There's good reason for such precautions. A disaster simulation at RCA's New York City DP center indicated that it would take 9.2 man-years and 478 computer hours to reconstruct the master files and documentation.

Even so, such countermeasures can prove of limited value. One midwest company that maintained extensive redundant files of equipment inventories was left with just that after a disastrous fire: backup catalogs of hardware that no longer existed. As this incident illustrates, untested off-site files might well be unusable files. Or to put it another way, put a price on your data before investing in elaborate bomb shelters and underground vaults.

Care should also be taken in the selection of delivery and courier services that transport materials to and from archival storage. It is all too easy for an imposter to appear at the appointed time and make off with a proprietary printout. Why bother investing in a fortress-like DP center if a commercial messenger service, which is highly vulnerable to theft and fraud, has been entrusted with the backup files?

With physical security, as with the other areas that have been discussed, there is a tendency to overlook the obvious. All too often, the barn door has been left wide open while security consultants explore the feasibility of complex cryptographic and password schemes. Some firms, on the other hand, can become paranoid about physical security measures. This writer was denied access to one DP center until he agreed to leave his notebook behind.

THREAT MONITORING

Threat monitoring permits detection of attempted or actual penetrations of the system—to provide either real-time responses to the system supervisor or identification and tracing of penetration attempts. Threat monitoring may include all attempts to enter the file, only rejected attempts that use illegal access procedures, attempts to write into protected files, or any unusual activity involving a certain file. Any of these activities other than a valid sign-on requires some reaction by the system—if only a record of the attempt in a log. Details of all violations should be provided to the security officer for a particular file owner.

Commercial monitoring systems are also available. The Data Sentinel, a security monitor developed by Burns International Security

Services, Inc., of San Francisco, uses a minicomputer to monitor the job stream of large computer installations. The Sentinel can examine each program as the main computer is being loaded or can monitor the data flow. If a preestablished set of performance parameters is exceeded, the system activates an alarm, which is displayed at a guard's console. Alarms range from a deviation from standard procedure, which requires only that the guard push a button if he thinks everything is in order, to an alarm that indicates that the monitor itself is being tampered with. An audit trail of operations on tape and printout provides a log of all computer job sequences and program changes. A typical system sells for $100,000.

CERTIFICATION AND AUDIT

How does a DP manager demonstrate that a computer environment is secure? Theoretically, all he needs to do is verify that hardware, software, procedural, and physical safeguards respond properly to all threats. But this is easier said than done. Clark Weissman of the System Development Corp. tried to gain certification for the Adept system and came to the conclusion that "certification today is a mystic's occupation! There are no guidelines, rules, policies, agencies, tests, models, or active lobbyists encouraging the development of information system certification. The serious designer must 'solo' from the beginning or hire a professional consultant who makes a living 'breaking' systems."

Weissman regards this as a shortcoming that will be rectified only as security failures in information systems become more widespread. He recommends the creation of a governmental agency to grant information systems "secureworthiness," not unlike the way in which the U.S. Federal Aviation Administration regulates aircraft airworthiness.[11]

Computer Audit Systems' Joseph Wasserman, a consultant who breaks systems, views the problem of certification somewhat differently. Wasserman's firm has already tested the level and effectiveness of controls and security for General Electric's Information Networks Department and several other firms. After determining that these companies are maintaining an acceptable standard of protection, Computer Audit issues a statement to this effect. Included in the tests that lead to this statement of "certification" are an evaluation of environmental conditions, of control of access of the computer center, and of the adequacy and use of written operating procedures and standards.

Internal auditing, the remaining control element in Figure 1, has become a matter of serious concern now that the classic paper-audit trail has been replaced by invisible arrangements of molecules in an iron-oxide coating on tape or drum. How does a company evaluate internal control procedures? Appraise testing and conversion procedures? Insure the future auditability of a computer system? Joe Wasserman suggests several techniques: sampling every nth record, using a test deck to evaluate system functions, comparing known data from the system with test data from a fictitious "mini" company, and using the computer utility programs to perform such functions as extraction, sampling, mathematical functions, comparison, and sorting.[16] Wasserman has also developed a computerized audit retrieval system (CARS) that is already being used by the U.S. Naval Audit Service. CARS is essentially a program that will extract data, sample, compare two files, perform arithmetic computations, summarize, and print the results.

THE HUMAN ELEMENT

Most security experts admit that hardware and software certification is feasible, but only if industry and government can agree on the need for a certificate of "secureworthiness" and a procedure for implementing such an evaluation. Regardless of what decisions are reached, however, a "100 percent secure" rating will be meaningless as long as the human element in a computer system is ignored. As Figure 2 illustrates, the programmer, operator, and maintenance man all pose a very real threat to system security. Qualities such as competence, loyalty, and integrity are system parameters that cannot be quantitatively measured. Hardware and software integrity can be maintained by applying many of the countermeasures and audit procedures just discussed. But what about personnel integrity?

The recent public outcry over privacy and data banks may well indicate an anxiety caused by ignorance of and lack of participation in the decision-making processes that make use of computer-stored data, rather than a concern over the information to be stored. Computer security, then, may be viewed as an extension of a problem that has been around for some time. In short, you can build locks, but who gets the key?

The author wishes to thank Major W. S. Bates of the U.S. Marine Corps Computer Science School, Dr. William F. Brown of the AVCO Corp., Dr. A. Michael Noll of the White House Office of Science and

Technology, and Dr. John W. Weil of Honeywell Information Systems, Inc., for their cooperation and assistance in the preparation of this article.

REFERENCES

1. W. H. Ware, "Security and privacy in computer systems," Proc. Spring Joint Computer Conf., vol. 30, pp. 279–282, 1967.
2. The Considerations of Data Security in a Computer Environment, IBM Corp., White Plains, N.Y., 1970.
3. W. A. Garrison and C. V. Ramamoorthy, "Privacy and security in data banks," Tech. Memo. 24, Electronics Research Center, Univ. of Texas at Austin, 1970.
4. J. M. Carroll, et al., "Multidimensional security program for a generalized information retrieval system," Proc. Fall Joint Computer Conf., vol. 39, 1971.
5. C. Weissman, "Security controls in the Adept-50 time-sharing system," Proc. Fall Joint Computer Conf., vol. 35, pp. 119–133, 1969.
6. L. J. Hoffman, "The formulary model for flexible privacy and access controls," Proc. Fall Joint Computer Conf., vol. 39, 1971.
7. J. D. Babcock, "A brief description of privacy measures in the RUSH time-sharing system," Proc. Fall Joint Computer Conf., vol. 30, pp. 301–302, 1967.
8. H. E. Petersen and R. Turn, "System implications of information privacy," Proc. Spring Joint Computer Conf., vol. 30, pp. 291–299, 1967.
9. P. Maitland, "Data transmission privacy: Vulnerability and protection," presented at the 43rd Annual Conf. of the Petroleum Industry Electrical Association, Apr. 1971.
10. D. Kahn, The Codebreakers. New York: Macmillan, 1967.
11. C. Weissman, "Trade-off considerations in security system design," System Development Corp. Doc. SP-3548, 1970.
12. P. L. Peck, "Survey of applicable safeguards for insuring the integrity of information in the data processing environment," Mitre Corp. Doc. MTP-356, 1971.
13. L. M. Molho, "Hardware aspects of secure computing," Proc. Spring Joint Computer Conf., vol. 36, pp. 135–141, 1970.

14. M. D. Schroeder and J. D. Saltzer, "A hardware architecture for implementing protection rings," presented at 3rd Annual ACM Symp. on Operating Systems Principles, Oct. 1971.

15. L. J. Hoffman, "Computers and privacy: A survey," Computer Surveys, vol. 1, pp. 85–103, June 1969.

16. J. J. Wasserman, "Plugging the leaks in computer security," Harvard Bus. Rev., vol. 47, pp. 119–29, Sept. 1969.

Security Considerations for
Operations Management

The systems design and operations management aspects of a secure data processing installation are almost totally interdependent. Unless operations management maintains physical, procedural and personnel safeguards, the system's security will constantly be at risk, no matter how much protection has been programmed in.

PHYSICAL SECURITY

The central computing facility, its related tape/disk libraries, the data preparation area and the supporting clerical control departments should be considered as one unit for security purposes.

A secure data processing system may need physical guards on the computer center, possibly also on some terminal locations. It may need a security staff to keep intruders out, assure that tape or disk stores are locked and perform periodic inspections.

The ready availability of cameras, microphones and other accouterments of eavesdropping requires that consideration be given to the physical location of such system components as terminals, consoles and printers. Both the casual viewer at an open door and the more sophisticated intruder with a telephoto lens or parabolic microphone can be deterred when system components are kept away from open windows, doors and the glass walls that frequently surround machine rooms.

Physical access to the computer room should also be restricted to only those people actually engaged in support of

SOURCE: IBM Booklet G520-2169-0. Reprinted by permission from "The Considerations of Data Security in a Computer Environment." © 1970 by International Business Machines Corporation.

computer operations. At least one senior person per shift should be designated responsible and accountable for maintaining security precautions.

Locked cabinets or vaults should be used to store sensitive data files, backup files, associated operating procedures and documentation. The tape and disk librarian should maintain a log that records, at a minimum, exactly when and by whom sensitive material is removed and returned.

Program decks, documentation, test cases, sample outputs and procedures which operate on sensitive data should be treated as securely as the data themselves. To avoid the possibility of both error and loss of security, prior versions of such material should be clearly labelled, held secure and then destroyed as soon as the new system is fully operational.

OPERATING PROCEDURES

Security routines are often programmed as integral parts of the operating system's control program, access methods and data management. Therefore, procedures are needed to verify that the system is intact after all changes, customer engineering activity and testing sessions. The procedures should be employed as a normal part of the daily start-up and close-down of the system, as well as after any system outage requiring recovery and restart.

Logs should be maintained to record each running of a sensitive job. These should report any significant action taken, such as an operator decision to override tape/disk labels or passwords.

Program testing aids and procedures are normally designed to provide the maximum information possible to facilitate debugging. The presence of sensitive data, either on-line or off-line but accessible, may require restrictions on full storage printouts, on the use of stand-alone utilities which modify files and on requests for file dumps that may compromise the security of data within the system. (A major concern is that stand-alone programs are, by their nature, independent of controls built into the operating system.) In some highly secure systems, program testing is permitted only with artificial data and only when actual data is physically off-line.

Both manual and computer restart and recovery procedures should be designed so that checkpoints, core dumps, and/or the entire restart procedure do not provide a road map to the system's security controls.

Demonstration programs also, whenever practicable, should be limited to data sets containing artificial data, to prevent not only disclosure of sensitive data, but possible loss due to errors.

If necessary, the demonstrations themselves, whether at remote terminals or within the computer facility, should be limited to an audience with a need to know.

PERSONNEL

Maintenance of security demands competence, loyalty and integrity from systems operators and machine room personnel. In addition, it requires continuing training for them, both in operating procedures and security measures. The purpose of this training is to insure that each individual recognizes his vital role in installation security and does not—through familiarity—become careless.

No one, regardless of level of competence or job responsibility, should be able to circumvent the security procedures, logs and audit trail.

The control of employees of other departments, as well as outsiders, may require special precautions such as sign-in registers, badges or special escorts. As computing systems and peripheral devices become increasingly more complex, the nature and variety of these outsiders expands significantly beyond those who traditionally participate in data processing. And usually these people are most deeply involved during times of crisis—a conversion or a system malfunction—when the urge to bypass security in order to get the system operational is very great and must be resisted.

Success in managing a secure installation is only possible through consistent and continuous adherence to the security measures. All indications of both successful and attempted violations must appear on the logs and audit trail. The review of these should be a combined effort by operations management, systems design and the security administration officer to determine and implement whatever improvements the system may require—physical, procedural, personnel or programming.

System Implications of Information Privacy

H. E. PETERSEN
R. TURN

INTRODUCTION

Recent advances in computer time-sharing technology promise information systems which will permit simultaneous on-line access to many users at remotely located terminals. In such systems, the question naturally arises of protecting one user's stored programs and data against unauthorized access by others. Considerable work has already been done in providing protection against accidental access due to hardware malfunctions or undebugged programs. Protection against deliberate attempts to gain access to private information, although recently discussed from a philosophical point of view,[1-4] has attracted only fragmentary technical attention. This paper presents a discussion of the threat to information privacy in non-military information systems, applicable countermeasures, and system implications of providing privacy protection.

The discussion is based on the following model of an information system: a central processing facility of one or more processors and an associated memory hierarchy; a set of information files—some private, others shared by a number of users; a set of public or private query terminals at geographically remote locations; and a communication network of common carrier, leased, or private lines. This time-shared, on-line system is referred to throughout as "the system."

SOURCE: Spring Joint Computer Conference, 1967, Proceedings. Reprinted by permission of the publisher, American Federation of Information Processing Societies Press.

Threats to Information Privacy

Privacy of information in the system is lost either by accident or deliberately induced disclosure. The most common causes of accidental disclosures are failures of hardware and use of partially debugged programs. Improvements in hardware reliability and various memory protection schemes have been suggested as countermeasures. Deliberate efforts to infiltrate an on-line, time-shared system can be classified as either passive or active.

Passive infiltration may be accomplished by wiretapping or by electromagnetic pickup of the traffic at any point in the system. Although considerable effort has been applied to counter such threats to defense communications, nongovernmental approaches to information privacy usually assume that communication lines are secure, when in fact they are the most vulnerable part of the system. Techniques for penetrating communication networks may be borrowed from the well-developed art of listening in on voice conversations.[5, 6] (While the minimum investment in equipment is higher than that required to obtain a pair of headsets and a capacitor, it is still very low since a one-hundred-dollar tape recorder and a code conversion table suffice.) Clearly, digital transmission of information does not provide any more privacy than, for example, Morse code. Nevertheless, some users seem willing to entrust to digital systems valuable information that they would not communicate over a telephone.

Active infiltration—an attempt to enter the system to directly obtain or alter information in the files—can be overtly accomplished through normal access procedures by:

- Using legitimate access to a part of the system to ask unauthorized questions (e.g., requesting payroll information or trying to associate an individual with certain data), or to "browse" in unauthorized files.
- "Masquerading" as a legitimate user after having obtained proper identifications through wiretapping or other means.
- Having access to the system by virtue of a position with the information center or the communication network but without a "need to know" (e.g., system programmer, operator, maintenance, and management personnel).

Or an active infiltrator may attempt to enter the system covertly i.e., avoiding the control and protection programs by:

- Using entry points planted in the system by unscrupulous programmers or maintenance engineers, or probing for and discovering "trap doors" which may exist by virtue of the combinatorial aspects of the many system control variables (similar to the search for "new and useful" operation codes—a favorite pastime of machine-language programmers of the early digital computers).
- Employing special terminals tapped into communication channels to effect:

  —"piggy back" entry into the system by selective interception of communications between a user and the processor, and then releasing these with modifications or substituting entirely new messages while returning an "error" message;

  —"between lines" entry to the system when a legitimate user is inactive but still holds the communication channel;

  —cancellation of the user's sign-off signals, so as to continue operating in his name.

  In all of these variations the legitimate user provides procedures for obtaining proper access. The infiltrator is limited, however, to the legitimate user's authorized files.

More than an inexpensive tape recorder is required for active infiltration, since an appropriate terminal and entry into the communication link are essential. In fact, considerable equipment and know-how are required to launch sophisticated infiltration attempts.

The objectives of infiltration attempts against information systems have been discussed by a number of authors[1-3,7] from the point of view of potential payoff. We will merely indicate the types of activities that an infiltrator may wish to undertake:

- Gaining access to desired information in the files, or discovering the information interests of a particular user.
- Changing information in the files (including destruction of entire files).
- Obtaining free computing time or use of proprietary programs.

Depending on the nature of the filed information, a penetration attempt may cause no more damage than satisfying the curiosity of a potentially larcenous programmer. Or it may cause great damage and result in great payoffs; e.g., illicit "change your dossier for a fee," or industrial espionage activities. (See Table I for a summary of threats to information privacy.)

More sophisticated infiltration scenarios can be conceived as the stakes of penetration increase. The threat to information privacy

TABLE I.   Summary of Threats to Information Privacy

Nature of Infiltration	Means	Effects
Accidental	Computer malfunctioning; user errors; undebugged programs	Privileged information dumped at wrong terminals, printouts, etc.
Deliberate Passive	Wiretapping, electromagnetic pickup, examining carbon papers, etc.	User's interest in information revealed; content of communications revealed
Deliberate Active	Entering files by: "Browsing" "Masquerading" "Between lines" "Piggy-back" penetration	Specific information revealed or modified as a result of infiltrator's actions

should not be taken lightly or brushed aside by underestimating the resources and ingenuity of would-be infiltrators.

Countermeasures

The spectrum of threats discussed in the previous section can be countered by a number of techniques and procedures. Some of these were originally introduced into time-shared, multi-user systems to prevent users from inadvertently disturbing each other's programs[8] and then expanded to protect against accidental or deliberately induced disclosures of information.[8,9] Others found their beginning in requirements to protect privacy in communication networks.[10] In the following discussion, we have organized the various countermeasures into several classes.

Access Management.   These techniques are aimed at preventing unauthorized users from obtaining services from the system or gaining access to its files. The procedures involved are authorization, identification, and authentication. Authorization is given for certain users to enter the system, gain access to certain files, and request certain types of information. For example, a researcher may be permitted to compile earnings statistics from payroll files but not to associate names with salaries. Any user attempting to enter the system must first identify himself and his location (i.e., the remote terminal he is using), and then authenticate his identification. The latter is essential if information files with limited access are requested; and is desirable to avoid mis-charging of the computing costs. The identification-authentication steps may be repeated any number of times (e.g., when particularly sensitive files are requested).

Requirements for authentication may also arise in reverse, i.e., the processor identifies and authenticates itself to the user with suitable techniques. This may satisfy the user that he is not merely conversing with an infiltrator's console. Applied to certain messages from the processor to the user (e.g., error messages or requests for repetition) these could be authenticated as coming from the processor and not from a piggy-back penetrator.

Processing Restrictions. Although access control procedures can eliminate the simple threats from external sources, they cannot stop sophisticated efforts nor completely counter legitimate users or system personnel inclined to browse. An infiltrator, once in the system will attempt to extract, alter, or destroy information in the files. Therefore, some processing restrictions (in addition to the normal memory protection features) need to be inposed on files of sensitive information. For example, certain removable files may be mounted on drives with disabled circuits, and alterations of data performed only after requests are authenticated by the controller of each file. Copying complete files (or large parts of files) is another activity where processing control need to be imposed—again in the form of authentication of file controllers.

In systems where very sensitive information is handled, processing restrictions could be imposed on specific users in instances of "suspicious" behavior. For example, total cancellation of any program attempting to enter unauthorized files may be an effective countermeasure against browsing.[9]

Threat Monitoring. Threat monitoring concerns detection of attempted or actual penetrations of the system or files either to provide a real-time response (e.g., invoking job cancellation, or starting tracing procedures) or to permit post facto analysis. Threat monitoring may include recording of all rejected attempts to enter the system or specific files, use of illegal access procedures, unusual activity involving a certain file, attempts to write into protected files, attempts to perform restricted operations such as copying files, excessively long periods of use, etc. Periodic reports to users on file activity may reveal possible misuse or tampering, and prompt stepped-up auditing along with a possible real-time response. Such reports may range from a page by page synopsis of activity during the user session, to a monthly analysis and summary.

Privacy Transformations. Privacy transformations[10,11] are techniques for coding the data in user-processor communications or in files to conceal information. They could be directed against passive (e.g., wiretapping) as well as sophisticated active threats (e.g., sharing a user's identification and communication link by a "piggy-back" infiltrator), and also afford protection to data in removable files against unauthorized access or physical loss.

A privacy transformation consists of a set of reversible logical operations on the individual characters of an information record, or on sets of such records. Reversibility is required to permit recovery (decoding) of the original information from the encoded form. Classes of privacy transformations include:

- Substitution—replacement of message characters with characters or groups of characters in the same or a different alphabet in a one-to-one manner (e.g., replacing alphanumeric characters with groups of binary numerals).
- Transposition—rearrangement of the ordering of characters in a message.
- Addition—using appropriate "algebra" to combine characters in the message with encoding sequences of characters (the "key") supplied by the user.

Well-known among a number of privacy transformations of the "additive" type[11] are the "Vigenere cipher," where a short sequence of characters are repeatedly used to combine with the characters of the message, and the "Vernam system," where the user-provided sequence is at least as long as the message. Successive applications of several transformations may be used to increase the complexity.

In general, the user of a particular type of privacy transformation (say, the substitution of characters in the same alphabet) has a very large number of choices of transformations in that class (e.g., there are 26 factorial—4×10^{26}—possible substitution schemes of the 26 letters of the English alphabet). The identification of a particular transformation is the "key" chosen by the user for encoding the message.

Any infiltrator would naturally attempt to discover the key—if necessary, by analyzing an intercepted encoded message. The effort required measures the "work factor" of the privacy transformation, and indicates the amount of protection provided, assuming the key cannot be stolen, etc. The work factor depends on the type of privacy transformations used, the statistical characteristics of the message language, the size of the key space, etc. A word of caution against depending too much on the large key space: Shannon[11] points out that about 3×10^{12} years would be required, on the average, to discover the key used in the aforementioned substitution cipher with 26 letters by an exhaustive trial-and-error method (eliminating one possible key every microsecond). However, according to Shannon, repeatedly dividing the key space into two sets of roughly an equal number of keys and eliminating one set each trial (similar to coin-weighing problems) would require only 88 trials.

The level of work factor which is critical for a given information system depends, of course, on an estimate of the magnitude of threats and of the value of the information. For example, an estimated work factor of one day of continuous computation to break a single key may be an adequate deterrent against a low-level threat.

Other criteria which influence the selection of a class of privacy transformations are:[11]

- Length of the key—Keys require storage space, must be protected, have to be communicated to remote locations and entered into the system, and may even require memorization. Though generally a short key length seems desirable, better protection can be obtained by using a key as long as the message itself.

- Size of the key space—The number of different privacy transformations available should be as large as possible to discourage trial-and-error approaches, and to permit assignment of unique keys to large numbers of users and changing of keys at frequent intervals.

- Complexity—Affects the cost of implementation of the privacy system by requiring more hardware or processing time, but may also improve the work factor.

- Error sensitivity—The effect of transmission errors or processor malfunctioning may make decoding impossible.

Other criteria are, of course, the cost of implementation and processing time requirements which depend, in part, on whether the communication channel or the files of the system are involved.

Integrity Management. Important in providing privacy to an information system is verification that the system software and hardware perform as specified—including an exhaustive initial verification of the programs and hardware, and later, periodic checks. Between checks, strict controls should be placed on modifications of software and hardware. For example, the latter may be kept in locked cabinets equipped with alarm devices. Verification of the hardware integrity after each modification or repair should be a standard procedure, and inspection to detect changes of the emissive characteristics performed periodically.

Integrity of the communication channel is a far more serious problem and, if common carrier connections are employed, it would be extremely difficult to guarantee absence of wiretaps.

Personnel integrity (the essential element of privacy protection) poses some fundamental questions which are outside the scope of this paper. The assumptions must be made, in the interest of realism, that not everyone can be trusted. System privacy should depend on the integrity of as few people as possible.

System Aspects of Information Privacy

As pointed out previously, not all parts of an information system are equally vulnerable to threats to information privacy, and different countermeasures may be required in each part to counter the same level of threat. The structure and functions of the information processor, the files, and the communication network with terminals are, in particular, sufficiently different to warrant separate discussion of information privacy in these subsystems.

Communication Lines and Terminals. Since terminals and communication channels are the principal user-to-processor links, privacy of information in this most vulnerable part of the system is essential.

Wiretapping: Many users spread over a wide area provide many opportunities for wiretapping. Since the cost of physically protected cables is prohibitive, there are no practical means available to prevent this form of entry. As a result, only through protective techniques applied at the terminals and at the processor can the range of threats from simple eavesdropping to sophisticated entry through special terminals be countered. While a properly designed password identification-authentication procedure is effective against some active threats, it does not provide any protection against the simplest threat—eavesdropping—nor against sophisticated "piggy-back" entry.

The only broadly effective countermeasure is the use of privacy transformations.

Radiation: In addition to the spectrum of threats arising from wiretapping, electromagnetic radiation from terminals must be considered.[12]

Electromagnetic radiation characteristics will depend heavily on the type of terminal, and may in some cases pose serious shielding and electrical-filtering problems. More advanced terminals using cathode ray tubes for information display may create even greater problems in trying to prevent what has been called "tuning in the terminal on Channel 4."

Use of privacy transformations also helps to reduce some of the problems of controlling radiation. In fact, applying the transformation as close to the electromechanical converters of the terminal as possible minimizes the volume that must be protected, and reduces the extent of vulnerable radiation characteristics.

Obviously, the severity of these problems depends upon the physical security of the building or room in which the terminal is housed. Finally, proper handling and disposal of typewriter ribbons, carbon papers, etc., are essential.

Operating modes: Whether it would be economical to combine both private and public modes of operation into a single standard terminal is yet to be determined; but it appears desirable or even essential to permit a private terminal to operate in the public mode, although the possibility of compromising the privacy system must be considered. For example, one can easily bypass any special purpose privacy hardware by throwing a switch manually or by computer, but these controls may become vulnerable to tampering. The engineering of the terminal must, therefore, assure reasonable physical, logical, and electrical integrity for a broad range of users and their privacy requirements.

Terminal identification: An unambiguous and authenticated identification of a terminal is required for log-in, billing, and to permit system initiated call-back for restarting or for "hang-up and redial"[13] access control procedures. The need for authentication mainly arises when the terminal is connected to the processor via the common-carrier communication lines, where tracing of connections through switching centers is difficult. If directly wired connections are used, neither authentication nor identification may be required, since (excluding wiretaps) only one terminal can be on a line.

Identification of a terminal could involve transmission of an internally (to the terminal) generated or user-entered code word consisting, for example, of two parts: one containing a description or name of the terminal; the other, a password (more about these later) which authenticates that the particular terminal is indeed the one claimed in the first part of the code word. Another method suggested for authenticating the identity of a terminal is to use computer hang-up and call-back procedures.[13] After terminal identification has been satisfactorily established, the processor may consult tables to determine the privacy level of the terminal; i.e., the users admitted to the terminal, the protection techniques required, etc.

User identification: As with a terminal, identifying a user may require stating the user's name and account number, and then authenticating these with a password from a list, etc.

If the security of this identification process is adequate, the normal terminal input mechanisms may be used; otherwise, special features will be required. For example, hardware to accept and interpret coded cards might be employed, or sets of special dials or buttons provided. Procedures using the latter might consist of operating these devices in the correct sequence.

In some instances, if physical access to a terminal is appropriately controlled, terminal identification may be substituted for user identification (and vice versa).

Passwords: Clearly, a password authenticating a user or a terminal would not remain secure indefinitely. In fact, in an environment of potential wiretapping or radiative pickup, a password might be compromised by a single use. Employing lists of randomly selected passwords, in a "one-time-use" manner where a new word is taken from the list each time authentication is needed has been suggested as a countermeasure under such circumstances.[9] One copy of such a list would be stored in the processor, the other maintained in the terminal or carried by the user. After signing in, the user takes the next word on the list, transmits it to the processor and then crosses it off. The processor compares the received password with the next word in its own list and permits access only when the two agree. Such password lists could be stored in the terminal on punched paper tape, generated internally by special circuits, or printed on a strip of paper. The latter could be kept in a secure housing with only a single password visible. A special key lock would be used to advance the list. Since this method of password storage precludes automatic reading, the password must be entered using an appropriate input mechanism.

The protection provided by use of once-only passwords during sign-in procedures only is not adequate against more sophisticated "between lines" entry by an infiltrator who has attached a terminal to the legitimate user's line. Here the infiltrator can use his terminal to enter the system between communications from the legitimate user. In this situation the use of once-only passwords must be extended to each message generated by the user. Automatic generation and inclusion of authenticating passwords by the terminal would now be essential for smoothness of operation; and lists in the processor may have to be replaced by program or hardware implemented password generators.

Privacy transformations: The identification procedures discussed above do not provide protection against passive threats through wiretapping, or against sophisticated "piggy-back" entry into the communication link. An infiltrator using the latter technique would simply intercept messages—password and all—and alter these or insert his own (e.g., after sending the user an error indication). Authentication of each message, however, will only prevent a "piggy-back" infiltrator from using the system after cancelling the sign-off statement of the legitimate user.

Although it may be conceivable that directly wired connections could be secured against wiretapping, it would be nearly impossible to secure common-carrier circuits. Therefore, the use of privacy transformations may be the only effective countermeasures against wiretapping and "piggy-back" entry, as they are designed to render encoded messages unintelligible to all but holders of the correct key. Discovering the key, therefore, is essential for an infiltrator. The effort required to do this by analyzing intercepted encoded messages (rather than by trying to steal or buy the key) is the "work factor" of a privacy transformation. It depends greatly on the type of privacy transformations used, as well as on the knowledge and ingenuity of the infiltrator.

The type of privacy transformation suitable for a particular communication network and terminals depends on the electrical nature of the communication links, restrictions on the character set, structure and vocabulary of the query language and data, and on the engineering aspects and cost of the terminals. For example, noisy communication links may rule out using "auto key" transformation[11] (e.g., those where the message itself is the key for encoding); and highly structured query languages may preclude direct substitution schemes, since their statistics would not be obscured by substitution and would permit easy discovery of the substitution rules. Effects of character-set restrictions on privacy transformations become evident where certain characters are reserved for control of the communication net, terminals, or the processor (e.g., "end of message," "carriage return," and other control characters). These characters should be sent in the clear and appear only in their proper locations in the message, hence imposing restrictions on the privacy transformation.

A number of other implications of using privacy transformations arise. For example, in the private mode of terminal operation the system may provide an end-to-end (terminal-to-processor) privacy transformation with a given work factor, independently of the user's privacy requirements. If this work factor is not acceptable to a user, he should be permitted to introduce a preliminary privacy transformation using his own key in order to increase the combined work factor. If this capability is to be provided at the terminal, there should be provisions for inserting additional privacy-transformation circuitry.

Another possibly necessary feature might allow the user to specify by appropriate statements whether privacy transforms are to be used or not. This would be part of a general set of "privacy instructions" provided in the information-system operating programs. Each change from private to public mode, especially when initiated from the terminal, should be authenticated.

Files

While the above privacy-protection techniques and access-control procedures for external terminals and the communication network may greatly reduce the threat of infiltration by those with no legitimate access, they do not protect information against (1) legitimate users attempting to browse in unauthorized files, (2) access by operating and maintenance personnel, or (3) physical acquisition of files by infiltrators.

A basic aspect of providing information privacy to files is the right of a user to total privacy of his files—even the system manager of the information center should not have access. Further, it should be possible to establish different levels of privacy in files. That is, it should be feasible to permit certain of a group of users to have access to all of the company's files, while allowing others limited access to only some of these files.

In this context certain standard file operations—such as file copying—would seem inappropriate, if permitted in an uncontrolled manner, since it would be easy to prepare a copy of a sensitive file and maintain it under one's own control for purposes other than authorized. Similarly, writing into files should be adequately controlled. For example, additions and deletions to certain files should be authorized only after proper authentication. It may even be desirable to mount some files on drives with physically disabled writing circuits.

Access control: Control of access to the files would be based on maintaining a list of authorized users for each file, where identification and authentication of identity (at the simplest), is established by the initial sign-in procedure. If additional protection is desired for a particular file, either another sign-in password or a specific file-access password is requested to reauthenticate the user's identity. The file-access passwords may be maintained in a separate list for each authorized user, or in a single list. If the latter, the system would ask the user for a password in a specific location in the list (e.g., the tenth password). Although a single list requires less storage and bookkeeping, it is inherently less secure. Protection of files is thus based on repeated use of the same requirements—identification and authentication—as for initial access to the system during sign-in. This protection may be inadequate, however, in systems where privacy transformations are not used in the communication net (i.e., "piggy-back" infiltration is still possible).

Physical vulnerability: An additional threat arises from possible physical access to files. In particular, the usual practice of maintaining backup files (copies of critical files for recovery from drastic system failures) compounds this problem. Storage, transport, and preparation of these files all represent points of vulnerability for copying, theft, or an off-line print out. Clearly, possession of a reel of tape, for example, provides an interloper the opportunity to peruse the information at his leisure. Applicable countermeasures are careful storage and transport, maintaining the physical integrity of files throughout the system, and the use of privacy transformations.

Privacy transformations: As at the terminals and in the communication network, privacy transformations could be used to protect files against failure of normal access control or physical protection procedures. However, the engineering of privacy transformations for files differs considerably:

- Both the activity level and record lengths are considerably greater in files;
- Many users, rather than one, may share a file;
- Errors in file operations are more amenable to detection and control than those in communication links, and the uncorrected error rates are lower;

- More processing capability is available for the files, hence more sophisticated privacy transformations can be used;
- Many of the files may be relatively permanent and sufficiently large, so that frequent changes of keys are impractical due to the large amount of processing required. Hence, transformations with higher work factors could be used and keys changed less frequently.

It follows that the type of privacy transformation adequate for user-processor communications may be entirely unacceptable for the protection of files.

The choice of privacy transformations for an information file depends heavily on the amount of file activity in response to a typical information request, size and structure of the file (e.g., short records, many entry points), structure of the data within the file, and on the number of different users. Since each of these factors may differ from file to file, design of a privacy system must take into account the relevant parameters. For example, a continuous key for encoding an entire file may be impractical, as entry at intermediate points would be impossible. If a complex privacy transformation is desired additional parallel hardware may be required, since direct implementation by programming may unreasonably increase the processing time. In order to provide the necessary control and integrity of the transformation system, and to meet the processing time requirements, a simple, securely housed processor similar to a common input-output control unit might be used to implement the entire file control and privacy system.

The Processor

The processor and its associated random-access storage units contain the basic monitor program, system programs for various purposes, and programs and data of currently serviced users. The role of the monitor is to provide the main line of defense against infiltration attempts through the software system by maintaining absolute control over all basic system programs for input-output, file access, user scheduling, privacy protection, etc. It should also be able to do this under various contingencies such as system failures and recovery periods, debugging of system programs, during start-up or shut-down of parts of the system, etc. Clearly, the design of such a fail-safe monitor is a difficult problem. Peters[9] describes a number of principles for obtaining security through software.

Penetration attempts against the monitor or other system programs attempt to weaken its control, bypass application of various countermeasures, or deteriorate its fail-safe properties. Since it is unlikely that such penetrations could be successfully attempted from outside the processor facility, protection relies mainly on adequate physical and personnel integrity. A first step is to keep the monitor in a read-only store, which can be altered only physically, housed under lock and key. In fact, it would be desirable to embed the monitor into the basic hardware logic of the processor, such that the processor can operate only under monitor control.

Software integrity could be maintained by frequent comparisons of the current systems programs with carefully checked masters, both periodically and after each modification. Personnel integrity must, of course, be maintained at a very high level, and could be buttressed by team operation (forming a conspiracy involving several persons should be harder than undermining the loyalty of a single operator or programmer).

Integrity management procedures must be augmented with measures for controlling the necessary accesses to the privacy-protection programs; or devices for insertion of passwords, keys, and authorization lists; or for maintenance. These may require the simultaneous identification and authentication of several of the information-center personnel (e.g., a system programmer and the center "privacy manager"), or the use of several combination locks for hardware-implemented privacy-protection devices.

Hierarchy of privacy protection: Privacy protection requires a hierarchy of system-operating and privacy-protection programs, with the primary system supervisor at the top. Under this structure, or embedded in it, may exist a number of similar but independent hierarchies of individual users' privacy-protection programs. It is neither necessary nor desirable to permit someone who may be authorized to enter this hierarchy at a particular level to automatically enter any lower level. Access should be permitted only on the basis of an authenticated "need to know." For example, if privacy transformations are employed by a particular user, his privacy programs should be protected against access by any of the system management personnel.

Time-sharing: Various modes of implementing time-sharing in the information system may affect the privacy of information in the processor. In particular, copying of residual information in the dynamic portions of the storage hierarchy during the following time-slice seems likely. Since erasing all affected storage areas after each time-slice could be excessively time consuming, a reasonable solution may be to "tag" pages of information and programs as "private," or to set aside certain areas of the core for private information and erase only those areas or pages after each time-slice. Only the private areas or pages would need to be erased as part of the swapping operation.[14]

Also important is the effect of privacy transformations on processing time. Sophisticated privacy transformations, for example, if applied by programmed algorithms, may require a significant fraction of each time-slice. It may be necessary, therefore, to use hardware implementation of privacy transformations by including these in the hardware versions of the monitor or through the use of a separate parallel processor for all access-control and privacy-transformation operations.

Hardware failures: With respect to integrity management, there is one aspect of hardware integrity which is the responsibility of the original equipment manufacturer, viz., a hardware failure should not be catastrophic in the sense that it would permit uncontrolled or even limited access to any part of the system normally protected. Whether this entails making the critical parts of the hardware super-reliable and infallible, or whether the system can be designed for a fail-safe form of graceful degradation is an open question. It is important to assure the user that the hardware has this basic characteristic.

CONCLUDING REMARKS

It should be emphasized again that the threat to information privacy in time-shared systems is credible, and that only modest resources suffice to launch a low-level infiltration effort. It appears possible, however, to counter any threat without unreasonable expenditures, provided that the integrity and competence of key personnel of the information center is not compromised. Trustworthy and competent operating personnel will establish and maintain the integrity of the system hardware and software which, in turn, permits use of their protective techniques. A concise assessment of the effectiveness of these techniques in countering a variety of threats is presented in Table II.

Privacy can be implemented in a number of ways ranging from system enforced "mandatory privacy," where available privacy techniques are automatically applied to all users with associated higher charges for processing time, to "optional privacy" where a user can specify what level of privacy he desires, when it should be applied, and perhaps implement it himself. The latter privacy regime appears more desirable, since the cost of privacy could be charged essentially

TABLE II. Summary of Countermeasures to Threat to Information Privacy

Threat \ Countermeasure	Access Control (passwords, authentication, authorization)	Processing Restrictions (storage, protect, privileged operations)	Privacy Transformations	Threat Monitoring (audits, logs)	Integrity Management (hardware, software, personnel)
Accidental: User error	Good protection, unless the error produces correct password	Reduce susceptibility	No protection if depend on password; otherwise, good protection	Identifies the "accident prone"; provides post facto knowledge of possible loss	Not applicable
System error	Good protection, unless bypassed due to error	Reduce susceptibility	Good protection in case of communication system switching errors	May help in diagnosis or provide post facto knowledge	Minimizes possibilities for accidents
Deliberate, passive: Electromagnetic pick-up	No protection	No protection	Reduces susceptibility; work factor determines the amount of protection	No protection	Reduces susceptibility
Wiretapping	No protection	No protection	Reduces susceptibility; work factor determines the amount of protection	No protection	If applied to communication circuits may reduce susceptibility
Waste Basket	Not applicable	Not applicable	Not applicable	Not applicable	Proper disposal procedures
Deliberate, active: "Browsing"	Good protection (may make masquerading necessary)	Reduces ease to obtain desired information	Good protection	Identifies unsuccessful attempts; may provide post facto knowledge or operate real-time alarms	Aids other countermeasures
"Masquerading"	Must know authenticating passwords (work factor to obtain these)	Reduces ease to obtain desired information	No protection if depends on password; otherwise, sufficient	Identifies unsuccessful attempts; may provide post facto knowledge or operate real-time alarms	Makes harder to obtain information for masquerading; since masquerading is deception, may inhibit browsers
"Between lines" entry	No protection unless used for every message	Limits the infiltrator to the same potential as the user whose line he shares	Good protection if privacy transformation changed in less time than required by work factor	Post facto analysis of activity may provide knowledge of possible loss	Communication network integrity helps
"Piggy-back" entry	No protection but reverse (processor-to-user) authentication may help	Limits the infiltrator to the same potential as the user whose line he shares	Good protection if privacy transformation changed in less time than required by work factor	Post facto analysis of activity may provide knowledge of possible loss	Communication network integrity helps

(Continued)

TABLE II.   (Continued)

Threat \ Countermeasure	Access Control (passwords, authentication, authorization)	Processing Restrictions (storage, protect, privileged operations)	Privacy Transformations	Threat Monitoring (audits, logs)	Integrity Management (hardware, software, personnel)
Entry by system personnel	May have to masquerade	Reduces ease of obtaining desired information	Work factor, unless depend on password and masquerading is successful	Post facto analysis of activity may provide knowledge of possible loss	Key to the entire privacy protection system
Entry via "trap doors"	No protection	Probably no protection	Work factor, unless access to keys obtained	Possible alarms, post facto analysis	Protection through initial verification and subsequent maintenance of hardware and software integrity
Core dumping to get residual information	No protection	Erase private core areas at swapping time	No protection unless encoded processing feasible	Possible alarms, post facto analysis	Not applicable
Physical acquisition of removable files	Not applicable	Not applicable	Work factor, unless access to keys obtained	Post facto knowledge from audits of personnel movements	Physical preventative measures and devices

to those users desiring protection. For example, if a user feels that simple passwords provide adequate protection, his privacy system can be implemented in that way, with probable savings in processing time and memory space.

Implementation of "optional" privacy could be based on a set of "privacy instructions" provided by the programming and query languages of the system. Their proper execution (and safeguarding of the associated password lists and keys) would be guaranteed by the system. The cost of their use would reflect itself in higher rates for computing time. For example, the AUTHENTICATE, K,M instruction requests the next password from list K which has been previously allocated to this user from the system's pool of password lists (or has been supplied by the user himself). The operating program now sends the corresponding message to the user who takes the correct password from his copy of the list K and sends it to the processor. If the comparison of the received password with that in the processor fails, the program transfers to location M where "WRITE LOG, A" instruction may be used to make a record of the failure to authenticate in audit log A. Further instructions could then be used to generate a real-time alarm at the processor site (or even at the site of the user's terminal), terminate the program, etc. Other privacy instructions would permit application of privacy transformations, processing restrictions, etc.

The privacy protection provided by any system could, of course, be augmented by an individual user designing and implementing privacy protection schemes within his programs. For example, he may program his own authentication requests, augmenting the system-provided instructions for this purpose; and use his own schemes for applying privacy transformations to data in files or in the communication network. Since these additional protective schemes may be software implemented they would require considerable processing time, but would provide the desired extra level of security.

Further work: This paper has explored a range of threats against information privacy and pointed out some of the systems implications of a set of feasible countermeasures. Considerable work is still needed to move from feasibility to practice, although several systems have already made concrete advances. Special attention must be devoted to establishing the economic and operational practicality of privacy transformations: determining applicable classes of transformations and establishing their work factors; designing economical devices for encoding and decoding; considering the effects of query language structure on work factors of privacy transformation; and determining their effects on processing time and storage requirements.

Large information systems with files of sensitive information are already emerging. The computer community has a responsibility to their users to insure that systems not be designed without considering the possible threats to privacy and providing for adequate countermeasures. To insure a proper economic balance between possible solutions and requirements, users must become aware of these considerations and be able to assign values to information entrusted to a system. This has been done in the past (e.g., industrial plant guards, "company confidential" documents, etc.), but technology has subtly changed accessibility. The same technology can provide protection, but we must know what level of protection is required by the user.

REFERENCES

1. The computer and invasion of privacy, Hearings Before a Sub-committee on Government Operations, House of Representatives, July 26–28, 1966, U.S. Government Printing Office, Washington, D.C., 1966.

2. P. Baran, "Communications, computers, and people," AFIPS Conference Proceedings, Fall Joint Computer Conference, Part 2, Vol. 27, 1965.

3. S. Rothman, Centralized government information systems and privacy, Report for the President's Crime Commission, September 22, 1966.

4. E. E. David and R. M. Fano, "Some thoughts about the social implications of accessible computing," AFIPS Conference Proceedings, Fall Joint Computer Conference, Part 1, Vol. 27, pp. 243–251, 1965.

5. S. D. Pursglove, "The eavesdroppers: fallout from R & D," Electronic Design, Vol. 14, No. 15, pp. 35–43, June 21, 1966.

6. S. Dash, R. F. Schwartz, and R. E. Knowlton, The eavesdroppers, Rutgers University Press, New Brunswick, N.J., 1959.

7. W. H. Ware, "Security and privacy: similarities and differences," presented at SJCC 67, Atlantic City, New Jersey.

8. R. C. Daley and P. G. Neumann, "A general-purpose file system for secondary storage," AFIPS Conference Proceedings, Fall Joint Computer Conference, Part 1, Vol. 27, p. 213, 1965.

9. B. Peters, "Security considerations in a multi-programmed computer system," presented at SJCC 67, Atlantic City, New Jersey.

10. P. Baran, On distributed communications: IX. Security, secrecy and tamper-free considerations, RM-3765-PR, The RAND Corporation, Santa Monica, California, August 1964.

11. C. E. Shannon, "Communications theory of secrecy systems," Bell System Technical Journal, Vol. 28, No. 4, pp. 656–715, October 1949.

12. R.L. Dennis, Security in computer environment, SP2440/000/01, System Development Corporation, August 18, 1966.

13. D. J. Dantine, "Communications needs of the user for management information systems," AFIPS Conference Proceedings, Fall Joint Computer Conference, Vol. 29, pp. 403–422, 1966.

14. R. L. Patrick, private communication.

Section III
PRIVACY
TRANSFORMATIONS

In this section we examine in some detail privacy transformations, also called encryption or scrambling. These are reversible encodings of data used to conceal information. They are operations which take data in its natural form (or cleartext) and transform the data so that it is (hopefully) unrecognizable by unauthorized persons. Privacy transformations are especially effective against communication line infiltration and against unauthorized access to data in removable files. Even simple privacy transformations are very effective against most users.

It is impossible to include in a collection of readings more than a small amount of the interesting literature on encryption, especially since this topic has fascinated many inquisitive minds down through the centuries. As David Kahn points out in his outstanding book The Codebreakers [12], cryptographic systems for hiding messages were used not only in modern times, but also by Venice's ruling body (The Council of Ten) in the sixteenth century, and even as early as the fifth century B.C. by the Spartans.

Some of the work which laid mathematical foundations for cryptography is not computer-oriented, since computers were not widely used when these papers were published. These path-finding (for their time) works dealt with cryptographic systems which have been somewhat obsoleted by the arrival of the computer. For that reason we decided not to include these seminal papers [13,14] in this book of readings. Another interesting article which we omitted due to space limitations is an account of recent work at IBM on encryption [15].

Paul Baran in his paper proposes a departure from traditional security concepts with the idea that the methods of building a secure system should not be kept secret. Rather, the system should be exposed to widespread security tests and to scrutiny by clever minds of diverse backgrounds. The more bright people who critically review a system, the greater the chance of discovering significant points of potential weakness—before the interloper does. The only secret should be the encryption key(s) and priming parameters. The ADEPT-50 system for the IBM 360/50 was based on this philosophy; it is described in Section IV.

Ralph Skatrud in his article proposes a cryptographic technique which he claims would be unbreakable in theory and achievable without using great amounts of keys. This system is based on the digital substitution method and is achieved using a relatively small amount of memory space.

Pseudo-random number techniques are certainly much more effective in concealing data than the traditional cryptographic methods of addition, transposition, substitution, and their combinations. However, pseudo-random number generators have the drawback that after a certain point the keys repeat. For large quantities of data this could allow breaking of the key and discovery of the cleartext message. To prevent this, J. M. Carroll and P. M. McLellan introduce what they call "infinite key" privacy transformations. These transformations provide extremely long key strings which are essentially "infinite"; these go a long way toward solving this problem.

There has been little work to date in assessment of the cost or speed of encryption. It is therefore worth noting Carroll and McLellan's figure of 37,000 bytes per CPU second for scrambling on a PDP-10/50 system. The editor has obtained similar results at Berkeley.

On Distributed Communications: IX. Security, Secrecy, and Tamper-Free Considerations

PAUL BARAN

SUMMARY

One key difference between a civilian and a military communications system is the provision made in the latter for the preservation of secrecy and for immunity from destructive tampering. These considerations are most effectively integrated into a network as an integral part of the switching mechanism, rather than in the form of "black boxes" tacked on as an afterthought. This Memorandum is an examination of the proposed Distributed Adaptive Message Block Network's use of this integrated design approach to the problem of providing cryptographic security.

It is acknowledged that the approach represents a departure from conventional practices, which have traditionally maintained a separation between the design of the communications network itself (which is most often a slight modification of a system originally designed for civilian use) and the design and implication of cryptographic safeguards. The rationale is stated that recent major advances in digital computer technology now make it technically feasible and economically desirable to consider a system designed primarily with military applications in mind, and which from the outset of design is cognizant of cryptographic requirements.

SOURCE: The Rand Corporation, Memorandum RM-3765-PR, August 1964. Reprinted by permission.

As a prelude to the proposal, however, the view is expressed that if one cannot safely describe a proposed system in the unclassified literature, then, by definition, it is not sufficiently secure to be used with confidence. A totally secure system design requires a full understanding of the problem by everyone involved with every part of the system—even those who would not normally hold any security clearance.

As applied to the proposed distributed network system, the specified integrated design would include various combinations of:

(1) End-to-end cryptography.

(2) Link-by-link cryptography.

(3) Use of automatic error-detection and repeat transmission (allowing use of more powerful cryptographic transformations).

(4) Transmission of successive Message Blocks by ever changing paths.

(5) Use of a cryptographic scheme which requires complete and correct reception of all previous traffic in a conversation in order to decrypt subsequent Message Blocks, and which suppresses silence periods in voice and data transmission.

(6) An initial system design which assumes potential infiltration by enemy agents having access to portions of the system and the cryptographic key bases:

   (a) Use of key bases split into separate parts and delivered by two or more individuals.

   (b) Non-acceptance of a Message Block for processing (and non-advancement of the crypto synchronization count) until preliminary filtering tests for validity of source and timing have been accomplished.

   (c) Use of an essentially new key for each separate conversion (permitting intermingling of classified and unclassified traffic without fear of security compromises).

   (d) Encouraging heavy use of the system for unclassified traffic, and the processing of all traffic as if it were of the highest secrecy level (perhaps even to the extent of intentionally adding fraudulent traffic between fictitious subscribers).

I. INTRODUCTION

Historically, military communications networks have been based on techniques and practices originated to meet civilian needs. And, although the military security environment is more demanding, as a practical matter there have always been technological limitations forcing the erection of "make do" patchworks for its communications systems. Starting with an essentially civilian-based system, a little is added here and a little there until we convince ourselves that the remaining security shortcomings are due to either technological or to economic lags in the state-of-the-art.

The last few years have witnessed major breakthrough upon major breakthrough in the digital computer technology. In light thereof, it is now pertinent to reconsider the ways in which we would like to build communications systems, taking advantage of these new developments.

An entire Memorandum in this series is being devoted to the problem of security alone because of its underlying importance both to the system and in the large, and due to a relative underdevelopment of the subject in general. For example, Bloom, Mayfield, and Williams in a survey on the problems of military communications report that Army officers most often cite security as their primary communications problem.*

In the proposed system synthesis, the constraints of existing practices have been purposely avoided in order to better consider an entire system from scratch. First considered are the military requirements, following which the discussion moves toward a hardware synthesis making use of this new era's rapidly advancing computer technology.

However, before discussing the proposed direction of solution, it is desirable to digress and touch upon a subject rarely seen in the unclassified literature, but one that must be understood in order to fully appreciate what is being proposed: the problem of the Secrecy about Secrecy.

II. THE PARADOX OF THE SECRECY ABOUT SECRECY

The Assumption of a Clear Dichotomy Between Classified and Unclassified Subject Matter

Present-day security laws divide all military information into two non-intersecting categories: information is either classified, or it is not. If it is, we go to great extremes and much expense to keep it

---

*Bloom, Joel S., Clifton E. Mayfield, and Richard M. Williams, Modern Army Communications, Final Report, The Franklin Institute Laboratories for Research and Development, Philadelphia, January 1962, p. 32.

secret, while relatively little, if any, attempt is made to protect "unclassified" information from untoward disclosure. If, by an almost metaphysical process, a subject is deemed to be slightly to the non-applicable side of a fuzzy classification line, it is often made freely available to all.

It is interesting to note that private "proprietary" trade secrets are often better kept than are secrets affecting national security (if the time between first disclosure and open publication "leak" is used as a measure). Yet, the weight of stringent penalties (not to mention the pressures of patriotism) exists to protect government secrets. Furthermore, most companies allow their civilian secrets to be locked in thin wooden desk drawers, to be discussed with people whose backgrounds haven't been investigated, and even to be discussed over the civilian telephone networks. Perhaps the difficulty in preserving military secrets is caused, at least in part, by the high price and inflexibility of present-day cryptographic equipment, combined with the imposition of rules that in fact hamper expeditious handling of military communications.

Cost and Result of Present-Day Cryptographic Equipment

Present-day communications cryptographic equipment is very expensive; as a result, it is not economically feasible to provide all the cryptographically-secure channels which might be otherwise considered necessary. For example, it has been said that the cost of providing cryptographic security on every communication link carrying sensitive military traffic could exceed the total expenditure for the entire remainder of the system. Thus, our present, and not very satisfactory, response to this dilemma is to force large volumes of "unclassified" military traffic to be sent out over the communications networks in the clear, accessible to all.

The writer has heard military communicators comment that the higher the rank of an officer using an unclassified communication circuit, the greater the probability that highly classified information will be discussed in the clear. Further, the greater the military tension, the higher the probability. Again, the reasons appear quite valid and overriding—particularly in military crises (and in more remote countries) the commander is so grateful to have any communications resource, that he does not demand (and indeed, given the situation, such demand would probably be unreasonable) the non-crisis-period luxury of voice cryptography.

In present-day communication networks, a circuit carrying information between two stations is usually routed over the same links day in and day out. It is only slightly more difficult to eavesdrop on networks containing switching nodes, inasmuch as the number of alternate paths is highly proscribed. It appears to be a relatively easy task to predict which links will convey traffic between any given station and any end destination.

On Secrecy of Secrecy

Discussions of the problems of security and secrecy with regard to military electronics equipment are more often found only in highly classified documents. It should be noted that this Memorandum has been purposely written to be unclassified, for we feel that unless we can freely describe the detailed workings of a proposed military communications system in the open literature, the system hasn't successfully come to grips with the security problem. No violation of security can occur with this procedure because the only background information used is that found in the unclassified literature, including patents, hardware development progress reports, advertisements, newspaper and journal articles, etc. Therefore we assume we have available to us less information concerning U.S. communications security procedures than does our enemy counterpart, giving us freedom to talk without fear of saying anything not otherwise obvious. Further, this material was prepared without our holding a cryptographic clearance* (which we do not want, in any case) and, therefore, without access to information thereby restricted. If we had such a clearance, we would be so constrained as to be unable to discuss this subject without fear of loss of the clearance.

Without the freedom to expose the system proposal to widespread secutiny by clever minds of diverse interests, is to increase the risk that significant points of potential weakness have been overlooked. A frank and open discussion here is to our advantage.

The overall problem here is highly reminiscent of the atomic energy discussions in the 1945-55 era—only those who were not cleared were able to talk about "classified" atomic weapons. This caused security officers to become highly discomfitured by the ease with which unclassified clues were being combined to deduce highly accurate versions of material residing in the classified domain. This

---

*Industrial Security Manual, Department of Defense, U.S. Government Printing Office.

points up a commonly recurring difference of opinion (or philosophy) between the security officer and the technically trained observer. The more technical training an individual possesses, the less confidence he seems to have of the actual value of secrecy in protecting the spread of new developments in a ripe technology. True security does not always equate to blanket unthinking secrecy. While the security value of effective secrecy can be high, we must be realistic and acknowledge the constraints of living in a free society where effective secrecy in peacetime is almost impossible. Avoiding a touchy subject by falling back on edicts rather than rationality may automatically insure the continued existence of the touchy subject.

Secrecy of Cryptographic Design. If the distributed network described in this series is to be built, many people must become involved in its design, manufacture, maintenance, and operation. It would be foolhardy to think that we can actually withhold the hardware details from our enemies. The network would be essentially worthless unless it were so designed that its operations could be discussed openly without resorting to the make-believe game of security in which we all agree to avoid talking about weaknesses—even if these weaknesses are obvious to all. Secrecy of cryptographic design can be self-defeating if it is maintained by blanket edicts in lieu of judicious restraint. The more bright people we can get to review this system now—particularly computer trained individuals—the less trouble we need expect in the future.

The Assumption of Almost-Infinite Effort in Code-Breaking. Part of the reason that current crypto systems are expensive is found in the requirement that they totally survive the efforts of a determined enemy, applying all his energies to break the code. The thought occurs that the money now being spent to insure a high degree of security in cryptographic devices might be better spent buying many more lower-quality cryptographic devices.

If it were not for the almost unyielding requirement for absolute security, we would be able to consider using many low-cost cryptographic schemes providing capability for handling all traffic. While these lower-protection-rate ciphers might yield to a determined enemy, extreme cipher-breaking activity could be made to extract such a high price, that in the long run, a lesser volume of really secret data would be lost. Such less-powerful crypto devices could help reduce the burden of the human classification decision and would speed communications.

Part of the delay in today's hard-copy communications system is the time spent in deciding whether text should be classified or not. Anything that reduces this inordinately heavy burden of deciding whether something is or is not classified, makes the goal of having all military traffic encrypted a highly desirable one in itself.

The proposed network is a universal high-secrecy system, made up of a hierarchy of less-secure sub-systems. It is proposed that the network intentionally treat all inputs as if they are classified, in order to raise the intercept price to the enemy to a value so high that interception would not be worth his effort. Of course, the extra layer of conventional cryptography would be maintained for use in those extremely sensitive cases where the proposed approach might seem risky.

Thus, fullest advantage is taken of the mechanism within the proposed system that takes a channel or a message and chops it into small pieces (like a fruit salad), transmitting it on as a series of message blocks, each using a different path. Additionally, much unclassified material is purposely transmitted cryptographically, and perhaps even a light dose of obsolete traffic is mixed in. Given a big enough bowl, it becomes very difficult to separate the garbage from the salad.

III. SOME FUNDAMENTALS OF CRYPTOGRAPHY

Digital Transmission

One reason cryptographic equipment is expensive is that it is necessary to convert all signals into digital form. (Digital operations permit complex cryptographic operational transformation of the data stream without irrevocable added distortion.) Today's cryptographic devices have not been designed as an integral part of any particular communications system, but, rather, are "black boxes" added onto communications networks designed for other purposes and other times.

In the all-digital system concept being developed, a potential savings occurs by combining the digital switching equipment together with digital cryptographic equipment. Such a combination, irrespective of potential savings offered, is not implemented without difficulty, for it represents the merging of two design areas historically kept apart, both managerially and technically. Probably, a prime reason that on-line cryptography has been so slow in developing is due to the tendency to fund communications systems under the service budgets, while the cryptographic devices used by these systems are supplied as government-furnished equipment by the National Security Agency (NSA). Hence, the true cost of the cryptographic equipment in a system is often not appreciated by the communications system designer, and feedback which would encourage better overall design of future systems by reducing the high cost of the cryptographic gear is lacking. Perhaps better systems would result if this suboptimization were avoided by making the hidden cost of the cryptographic equipment in each communications more visible. Thus, in the development of the distributed network concept, it was felt desirable to include the cost of the cryptographic equipment as an integral part of the switching equipment.

Layers of Encryption

On-line cryptographic communications operation is defined as one in which information is inserted into a network in real-time, converted by cryptographic transformation, transmitted, received, decrypted, and output to the recipient without appreciable delay.

On-line communications traffic can be encrypted at several different stages. These choices might be labeled end-to-end, link-by-link, and, a combination of the two, double encryption (see Figure 1).

End-to-End Encryption. In the end-to-end encryption, a cryptographic device is connected adjacent to the user and a reciprocal transformation device at the receiver. It is an economical way of using cryptographic gear where the two end-points have sufficient volume to warrant tying up the special terminal equipment on a full-time basis. Figure 1a depicts end-to-end encryption, in which the message and the crypto encoder reside in a secure area, as does the end addressee. The same data transformation device (key) must be available to both crypto units.

Cryptographic Data Transformations. A canonical form of cryptographic transformation uses two synchronized pseudo-random binary streams generated by two "key generators," one at the transmitting site, the other at the receiving site. Figure 2 shows the operation of this process. A short key-base contains the starting and modification parameters of a key generator. The key generator creates a long non-repeating digital stream. This stream is then combined with the outgoing message by some logical transformation and the resulting stream, comprising the encrypted text, is transmitted. There are a

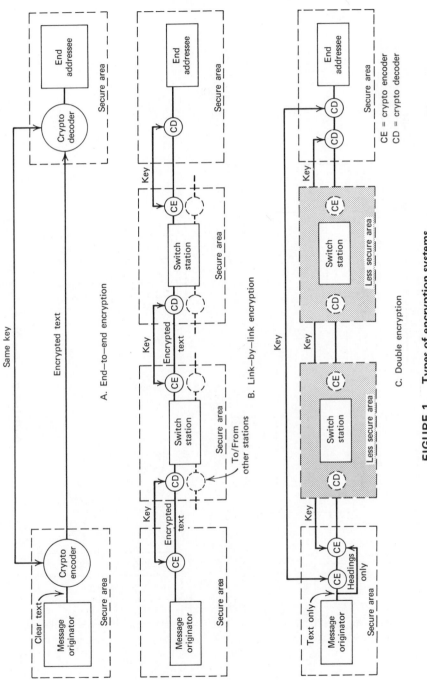

FIGURE 1. Types of encryption systems.

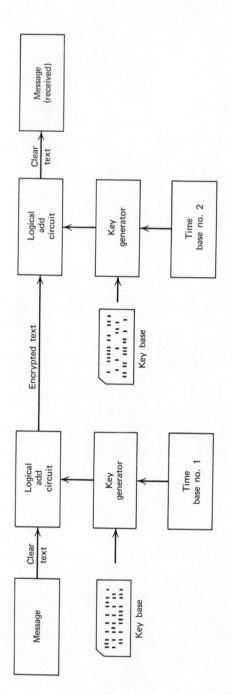

1 1 0 0	Message
1 0 1 0	Key
0 1 1 0	Input

0 1 1 0	Output
1 0 1 0	Key
1 1 0 0	Message

FIGURE 2.   The Crypto process.

few important points to be kept in mind. First, the key generator is presumed to have statistical properties that make it appear as a totally-random digital noise generator. Secondly, in this scheme it is necessary that both key generators be fully synchronized, and that means be provided to cause the time base at the receiving end to coincide with the clock rate at the transmitter end. Third, the logical function combining text and key be such as to provide the same probability of transmitting a "1" for a "0" as for a "1". In Figure 2, a "logical-add" circuit is used to perform the equal probability of transformation that allows reciprocal operation at the receiver. That is,

$$M \oplus K = E$$
$$E \oplus K = M$$

where   M   = the original message
        K   = the key
        E   = encrypted text
        $\oplus$ = the logical-add transformation.

The truth table for the logical-add ($\oplus$) is shown at the bottom of Figure 2. If the message bit is "0" and the key bit is "0", the output is "0"; if the message bit is "0" and the key bit is "1", the output is a "1"; if the message bit is a "1" and the key bit is "0", the output is "1"; etc. It can be seen, therefore, that the logical-add operation is perfectly reciprocal when the key is again added to the encrypted text. The message bits emerge in their original form. Other more complicated "operators" can be used in lieu of the logical-and circuit. (For example, see the Appendix.)

While it is theoretically possible to write an unbreakable cipher merely by using an infinite-length nonrepeating key, it would be necessary to have a copy of this key at both the transmitting station and at the receiving station. At the high data rates being considered, this data storage requirement proves to be impractical. Therefore, the alternative of creating a long key from a relatively short key base has been chosen. It is possible to generate a long mathematical series or string of bits from a moderate-length key base. The length of the key should be chosen such that the series does not repeat or reveal periodicity before the time the key is changed. Thus, for example, a new key base can be inserted into the key generator daily and the receiving crypto system synchronized to match the time base at the transmitting station. The length of a series that can be generated by a set of digital elements cannot be greater* than $N2^N$, where N is equal to the number of flip-flops or storage elements used in the circuit creating the series. This means that extremely long sequences can be created that do not repeat, using a relatively small number of storage cells. For example, if $N = 50$, then $N2^N$ is equal to more than 50,000,000,000,000,000. Or, maximal sequences up to this length can be created. Not all such sequences would, however, be usable, because their statistical properties would reveal the construction of the generator function.

Link-by-Link Encryption. Link-by-link encryption, as shown in Figure 1b, is used when there is not sufficient traffic to warrant a full-time cryptographically-secure circuit between two subscribers. Thus, one key is used between the subscriber and his relay station, separate keys between each pair of relay stations. In such a system, there is an underlying assumption made that each switching center, together with its cryptographic equipment, is located in a secure area and only trustworthy, cleared personnel ever have access to the text which may be in the clear while passing through the switching center. Because of the different transmission time delays and the problems associated in providing a separate set of keys between each originator and every possible end addressee, it must be assumed that each switching center or station, together with its crypto equipment, is located in a secure area. Thus, messages generated in the clear are encrypted and sent to a switching center. Next, each message is decrypted, the address is used to set up the proper outgoing line connection, and the message is sent to the next station. The assumption of absolute security is not always a safe one to make in handling extremely sensitive information. Thus, it might be said that the chief limitation of link-by-link encryption is in the reduced security offered messages passing through several tandem switching centers. Traffic flowing throughout the entire network is openly readable by those inside any switching center—a highly undesirable possibility. Worse yet, as the complexity of the switching networks increases, the number of intermediate switching stations also increases. A point is reached where it becomes almost foolhardy to rely upon this technique alone for protection.

Double Encryption. Double encryption is a combination of end-to-end encryption for the text and link-by-link encryption for the message heading plus the encrypted text.

---

*Assuming that the sequence generator is exactly equivalent to a nonlinear shift register.

Figure 1c exemplifies double encryption. The first encryption operation is for text only, the second layer of encryption is for both the text and the heading. Headings must be available in the clear at the switching center in order that the switching center have the necessary information to route traffic.

IV. IMPLICATIONS FOR THE DISTRIBUTED NETWORK SYSTEM

As it will be necessary to pass through very many switching centers in the proposed distributed network, the limitations of link-by-link encryption are strongly felt. A system with several hundred nodes, depending solely upon link-by-link encryption, would probably be considered inadequate except perhaps for the transmission of semi-classified data—data that would probably be sent in the clear today. Further, end-to-end encryption alone is also unsatisfactory, as the heading on each message block would be in the clear.

Thus, the distributed network shall use both link-by-link and end-to-end encryption. Rather than adding boxes to each switching center, the cipher encoder and decoder circuits shall be designed as an integral part of the Switching Nodes and Multiplexing Stations.

Link-by-Link Cryptography in the Distributed Network

The link-by-link crypto used in the distributed network is described in detail in ODC-VII.* Identical pseudo-random flip-flop chains exist at adjacent Switching Nodes. A logical operation combines the key and the text; timing is established from a piezoelectric clock. Each sequential Message Block contains a "Crypto Serial Number" in the clear derived from the time base.

Timing is established by shifting the local timing so that incoming Message Blocks arrive synchronized to the "start of Message Block" point of the local counter. Then, the difference between the Crypto Serial Numbers is measured by a digital subtraction and the local timing rate is increased or decreased accordingly. The process is repeated until the link has been pulled into synchronization. Synchronization is automatic for link outages up to at least 12 hours duration.

---

*ODC is an abbreviation of the series title; the number following refers to the particular volume in the series.

It is anticipated that the key at each Switching Node will be changed on the order of once per week, or thereabouts. Storage for two alternatively assigned key phases is anticipated to eliminate the need for personnel to be at two or more Switching Nodes at the same time.

It should be emphasized that the link-by-link cryptography serves primarily to keep message headings secret from the eavesdropper.

During the periods in which no valid traffic is being transmitted, a "dummy" or filler stream of bits is sent, not only concealing traffic loading, but also for maintaining the timing synchronization. The dummy stream is created by an electronic noise generator tube feeding several stages of a pseudo-random counter.

The keys used for the link-by-link crypto are in the form of cards, statically read out.

While the crypto stream would be rather hard to "break," it will be seen that comparatively little damage will result should such an event occur.

End-to-End Cryptography in the Distributed Network

The end-to-end crypto built into the Multiplexing Station (see ODC-VIII) is more complicated than that used on the links between the Switching Nodes (and the links from the Multiplexing Station to the Switching Nodes). The added complexity is due to the fact that Multiplexing Station cryptography must permit any subscriber "to talk" to any other subscriber. As the number of potential subscribers is in the millions, the requirement for key storage can become overwhelming. Therefore, an alternative approach has been chosen of storing at each Multiplexing Station key bases only to other Multiplexing Stations. Since we anticipate a maximum of 1024 Multiplexing Stations, only this number key bases need be stored at each Multiplexing Station. We will also assume that any pair of subscribers will desire connections to be kept open for periods ranging from a few seconds to a full day. Such connections, called "pseudo-circuits," are discussed in detail in ODC-VIII.

The first few Message Blocks in any "conversation" exchange housekeeping information necessary for rapid processing of subsequent Message Blocks. This interchange will require on the order of perhaps two seconds. Every time a new call is placed by a subscriber, the originating Multiplexing Station notes which Multiplexing Station is being called and increments its corresponding stored Serial Call Number for the called Multiplexing Station. This serial number is used by both Multiplexing Stations as a crypto start point for synchronization. Since each Multiplexing Station contains a powerful computing engine, and as one second is a long time in the life of a fast computer, sufficient time and capability exist for creating a new pseudo-random number for each new call with no apparent relationship to the key base used on previous calls. Thus, information concerning one call is of no use whatsoever in breaking subsequent calls. This is important in a system with widespread entry, and even allows civilian traffic to be combined with military traffic without weakening the secrecy protection offered.

Modification of the Derived Key Base. To this point, both Multiplexing Stations are synchronized and are using the same derived key bases. (Means are also included to handle errors and reset (advance only) the counters in the rare event of system malfunction. However, in no circumstance is the same derived key base ever used for more than a single conversation call.) After the setup interval, Message Blocks will arrive at a very high rate. It is necessary to create a key from the derived key base at a very rapid rate, leaving very little time for processing. As this is a routine continuous operation, a "stamping mill" processor, with a portion of the Multiplexing Station equipment working full time on this operation, is utilized. The Multiplexing Station uses a drum or similar recirculating register to store the key bases, the derived keys, and the Message Blocks. Figure 3 shows the cryptographic processing of a drum operating on incoming encrypted text. The processing scheme used depends primarily upon a very low Message Block error rate at the Multiplexing Stations. Unfiltered errors and lost Message Blocks are expected to be such rare events, that we shall intentionally "knock down" a quasi-circuit if a single bad Message Block slips by the error-detection filters. (It should be understood that such a rigorous response to errors is infeasible in conventional transmission systems because of their relatively high error rates.)

Incoming encrypted text alternately fills one of the two assigned registers while the other register is simultaneously being read out and "logically-added" to the key base. The clear output text is then stored on one of two alternately assigned registers reserved for this purpose. Meanwhile, the clear text and the incoming text operate upon one another in a controlled manner to produce a new key base,

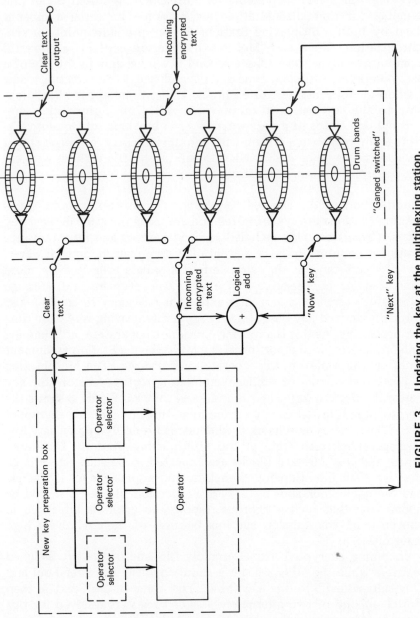

FIGURE 3. Updating the key at the multiplexing station.

based upon the previous key base used. This procedure may appear to be similar to the conventional "autokey"* procedure, but it should be noted that the next key is related to its previous one by a very complex and unknown mathematical operation. Even having the entire encrypted text and a sample of clear text will not facilitate ascertaining subsequent samples of clear text.

Thus, very high speed processing of Message Blocks with high cryptographic security for 1024 separate subscribers per Multiplexing Station does not appear particularly difficult to accomplish. All the equipment required for these operations is included in the parts breakdown in ODC-VIII.

It should be pointed out that the detailed implementation described may or may not be the precise method used. The present detailed description seeks only to point out that secure cryptographic processing at extremely high data rates appears technically possible. The actual choice, and detailed selection of the cryptographic operators, is left to the appropriate agency at the appropriate time.

Message Block Pre-Filtering Key. In order to prevent interruption of the sequence of Message Blocks arriving at the Multiplexing Station by false Message Blocks, means to detect and eliminate acceptance of "counterfeit" Message Blocks are included. Such false Message Blocks might conceivably be generated by a sophisticated enemy agent who has somehow managed to break the link-by-link crypto.

It will be recalled that the Message Block comprises 1024 bits, of which 128 are reserved for various housekeeping functions. Twenty of these housekeeping bit positions are set aside to act as a Pre-Filter Key.** Both the transmitting and receiving Multiplexing Stations generate these keys simultaneously. If, and only if, the incoming Pre-Filtering Key matches the <u>next</u> expected short Pre-Filtering Key, will the Message Block be accepted for further processing and the crypto key count be advanced. If any Message Block arrives that does not meet this test, it is transmitted to the human intercept position at the receiving Multiplexing Station for intervention checking.

---

*Shannon, Claude E., "Communications Theory of Secrecy Systems," <u>Bell Systems Technical Journal</u>, Vol. 28, No. 4, October 1949, p. 668.
**Twenty bits are sufficient to detect better than 1,048,575 out of 1,048,576 random fraudulent Message Blocks.

Genealogy of the Keys

A hierarchical development is being employed to create a very long key from a relatively short key base and caution must be exercised. If too long a sequence is generated from a single key base, it might be possible to deduce other keys derived from the same base. Therefore, let us examine the sequence lengths required by this system to insure that they are very much shorter than would reveal the nature of the generator function.

(1)	Number of Multiplexing Stations	1,024
(2)	Number of new subscriber-to-subscriber calls per key-change period between the ith and the jth Multiplexing Station	100,000*
(3)	Maximum length of time between key changes	48 hr
(4)	Maximum length of time for connection of a "quasi-circuit"	24 hr
(5)	Acceptable probability of breaking and entering a Switching Node, analyzing Message Block headings, and spending full time on a single link attempting to interrupt a single call in progress by creating false Message Blocks	$<10^{-6}$
(6)	Average time between potential interruptions (= 2/3 ms per Message Block $\times$ 10^6)	>10 min
(7)	Maximum number of Message Blocks exchanged between any two subscribers on any single call	1,960,000**

If the active part of the crypto key base used per call is 866 bits, then the longest generated sequence can be as great as 2^{866}, or about 10^{300}.***

Generation and Distribution of Keys

A constant supply of key bases is required to keep the distributed network system operating. One possible plan is shown in Figure 4,

---

*However, the design is based on 1,000,000+.

**The highest normally expected data rate per subscriber is:
    (19,600 bits/sec) (3600 sec/hr) (24 hr)
    = 1.693×10^9 bits per key change
    = 1.824×10^6 Message Blocks.

***For comparison, recall that there are only about 10^{80} electrons in the universe.

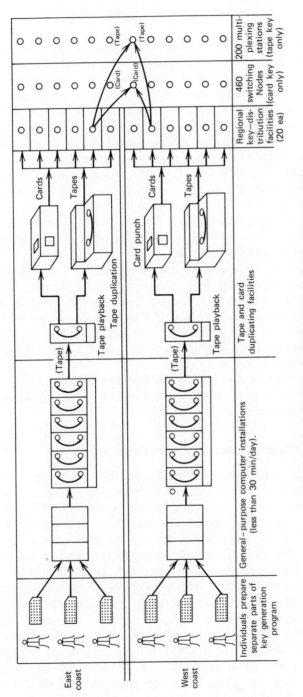

FIGURE 4. One method of preparing and distributing key bases.

in which two major key preparation stations are depicted, one in the East and one in the West. Each such station contains a large general-purpose computer with about six tape units. Separately written, highly complex, random number generating programs are used by each key preparation site. Choice parameters which modify the random number generator are inserted by three individuals at each site working independently. Conventional one-inch magnetic computer tapes, recorded at high speed, are played back into a ¼" tape duplicator for preparation of the 300-ft spools of ¼" tape used in the Multiplexing Stations. The one-inch computer tape outputs are also used to drive an off-line card punch to prepare the shorter set of key bases used by the Switching Nodes. The output of each of the two sites' tapes and card duplicating facilities are stored in about twenty geographically distributed sites.

The Switching Node and Multiplexing Station keys are comprised of two parts, one coming from the distribution site prepared by the East unit, and the other part coming from the West unit via different distribution sites. Each member of a two-man team has mechanical key access to only his own part of the key base. Thus, the system is relatively secure from a <u>single</u> enemy agent having access to an entire key base for any unit.

In the next section it will be shown that even if an enemy were, somehow, able to gain access to the full key, he would still probably not be able to reconstruct traffic.

Protection Offered by Semi-Random Path Choice

In the distributed network, each Message Block usually travels by a path distinctly different than that taken by the previous Block. Path selection is determined on a Switching-Node-by-Switching-Node basis. Each Switching Node chooses the "best" path for each Message Block. If the "best" locally connected link is busy or inoperative, the next best link is used; the heavier the network loading, the more circuitous and varied are the paths taken.

It will be recalled that it is <u>impossible</u> to decrypt a stream of Message Blocks unless all preceding Message Blocks have been correctly received. An eavesdropper, even one equipped with <u>both</u> the link-by-link <u>and</u> the end-to-end keys, cannot decipher any "quasi-channel" or stream of Message Blocks unless he has correctly received all previous Message Blocks. Thus, unless the interceptor records <u>all</u> outgoing links from the Switching Node for a single Multiplexing Station and has <u>all</u> keys, he will not be able to decrypt the sequence of Message Blocks.

It will also be recalled that the links used in the system can have a rather poor unfiltered error rate—one error per 1000 Message Blocks.* The filtered error rate is extremely low—some five orders of magnitude or so better. This, however, is obtained only by the use of an automatic error detection facility and allowance being made for requests for repeat transmissions. An eavesdropper, even one equipped with all keys, cannot very well ask for repeat transmissions. Thus, he is at a decided disadvantage in deciphering the stream of Message Blocks, because his streams will contain errors.

Further, devices able to record 1.5 million bits per second with an adequately low error rate are on the fringe of 1963 state-of-the-art. Lastly, it will be remembered that all silence periods in voice transmissions greater than about 1/20 sec will be suppressed, making the determination of the sequence of Message Blocks extremely difficult and time consuming (see ODC-VIII).

V. A "DEVIL'S ADVOCATE" EXAMINATION

The secrecy provisions for the distributed network system are not being described in full and complete detail in this Memorandum. For example, some preliminary thinking about methods of extending the zone of full secrecy to individual subscribers remote from the Multiplexing Station has been omitted. One reason for such omissions is the fact that the basics of the problem are still being examined.

A key rationale for writing this Memorandum has been to fulfill the need for a working paper which would impart to the reader a feeling for the detailed secrecy measures necessary in the proposed system and to aid in a subsequent "devil's advocate" examination of the system as a whole. The proposed network must successfully operate in a hostile environment, and therefore the system design should be made always keeping in mind potential system weaknesses. We are concerned lest a clever and determined enemy find in it an Achilles heel. As an acid test, we elicit and encourage a response from the reader who will "don the hat of an enemy agent" and try to discover weak spots in the proposed implementation. Such an enemy is assumed to have a limited number of highly competent cohorts plus all the equipment he can transport. Further, it is assumed that the fundamental human inadequacies of our, or any security clearance system will permit infiltration by some at least minimal number of enemy agents who will gain a complete and detailed understanding of the workings of the system.

*See ODC-VI for link error rate determination.

Inasmuch as few people have ready access to the crypto keys and since the keys are changed on a short-time basis, it can be assumed that the subversive agent will generally not have access to more than a portion of the key—unless he resorts to force in obtaining the key, thereby tipping his hat.

As more and more about the limitations of the proposed implementation is learned, we plan to add more and more safeguards to complicate the task of the enemy agent, until a point is reached where we can safely say, "It is now unreasonably difficult for an enemy, or a friend, to interfere with the operation of this network."

The rationale for a limitation on the number of cooperating agents in the pay of an enemy lies in the high probability that any locally recruited agent will be, in fact, a double agent. Hence, the number of agents who know of any proposed operation must be limited for fear of revealing the attack plan.

APPENDIX.   USE OF A FUNCTION OF N-BOOLEAN VARIABLES AS A SECOND-ORDER MODIFIER FOR "NEXT-KEY" GENERATION

In the foregoing text, little was said about the types and the range of operations possible in modifying the key in the end-to-end auto-key subsystem. This Appendix lends some insight into the added complexity of analysis that can be created for the eavesdropper by simply varying the logical addition operator.

In Figure 5 three drum bands, each containing 866 bits, are shown. The first band contains the key used to decrypt the last Message Block; the second drum stores text in the clear that has been derived by use of the old key; and the third drum band stores a new key computed by a "black box," labeled "Z".

A, B, and C, could, for example, represent three magnetic heads on the Multiplexing Station drum, 16 bits apart. Similarly, D, E, and F, would represent a second set of three heads. The box, Z, contains Boolean logic which performs "some" operational function upon the old key for the sake of increasing complexity. Consider the six separate heads to form six separate inputs. We ask, "How many different ways can six inputs be logically organized to form separate and distinct output functions?"

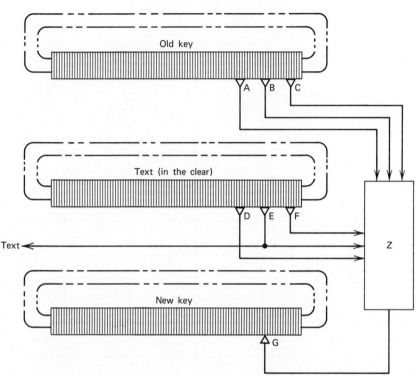

FIGURE 5. The generation of a new key using a function of N-Boolean variables as a transformation operator.

Any Boolean function can be expressed as the logical addition of a series of "min-terms."* Each min-term is a logical product of each of the fundamental inputs or its logical complement. Any logical function can be expressed as a series of points on a Veitch Diagram (see Figure 6). Thus we can have

$$2^{2^N} = 2^{64} \simeq 10^{64/3 \cdot 2} \simeq 10^{20}, \text{ or}$$
$$\sim 100{,}000{,}000{,}000{,}000{,}000{,}000$$

allowable combinations for only six variables. This number almost "explodes" when the number of variables is raised. For example, let N equal the number of variables and compute the number of separate logical functions possible:

*See: Ware, W. H., Digital Computer Technology and Design, Vol. I, Wiley, New York, 1963, pp. 4.13–4.16.

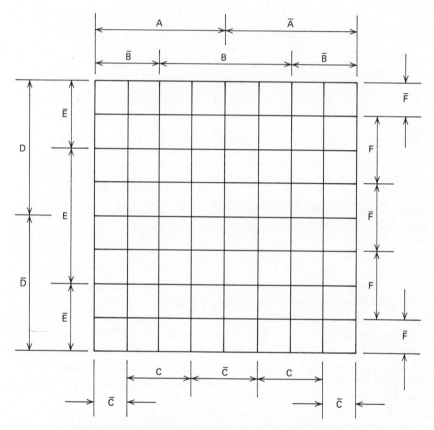

FIGURE 6.   Possible min-terms for six Boolean variables.

N	2^N	2^{2^N}	Number of Functions, Decimal Value
6	64	2^{64}	$\sim 10^{20}$
7	128	2^{128}	$\sim 10^{40}$
8	256	2^{256}	$\sim 10^{60}$
9	512	2^{512}	$\sim 10^{80}$
10	1024	2^{1024}	$\sim 10^{100}$

As any single one of the six input min-terms can be implemented with only six diodes, and as all combinations of min-terms can be implemented with 64 or fewer min-terms, it follows that every complicated function possible can be implemented with two-level logic, requiring 384 diodes (six diodes per min-term, times 64 diodes for all min-terms), for any of the $\sim 10^{20}$ functions possible for six variables.

Of course, rather complex logic circuitry is required for many of these combinations, but many of the functions can be created with only a small portion of the full complement of 384 diodes.

Thus, it is seen that rather simple straightforward techniques can be used at this point to add another layer of complexity, further compounding the problems of the would-be eavesdropper.

A Consideration of the Application of Cryptographic Techniques to Data Processing

R. O. SKATRUD

INTRODUCTION

Two digital cryptographic techniques are described which may have potential applications in Data Processing Systems. A method of digital substitution analogous to a Vernan double tape system is presented, using a controlled combination of data and the contents of two memories. The second method uses a digital route transposition matrix using a combination of row and column transposition under memory control. Possible ways of achieving key leverage in each ciphering process are described.

The large growth in digital computers and computer usage proliferating to time-shared remote systems presents an increasing need to provide data security within a system as well as applying it to data transmitted over communications media.[1] Two fundamental approaches to producing security in data use are developed in this presentation. One is a digital-substitution technique and the second involves a digital-matrix transposition.

Some of the earliest practical cryptographic systems were the monoalphabetic substitution systems used by the Romans.[2] In these, one letter is substituted for another. For example, an A might be replaced by a C. By the fifteenth century, an

SOURCE: Fall Joint Computer Conference, 1969, Proceedings. Reprinted by permission of the publisher, American Federation of Information Processing Societies Press.

Italian by the name of Alberti came up with a technique of crypto-analyzing letters by frequency analyses. As a result, he invented probably the first polyalphabetic substitution system using a cipher disk. Thus, he would encode several words with one substitution alphabet, then he would rotate the disk and encode several more words with the next substitution alphabet.

Early in the sixteenth century Trithemius, a Benedictine Monk, had the first printed book published on cryptology. Trithemius described the square table or tableau which was the first known instance of a progressive key applied to polyalphabetic substitution. It provided a means of changing alphabets with each character. Later in the sixteenth century, Vigenere perfected the autokey: a progressive key in which the last decoded character led you to the next substitution alphabet in a polyalphabetic key. These were basically the techniques that were widely applied in the crypto-machines in the first half of the twentieth century. Various transposition techniques have been employed including the wide use of changing word order and techniques such as rail transcriptions (used in the Civil War).

In 1883, Auguste Kerckhoffs, a man born in Holland but a naturalized Frenchman, published a book entitled La Cryptographic Militaire. In it, he established two general principles for cryptographic systems. They were:

1. A key must withstand the operational strains of heavy traffic. It must be assumed that the enemy has the general system. Therefore, the security of the system must rest with the key.
2. Only cryptoanalysts can know the security of the key. In this, he infers that anyone who proposes a cryptographic technique should be familiar with the techniques that could be used to break it.

From these two general principles, six specific requirements emerged in his book:

1. The key should be, if not theoretically unbreakable, at least unbreakable in practice.
2. Compromise of the hardware system or coding technique should not result in compromising the security of communications that the system carries.
3. The key should be remembered without notes and should be easily changeable.

4. The cryptograms must be transmittable by telegraph. Today this would be expanded to include both digital intelligence and voice (if voice scramblers are employed) utilizing either wire or radio as the medium.

5. The apparatus or documents should be portable and operable by a single person. This requirement is met in the systems proposed in this paper by the portability of the key in a dense storage medium (such as magnetic tape), installable in a processing system by one man.

6. The system should be easy, neither requiring knowledge of a long list of rules nor involving mental strain. In the proposed systems, the key is an automatic-machine-controlled process until a key change occurs.

In 1917 Gilbert S. Vernan, a young engineer at American Telephone and Telegraph Company, using the Baudot code (teletype) invented a means of adding two characters (exclusive or). Vernan's machine mixed a key with text as illustrated by the following:

Clear Text	1	0	1	1	1
Key	0	1	0	1	0
Coded Character	1	1	1	0	1

To derive the text from the coded character, all that was required was the addition of the key again to the coded character.

Coded Character	1	1	1	0	1
Key	0	1	0	1	0
Clear Text	1	0	1	1	1

His machines used a key tape loop about eight feet long which caused the key to repeat itself over a high volume of traffic. This allowed cryptanalysts to derive the key. William F. Friedman, in fact, solved cryptograms using single-loop code tapes but appears to have been unsuccessful when two code tapes were used. Major Joseph O. Mauborgne (U.S. Army) then introduced the one-time code tape derived from a random noise source. This was one of the first theoretically (and in practice) unbreakable code systems. The major disadvantage of the system was the enormous amounts of key required for high-volume traffic.

During the 1920's and 1930's, the rotor-code machines having five and more rotors, each rotor representing a scrambling step, were developed. They proved relatively insecure, requiring only high-traffic volume for the cryptanalyst to break them. In fact, the Japanese used a code-wheel-type machine for their diplomatic communications well into World War II. It was vulnerable to cryptoanalysis, and William F. Friedman and his group not only solved the code but reconstructed a model of the machine to break Japanese diplomatic correspondence. Thus, President Roosevelt and others were aware of the impending break in diplomatic relations with Japan just prior to World War II.

The code wheels (or rotors) were nothing more than key memories storing quantities of key which could easily be changed by interchanging rotor positions, specifying various start points for each rotor, and periodically replacing a set of rotors. This provided a means of producing what I will call a key leverage.

Digital Substitution

A system which uses the "exclusive or" technique developed by Gilbert S. Vernan, applied directly to data stored and distributed by a computer, is shown in Figure 1.

Instead of using two tapes, this system would use two key memories and an address memory. Synchronization would be achieved by use of the address memory which would be addressed by the first transmitted intelligence. The contents of the two addresses obtained could come into the address registers which would pull key words from the associated addresses in each of the two key memories. Data to be transmitted would be first exclusive ORed with the contents of the first memory location and then with the contents of an address of the second memory. Each character transmitted would thus be encoded twice.

This would represent an element of security dependent on the contents of the two key memories. Order-of-address usage of the key would be dependent on the contents of the address memory. To derive the key, contents of the key memories and address memory would have to be solved. The larger the memory contents, the harder these would be to determine. A large volume of traffic, where starting points in the address control memory would be repeated, could begin to provide clues that could be used to derive the key. Therefore, one would, at frequent intervals determined by usage, change the content of the address memory.

At less frequent intervals, one would change the contents of the key memories. These intervals would be chosen again on the basis of data traffic using the system and the type of security expected from the system.

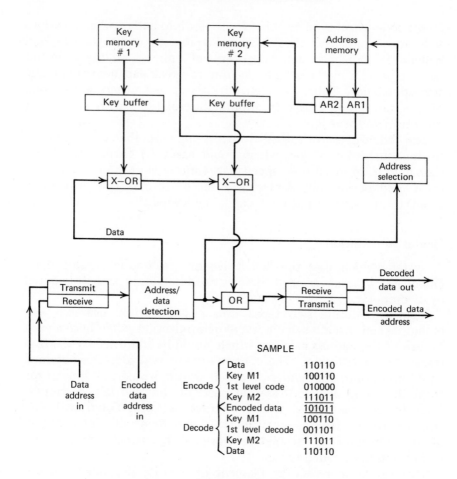

FIGURE 1.   Digital substitution logic.

The relative security of the system would be a function of the amount of memory. If a memory of n bits is considered, total permutations available in the memory of those bits would be 2^n. If the key is derived from a random noise source, probabilities of getting all 0's or all 1's in the memory are very small, as would large imbalances existing between 0's and 1's. Therefore, each key memory would have a distribution in the total bit field available approximating a distribution of bits whose permutations in practice would be more in the neighborhood of $2^{n/2}$. Each of the two key memories would have one of that many practically usable permutations, each one of which could operate on the other in the encoding process. Therefore, by probability theory, the probable permutations would be the product of the two memory potentials or $(2^{n/2})$ $(2^{n/2})$ or a potential key field of 2^n permutations.

The 2^n possible permutations of the key memories would also be acted on by the m addresses of each memory which would all exist in any order in the address memory. Possible permutations of addresses, taking them m at a time, would be m factorial for each of the memories. Therefore, one would achieve the possibility of each of the m-factorial, possible addresses for one memory being able to operate on each of the m-factorial, possible permutations of the other memory. This would represent a total of $(m!)^2$ possible permutations of the addresses.[3]

Therefore, if one were to completely break the key, one would have to derive the one permutation used out of a potential of a total possible equal to $(m!)^2 2^n$. Heavy traffic on the system, with repetition of the key, would however, give handles to the crypto-analyst in deriving the key so it could not be considered unbreakable.

It is possible to achieve a system which would be unbreakable in theory and achievable without using great amounts of key. This is achievable by using a one-time key with techniques of producing key leverage. Since two memories are used for key, and each memory has addresses associated with it in the address memory, one can achieve key leverage by the fact that different combinations of the contents of the addresses of the key give different coding results. Proper choice of address usage in the address memory will insure that each message that is transmitted would be encoded with a unique code until all the combinations of the addresses were used for the two key memories.

It is known that the Address Memory contains one of m! permutations possible in the m addresses for each key memory. If it is assumed that each memory location contains a character in key memory, that somewhere in the address memory is the address of that character, and that each address is one address memory location, then a practical means of control begins to emerge. If, for example, m is considered to be 1,000 addresses and a usage scheme is used similar to that outlined in Table I, synchronization would be achieved by message numbering consecutively from 000 to 999.

The first character transmitted would use the contents of address 000 for Key Memory 1 and 000 for Key Memory 2. The second character transmitted would use the contents of address 001 in Address Memory 1, and the contents of address 001 in Address Memory 2. This progression could continue to address-memory-location 999 for each of the two address-memory slots.

TABLE I. Address Memory Usage

Message Number	Address Memory 1	Address Memory 2
000	000	000
	001	001
	002	002
	∫	∫
	999	999
001	000	001
	001	002
	002	003
	∫	∫
	999	000
002	000	002
	001	003
	∫	∫
	999	001
∫	∫	∫
500	000	500
	001	501
	∫	∫
	999	499
999	000	999
	001	000
	002	001
	∫	∫
	999	998

Refresh Address Memory and repeat cycle.

The second message transmitted would be numbered 001. The address-register pairs for message number 2 would now be 000, and 001 for the first character. The second character would be 001 and 002. The address register would therefore be using different address pairs for the second message than it did on the first.

At the 501st message, it would bear number 500. The address pairs for the first character transmitted would now be 000 and 500. The second character transmitted would use address-memory locations 001 and 501.

Therefore, it can be seen that by continuing the sequence through message 1000 bearing number 999, no repetition of address pairs will exist. Therefore, with m equal to 1,000 and two key memories and 2 address memories, the system limit—if used in this way—is 1,000 messages of 1,000 characters each.

At the time the system limit is reached, one would change the address memory by supplying a new permutation of addresses for each of the two address-memory slots. This would provide the capability of transmitting and receiving another 1,000 messages of 1,000 characters each. It can be seen that the system employs a progressive-key system and, in theory, one could use m! combinations of addresses in each of the two address-memory slots before obvious key repetition would begin, without changing the contents of the key memories. In practice however, one would, at predetermined intervals, change the contents of the key memories.

It can be shown that the system is modular. By adding a third key memory and a third address-memory slot, the system would be expanded to 1,000,000 messages each with a capacity of 1,000 characters. It can also be shown that a trade-off exists between message length and number. For example, if message length were defined to be a maximum of 100 characters instead of 1,000 the message count on the expanded system could go to 10,000,000 messages before the key would be repeated.

In a system using two levels of encoding and m = 1,000 at a transmission rate of 2,000 bits per second, the key will last for 1.4 hours of continuous transmission before the address slots in the address memory would have to be changed. This assumes that 10 bits are present in each key memory address. If transmission loading was 50%, this figure would go to 2.8 hours. Therefore, with heavy traffic, the Address Memory Contents would have to be changed two or three times per day. This could be arranged by pre-storing numbers of changes on a dense-storage medium such as magnetic tape.

Higher usage rates would require higher rates of change for the Address Memory and/or a modular expansion of the key system. Therefore, the system is applicable to any rate of key usage that is in use today. It is also modular, as can be seen, by choice of m.

Thus, it is possible to use a system of digital substitution in a cryptographic computer system which would, if system design parameters were properly chosen, deny access to data in a system to all who did not possess the cryptographic key. The system described here is basically a polyalphabetic substitution system. It employs the fundamental techniques employed by Vernan and would also include some of the characteristics of the rotor machines in achieving leverage in the number of permutations available on data. It is, however, different since we are now operating on the digital makeup of the intelligence rather than on the character as an entity, and we use electronics instead of the mechanical rotor. We also avoid repetitive use of the key which was the reason that rotor-machine codes were finally broken.

Digital Route Transposition

Transposition techniques can also be used in conjunction with data processing. If the route transposition technique is applied to the read-in and read-out of digital data from a matrix, it is possible to achieve the results of polyalphabetic substitution without a direct substitution key being required. It can be shown that key usage is far less than that required for direct substitution. With the data-key leverage obtained, some interesting possibilities on key transmission can be obtained. With these, it becomes more feasible to explore the possibility of single-use keys.

To illustrate the method, let us consider an n^2 matrix where n = 8. The matrix will be made up of 8 rows and 8 columns. Information can be read into and out of the 8 columns of the matrix in any order.

The information would be transmitted into the receiving-matrix columns in the same order that it left the transmitting matrix. To complete the data reconstruction, the information in the receiving matrix now would be read out in the same row order that it entered the transmitting matrix. Therefore, the process is reversible.

Figure 2 shows the base matrix. If an 8-by-8 matrix is considered, there are 8 factorial different orders possible in both the rows and columns. For any one matrix of information (64 bits), there are a possible $(8!)^2$ ways of seeing this information when transmitted.[2] Eight factorial squared gives an approximate 1.6×10^9 possible

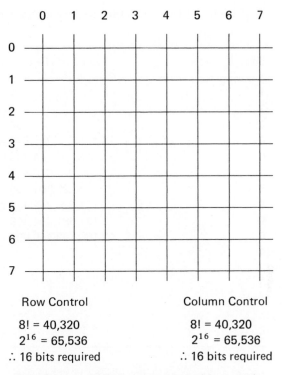

Row Control

8! = 40,320

2^{16} = 65,536

∴ 16 bits required

Column Control

8! = 40,320

2^{16} = 65,536

∴ 16 bits required

FIGURE 2.   Digital route transposition matrix.

permutations on each matrix. Since it would be the function of the key to select matrix permutation, each matrix would be transmitted with a different key. Table II shows the effect of varying matrix size in terms of available permutations on the data.

The elements of control required for the rows and columns of the matrix must be independent. To keep control independent, Row Key and Column Key Memories can be used. Since in the example chosen there are 8 rows and 8 columns, there are 8! different possible orders to read into or out of each matrix. Thus 2^{16} is approximately equal to 8!. It can be shown that 16 bits will be sufficient for reading information into or out of the rows of the matrix. Likewise, 16 bits will allow information to be read into or out of the 8 columns. Therefore, 32 bits of key are required to encode and decode 64 bits of information using a Digital Route Transposition Matrix.

By looking at direct key usage and comparing it to key usage described on Digital Substitution, we find that key consumption

TABLE II.   Effect of Matrix Size on Permutations

Matrix Size: n	Read-Write Permutations: $(n!)^2$
1	$1 = 1.0 \times 10^0$
2	$4 = 4.0 \times 10^0$
3	$36 = 3.6 \times 10$
4	$576 = 5.8 \times 10^2$
5	$14{,}400 = 1.4 \times 10^4$
6	$518{,}400 = 5.2 \times 10^5$
7	$25{,}401{,}600 = 2.5 \times 10^7$
8	$1{,}625{,}702{,}400 = 1.6 \times 10^9$
9	$131{,}681{,}894{,}400 = 1.3 \times 10^{11}$
10	$13{,}168{,}189{,}440{,}000 = 1.3 \times 10^{13}$
11	$= 1.6 \times 10^{15}$
12	$= 2.4 \times 10^{17}$
13	$= 3.9 \times 10^{19}$
14	$= 7.7 \times 10^{21}$
15	$= 1.7 \times 10^{24}$
16	$= 1.4 \times 10^{26}$

per transmitted bit is reduced by a factor of 4. For each 64 bits transmitted by the Digital Route Transposition Matrix, 32 bits of key are used. With Digital Substitution 2 bits of key are used for each bit transmitted.

If 1,000 addresses are assumed in each of two address slots in Address Memory, the potential for applying them to something analogous to message number again exists. However, since each step of the Address Memory now transmits a full matrix of information synchronization would now be achieved by matrix count instead of message number. Therefore, one would step through the address count. If 1,000 addresses were used in each of the row and column memories, one would step through the address-register counts 1,000,000 times, pairing up a different row and column address count every step. In terms of usable bits available for transmission, this would yield 64,000,000 data bits. If the system were transmitting 2,000 bits per second, this would represent 8.8 hours of continuous transmission. If transmission utilization was 50%, this would represent 17.6 hours of transmission. It would be applicable to any data rate by varying the address memory-change rate. At the end of the 64,000,000 bits, the address memories would be refreshed with a new permutation and the process would continue. Thus, no key repetition would occur.

If data rates were very high, one could consider transmitting the address information encoded in the one-time key. This could be accomplished by the addition of an Address Buffer Memory which would be loaded prior to the point where the system ran out of address permutations. At the point of run-out, a new permutation would be moved out of the Address Buffer into the Address Memory and the process would continue. Since both ends of a system must be synchronized, the transfer would always occur simultaneously at both ends of the system.

After some predetermined number of address-permutation changes, the key would be changed in the Row and Column Key Memories. This change would not have to be frequent unless a key compromise was suspected. Frequency of change will normally be determined by choice of memory size and other design parameters in the system.

Figure 3 represents a diagram of the transmitting function for a Digital Route Transposition Matrix. An address followed by data would come into the system. The starting address for the address memory would be also transmitted to the receiving station. The station would select a pair of key addresses in the address memory which would pull the contents from Row-Key and Column-Key memories to activate the row- and column-scan selection control.

The row-scan selection control would activate read-in to one matrix of data, which would fill all of its rows with data. At that point in time, column-scan selection control would take over and begin transmitting data from the first filled matrix. While the first matrix is transmitting, a new row-key word would be brought out by stepping the address-selection logic to get the next row key from Row-Key Memory.

When the first matrix has finished transmitting, address-selection would supply the second address for the Column-Key Memory. With proper choice of timing relationships, continuous data transmission would occur by permitting encoded data from matrix A or B to enter the line. While one matrix is transmitting, the second would be filling with data.

The receive function would be the reverse of the transmitting function. It can be seen that a double matrix is required to secure continuous transmission.

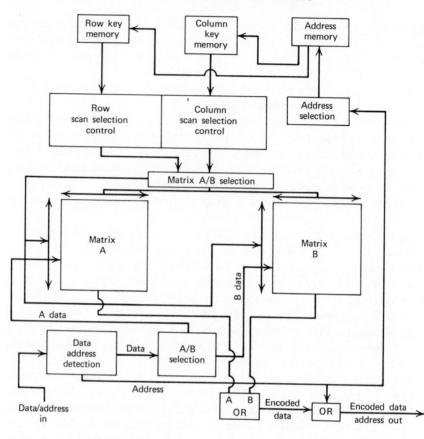

FIGURE 3. **Digital route transposition matrix.**

Error Detection and Recovery

Existing techniques of error detection could be employed. When techniques of ciphering are used on a system employing transmission lines, it would be possible to use a polynomial accumulation which comes very close to being unique for each block of data transmitted. The one- or two-character accumulation would be transmitted at the end of the block and compared to that generated by the received data. An error would be assumed only if there was a difference.

Error recovery would be initiated by transmittal of a negative acknowledgment to that block of data. Action at the transmitting end would then consist of retransmission of the data block with the same address designations for key usage being held. This would be necessary to prevent the same text from being transmitted twice with different keys. Transmission twice with different keys could provide information to a cryptoanalyst which could possibly permit breaking a portion of a key.

Polynomial accumulations would be equally applicable to either the double substitution or transposition technique. Accumulations could be done either before or after encoding, depending on the handling of transmission control characters.

Another possible error detection technique, particularly with a transposition matrix, would be the utilization of horizontal and vertical parity assignments. The reliability of the technique would require evaluation for the particular application to determine what types of multiple-bit errors would result in lack of error detection. It would be used only if the probability of detection were sufficiently high for the application. Again, detection of the error would require re-transmission by the same key-address designators that were used for the original transmission.

Both systems would satisfy all the criteria and principles established by Auguste Kerckhoff's book published in 1883. There would be no requirement for manual intervention unless maintenance was required. Since a one-time code would be used, it is in theory unbreakable. The security of the system rests with the key, not the hardware. In operation, the key is undergoing continuous change automatically and/or under control of an operator, depending on application and specific hardware design. Both systems would be simple, and for all practical purposes, transparent to the operators. Operators would handle the clear information as is done today, even in the most confidential types of operations.

Selection of operators would remain a management function, as it is today. This system would be designed to prevent unauthorized proliferation of confidential information by direct access from other I/O devices that do not possess the key, in spite of the fact that they may have the hardware.

With integrated circuits becoming available and the cost per circuit function decreasing, it becomes possible to consider undertaking designs that would offer relatively high degrees of privacy in computer systems at reasonable cost. High-density memories and the technology to support the logical control of cryptographic systems exist today.

REFERENCES

1. A. Westin, Privacy and freedom, Atheneum, 1967.
2. D. Kahn, The code breakers, The Macmillan Co., 1967.
3. C. H. Richardson, An introduction to statistical analysis, Harcourt Brace and Co., 1934.

Fast "Infinite-Key" Privacy Transformation for Resource-Sharing Systems

J. M. CARROLL

P. M. McLELLAN

INTRODUCTION

In all systems affording real-time multiple access to shared computing resources, there exists the risk that information belonging to one user, may, contrary to his intent, become available to other users, and there is the additional risk that outside agencies may infiltrate the system and obtain information. Protection of information within central processors, auxiliary storage (disk, drum), and on-site bulk storage (tape), is a responsibility of the system; the responsibility for the protection of information in external communication links seems presently to devolve by default upon the user. The crux of the privacy issue is the design, evaluation, and implementation of hardware, software, and operating procedures contrived to discharge both of these responsibilities.

This paper describes a real-time software system for privacy transformation applicable to the problems of both system and user. It will be presented within the context of known threats to privacy, presently available counter-measures, and the current operational environment.

SOURCE: Fall Joint Computer Conference, 1970, Proceedings. Reprinted by permission of the publisher, American Federation of Information Processing Societies Press.

THREATS TO PRIVACY

The challenges to the privacy of information in a computer system may be accidental or deliberate; this discussion relates specifically to deliberate challenges, although the software developed may afford some protection against the undesired consequences of accidental compromise.

The objectives of deliberate infiltration include:

1. Gaining access to information in files.
2. Discovering the information interests of users.
3. Altering or destroying files.
4. Obtaining free use of system resources.

The nature of deliberate infiltration will be discussed within the framework presented by Peterson and Turn,[1] who established the following categories:

A. Passive Infiltration
    1. Electro-magnetic pickup (from CPU or peripheral devices).
    2. Wiretapping (on communications lines or transfer buses).
    3. Concealled transmitters (CPU, peripheral devices, transfer buses, communications lines).

B. Active Infiltration
    1. Browsing.
    2. Masquerading.
    3. Exploitation of trap doors.
    4. "Between-lines" entry.
    5. "Piggy back" infiltration.
    6. Subversive entry by centre staff.
    7. Core dumping.
    8. Theft of removable media.

Browsing is defined as the use of legitimate access to the system to obtain unauthorized information.

Masquerading consists of posing as a legitimate user after obtaining proper identification by subversive means.

Trap doors are hardware or software deficiencies that assist the infiltrator to obtain information having once gained access to the system.

Between-lines entry consists of penetrating the system when a legitimate user is on a communications channel, but his terminal is inactive.

Piggy-back infiltration consists of selectively intercepting user-processor communications and returning false messages to the user.

EXISTING COUNTERMEASURES

Methods to enhance privacy are roughly classified as follows:

1. Access control.
2. Privacy transformations.
3. Processing restrictions.
4. Monitoring procedures.
5. Integrity management.

Access control consists of authorization, identification, and authentication and may function on the system or file level. Authorization to enter the system or files is generally established by possession of an account number or project number. The user may be identified by his name, terminal, or use of a password. The user may be required to perform a privacy transformation on the password to authenticate his identity. Peters[2] recommends use of one-time passwords.

Passwords may also include authority codes to define levels of processing access to files (e.g., read only, write, read-write, change protection).

Privacy transformations include the class of operation which can be used to encode and decode information to conceal content. Associated with a transformation is a key which identifies and unlocks the transformation to the user and a work factor, which is a measure of the effort required of an infiltrator to discover the key by cryptanalysis.

Processing restrictions include such functions as provisions to zero core before assigning it to a second user, mounting removable files on drives with disabled circuitry that must be authenticated before accessing, automatic cancellation of programmes attempting to access unauthorized information, and software which limits access privileges by terminal.

Monitoring procedures are concerned with making permanent records of attempted or actual penetrations of the system or files. Monitoring procedures usually will not prevent infiltration; their protection is ex post facto. They disclose that a compromise has taken place, and may help identify the perpetrator.

Integrity management attempts to ensure the competence, loyalty, and integrity of centre personnel. In some cases, it may entail bonding of some staff.

EFFECTIVENESS OF COUNTERMEASURES

The paradigm given in Figure 1, grossly abridged from Peterson and Turn, characterizes the effectiveness of each countermeasure against each threat.

Threat	Directed Against	Countermeasures				
		Access Control	Privacy Transform.	Process. Restrict.	Threat Monitor.	Integrity Manage.
Passive	CPU	NONE	NONE	NONE	NONE	FAIR
	DEVICES	"	GOOD	"	"	"
	LINES	"	"	"	"	NONE
Browsing	SYSTEM	GOOD	GOOD	GOOD	GOOD	NONE
Masquerade	"	FAIR	FAIR	FAIR	GOOD	FAIR
Between-Lines	"	NONE	GOOD	FAIR	FAIR	NONE
Piggy-Back	"	NONE	FAIR	FAIR	FAIR	NONE
Trap-Doors	CPU	NONE	NONE	NONE	FAIR	NONE
	DEVICES	FAIR	GOOD	FAIR	"	"
Systems Entry	CPU	NONE	NONE	NONE	NONE	GOOD
	DEVICES	"	FAIR	"	FAIR	"
Core Dump	CPU	NONE	NONE	NONE	GOOD	GOOD
Theft	DEVICES	NONE	GOOD	NONE	FAIR	GOOD

FIGURE 1. Threat-countermeasure matrix.

We independently investigated each cell of the threat-countermeasure matrix in the real-time resource-sharing environment afforded by the PDP-10/50 at Western (30 teletypes, 3 remote batch terminals). Our experience leads to the following observations:

Passive Infiltration: There is no adequate countermeasure except encipherment and even this is effective only if enciphered traffic flows on the bus or line attacked by the infiltrator. Competent, loyal personnel may deter planting wireless transmitters or electro-magnetic pickups within the computer centre.

Browsing: All countermeasures are effective; simple access control is usually adequate.

Masquerading: If the password is compromised, most existing countermeasures are rendered ineffective. Use of authentication, one-time passwords, frequent change of password, and loyalty of systems personnel help to preserve the integrity of passwords. Separate systems and file access procedures make infiltration more difficult, inasmuch as two or more passwords must be compromised before the infiltrator gains his objective. Monitoring procedures can provide ex post facto analysis.

Between-Lines Entry: Only encipherment of files, or passwords applied at the message level rather than for entire sessions, provide adequate safeguards. Monitoring may provide ex post facto analysis.

Piggy-Back Techniques: Encipherment provides protection unless the password is compromised. Monitoring may provide ex post facto analysis.

Trap-doors: There is no protection for information obtainable from core, although monitoring can help in ex post facto analysis. Encipherment can protect information contained in auxiliary storage.

Systems entry: Integrity management is the only effective counter-measure. There is no other protection for information in core; even monitoring routines can be overridden. Encipherment protects infor-mation in virtual storage only to the extent that passwords are pro-tected from compromise.

Core dump: There is no effective protection except integrity management, although monitoring procedures can help in ex post facto analysis.

Theft: Encipherment protects information stored in removable media.

Our initial study persuaded us that privacy transformation coupled with password authentication would afford the best protection of information. Integrity management procedures were not within the scope of this research.

PRIVACY ENVIRONMENT: MANUFACTURERS

Our next task was to investigate the privacy environment of resource-sharing systems. Five manufacturers of equipment, doing business in Canada, participated in our study. Their contributions are summarized in the following points:

1. The problem of information security is of great concern to all manufacturers of resource-sharing equipment.
2. Most manufacturers are conducting research on privacy; only a small minority believes that the hardware and software currently supplied are adequate to ensure the privacy of customer information.
3. The password is the most common vehicle of system access control; dedicated direct lines are recommended in some special situations.
4. At least two manufacturers have implemented password authentication at the file level.
5. There appears to be no customer demand for implementation of hardware or software privacy transformations at this time.
6. Most manufacturers stress the need for integrity management.
7. Two large manufacturers emphasize the need for thorough log-keeping and monitoring procedures.
8. Communication links are seen as a major security weakness.

We next surveyed 25 organizations possessing hardware that appeared to be suitable for resource-sharing. Sixteen organizations participated in our study, representing about 75 percent by traffic volume of the Canadian time-sharing industry. From information furnished by them, we were able to obtain a "privacy profile" of the industry.

The average resource-sharing installation utilizes IBM equipment (Univac is in second place). The typical system has over 512 thousand bytes of core storage and 175 million bytes of auxiliary storage. The system operates in both the remote-batch and interactive modes. It has 26 terminals communicating with the central processors over public (switched) telephone lines.

In seven systems, authorization is established by name, account number, and project number. Five systems require only an account number. Nine systems require a password for authority to enter the system; the password is protected by either masking or print-inhibit.

Identification is established by some combination of name, account number, project number, or password; in no case is identification of the terminal considered. No use is made of one-time passwords, authentication, or privacy transformations. In no system is a password required at the file level; seven systems do not even require passwords. Access control provisions of 16 Canadian systems are summarized in Figure 2.

RESOURCE-SHARING SYSTEMS

Number of Systems	Authorization	Identification	Authority
4	Account # Project #	Name	Password
3	Account #	—	Password
3	Account # Project #	Name	—
2	Account #	—	—
1	Account #	Name	Password
1	Project #	Name	—
1	—	—	Password
1	Project #	—	—

FIGURE 2.   Access control in 16 Canadian resource-sharing systems.

Only two systems monitor unsuccessful attempts to gain entry. In nine systems, both centre staff and other users have the ability to read user's files at will. In six systems, centre staff has unrestricted access to user files. Only three organizations have implemented integrity management by bonding any members of staff.

The state of privacy, in general, in the Canadian resource-sharing industry, can be described as chaotic and, with few exceptions, the attitude of systems operators towards privacy as one of apathy.

PRIVACY TRANSFORMATION:
FUNCTIONAL SPECIFICATIONS

It was decided, therefore, to begin development of a software system for privacy transformation that would be synchronized by an authenticated password, anticipating that sooner or later some users will demand a higher degree of security in resource-sharing systems than is currently available. Such an authentication-privacy transformation procedure would afford the following advantages:

1. Provide protection for the password on communications channels.
2. Implement access control at the file level.
3. Obviate the need for storing passwords as part of file headings.
4. Afford positive user identification since only authorized users would be able to synchronize the keys of the privacy transformation.
5. Furnish "work factor" protection of files against browsing, "between-lines" entry, "piggy-back" infiltration, "trap doors" to auxiliary storage, entry of systems personnel to auxiliary storage, eavesdropping on transfer buses, and theft of removable media.

The technique of privacy transformation that seemed most promising was a form of the Vernan cipher, discovered in 1914 by Gilbert S. Vernan, an AT&T engineer. He suggested punching a tape of key characters and electromagnetically adding its pulses to those of plain text characters, coded in binary form, to obtain the cipher text. The "exclusive-OR" addition is used because it is reversible.

The attractive feature of the Vernan cipher for use in digital systems is the fact that the key string can readily be generated by random number techniques. For maximum security (high work factor) it is desirable that the cipher key be as long as the plain text to be encrypted. However, if the flow of information is heavy, the production of keys may place extreme loads on the arithmetic units of processors—the rate of message processing may then be too slow to be feasible. Two solutions have been proposed.

In the first, relatively short (e.g., 1,000 entries) keys are produced and permutations of them used until repetition is unavoidable. A second approach is to use an extremely efficient random number generator capable of producing strings that appear to be "infinite" in length, compared to the average length of message to be transformed.

PRIOR WORK (SHORT-KEY METHOD)

An algorithm for a short key method presented by Skatrud[3] utilizes two key memories and an address memory. These are generated off-line by conventional random number techniques. Synchronization of an incoming message and the key string is achieved by using the first information item received to address an address memory location. The contents of this memory location provides a pair of address pointers that are used to select key words from each of the key memories. The key words are both "exclusive-OR'ed" with the next data item, effectively providing double encryption of it. The address memory is then successively incremented each time another data item arrives. Each address location provides two more key address pointers and each key address furnishes two key words to be "exclusive-OR'ed" with the current data item. Key word pairs are provided on a one-for-one basis with input data items until the entire message has been processed. For decoding, the procedure is completely reversible.

PRESENT WORK ("INFINITE" KEY METHOD)

We decided to use the infinite key approach because it would:

1. Reduce storage requirements over those required by short key methods. This will tend to reduce cost where charges are assessed on the amount of core used; and, more importantly, will permit implementing the transformation on small computers (e.g., one having a 4096-word memory) located within the user's work space.
2. Obviate the need for off-line key production and virtual storage of superseded keys [or reencipherment of existing files after a key memory change].
3. Provide extremely long key strings for improved work-factor protection of information.

Our privacy transformation combines the speed of the arithmetic congruential method of random-number generation with the previously established randomness of a mixed multiplicative congruential generator. The length and composition of the seed for the key string are determined by the password of the file to be coded or decoded. Each unit of input text is "exclusive-OR'ed" with the next random number of the key in a one-to-one manner until the input plain text has been fully processed. The system has been implemented on a PDP-10/50 computer; the "unit of input text", in this case, is a 36-bit word.

There are two programmes; the input/output (CRYPTO.IO) which handles password authentication; and the privacy transformation (CRYPTO.2).

In the first programme, the user calls the name of the file to be processed. The user's directory, CRYPTO.UFD, which is maintained as a protected file on the system disk area, is searched to verify that a password exists. (A user must contact the system security officer to have a file password entered.) If no password exists, the user receives an error message. Otherwise, the 6-digit password is retrieved from disk to core, and the file name is stored in core for future reference.

The user is now challenged to authenticate his identity. A random 5-digit octal number is transmitted to user's terminal, and he is expected to effect on this number a pre-determined transformation, dependent on the file password, and transmit the result to the processor. If the transformation is incorrect, an error message will be transmitted and the user line dropped. (A date-time group may be made part of this transformation to afford additional protection against "piggy-back" infiltration.)

If the transformation is correct, the file is initialized for output, a call is generated for the transformation routine, and the file name and password are supplied. Upon return of control from the transformation subroutine, the run is terminated. Figure 3 is a logic flowchart for this procedure.

IMPLEMENTATION ON A LARGE COMPUTER

The privacy transformation makes use of a two-stage random number generator, IRAND, which supplies key strings dynamically in 512-word blocks. Each word is exclusively OR'ed with an input string of five 7-bit ASCII characters to realize encryption or decryption, as the case may be. Synchronization of the key strings with text is achieved by using the 6-digit password as the starting seed S_0 for the seed-string generator, which is one stage of the two-stage random number generator.

A key string of N random numbers is generated using the additive congruential method

$$X_{i+1} \equiv X_i + X_{i-L} \pmod{m}$$

where $m = 2^b$ and b is 35, the bit length of the computer word; and where

$$X_1, \ldots, X_L$$

is the sequence

$$S_1, \ldots, S_L$$

which is called the seed string.

The seed string is generated by using a conventional mixed multiplicative congruential generator of the form

$$S_{i+1} \equiv aS_i + C \ (\mathrm{mod} \ m)$$

where

$$a \equiv \pm 3 \ (\mathrm{mod} \ 8)$$

and is a value close to $a = 2^{b/2}$, to satisfy the Conveyou-Greenburger criterion.[5,6] The value 131,069 has been found to be satisfactory.

The value of C was selected to be $<a$ and relatively prime to m. The value 7 was found to be satisfactory.

The length of the seed string is variable but selected to fall within the range $16 \leqslant L \leqslant 79$, in accordance with the suggestions set forth by Green, Smith, and Klem.[7] Its length is determined by adding 16 to the six lower order bits of the password.

The period of usage of the seed string (N) is determined by adding 2^K to the K low-order bits of S_L, and is within the range

$$2^K \leqslant N < 2^{K+1}$$

For high-security applications, K = 18; for lower-security applications K = 12 to decrease the load on the arithmetic unit of the processor.

After N random numbers have been generated in this fashion, the procedure is repeated using the current value of S_L instead of the password (S_0). Thus the complete contents of a file may be enciphered with a vanishingly small probability that any portion of the key string will repeat.

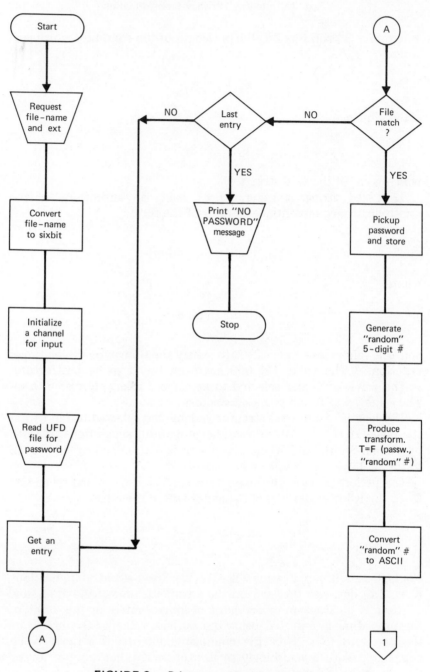

FIGURE 3. Privacy transformation routines.

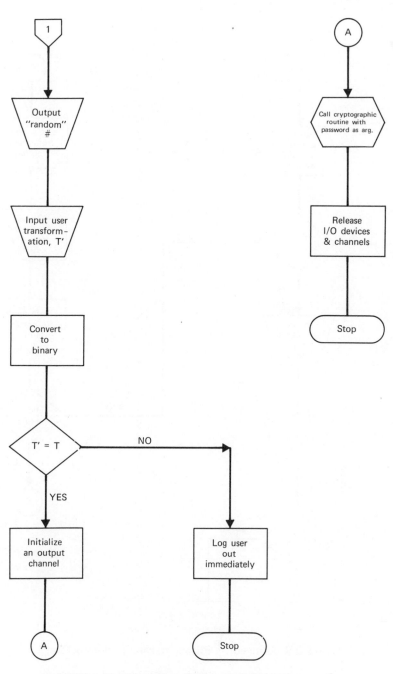

FIGURE 3 (Continued).   Privacy transformation routines.

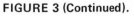

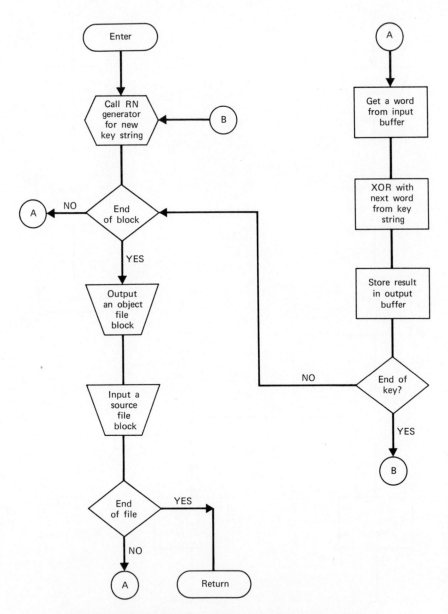

FIGURE 3 (Continued).   Privacy transformation routines.

IMPLEMENTATION ON A SMALL COMPUTER

Implementation of this privacy transformation on a small computer such as the PDP-8I (12-bit word, 4096-word memory), requires certain modifications in the procedure. Two additive congruential generators are used so that all operations may be kept within the limitations of the machine's basic arithmetic capability (two's complement add).

The seed of the second generator is stored as a string of 64 4-digit octal numbers. (We have found that digits of the expansion of pi work well; any random string can be used.)

The second generator randomly initializes itself by cycling for a number of periods determined by the 12 low-order bits of the password. It then generates a seed $S_1, \ldots, S_L$, for the first generator. The length of the seed is determined by the six low-order bits of the password. The length of key string (e.g., period of the first generator) is determined by the value of the four octal digits of S_L. (Note: all operations are carried out in octal arithmetic modulo 4096). At the end of this period, S_0 is set equal to S_L and the process is repeated.

EVALUATION

Three tests were conducted on our privacy transformation programme as implemented on the PDP-10/50. The first two tested in cipher key for random characteristics, comparing it with a mixed multiplicative congruential generator described in IBM,[8] which we knew from experience in our Simulation Laboratory to have acceptably random characteristics. The tests evaluated goodness-of-fit to a uniform distribution, and serial autocorrelation lagged 1 to 5 (the second test thus has five distinct parts).

The third test was for speed of producing encoded words.

The randomness tests were conducted according to procedures attributed to I. J. Good[9,10] as described in Naylor[11] and Lewis.[12] Each part of each test used 100 random blocks of 1,000 numbers each, sampled from the "infinite" cipher key string. The 100 resulting values of chi^2 (one value for each block), calculated under the assumption of a flat distribution in the first case, and no serial autocorrelation in the second, were then tested for goodness-of-fit to a chi^2 distribution having 99 degrees of freedom. The criterion value, the 95 percent confidence level for chi^2 with 9 degrees of freedom, was 16.9. Values of chi^2 lower than this were deemed to signify that the outcome of a test was satisfactory.

The test results are tabulated in Figure 4. It can be seen that the high-security cipher (K-18) is superior to the low-security cipher (K-12) with respect to both goodness-of-fit to a uniform distribution, and absence of serial autocorrelation lagged 1 to 5. Both cipher key strings were found to be superior in these qualities of randomness to the conventional mixed multiplicative congruential generator. In addition, no evidence of cycling was observed in either cipher key string.

(VALUES OF chi^2)

Method		Test				
	Goodness of fit		Serial Autocorrelation			
		Lag 1	2	3	4	5
High Security	5.4	8.2	12.0	15.4	8.0	7.6
Low Security	9.6	9.6	11.2	12.2	18.2	14.2
MMC Generator	12.8	12.8	16.6	16.4	26.4	11.2

(Acceptable chi^2 = 16.9)

FIGURE 4. Evaluation of the randomness of cipher key strings.

The test of processing speed was carried out in the time-sharing environment of the PDP-10/50 system under full load with "swap" times included. It was found that 135,168 five-byte words were produced in 18.28 seconds (37,000 bytes per second) using the high-security (slower) procedure. It is felt that this test represents worst case conditions and that double the observed speed can easily be realized.

SUMMARY

The two-stage random number generator used in this privacy transformation procedure appears to possess excellent characteristics of randomness and is capable of producing a cipher key string that is effectively infinite in length. These characteristics should ensure high "work factor" security against cryptanalytic attack. (Actually, it is a rather good random number generator for general simulation work.)

The speed of the encipherment routine is sufficient to keep up with normal data transfers between the processor and peripheral devices.

Use of an authenticated password to synchronize the cipher key string affords several advantages:

1. Differential access to files is achieved by assigning a unique password to each file and investing only authorized users with it.
2. Differential access at lower levels (e.g., records) requires only using more of these 6-digit passwords.
3. Storage of the passwords in a separate user file directory conserves space in user files and helps preserve the integrity of passwords.
4. The authenticating transformation effected on the password ensures that it never appears in clear on communications lines.
5. Possession of the password and authenticating transformation positively establishes the bona fide authority of the user.

Existence of high- and low-security modes for the privacy transformation allows the user to trade-off "work factor" protection against load on the processor's arithmetic unit at will.

When the privacy transformation is modified to utilize two arithmetic congruential generators, the user is able to implement it on a computer having minimal word length, storage, and computational capability. He can, therefore, encipher his traffic on external switched lines at a hardware cost of roughly $10,000.

It is felt that the authentication—privacy transformation system described provides a flexible, efficient, and economical method for ensuring the privacy of information in resource-sharing computer environments.

[An additional benefit arising from our research was the discovery of two "trap doors" in the PDP-10/50 monitor, which were nailed shut by relatively simple programming fixes. This experience suggests to us that the security officer for a system handling sensitive information might find it worthwhile to assign at least one competent systems programmer as a "counter-infiltration" specialist with the assigned mission of discovering and repairing similar deficiencies.]

ACKNOWLEDGMENTS

This work was supported in part by the Canada Council, Social Sciences and Humanities Division, under grant number 69-0671 (Privacy and the Computer) and by the Defense Research Board

(Canada) under grant number 9931-23 (Protection Methods for Real-Time Computer Systems).
The additive congruential generator for a short word length machine was programmed and tested by G. M. Dawdy of the Computer Science Department.

REFERENCES

1. H. E. Petersen and R. Turn, "System implications of information privacy," AFIPS Conference Proceedings, Spring Joint Computer Conference, Vol. 30, pp. 291–300, 1967.
2. B. Peters, "Security considerations in a multi-programmed computer system," AFIPS Conference Proceedings, Spring Joint Computer Conference, Vol. 30, 1967.
3. R. O. Skatrud, "The application of cryptographic techniques to data processing," AFIPS Conference Proceedings, Spring Joint Computer Conference, Vol. 35, pp. 111–118, 1969.
4. T. E. Hull and A. R. Dobell, "Mixed congruential random number generators for binary machines," J. ACM., Vol. 11, No. 1, pp. 230–254, 1964.
5. R. R. Coveyou, "Serial correlation in the generation of pseudo-random numbers," J. ACM., Vol. 7, pp. 72–74, 1960.
6. M. Greenburger, "An a priori determination of serial correlation in computer generated random numbers," Math of Computation, Vol. 15, pp. 383–389, 1961.
7. B. F. Green, J. Smith, and L. Klem, "Empirical tests of an additive random number generator," J. ACM., Vol. 6, No. 4, pp. 527–537, 1959.
8. Random number generation and testing, IBM Corp., Form C20-8011, White Plains, N.Y., 1959.
9. I. J. Good, "The serial test for sampling numbers and order tests of randomness," Proc. Camb. Phil. Soc., Vol. 49, pp. 276–284, 1953.
10. I. J. Good, "On the serial test for random sequences," Annals of Math Stat., Vol. 28, pp. 262–264, 1957.
11. T. H. Naylor, J. L. Balintfy, D. S. Burdick, and K. Chu, Computer Simulation Techniques, John Wiley & Sons, Inc., New York, pp. 52–53, 1966.
12. P. A. W. Lewis, A. S. Goodman, and J. M. Miller, "A pseudo-random number generator for the systems 360," IBM Syst. J., Vol. 8, No. 2, p. 136, 1969.

Section IV
MODELS FOR
SECURE SYSTEMS

This section presents models for various security systems. The first four papers describe proposed or implemented software systems which were designed with security in mind from the very start. They therefore avoid some of the horrendous problems one encounters when adding code to an operating system at some later point in time. The last paper presents a more global model of databank systems which attempts to shed some light on protector-intruder interactions.

T. D. Friedman's model uses as its primary source of authorization information a collection of security profiles which allow users to access data in various protection groups. These protection groups compartmentalize all the data in a data base. Friedman also gives some interesting quantitative projections concerning overhead for a system based on his model.

Our own formulary model, developed independently, shares one common central concept with Friedman's, that of the user control block. Our model is independent of both machine and data base structure. It introduces arbitrarily complex decision procedures which are invoked at run time. If desired, access can be controlled at arbitrarily low levels, even at the bit level. Possibly the most important contribution is that the formulary model puts all security information in one place. It attempts to avoid the situation where one secures one part of the operating system and quashes one particular problem only to have as a result some other problem pop up somewhere else, far removed, in the operating system. It is also, we believe, sufficiently modular to allow cost effectiveness studies for various kinds of access mechanisms to be carried out easily.

157

Weissman in his very important ADEPT-50 system introduces at least three interesting features:

1. A well-defined method of initialization of security profiles which allows the security control mechanism to be freely discussed. It remains unclassified (not secret) until primed by the security configuration parameters, as Baran had suggested.
2. Automatic file classification based upon the cumulative security history of referenced files—the concept of <u>high water mark</u>.
3. The security umbrella of the ADEPT job, whereby the job is assigned security based on the security allocated to the user, terminal, and files involved.

Weissman's paper starts with a formal model for security, probably the first of its type, which will certainly be of interest to theoretically-minded readers.

The paper by Conway, Maxwell, and Morgan finds all the previous security systems deficient in their inability to separate data-dependent and data-independent conditions. The major advantage of their model is its ability to make access decisions that are independent of the data value once (at compile time), rather than every time the data is accessed at run time. The authors compare their system with both formularies and with Graham's ring structures (see Section VI). They point out that to implement their model, one must not allow programming in lower level languages, and one must provide some way of protecting compiled object code before it is run so that the user cannot modify it during this interval. They also go into some detail on what would be necessary to modify an existing operating system to make use of their ideas.

The last paper in this section by Turn and Shapiro formulates a structural model of databank systems and presents a model of the economic interactions of the databank protector and potential intruders. The variables here are the value of information to the subjects, protector, and intruders; expenditures by each of these parties; and the effectiveness of various security and intrusion techniques. This is one of the first global models which gives us the opportunity, if we desire, to place a money value on various types of information and to determine, using this money value, how much we are willing to spend to protect that information.

The Authorization Problem in Shared Files

T. D. FRIEDMAN

Time-sharing computer systems permit large numbers of users to operate on common sets of data and programs. Since certain of this material may be sensitive or proprietary, protective measures are required to prevent disclosures to persons lacking proper authority. In current time-sharing systems, protection is often inadequate. A central concern in protection is the authorization problem[1-3] which involves determining whether a user who is recognized by the system should be allowed access to information he desires. An authorization system must include a mechanism for withholding or releasing the information after the determination is made. This mechanism is closely associated with access mechanisms and operating systems.

This paper considers authorization, as far as possible, apart from specific access mechanisms or operating systems, and suggests directions for study and research. Observations are made about information protection in general-purpose, time-sharing systems. Authorization is then considered in detail, and guidelines for dealing with this problem are discussed. A hypothetical model of an authorization system is described.

Information Protection

Authorization is part of the more general problem of information protection in computers,[4,5] which consists of both

SOURCE: Reprinted by permission from T. Friedman, "The Authorization Problem in Shared Files," IBM Systems Journal, Vol. 9, No. 4. © 1970 by International Business Machines Corporation.

protecting data and programs from destruction and securing them against improper disclosure. In providing comprehensive protection, the following four objectives should be considered:

- System integrity. Hardware, operating system, channels, and switching centers must operate reliably and resist penetration. Areas of particular vulnerability are storage protection, privileged instruction control, page roll-in/roll-out, management of dumps, system failure and recovery procedures, and the handling of removable files. Integrity also depends on the physical isolation of the machine room, communication lines, and remote devices. Personnel selection and computer center policies require attention as well.

- User identification. Users at remote terminals must be correctly identified when they log on, and their identities must continue to be assured throughout the execution of their jobs. Various identification mechanisms have been proposed, including secret passwords, locks and keys, badge readers, and automatic voice recognition. If user identities are not adequately verified, all other protection measures are rendered ineffectual because an intruder may penetrate the system by masquerading as a known user.

- Audit trails. Accesses to protected data should on occasion—or perhaps at all times—be recorded. In this way, infiltration attempts may be detected, and the threat of discovery should discourage mischief.

- Authorization. Methods to share data selectively among users is the subject of this paper.

THE PROBLEM

It would be desirable to provide selective sharing of information in main storage. However, the required authorization may hamper performance or increase costs since elaborate checking and disabling processes may have to be introduced into every storage access. Current time sharing systems do in fact achieve some degree of protection in main storage, but sharing is permitted only at the level of large storage segments rather than individual fields.[6]

This paper addresses the more tractable problem of providing authorization for accesses to secondary, or auxiliary, storage media. Small delays in auxiliary storage accesses may be tolerable because of the slower operation of these media as well as their lower frequency of access. In this discussion, authorization refers only to the protection of access to shared auxiliary files. The separate objectives of system integrity, user identification, and audit trails are not treated in detail, nor are the problems of operating system design, access methods, data management, and field handling. These topics, however, affect authorization critically and require attention.

Authorization involves the comparison of restrictions placed on information—data and programs—in files with privileges of users requesting access of this information. In the past, this requirement did not arise because files were not shared; users exchanged information only off line. Proprietary files were protected by being stored on removable tapes or disks, which could be held under lock and key when not in use. During runs, the entire computing center could be made secure.

The true authorization problem arises when several users must access a common file, subject to the constraint that not all users are permitted access to all data. Such a requirement may arise in police networks, government data centers, banking data centers, management information systems, or credit bureaus. Conceivably, some future computer center may simultaneously serve several of these applications.

Efficiency

Authorization is not so much a theoretical problem as one of efficiency.[7] The problem increases when there are large numbers of data sets, protection categories, and users. Authorization may then be considered as a mapping function of users to data. But in some future computer systems, such a mapping function might well become unmanageable. Imagine, for example, a system supporting 20,000 users, 2,000 of whom may be on line simultaneously. They may be processing data from a common bank containing perhaps trillions of records. It would seem to be a formidable task to screen each file access according to all restrictions that may have been placed on the data versus all privileges that the user may hold. Possibly the process could be shortened by consolidating the diverse privileges and restrictions or assigning them to a hierarchy. Nevertheless such a scheme creates interdependencies of categories that make later modifications cumbersome. A file that cannot be easily modified is likely to suffer early obsolescence.

Specialized Applications

There may be little need to make major modifications, however, in files dedicated to various specialized applications. Many management information systems are of this type in which all data is maintained by a central administrator. Formats and data organization in these systems are well-defined and relatively fixed, and the classes of users are also restricted and easily described. All types of protection and privileges can be determined in advance. The authorization process may be organized in a straightforward manner because only a small fixed number of protection categories are needed for information in the file, and a fixed number of user classes with their associated privileges are required.

A variety of techniques could serve to simplify authorization in such systems. Because the format of data fields is fixed, the individual fields need not be tagged. Protection could be provided by reference to a single format descriptor. Sets of protections and privileges could be combined, and specific combinations could be represented in terms of such logical connectives as AND, OR, and NOT. Greater convenience and efficiency could thereby be provided than is possible with exhaustive lists of protections or privileges. Protection may also be defined in terms of the value of certain fields, such as "Salaries over $10,000," which could prove quite useful. Systems of this type are gaining wide usage, and substantial activity is currently devoted to providing authorization for these applications.

General Systems

This paper, however, is concerned with large systems of a less centralized type intended to serve a variety of applications, such as the MIT Compatible Time-Sharing System (CTSS)[8] and the IBM System/360 Time-Sharing System (TSS/360).[9] A large number of dissimilar data sets may be maintained within storage, and the formats and organization of these data may not be known in advance. Indeed, new data sets in entirely unpredictable formats may be introduced by users at any time. In such systems, a more flexible authorization mechanism is required, and the specialized techniques previously discussed may, in these general systems, cause difficulties and inefficiencies. For example, protection according to value would require the authorization system to retrieve information about the formatting of records involved, which could cause large delays. Instead, the techniques considered here are intended for systems in which format, data organization, user categories, and applications are not fixed in advance.

In a general shared file system, complex and unsystematic relationships may develop between user privileges and data restrictions.

In management applications, for example, managers may possess the right to see their employees' pay records, but not, say, their health records. Corporate officers should have access to information within their provinces of authority. Since executive responsibilities may in part be duplicated, the privileges may be neither disjoint nor fall into a simple tree hierarchy, but instead may be overlapping. Moreover, privileges may change more or less continuously as users acquire or lose responsibilities in their assignments.

Enabling and Disabling Access

Thus, it may be shortsighted to base an authorization system on anticipated user relationships. Authorization simply requires that users be separated from information they lack privilege to access. A test for protection violations must be performed; if a user does not hold privilege to records he requests, access must be prevented.

To consider how access may be disabled, let us distinguish the following four functional steps in a read operation. (Analogous steps exist in write or update operations.)

1. User establishes connection to the system and is logged on.
2. User requests information.
3. System responds by selecting the information.
4. Information is transmitted to the user.

Methods for disabling (or enabling) access can thus be classified according to the step that is affected.

The highest degree of protection is provided by disabling the first step; i.e., a user is prevented from logging on altogether if he lacks privilege to any data on the system. This level of protection implies that sets of data having distinct protection requirements must be maintained on separate machines for different users. Such a scheme eliminates a major part of the protection problem, but it also eliminates the capability for time sharing. The result is unattractive not only because the processor and file system must be duplicated for each user group, but also because common updating operations are prohibited. Even so, this scheme may be the only acceptable approach to authorization where military security standards apply.

Alternatively, the user may be allowed to log on, but he is prevented from issuing unauthorized requests. This can be accomplished by restricting knowledge of the data names to persons privileged to those data. By this scheme, if someone knows what to ask for, it implies he has a right to see it.[10] This is a simple and easily realized approach. However, anyone who, through accident or design, acquires a secret name also acquires the ability to violate the protection. A refinement to this approach is not to conceal data names but to require the requester to supply an additional secret password for protected sets of data. The advantage of this scheme is that passwords can be made longer and more difficult to discover than would be convenient for data names. However, it burdens the user with remembering and communicating more terms. Moreover, the scheme still remains vulnerable to penetration by accidental discovery of the secret terms.

In a third approach, the user is allowed to log on and to request access. If he does not hold appropriate privilege, however, the selection mechanism is inhibited. The data protection techniques used in CTSS and TSS/360 fall into this category. Sensitive files outside the user's storage area can be selected only if he possesses special internal pointers in his directory to those records. The distinction between the preceding method and the method suggested here is that in this case the "passwords" (i.e., pointers) are supplied and maintained by the system rather than by the user. Because the user cannot change his own pointers, this system is more resistant to mischief than the previous one. Nevertheless, even here the test for violation is conducted on information specified in the request rather than on the information that is actually selected. If a machine error occurs after the test and during selection, then sensitive data may be made available to unauthorized persons. This protection method may thus fail in the event of a single error such as the alteration of an address.

Stronger protection is provided if the data transmission step rather than the selection step is disabled on detection of a violation. Then the test for violations may be conducted using the data that are actually selected from storage, but before they are made available to the user. In this case, protection failures would require at least two independent but coincidental mishaps: (1) unauthorized data are accessed in storage, and (2) these data are not recognized as unauthorized for the requester during the subsequent testing phase.

Rather than disabling the actual transmission of data, they could always be made available. If a violation occurs, however, the data would be presented in an unusable form. For example, sensitive records could be stored in cryptographically enciphered form, and be automatically deciphered during output using a key assigned to the user. Cryptographic techniques provide impressive levels of protection,[2,11-13] although the security of any cipher is never certain. Cryptography seems especially promising for protecting communication lines to remote terminals. Nevertheless, this approach may prove unacceptable for routine file processing because of the resulting delay in channel access.

In contrast to full-scale cryptography, an elementary scrambling process[14] has attracted interest because of its economy and speed. Scrambling consists of the replacement of characters in a record according to a simple, fixed substitution rule. As scrambled records are read from a file, they are simultaneously unscrambled according to a user's key. Improperly retrieved records are scrambled according to an unknown key and so are unreadable. Scrambling thus prevents one user from directly browsing through another user's data. However, it is a relatively trivial (as well as an entertaining) challenge to decipher such a code. Since scrambling does not offer significant protection, it may actually constitute a danger by providing an illusion of protection that does not exist.

Although these six methods do not exhaust the means of disabling access, they illustrate the wide choice of techniques possible. A combination of techniques may be stronger than any one alone, but this would be more costly and is not considered further here. Of the alternatives, protection by disabling the data transmission appears most promising because failure would require the concurrence of two independent mishaps.

Test for Violations

Consider now a test to detect protection violations. The test determines whether the requested access falls within the allowed privileges of the user. A straightforward approach is to scan a list of codes delegated to the user until a code is found that authorizes the requested access. More sophisticated approaches could involve the derivation of protection and privilege values indirectly by some algorithm.[6] Protection codes may be stored with the data, or alternatively, they may be held in separate attribute tables. Protection might even be defined as a function of the value of the data. According to one view, individual entries need no protection. Rather, the function of a protection system is to ensure that a user does not obtain certain combinations of entries that would enable him to discover sensitive facts. This last threat may be averted by requiring a user to hold privilege for all data in a category before he can see any of these data.

It is not possible to settle such application- and system-related issues in this general discussion. However, considerations such as simplicity, efficiency, and flexibility appear to recommend the less sophisticated method, namely, the systematic comparison of protection codes with privilege codes.

Privilege

Privilege may be described as the right of users to access sensitive information. However, it is often advantageous for a program to possess privileges different from those of the person who invoked it. The program's privileges may exceed those of the person. For example, a statistician may be prohibited from seeing individual salary records, but he could be permitted to execute a program that has the privilege of reading salaries in order to determine salary averages. Likewise, it would be desirable to deny a program certain access privileges held by the person using the program. In that way, a user could ensure that a program does not disturb certain of his data sets.

In the case of a program that possesses privileges not held by the person using it, such a program must have a kind of miniature security system built in to censor sensitive information from data returned to the user. Consequently, the user must be prevented from modifying the program, and perhaps prevented even from looking at it.

Furthermore, it would be useful if privileges and restrictions could be passed along selectively as programs invoke other programs. But then rather elaborate controls would be needed to keep track of the levels of privilege and restriction that apply at any moment. Before any access can be obtained, the authorization system would have to determine the result of all accumulated privileges and restrictions. Such capabilities would burden the authorization system with chores involving scoping rules and stacking. Because all file accesses would be affected, system performance might deteriorate.

The notion of privileged programs warrants further attention. Although they are not considered further here, privileged programs are discussed in Reference 10. In the remainder of this paper, privilege is referred to as an attribute of users, but of course, observations made regarding user privilege could also apply to program privilege.[15]

Planning for authorization should begin during the preliminary development of a system. It may not be sufficient to "patch up" an existing system by the addition of checking and monitoring features. Checking and monitoring, even when used extensively, do not necessarily make safe a vulnerable system. For example, if there are many access paths to certain sensitive data, a checking process could be introduced into each path. Nevertheless, unforeseen combinations of paths may provide "trap door" entrances, allowing resourceful human infiltrators to circumvent the protection.[2] Instead, it seems preferable to redesign such a system so that only one fully protected access path exists to the sensitive data.

Although it is clear that protection is mandatory for shared-file systems, it is not evident how extensive it should be. Commercial users, for example, do tolerate occasional disclosures under batch processing conditions. Occasionally, a user discovers that he has received someone else's output or that someone else has received his. On the other hand, extreme military levels of security[16] are more than appropriate for most nonmilitary applications.[17] Indeed, if a reasonably secure system could be realized, it might in time be accepted for certain military applications.

But what is reasonable? Application studies and user surveys could help to indicate the degrees of protection that customers will demand, the costs they will pay, and the penalties in processing speed and convenience they will tolerate. In the absence of this information, the discussion must be speculative.

AN IDEAL SYSTEM

At this point, let us consider features that would characterize an ideal authorization mechanism for a general-purpose, time-sharing system.

- Users should be assured that protected data, programs, or messages will not be disclosed to unauthorized parties, even in case of major hardware failure or loss of the operating system. On the other hand, users should never be denied access to information for which they are authorized.
- It should not be possible for any user to "break" the protection mechanism so as to discover secret data, even if he understands how the mechanism operates.
- Users should be able to enter data freely into a protected file, and they should be able to specify the individuals who are allowed access to those data, and the type of access permitted.
- All common types of file updating and processing should be permitted. Users should be able to create, modify, and delete data within their areas of responsibility.
- Response time for processes in the secure shared file should not be appreciably greater than the time required for any other processing.

- The authorization system should impose as few restrictions as possible on the operating system, file structure, time-sharing system, and hardware.
- It would be undesirable for users who have already been logged on and identified to be expected to remember long lists of passwords, secret keys, or special commands. People are inclined to write lists down, thereby compromising secrecy. Forgetful users may at length attempt to disable the protection mechanisms altogether in order to continue using the machine.
- The system should not depend upon continuous attention of a human security officer for its normal operation, since a human is likely to be overwhelmed during periods of high activity. However, a human authority should be notified in the event of irregularities, and he should be able to suspend any job on command.

Although we have indicated that a protection mechanism should, where possible, be independent of the hardware, operating system, and environment, a practical protection mechanism must reflect characteristics of the entire system including the file organization, channel switching, and record identification methods. Whereas some general recommendations may be advanced on the basis of the ideal system, those recommendations are suggested only if they can be provided compatibly with the specific system architecture. Possible difficulties resulting from these recommendations are pointed out later in this paper.

To discuss authorization, a basic unit of protected information is necessary. Accordingly, we define a protected field as a section of data or program in storage that is subjected to a uniform degree of protection, i.e., all bits of the field receive exactly the same protection. This unit should be distinguished from a physical record, which is defined as a separately retrievable unit of information from a given storage device. Protected fields in certain cases should also be distinguished from a logical record, which is considered a unit in terms of its content, function, or use.

This concept implies the existence of field handling within the data management system. However, it should be noted that field handling, which consists of identifying and extracting fields from larger physical or logical records, involves formidable design problems that may exceed the difficulties of the authorization system itself.

SYSTEM GUIDELINES

On the basis of the preceding considerations, the following guidelines are suggested by the author:

- Isolation of the authorization mechanism
- Access limitation
- Adjacent tagging
- Single-tag rule
- Compartmentalization

Isolation of the Authorization System

Although functions of authorization and the operating system often overlap, the authorization system should be organized as an isolated program module distinct from the remainder of the operating system. Protection would then be distinguished from other data management functions. The authorization system would be invoked as an independent task whenever access to data in the secured shared file is requested. This would allow the authorization system to be programmed as a limited, self-contained package so that it could be subjected to unusually thorough debugging and check-out.

The package should reside in a separate protected region of storage in order to eliminate "trap door" entrances into the routines. Attempts to branch into those programs, even when made by the operating system, would then be rejected automatically as violations of the storage bounds. Instead, the routines should be invocable only in response to a limited set of explicit requests.

The designer, however, should not disregard possible difficulties that isolation may impose. Separate "packaging" might increase the program size, and delays could also occur. Housekeeping and other utilities might have to be duplicated in such a package. Extra programming may also be required for routines to be made invocable functions, i.e., prologues, epilogues, or argument-passing mechanisms might be needed. Interruption handling and failure-recovery routines may present particular problems for such a package.

Access Limitation

The shared file itself must be isolated so that it will be impossible to access it except by means of the authorization system. One way to meet this requirement is to dedicate certain channels to the authorization system. That is, channels would be assigned permanently to the authorization programs. No way should be provided to reassign these channels by program control. It is possible, however, that a satisfactory level of security can be obtained as well by programmed access methods, without dedicated channels.

Adjacent Tagging

Some form of tagging is needed to designate data as "protected." The tags ought to be kept adjacent to the data themselves, provided this is consistent with the file organization. It is often convenient to carry data attributes in lists separated from the data. However, every interval separating a protected field from its protection presents a slight but real opportunity for errors of reference to arise. Since the goal is to minimize risk, physical separation should be avoided. A possible disadvantage is that the arrangement may make the process of checking the tag less efficient, and thereby impede performance.

Single-Tag Rule

If protection tags are carried along with data, the tags will consume file space. Such space is likely to be costly because of the exceptional treatment given this file. Also, since each tag increases the quantity of information contained in the file, additional time may be required to locate a given protected field.

To conserve file space no more than a single protection tag should be attached to any such field. Thus if further protection is desired for a field that is already protected, instead of adding a second tag to the field, a single new tag must replace the old one. The new tag will signify the combination of the old and the new protections. This procedure prevents long lists of tags from being attached to data in the file.

The single-tag rule may, however, prove to be impracticable if the length of the average protected field does not greatly exceed the length of the tag. A major part of the file space would then be allotted to the protection tags, a requirement that is undesirable. If this is the case, it may be necessary to limit protected fields to larger units, or alternatively, to impose restrictions on format. As a third possibility, the number of protected categories could be restricted.

Compartmentalization

However, if the single-tag rule is followed, each distinctly protected segment of data will possess one tag, and that tag alone must serve to identify all specific restrictions placed upon the segment. It is convenient to make use of the tagging system to organize the protection classification scheme, so that each tag itself constitutes a protection category. All data that are similarly restricted to certain users are assigned a common protection tag. Therefore, those data are assigned to a common protection category.

For convenience, such a category of data is called a group, which we define as the most elementary, atomic protection category. There are no subcategories within groups with respect to protection. Privilege to any information within a group implies privilege to all information in that group.

Protection groups are discrete and compartmentalized. Any item of protected data is assigned to one and only one group. Every group is an independently existing entity, and is not affected by changes in other groups. This strategy is similar to the scheme devised by Hsiao,[18] except that in our case protection applies to individual records rather than to files as a whole.

The compartmentalized scheme contrasts with the concept of a stratified or multilevel security classification scheme.[16] There can be no levels or structures in the compartmentalized system. Every protected record is as absolutely restricted to its delegated users as any other. The notion of levels of security, such as CONFIDENTIAL, SECRET, or TOP SECRET, does not apply in the compartmentalized system. In a compartmentalized scheme, such levels simply constitute nonfunctional information to be carried in addition to the protection categories.

Compartmentalized protection groups correspond to the military notion of NEED TO KNOW. It is undesirable to automatically release data with, say, CONFIDENTIAL protection to anyone who has access to SECRET data. There may be an occasion when certain SECRET data has to be disclosed to someone who is not authorized to see certain CONFIDENTIAL data. However, a NEED TO KNOW for one category of data does not imply a NEED TO KNOW for another category. In other words, protections should not have interdependencies or hierarchy. Weissman[6] and Graham[7] have described schemes combining NEED TO KNOW and protection levels. It is not evident, however, whether these approaches are more useful than compartmentalization alone.

The compartmentalized, single-tag approach requires a less complex test for violations than some alternative methods. For example, if a field has more than one associated protection tag, a non-trivial test may be required to determine whether a request for access is permissible. In contrast, if each field has only one tag, the test could consist only of comparison of that tag with the explicit privileges of the requester, which may reduce the processing time to approve the request.

The compartmentalized system also provides a high degree of flexibility. As previously noted, users' privileges to data may be complex, changing, and without a well-defined hierarchy. If any associations of protection groups and users are built into the basic file organization, small changes in relationships could require reconstructing much of the file. A compartmentalized system, on the other hand, makes possible the association of any record with any clique of users. A distinct user clique is definable for each group of records.

The term clique refers to a set of users such as "Department Managers" or "Corporation Attorneys," in contrast to a group, which is defined as a set of data requiring a common type of protection. The protection of a group always consists of granting to some user clique the exclusive privilege to that data group; thus there may be a one-to-one correspondence of groups and cliques. Two terms are used here because it is sometimes desirable to make the same data available in different ways to different users. A certain group of data, for example annual salaries, may be released to the clique of payroll department members on a read-only basis, whereas those same data may be released to the clique of payroll clerks on a read-write basis. Incidentally, that second clique might consist of only one individual.

Compartmentalized data would be partitioned into a multitude of disjoint groups, thereby providing complete freedom to associate individuals with protected data. Changes could be readily made. An individual would be delegated privilege to a specific set of data by adding the explicit protection code for that data group to his security profile. Privilege is revoked by divesting his profile of that protection code. Such operations do not affect the individual's privileges to any data except those explicitly delegated or revoked. If a subset of some previously defined group of data is to be altered in respect to its restrictions to users, the original protection group must be redefined as two groups according to this distinction.

The compartmentalized protection scheme has the disadvantage that it might lead to the proliferation of protection groups, which may impose an administrative burden on the authorization system.[4] However, this burden may be tolerable, as will be described later in this paper. To aid processing, an auxiliary table of the interrelations of protection groups may be maintained in addition to the primary classification system. Such a table would serve as a convenience and would be distinct from the primary system.

The primary directory of the authorization system is a matrix of profiles, in which data group privileges are listed with respect to each user. Of course, such a matrix could be represented as well in transposed form, whereby all privileged users would be listed with respect to each data group. In the latter case, when access is requested, the list of privileged users for the requested data group would be searched for the user who issued the request. If there are many more data groups than users, searching a row of the transposed matrix would usually be shorter than searching the untransposed matrix. However, there would be more rows in the transposed matrix, so that it might take longer to locate the appropriate row.

A SYSTEM MODEL

The foregoing guidelines are now expanded into an illustrative model of an authorization system. This system is necessarily hypothetical, because any implementation must take account of specific hardware, software, applications, load considerations, and file organization. The organization of the system is shown in Figure 1.

We assume that the computer runs under an operating system that supports several remote-terminal users who carry on separate jobs simultaneously. For work space, each user is allocated a private bounded region of the computer's main storage. Within his region, the user may conduct whatever interactive processing he desires, but he cannot directly access anything outside his region except the system supervisor.

The operating system resides in a distinct, protected region of main storage. The authorization system resides in yet another main storage region, which is inaccessible not only from the user regions but also from the operating system. Authorization programs may only be invoked by a limited set of explicit requests. The storage protection scheme must be effective in preventing intrusions into the authorization program region.

The secured shared file resides in an auxiliary storage medium, or possibly a set of auxiliary media, which are accessible only to the authorization system. These media (indicated in Figure 1 as a disk storage) and their associated channels should be protected against invasion, bugging, or physical removal. It must not be possible for a user to switch the secured shared file to normal channels so as to circumvent the authorization system.

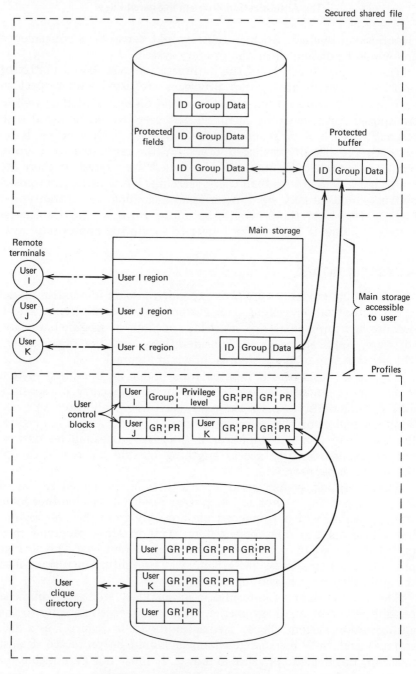

FIGURE 1.   Model authorization system.

Group Tags and ID

There may be normal, freely accessible channels for files that are neither secured nor shared. These files are not under control of the authorization system. To avoid overburdening secured shared files, users could be directed to use them only for data they expect to share selectively. However, in an actual system it may be more economical to use the secured shared-file mechanism for all secondary files even though the mechanism is not required in each case. According to the suggested guidelines, protection information is carried adjacent to the data in the file. This protection information, shown in the figure as GROUP and GR, is termed the "group tags." All data that are to be similarly restricted to a common set of users should be assigned the same unique group tag. As the system is used, it may happen that more than one group of data may be defined that are similarly restricted to the same users. The authorization system searches the files periodically to discover such equivalent groups, and then adjusts those group tags to be identical.

As suggested, each protected field possesses a single group tag. Again these fields need not correspond to physical records of the storage medium. They may be of different length from physical records, nor need the protected fields be of fixed length. Means must be provided, however, to identify these fields. The identification, ID, serves to distinguish protected fields within a single group or within distinct groups. Precise identification conventions are more properly a topic of file organization and accessing, and are not considered in this discussion. The ID could be carried along with the field, as shown in Figure 1, or alternatively, the ID could be held in a separate directory. It is, however, desirable to keep the group tag distinct from the ID, since the ID provides the name of a protected field in the files, whereas the group tag serves to protect the field. By means of this distinction, a protected field that had been improperly selected through an error of identification can, nevertheless, still be detected, and then withheld during the testing period.

Public Status

Testing may sometimes be omitted by the use of special public status categories of the tag. A public status tag indicates that normal protection is not required. The categories could be indicated when a tag value falls within certain numeric ranges, as shown by Table I.

TABLE I

Tag	Status
0	Default tag for a completely unprotected field. Any user may read, alter, or write.
1 to 20,000	Publicly available for reading or updating, but may not be deleted except by users with appropriate privilege.
20,001 to 40,000	Publicly available for reading only.
40,001 to 60,000	Publicly available as an executable program only.
Over 60,000	Fully private.

Profiles

In addition, there could be a category permitting public availability for updating but not reading, although it is questionable whether such a category is desirable. The actual tag ranges should be determined by statistical studies of the usage of public categories. The authorization system also must provide a security profile for each user. Such a profile consists of a complete list of data protection groups for which the user has access privileges.

When a user logs on and is properly identified, the authorization system copies that user's security profile into a control block located in a protected main storage region, as shown by the heavy arrow at the bottom of the figure. By holding this copy in main storage, the authorization system can complete the confirmation of requests more quickly than otherwise. Whenever a user requests access to the secured shared file, the authorization system consults his profile to determine whether he has the required authority.

Privilege Levels

Associated with each group tag in the profile there is also a field to specify the level of privilege that the user has been granted for that group. (Privilege is indicated by "PR" in the profile area of the figure.) Four levels of privilege may be sufficient, which could be represented with a two bit code, as shown in Table II. If fields are available only as executable routines, the authorization system loads the fields into an inaccessible main storage region in preparation for execution. In other cases, fields are copied into the user's area.

TABLE II

Code	Privilege Level
00	Execute only. Fields are available only as programs for execution; they cannot be displayed or dumped.
01	Read only. User may execute and read, but not modify these fields.
10	Update. User may execute, read, and modify fields, but neither delete nor create new fields.
11	Full privilege. User may create new fields, delete existing fields, as well as execute, read, and update any field, and may delegate privileges.

Additional privilege levels may be desired as, for example, "create but not read," "update but not read," or "create but not delegate." Such categories, however, may lead users to enter material that they are unable to review or control. Consequently, the file may become cluttered with data of doubtful accuracy, and which cannot readily be verified, corrected, or removed. In contrast, the four privilege levels originally suggested can achieve the same objectives without causing these problems. The purpose of "create but not read," for example, is to prevent a user from browsing through data in a category even though he is authorized to enter data into that category. The same ends, however, would be served if each such user establishes a private group for recording data and then delegates privilege to an official (or to a privileged program) to copy his group into a special master table. The individual user would lack privilege to read that table, but he would be able to review and correct the original entries in his private file. Thus, users can prepare data for entry in the master table, although they are not able to read the table. Similarly, "update but not read" and "create but not delegate" could be realized by application of the four previously suggested privilege levels.

SYSTEM OPERATION

File Operation Mode

The model authorization system operates in two modes. In the file operation mode the system executes on demand when a user requests a service relating to the secured shared file. The background mode is used for inspecting and revising files for consistency. We first consider the file operation mode, which includes the following commands:

LOG ON/LOG OFF
DELEGATE (REVOKE) PRIVILEGE
READ
EXECUTE
READ FOR UPDATING
UPDATE
CREATE
DELETE

LOG ON and LOG OFF simply involve copying the user profile into his control block after he has been properly identified, and removing it after the user signs off. The DELEGATE (REVOKE) PRIVILEGE command operates on the user security profiles. When this command is given, the authorization system confirms that the requester has full privilege for the data group referred to; then the system attaches or removes the group tag from the profile of the specified user. Privilege at any level can be delegated. Although operations on user profiles should be executed rapidly, they need not be accomplished as quickly as operations on the secured shared file.

The READ, EXECUTE, READ FOR UPDATING, UPDATE, CREATE, and DELETE commands involve operations on the file that are each composed of the four steps: request, search, confirmation, and release.

READ

Request. The user calls the authorization system (heavy arrows between user and main storage on the left side of the figure), and he, or a program he calls, issues a read request that identifies a record in the secured file. Record identification is an aspect of file management, and could be accomplished by such methods as ID field, displacement from base, address, indirect reference, or structure. Optionally, the requester may supply the group name, so that a search of his profile for that group is initiated at the same time.

Search. The file accessing system initiates a search for the record. If group has been specified in the request, a simultaneous search for group privilege is initiated in the user control block.

Confirmation. When the record has been located in the secured file, the authorization system holds it in a protected buffer for confirmation, as indicated at the top of the figure. There may be several such buffers. If a record has public-read status, confirmation is omitted. Otherwise, the group name in the file entry is compared with group privileges listed for the user in the user control block (light arrow to the right of the figure). If confirmation is not achieved, the request may constitute an attempted violation, and should be recorded for audit.

Release. If confirmation is achieved, the portion of the buffer containing the field is copied into the user's space.

EXECUTE is similar to READ, except for the following factors. Confirmation may be omitted if the protected field has public-execute-only status. The authorization system loads the field into a special protected region of main storage rather than into the user's region. When an entire program—linkages, arguments, and pointers to data—has been loaded, the program is executed. If the user wants the program to process his protected files, he delegates privilege for those files to the program when he calls it.

The READ FOR UPDATING command is similar to READ except for the following provisions. An interlock must be provided so that no other user may update the field.[3] The original record is retained after release in the authorization system buffer to await the updated version. User confirmation is waived only if the field has public-updatable status. Otherwise, the user must have at least update privilege for this group. Finally, if the user logs off before completing an update, the field must have its interlock removed.

UPDATE

Request. This command is executable only if a READ FOR UP-DATING command had previously been executed for the same field by the user during the current run—otherwise the request is rejected. The same ID should be used as had been used previously in the READ FOR UPDATING. The authorization system compares this ID with the copy of the original record held in its protected buffer. If a match occurs, the user's updated data are copied into the buffer in place of the original data.

Search. As an added precaution, the original protected record must be read from the file again just prior to updating. Therefore, for certain storage media, a search may be initiated.

Confirmation. The same confirmation is required when rereading the entry from the file as was required in the READ FOR UPDATING; namely, the field should be public updatable or the user must have privilege for this group of at least update level. Also, the protected field's ID, status, and group must match those of the updated version held in the authorization system buffer.

Release. When confirmation is complete, the authorization system writes the updated entry into the file. If record sizes are fixed, writing could be accomplished by overwriting the space of the original record. Otherwise, the original record is deleted, and the updated record is added. The interlock is removed.

CREATE

Request. Any user may create an entry in the file. If a user issues a CREATE command, but does not specify group and status, a default group is automatically assigned to the field with private status. The default group name is taken directly from the user's own identification, thereby defining a group unique to that user. Of course, the user may also request the creation of a protected field with another group name or status. At request time, the desired entry is copied from the user space into the system buffer.

Confirmation. If the user has indicated his own name for his group, either explicitly or by default, confirmation is directly provided. If any other group is indicated, the authorization system first determines whether the user has full privilege for that group.

Release. After confirmation, the entry is copied into the secured shared file from the protected buffer.

The DELETE command is similar to CREATE in that identifications must match, and the user must have full privilege.

Background Mode

We now outline the background mode which includes the DEFINE GROUP and IDENTIFY CLIQUE commands. The DEFINE GROUP establishes a category of data, and the IDENTIFY CLIQUE command establishes a category of users. The background mode also includes regular inspections to determine that each group has an owner with full privilege, that equivalent groups are merged, and that privileges delegated to cliques of users are granted to each member of the clique.

The DEFINE GROUP command affects both the secured shared file and user profiles. By means of this command, an existing group can be fragmented into several groups, or several groups can be merged into one. A group may also be defined as being "public," in which case the tag value is assigned within the range of one of the special public categories.

Protected fields that have been filed under a user's private default group tag can be shared if the user explicitly delegates privilege for that group to other users. Alternatively, the sharing of protected fields may also be accomplished by designating certain fields to be in a group for which other users already possess privilege.

The DEFINE GROUP command is relatively slow in execution because it requires that the secured shared file be thoroughly searched for all fields tagged with the old group categories. These categories must be redesignated with the new categories. Also, all user profiles that include privilege to the obsolete group categories must be revised before regular processing proceeds. The DEFINE GROUP command, therefore, halts file processing, and should be performed only in a low priority mode. When issuing this command, the user must hold full privilege for the old groups and, if the new group categories already exist, he must hold full privilege for these groups as well.

Besides the secured shared file and user profile list, a table of user cliques may be provided. Privilege for a data group could thereby be delegated to a clique as a whole. Then when the IDENTIFY CLIQUE command is issued, the authorization system, in the background mode, goes through the list of clique members and attaches the privilege to each member's profile. Incidentally, the existing protection system can be used to protect this clique membership list. The list may simply be maintained as a secured shared file group. As a consequence, the list will then have explicit sets of users authorized to refer to it and change it.

Quantitative Projections

The system model is used for illustrative purposes and is not intended for inclusion in an existing or future shared computer without change. Performance of an authorization system can only be evaluated if it is a component of an actual time-sharing system. Although studies and experiments may in time provide empirical information on comparative authorization systems, it may be instructive to consider some projections based on our model.

Assume that the hypothetical system supports 20,000 recognized users from various independent organizations and that 2,000 terminals may be simultaneously connected on-line. If such a large general-purpose, secured shared file system becomes operational, a demand for an extensive exchanging and trading of data and programs may result. For our projections, let us assume that the average user holds privileges for 200 groups of protected data. (There may, of course, be a few users with privileges to all or almost all data groups.) The average user will originate perhaps ten groups of secured data. From these assumptions, it follows that there are 10 times 20,000 (or 200,000) data groups. To distinguish that number of groups, an 18-bit tag is required for each protected field. If we assume that an average entry is 50 bytes (400 bits), it follows that the proportion of information in the secured shared file devoted to protection is 18 bits divided by 400 bits, or 4.5 percent of the total file. (Parity bits or error correction bits, of course, are not included in these figures.) However, if the average protected field is considerably smaller than 50 bytes, the proportion of storage required for protection will grow, which may make the system unacceptable.

Each user's security profile consists of his personal identification field and a list of group privileges and privilege levels. Assume that each user's identification field consists of 15 bytes (120 bits). Of these, 18 bits are needed for each group code, and 2 bits for the privilege level indicator. An 18-bit field is also required to report the number of groups in the profile because the maximum is 200,000. Since the average user is assumed to hold privileges for 200 groups, storage for an average profile is 120 + 200 (18 + 2) + 18 (or 4,138) bits. Since 20,000 users are recognized, 82,760,000 bits or 10,345,000 bytes of storage are required for a complete set of profiles.

The authorization system will impose a delay, which is expected to be small in comparison with the file search delay. The most commonly used file commands are expected to be READ, READ FOR UPDATING, and UPDATE. In execution, delays will result from the following authorization system operations:

- Calling the authorization system.
- Copying the field into the buffer.
- Comparing the group tag with the user profile.

It is hoped that the authorization system can be programmed so that system calls involve only a few instructions. Copying a field into the buffer may involve only a single start-input/output instruction. Comparison of the group with the user profile involves executing a short program loop to scan the profile. Since the average user is assumed to hold privilege for 200 groups, an average of 100 loop iterations is expected. The average delay could be reduced by listing the most frequently used groups at the beginning of the profile. Iteration delay could be avoided by the user's supplying the group tag in his request, so that his profile is scanned while the file is searched.

The vulnerability of the hypothetical system should be considered. Only users who hold full privilege for groups can alter security profiles, and they may alter only references to those groups for which their full privilege applies. Otherwise people cannot affect their own or anyone else's profile. Users should not be able to interfere with the authorization system except by a rather unlikely combination of accidents. Even catastrophic system failures do not appear to provide opportunities for such lapses in protection.

CONCLUDING REMARKS

Selective sharing of information has been considered in this paper only with regard to auxiliary storage in a certain general type of time-sharing system. Further study is needed to provide an efficient authorization system within the central processor's main storage. Effort is also required to enable programs to pass privileges selectively when calling other programs.

ACKNOWLEDGMENT

The author wishes to thank P. S. Dauber for suggesting this study. He also acknowledges the aid of P. R. Schneider, C. J. Stephenson, M. A. Auslander, and M. E. Hopkins; of R. Courtney and L. Moss, who established the conceptual groundwork on which this paper is based; and of A. M. Pfaff for much constructive criticism.

REFERENCES

1.   The Consideration of Data Security in a Computer Environment, 520-2169, International Business Machines Corporation, Data Processing Division, White Plains, New York.

2.   H. E. Petersen and R. Turn, "System implications of information privacy," AFIPS Conference Proceedings, Spring Joint Computer Conference 30, Thompson Book Company, Washington, D.C., 291–300 (1967).

3. J. B. Dennis and E. C. van Horn, "Programming semantics for multi programmed computation," Communications of the Association for Computing Machinery 9, No. 3, 143–155 (March 1966).

4. L. J. Hoffman, "Computers and privacy: a survey," Computing Surveys 1, No. 2, 85–103 (1969).

5. W. H. Ware, "Security and privacy in computer systems," AFIPS Conference Proceedings, Spring Joint Computer Conference 30, Thompson Book Company, Washington, D.C., 279–282 (1967).

6. C. Weissman, "Security controls in the ADEPT-50 time-sharing system," AFIPS Conference Proceedings, Fall Joint Computer Conference 35, 119–133, AFIPS Press, Montvale, New Jersey (1969).

7. R. M. Graham, "Protection in an information processing utility," Communications of the Association for Computing Machinery 11, No. 5, 365–369 (May 1968).

8. P. A. Crisman, Editor, The Compatible Time-Sharing System—A Programmer's Guide, MIT Press, Cambridge, Massachusetts (1965).

9. System/360 Time-Sharing System, Concepts and Facilities, C28-2003, International Business Machines Corporation, Data Processing Division, White Plains, New York.

10. B. W. Lampson, "Dynamic protection structures," AFIPS Conference Proceedings, Fall Joint Computer Conference 35, 27–38, AFIPS Press, Montvale, New Jersey (1969).

11. W. F. Friedman, "Cryptology," Encyclopaedia Britannica 6, 844–851, Chicago, Illinois (1967).

12. C. E. Shannon, "Communication theory of secrecy systems," Bell System Technical Journal 28, No. 4, 656–715 (October 1949).

13. R. O. Skatrud, "A consideration of the application of cryptographic techniques to data processing," AFIPS Conference Proceedings, Fall Joint Computer Conference 35, 111–117, AFIPS Press, Montvale, New Jersey (1969).

14. P. Baran, "Communications, computers and people," AFIPS Conference Proceedings, Fall Joint Computer Conference 27, Part 2, Thompson Book Company, Washington, D.C., 45–49 (1965).

15. R. C. Daley and P. G. Neumann, "A general-purpose file system for secondary storage," AFIPS Conference Proceedings, Fall Joint Computer Conference 27, Part 1, Spartan Books, New York, New York, 213–229 (1965).

16. B. Peters, "Security considerations in a multiprogrammed computer system," AFIPS Conference Proceedings, Spring Joint Computer Conference 30, Thompson Book Company, Washington, D.C., 283–286 (1967).

17. W. H. Ware, "Security and privacy: simularities and differences," AFIPS Conference Proceedings, Spring Joint Computer Conference 30, Thompson Book Company, Washington, D.C., 287–290 (1967).

18. D. K. Hsiao, "A file system for a problem solving facility," Ph.D. Dissertation (Electrical Engineering), University of Pennsylvania, Philadelphia, Pennsylvania (1968).

The Formulary Model
for Flexible Privacy
and Access Controls

LANCE J. HOFFMAN

INTRODUCTION

This paper presents a model for engineering the user interface for large data base systems in order to maintain flexible access controls over sensitive data. The model is independent of both machine and data base structure, and is sufficiently modular to allow cost-effectiveness studies on access mechanisms. Access control is based on sets of procedures called formularies. The decision on whether a user can read, write, update, etc., data is controlled by programs (not merely bits or tables of data) which can be completely independent of the contents or location of raw data in the data base.

The decision to grant or deny access can be made in real time at data access time, not only at file creation time as has usually been the case in the past. Indeed the model presented does not make use of the concept of "files," though a specific interpretation of the model may do so. Access control is not restricted to the file level or the record level, although the model permits either of these. If desired, however, access can be controlled at arbitrarily lower levels, even at the bit level. The function of data addressing is separated from the function of access control in the model. Moreover, each element of raw data need appear only once, thus allowing considerable savings in memory and in maintenance effort over previous file-oriented systems.

SOURCE: Fall Joint Computer Conference, 1971, Proceedings. Reprinted by permission of the publisher, American Federation of Information Processing Societies Press.

Specifically not considered in the model are privacy problems associated with communication lines, electromagnetic radiation monitoring, physical security, wiretapping, equipment failure, operating system software bugs, personnel, or administrative procedures. Cryptographic methods are not dealt with in any detail, though provision is made for inclusion of encrypting and decrypting operations in any particular interpretation of the model.

Specific interpretations of the model can be implemented on any general-purpose computer; no special time-sharing or other hardware is required. The only proviso is that all requests to access the data base must be guaranteed to pass through the data base system.

ACCESS CONTROL METHODS

Access Control in Existing Systems

In most existing file systems which are concerned with information privacy, passwords[1,2] are used to provide software protection for sensitive data. Password schemes generally permit a small finite number of specific types of access to files. Each file (or user) has an associated password. In order to access information in a file, the user must provide the correct password. These methods, while acceptable for some purposes, can be compromised by wiretapping, electromagnetic radiation monitoring, and other means. Even if this were not the case, there are other reasons[3] why password schemes as implemented to date do not solve satisfactorily the problem of access control in a large computer data base shared by many users.

One of these reasons is that passwords have been associated with files. In most current systems, information is protected at the file level only—it has been tacitly assumed that all data within a file is of the same sensitivity. The real world does not conform to this assumption. Information from various sources is constantly coming into common data pools, where it can be used by all persons with access to that pool. A problem arises when certain information in a file should be available to some but not all authorized users of the file.

In the MULTICS system[4] for example, if a user has a file which in part contains sensitive data, he just cannot merge all his data with that of his colleagues. He often must separate the sensitive data and save that in a separate file; the common pool of data does not contain this sensitive and possibly highly valuable data. Moreover, he and those he permits to access this sensitive data must, if they also wish to make use of the nonsensitive data, create a distinct merged file, thus duplicating information kept in the system; if some of this duplicated data must later be changed, it must be changed in all files instead of only one. Figure 1, taken from Hoffman's survey[5] of computers and privacy, graphically illustrates this situation by depicting memory allocation under existing systems and under a more desirable system.

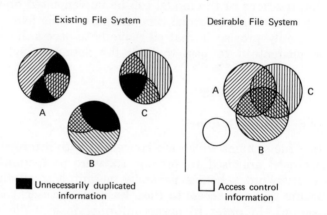

FIGURE 1.   Use of computer storage in file systems.

The file management problems presented and the memory wastage (due to duplication of data) tend to inhibit creation of large data bases and to foster the development of smaller, less efficient,* overlapping data bases which could, were the privacy problem really solved, be merged.

Several years ago Bingham[7] suggested the use of <u>User's Control Profiles</u> to associate access control with a user rather than a file. This allows users to operate only on file subsets for which they are authorized and to some extent solves the memory wastage problem. Weissman has recently described a working system at SDC which makes use of security properties of users, terminals, and files.[8] He presents a set-theoretic model for such a system. His model does not deal with access control below the file level.

Hsiao[9] has recently implemented a system using <u>authority items</u> associated with users. Hsiao's system controls access at the record

---

*A simple cost model for information systems is presented by Arvas.[6] He there derives a simple rule to determine when it is more efficient to consolidate files and when it is more efficient to distribute copies of them.

level, one step beneath the file level. In it, access control information is stored independently of raw data, and thus can be examined or changed without actually accessing the raw data. Hsiao's system and the TERPS system[10] at West Sussex County in England are two of the first working systems which control access at a level lower than the file level.

Access Control in Proposed Systems

Some other methods have been proposed for access control, but not yet implemented. These include Graham's scheme[11] which essentially assigns a sensitivity level to each program and data element in the system,* another which allows higher-level programs to grant access privileges to lower-level programs,[12] and still others which place access control at the segment level[13,14] via machine hardware and "codewords." These methods may prove acceptable in many contexts. However, they are not general enough for all situations. If distinct sensitivity levels cannot be assigned to data, as is sometimes the case, Graham's scheme cannot be used. The other methods, while working in principle on a computer with hardware segmentation, seem infeasible and uneconomical on a computer with another type of memory structure such as an associative memory[15-19] or a Lesser memory.[20] These objections are covered in more detail elsewhere.[5]

Desirable Characteristics for an Access Control Method

It seems desirable to devise a method of access control which does not impose an arbitrary constraint (such as segmentation or sensitivity levels) on data or programs. This method should allow efficient control of individual data elements (rather than of files or records only). Also, it should not extract unwarranted cost in storage or elsewhere from the user who wants only a small portion of his data protected. The method should be independent of both machine and file structure, yet flexible enough to allow a particular implementation of it to be efficient. Finally, it should be sufficiently modular to permit cost-effectiveness experiments to be undertaken. We would then finally have a vehicle for exploring the often-asked but never-answered question about privacy controls, "How much does technique X cost?"

We now present such a method.

---

*Evidently this scheme has now been implemented.

THE FORMULARY METHOD OF ACCESS CONTROL

We now describe the "formulary" method of access control. Its salient features have been mentioned above. The decision to grant or deny access is made at data access time, rather than at file creation time, as has generally been the case in previous systems. This, together with the fact that the decision is made by a program (not by a scan of bits or a table), allows more flexible control of access. Data-dependent, terminal-dependent, time-dependent, and user response-dependent decisions can now be made dynamically at data request time, in contrast to the predetermined decisions made in previous systems, which are, in fact, subsumed by the formulary method. Access to individual related data items which may have logical addresses very close to each other can be controlled individually. For example, a salary figure might be released without any identification of an employee or any other data.

For any particular interpretation, the installation must supply the procedures listed in Table I. These procedures can all be considered a part of the general accessing mechanism, each performing a specific function. By clearly delimiting these functions, a degree of modularity is gained which enables the installation to experiment with various access control methods to arrive at the modules which best suit its needs for efficiency, economy, flexibility, etc. This modularity also results in access control becoming independent of the

TABLE I.   Procedures Supplied by the Installation

FOR EACH INTERPRETATION, INSTALLATION MUST SUPPLY

- At Least One TALK Procedure
- Coding for the ACCESS Algorithm
- PRIMITIVE OPERATIONS
  - Fetch
  - Store
- At Least One FORMULARY, Consisting of
  - Control Procedure
  - Virtual Procedure
  - Scramble Procedure (may be null)
  - Unscramble Procedure (may be null)
- A FORMULARYBUILDER Procedure

---

remainder of the operating system, a desirable but elusive goal.[8] While the formulary model and its central ACCESS procedure remain unchanged, each installation can supply and easily change the procedures of Table I as desirable. These procedures are all specified in the body of this paper.

The basic idea behind the formulary method is that a user, a terminal, and a previously built formulary (defined below) must be linked together, or attached, in order for a user to perform information storage, retrieval, and/or manipulative operations. At the time the user requests use of the data base system, this linkage is effected, but only if the combination of user, terminal and formulary is allowed. The general linking process is described later in this section.

Virtual memory mapping hardware is not required to implement the model but the model does handle systems equipped with such hardware. It is assumed that enough virtual addressing capacity is available to handle the entire data base. Virtual addresses are mapped into the physical core memory locations, disc tracks, low-usage magnetic tapes, etc., by hardware and/or by the FETCH and STORE primitive operations (see below) for a particular implementation.

Definitions and Notation

The internal name of a datum is its logical address (with respect to the structure of the data base). The internal name of a datum does not change during continuous system operation.

Examples:

(1) A "tree name" such as 5.7.3.2 which denotes field 2 of branch 3 of branch 7 of branch 5 in the data base

(2) "Associative memory identifiers" such as (14, 273, 34) where 14 represents the 14th attribute, 273 represents the 273rd object, and 34 represents the 34th value, in a memory similar to the one described by Rovner and Feldman.[21]

A User Control Block, or UCB, is space in primary (core) storage allocated during the attachment process (described below). It contains the user identification, terminal identification, and information about the VIRTUAL, CONTROL, SCRAMBLE, and UNSCRAMBLE procedures of the formulary the user is linked to. (An entity with the same name and used similarly has recently been presented independently in a non-implemented model by Friedman.[22])

Usually this information is just the virtual address of each of these procedures. The virtual addresses are kept in primary storage in the UCB since a formulary, once linked to a user and terminal, will probably be (oft-) used very shortly. The first reference to any of these addresses (indirectly through the UCB) will trigger an appropriate action (e.g., a page fault on some computers) to move the proper program into primary storage (if it is not there already). It will then presumably stay there as long as it is useful enough to merit keeping in high-speed memory. The virtual addresses of procedures of a formulary cannot change while they are contained in any UCB. This constraint is easy to enforce using the CONTROL procedure described below which controls operations on any datums, including formularies. Each UCB always is in high-speed primary storage in the data area of the ACCESS procedure.

The ACCESS Procedure

All control mechanisms in the formulary model are invoked by a central ACCESS procedure. This ACCESS procedure is the only procedure which directly calls the primitive FETCH and STORE operations and which performs locking and unlocking operations on data items in the base. All requests for operations on the data base must go through the ACCESS procedure.

The ACCESS procedure is a very important element of the formulary model. It is described in full detail and its algorithm is supplied below.

The user communicates only indirectly with ACCESS. The bridge (see Figure 2) between the system-oriented ACCESS procedure and the application-oriented user is provided by the (batch or conversation) storage and retrieval program, TALK.

TALK, the application-oriented storage and retrieval procedure

To access a datum, the user must call upon TALK, the (non-system) application oriented storage and retrieval procedure. TALK converses with the user (or the user's program) to obtain, along with other information, (1) a datum description in a user-oriented language, and (2) the operation the user wishes to perform on that datum. TALK translates the datum description in the user-oriented language into an internal name, thus providing a bridge between the user's conception of the data base and the system's conception of the data base. The TALK procedure is described in more detail below.

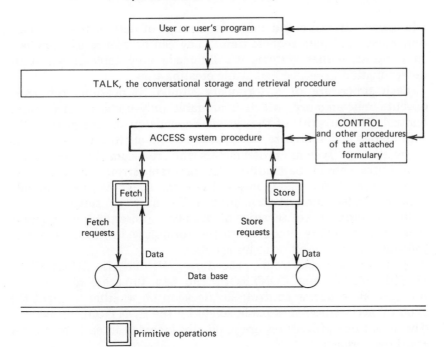

FIGURE 2.   User/data base interface.

Formularies—What They Are

A formulary is a set of procedures which controls access to information in a data base. These procedures are invoked whenever access to data is requested. They perform various functions in the storage, retrieval, and manipulation of information. The set of procedures and their associated functions are the essential elements of the formulary model of access control.

Different users will want different algorithms to carry out these functions. For example, some users will be using data which is inaccessible to others; the name of a particular data element may be specified in different ways by different users; some users will manipulate data structures—such as trees, lists, sparse files, ring structures, arrays, etc.—which are accessed by algorithms specifically designed for these structures. Depending on how he wishes to name, access, and control access to elements of the data base, each user will be attached to a formulary appropriate to his own needs.

Procedures of a Formulary.   In this subsection, we describe the procedures of a formulary. These procedures determine the accessibility, addressing, structure and interrelationships of data in the data base dynamically, at data request time. They can be arbitrarily complex. In contrast, earlier systems usually made only table-driven static determinations, prespecified at file creation time.

Each procedure of a formulary should, if possible, run from execute-only memory, which is alterable only under administrative control. The integrity of the system depends on the integrity of the formularies and therefore the procedures of all formularies should be written by "system" programmers who are assumed honest. These procedures should be audited for program errors, hidden "trap doors," etc., before being inserted into the (effective) execute-only memory under administrative control. Failure to do this may result in the compromising of sensitive data, since an unscrupulous programmer of a formulary could cause the formulary to "leak" sensitive information to himself or to his agents.

A formulary has four procedures: VIRTUAL, SCRAMBLE, UNSCRAMBLE, and CONTROL. The first three are relevant but not central to access control; the decision on whether to grant the type of access desired is made solely by the CONTROL procedure. The first three procedures are explicitly included in each formulary for three reasons:

(1)   to centralize in one place all functions dealing with addressing and access control;
(2)   to give the model the generality necessary to model existing and proposed systems; and
(3)   to provide well-delimited modules for cost/effectiveness studies and for experimentation with different addressing schemes and access control schemes.

a. The VIRTUAL procedure. VIRTUAL translates an internal name into the virtual address of the corresponding datum. VIRTUAL is a procedure with two input parameters:

(1)   the internal name to be translated
(2)   a cell which will sometimes be used to hold "other information" as described below.

VIRTUAL returns

(1)   the resulting virtual address
(2)   a completion code (1 if normal completion)

Recall that enough virtual addressing capacity is assumed available to handle the entire data base. Virtual addresses are mapped into the physical core memory locations, disc tracks, low-usage magnetic tapes, etc., by hardware and/or by the FETCH and STORE primitive operations for a particular implementation.

b. The SCRAMBLE procedure. SCRAMBLE is a procedure which transforms raw data into encrypted form. (In some specific systems, SCRAMBLE may be null.) SCRAMBLE has two input parameters:

(1)   the virtual address of the datum to be scrambled
(2)   the length of the datum to be scrambled

SCRAMBLE has three output parameters:

(1)   a completion code (1 if normal completion)
(2)   the virtual address of the scrambled datum
(3)   the length of the scrambled datum

Note that if an auto-key cipher (one which must access the start of the cipher-text, whether or not the information desired is at the start) is used, <u>all</u> of the information encrypted using that cipher, be it as small as a single field or as large as an entire "file," <u>must</u> be governed by the same access control privileges. Therefore, some applications may choose to use several (or many) auto-key ciphers within the same "file." It is inefficient and usually undesirable to scramble data items at other than the internal name level, e.g., scrambling as a block (to effectively increase key length) the data represented by several internal names. In cases where internal names represent data which fit into very small areas of storage, greater security may be obtained by other methods (e.g., use of nulls).

We do not discuss encrypting schemes in this paper. The interested reader is referred to work by Shannon,[23] Kahn,[24] and Skatrud.[25]

c. The UNSCRAMBLE procedure. UNSCRAMBLE is an unscrambling procedure which transforms encrypted data into raw form. (In some specific systems, UNSCRAMBLE may be null.) UNSCRAMBLE has two input parameters:

(1)   the virtual address of the datum to be unscrambled
(2)   the length of the datum to be unscrambled

UNSCRAMBLE has three output parameters:

(1)   a completion code (1 if normal completion)
(2)   the virtual address of the unscrambled datum
(3)   the length of the unscrambled datum.

d. The CONTROL procedure. CONTROL is a procedure which decides whether a user is allowed to perform the operation he requests (FETCH, STORE, FETCHLOCK, etc.) on the particular datum he has specified. CONTROL may consider the identification of the user and/or the source of the request (e.g., the terminal identification) in order to arrive at a decision. CONTROL may also converse with the requesting user before making the decision.

CONTROL has two input parameters and two output parameters. The two input parameters are:

(1)   the internal name of the datum
(2)   the operation the user desires to perform

The two output parameters are:

(1)   1 if access is allowed; otherwise an integer greater than 1
(2)   "other information" (explained below).

In some specific systems, data elements may themselves contain access control information. Consider three examples:

Example 1.

$$\text{DATUM} \quad \boxed{\text{R} \quad | \quad \text{W} \quad | \quad \text{30 bits of actual data}}$$

If bit R is on, DATUM is readable.
If bit W is on, DATUM is writeable.

Example 2.

$$\text{SALARY} \quad \boxed{\$25,000}$$

Reading or writing of salaries of $25,000 or over requires special checking. CONTROL must inspect the SALARY cell before it can do further capability checking and eventually return 1 or some greater integer as its first output parameter (see Figure 3). Note that return of an integer greater than 1 actually transmits some information to the user; if he knows that he will not be allowed to alter salaries which are $25,000 or over, a denial of access actually tells him that the salary in question is at least $25,000. In the formulary model, CONTROL can only make a yes or no decision about access to a particular datum. Any more complex decisions, such as one involving release of a count which is possibly low enough to allow unwanted identification of individual data[26] (e.g., "Tell me how many people the Health Physics Group treated for radiation sicknesses last year who also were treated by the Psychiatric Outpatient Department at the hospital"), can only be made by a suitably sophisticated TALK procedure.

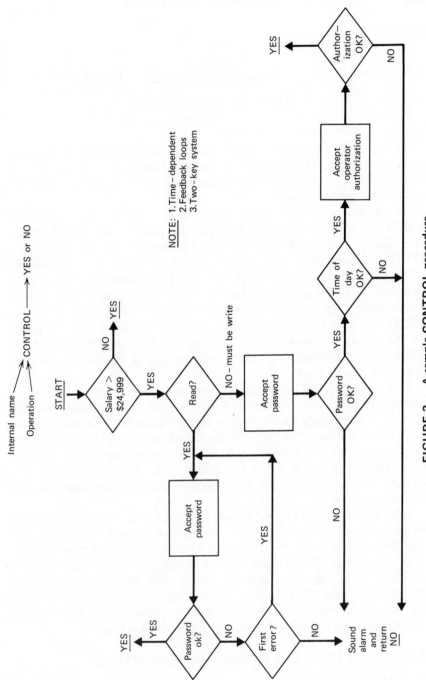

Internal name ———►
Operation ———►CONTROL ———►YES or NO

START

Salary > $24,999   NO ———► YES
        │ YES

Read?   NO – must be write ———► Accept password
        │ YES

Accept password

Password ok?   YES ———► YES
        │ NO

First error?   YES
        │ NO

Sound alarm and return NO

Password OK?   YES ———► Time of day OK?   YES ———► Accept operator authorization ———► Authorization OK?   YES
        │ NO   │ NO   │ NO

        NO

NOTE: 1. Time – dependent
      2. Feedback loops
      3. Two – key system

FIGURE 3. A sample CONTROL procedure.

Example 3.

Record N − 1		Record N	Record N + 1
	347	346 storage units of actual data	

The record contains its own length (and, therefore, also points to its successor). This type of record would appear, for example, in variable length sequential records on magnetic tape and in some list-processing applications.

In systems of this type, CONTROL might often duplicate VIRTUAL's function of transforming the internal name of a datum into that datum's virtual address. To achieve greater efficiency, CONTROL can (when appropriate) return the datum's virtual address as "other information." VIRTUAL, which is called after CONTROL (see the ACCESS algorithm below), can then examine this "other information." If a virtual address has been put there by CONTROL, VIRTUAL will not duplicate the possibly laborious determination of the datum's virtual address, since this has already been done. VIRTUAL will merely pluck the address out of the "other information" and pass it back.

Note that CONTROL can be as sophisticated a procedure as desired; it need not be merely a table-searching algorithm. Because of this, CONTROL can consider many heretofore ignored factors in making its decision (see Figure 3). For example, it can make decisions which are data-dependent and time-dependent. It can require two keys (or N keys) to open a lock. Also it can carry on a lengthy dialogue with the user before allowing (or denying) the access requested.

CONTROL is not limited to use at data request time. In addition to being used to monitor the interactive storage, retrieval, and manipulation of data, it can also be used at initial data base creation time for data edit picture format checking, data value validity checking, etc. Or, alternatively, one could have two procedures CONTROL1 and CONTROL2, in two different formularies, F1 and F2. F1 could be attached at data input time and F2 at on-line storage, retrieval, manipulation, and modification time.

Simultaneous Use of One Formulary by Multiple Users

Note that the same formulary can be used simultaneously by several different users with different access permissions. This is possible because access control is determined by the CONTROL procedure of the attached formulary. This procedure can grant different privileges to different users.

Building a Formulary

Before a formulary can be attached to a user and a terminal, the procedures it contains must be specified. This is done using the system program FORMULARYBUILDER. FORMULARYBUILDER converses with the systems programmer who is building a formulary to learn what these procedures are, and then retrieves them from the system library and enters them as a set into a formulary which the user names. The specifics of FORMULARYBUILDER depend on the particular system.*

The Attachment Process—The Method of Linking a Formulary to a User and Terminal

In order to allow information storage and retrieval operations on the data base to take place, a user, a terminal, and a formulary which has been previously built using FORMULARYBUILDER must be linked together. This linking process is done in the following manner.

At the first time ACCESS is called (by TALK) for a given user and terminal, it will only permit attachment of a formulary to the user and terminal (i.e., it will not honor a request to fetch, store, etc.). The attachment is permitted only if the CONTROL program of the default formulary allows. The default formulary, like all other formularies, contains VIRTUAL, CONTROL, SCRAMBLE, and UNSCRAMBLE procedures. For the default formulary, they act as follows:

CONTROL   CONTROL takes the internal name representing the formulary and decides whether user U at terminal T is allowed to attach the formulary represented by the internal name. U and T are maintained in the UCB and passed to CONTROL by ACCESS.

VIRTUAL   VIRTUAL takes the internal name representing the formulary and returns the virtual address of the formulary.

---

*An extension to FORMULARYBUILDER which would allow a user to grant capabilities to other users, and then allow these users to grant capabilities to still other users, etc., has been proposed by Victor Lesser. The formulary model does not currently adequately handle this area of concern.

SCRAMBLE   No operation.
UNSCRAMBLE   No operation.

The ATTACH attempt, if successful, causes information about the formulary specified by the user to be read into the UCB (which is located in the data area of the ACCESS procedure). ACCESS then uses this information (when it is subsequently called on behalf of this user/terminal combination) to determine which CONTROL, VIRTUAL, SCRAMBLE, and UNSCRAMBLE procedures to invoke.

Independence of Addressing and Access Control. After the attachment process, the User Control Block (UCB) contains the user identification U, terminal identification T, and information about (usually pointers to) the VIRTUAL, CONTROL, SCRAMBLE, and UNSCRAMBLE procedures of a formulary. Whether the user can perform certain operations on a given datum is controlled by the CONTROL program. The addressing of each datum is controlled by the VIRTUAL program. Addressing of data items is now completely independent of the access control for the data items.

Breaking an Attachment. An existing attachment is broken whenever

(1) the user indicates that he is finished using the information storage and retrieval system (either by explicitly declaring so or implicitly by logging out, removing a physical terminal key, reaching the end-of-job indicator in his input card deck, etc.), or

(2) the user, via his TALK program, explicitly detaches himself from a formulary.

Subdivision of Data Base Into Files Not Required

Note that while the concept of a data set (or a "file") MAY be used, the formulary method does not require this. This represents a significant departure from previous large-scale data base systems which were nearly all organized with files (data sets) as their major subdivisions. Under the formulary scheme, access to information in a data set is not governed by the data set name. Rather, it is governed by the CONTROL procedure of the attached formulary. Similarly, addressing of data in a data set is governed by the VIRTUAL procedure and not by the data set name. Subdividing a data base into data sets, while certainly permitted and often desirable, is not required by the formulary model.

Concurrent Requests to Access Data—The LOCKLIST

The problem of two or more concurrent requests for exclusive data access necessitates a mechanism to control these conflicts among competing users. This problem has been discussed and solutions proposed by several workers.[28,9,27] In the formulary model, data can be set aside (locked) dynamically for the sole use of one user/terminal combination in a manner similar to Hsiao's "blocking"[9] using a mechanism known as the LOCKLIST.

The locking and unlocking of data to control simultaneous updating is an entirely separate function from the access control function. Access control takes into account privacy considerations only. Locking and unlocking are handled by a separate mechanism, the LOCKLIST. This is a list of triplets maintained by the ACCESS program and manipulated by the FETCHLOCK, STORELOCK, UNLOCKFETCH, and UNLOCKSTORE operations. Each triplet contains (1) the internal name of a current item, (2) the identification of the user/terminal combination which caused it to be locked, and (3) the type of lock (fetch or store). Any datum represented by a triplet on the LOCKLIST can be accessed only by the user/terminal combination which caused it to be locked.

Data items which can be locked are atomic, i.e., subparts of these data items cannot be locked. This implies, for example, that if a user wishes to lock a tree structure and then manipulate the tree without fear of some other user changing a subnode of the tree, either

(1) the tree must be atomic in the sense that its subnodes do not have internal names in the data base system, or

(2) each subnode must be explicitly locked by the user and only after all of these are locked can he proceed without fear of another user changing the tree.*

The TALK Procedure—Details

To access a datum, the user must effectively call upon TALK, the (nonsystem) application-oriented storage and retrieval procedure. TALK converses with the interactive user and/or the user's program and/or the operating system to obtain

---

*A more general and elegant method of handling concurrent requests to access data is being developed by R. D. Russell as part of a general resource allocation method. Much of the housekeeping work currently done in the formulary model can be handled by his method.

(1) a datum description in a user-oriented language
(2) the operation the user wishes to perform on that datum
(3) user identification and other information about the user and/or the terminal where the user is located.

Depending on the particular system, the user explicitly gives TALK zero, one, two, or all three of the above parameters. TALK supplies the missing parameters (if any), converts (1) to an internal name, and then passes the user identification, the terminal identification, the internal name of the datum, and the desired operation to the ACCESS procedure, which actually attempts to perform the operation.

Note that one system may have available many TALK procedures. A user requests invocation of any of them in the same way he initiates any (nonsystem) program. Sophisticated users will require only "bare-bones" TALK procedures, while novices may require quite complex tutorial TALK procedures. They may both be using the same data base while availing themselves of different datum descriptions. As an example, one TALK procedure might translate English "field names" into internal names, while another TALK procedure translates French "field names" into internal names. This ability to use multiple and user-dependent descriptions of the same item is not available with such generality in any system the author is aware of, though some systems allow lesser degrees of this.[29,30]

Different TALK procedures also allow concealment of the fact that certain information is even in a data base, as illustrated in Figure 4. The remarks above about using different TALK procedures also apply if a system uses only one relatively sophisticated TALK

USER 1
_____

WHAT PROGRAM? talk1
TALK1 HAS BEGUN EXECUTION.
WHAT DATA WOULD YOU LIKE
    TO SEE? salary of robert d. jones
YOU ARE NOT PERMITTED READ
    ACCESS TO THE SALARY FIELD.

CONTROL determined that the user
    was not permitted read access,
    causing this reply to be given by
    TALK1.

USER 2
_____

WHAT PROGRAM? talk2
TALK2 HAS BEGUN EXECUTION.
WHAT DATA WOULD YOU LIKE
    TO SEE? salary of robert d. jones
NO FIELD NAMED SALARY.

TALK2 intentionally returned this
    reply to the user.

FIGURE 4. Concealment of the fact that a data base contains certain information.

procedure which takes actions dependent on the person or terminal using it at a given time.

The ACCESS Procedure—Details

ACCESS uses the VIRTUAL, CONTROL, UNSCRAMBLE, and SCRAMBLE procedures specified in the UCB to carry out information storage and retrieval functions. Its input parameters are:

(1) information about the user, terminal, etc., defined by the installation. This information is passed by the procedure that calls ACCESS;

(2) internal name of datum;

(3) an area which either contains or will contain the value of the datum specified by (2);

(4) the length of (3);

(5) operation to perform—FETCH, FETCHLOCK, STORE, STORELOCK, UNLOCKFETCH, UNLOCKSTORE, ATTACH, or DETACH. FETCHLOCK and STORELOCK lock datums to further fetch or store accesses respectively (except by the user/terminal combination for which the lock was put on). UNLOCKFETCH and UNLOCKSTORE unlock these locks. ATTACH and DETACH respectively create and destroy user/terminal/formulary attachments.

(6) a variable in which a completion code is returned by ACCESS.

ACCESS itself handles all operations of (5) except FETCH and STORE. For FETCH and STORE operations on the data base, it invokes the FETCH and STORE primitives specified below.

Note that some means must be provided to determine which formulary is attached so the CONTROL, SCRAMBLE, UNSCRAMBLE, and VIRTUAL procedures of that particular formulary can be invoked. One method is to have those procedures themselves determine which formulary is attached by examining data common to them and to the ACCESS procedure. These data are initially set by the ACCESS procedure and then are referenced by the other procedures. A working system using this method is illustrated in another report.[31] An alternative method, if ACCESS is written in a more powerful language or in assembly language, would be to use a common transfer vector.

Note that the procedures TESTANDSET and IDXLL and their corresponding calls can be removed from ACCESS if no user will ever have to lock out access to a datum which ordinarily can be accessed by several users at the same time or if the installation wishes to use another method to control conflicts among users competing for exclusive access to datums; this makes the procedure considerably shorter. Such a "no parallelism" version of the ACCESS algorithm is given elsewhere.[31]

An ALGOL algorithm for the ACCESS procedure follows. This procedure is quite important and should be examined carefully. The comments in the algorithm should not be skipped, as they often suggest alternate methods for accomplishing the same goals.

THE ACCESS ALGORITHM

procedure access (info, intname, val, length, opn, compcode);
integer array info, val; integer length, opn, compcode;
begin comment   If OPN = FETCH, VAL is set to the value of the datum represented by INTNAME.
                 If OPN = STORE, the value of the datum represented by INTNAME is replaced by the value in the VAL array.
                 If OPN = FETCHLOCK or STORELOCK, the datum is locked to subsequent FETCH or STORE operations by other users or from other terminals until an UNLOCKFETCH or UNLOCKSTORE operation, whichever is appropriate, is performed.
                 If OPN = UNLOCKFETCH or UNLOCKSTORE, the fetch lock or store lock previously inserted by a FETCHLOCK or STORELOCK operation is removed.
                 If OPN = ATTACH, the formulary represented by internal name INTNAME is attached to the user and terminal described in the INFO array.
                 If OPN = DETACH, the formulary represented by internal name INTNAME is detached from the user and terminal described in the INFO array.
                 VAL is LENGTH storage elements long.
                 Note that a FETCH (STORE) operation will actually attempt to fetch (store) LENGTH storage elements of information.
                 It is the responsibility of the TALK procedure to handle scrambling or unscrambling algorithms that return outputs of a different length than their inputs.

ACCESS returns the following integer completion codes in COMPCODE:

1   normal exit, no error
2   unlock operation requested by user or terminal who/which did not set lock
3   operation permitted but gave error when attempted
4   attempt to unlock datum which is not locked in given manner
5   cannot handle any more User Control Blocks (would cause table overflow)
6   attempt to detach nonexistent user/terminal/formulary combination
7   operation permitted for this user and terminal but could not be carried out since datum was locked (by another user/terminal) to prevent such an operation
8   cannot put lock on as requested since LOCK-LIST is full
9   datum already locked by this user and terminal
10 error return from VIRTUAL procedure
11 operation on the datum represented by INT-NAME not permitted by CONTROL procedure of the attached formulary
12 end of data set encountered by FETCH operation.

Note that by the time the user has left the ACCESS routine, the data may have been changed by another user (if the original user did not lock it). Note that ACCESS could be altered to allow scrambling and unscrambling to take place at external devices rather than in the central processor.
Important: ACCESS expects the following to be available to it. The installation supplies these in some way other than as parameters to ACCESS (for example, as global variables in ALGOL or COMMON variables in FORTRAN)—

(1) ISTDUCB   the default User Control Block. Its length is NUCB storage units.
(2) NUCB   see (1).

(3) UCB   a list of User Control Blocks (UCB's) initialized outside
ACCESS to ucb (1,1) = –2
ucb (i,j) = anything when
$\sim (i = j = 1)$
UCB is declared as
integer array [1:maxusers, 1:nucb].

(4) MAXUSERS   the maximum number of users which can be actively connected to the system at any point in time.

(5) ITALK   the length of the INFO array (which is the first parameter of ACCESS)—INFO contains information about the user and terminal which is used by ACCESS and also passed by ACCESS to procedures of the attached formulary.
INFO[1] contains user identification.

(6) LOCKLIST   a list of locks (each element of the LOCKLIST array should be initialized outside ACCESS to -1). LOCKLIST is declared as **integer array** [1:4, 1:maxllist].

(7) MAXLLIST   the maximum length of the LOCKLIST.

(8) CS1   a semaphore to govern simultaneous access to the critical section of the ACCESS procedure (initialized to 1 outside ACCESS).

ACCESS assumes that the variables FETCH, STORE, FETCHLOCK, STORELOCK, UNLOCKFETCH, UNLOCKSTORE, ATTACH, and DETACH have been initialized globally and are never changed by the installation;
integer array iucb [1:nucb], reslt [1:length];
integer i, ii, islot, j, yesno, other, n, datum;
integer procedure testandset (semaphore); **integer** semaphore;
begin comment TESTANDSET is an integer function designator. It returns –1 if SEMAPHORE was in the state LOCKED on entry to TESTANDSET. Otherwise, TESTANDSET returns something other than –1. In all cases, SEMAPHORE is in state LOCKED after the execution of the TESTANDSET procedure, and must be explicitly unlocked in order for it to be used again.

TESTANDSET is used to implement a controlling mechanism to prevent conflicts among users competing for the same resource, as discussed in work by Dijkstra.[27] It will NOT prevent "deadly embraces".[32] No explicit code is given here, since the function is machine-dependent.

This procedure can be removed if no user will ever have to lock out access to a datum which ordinarily can be accessed by several users at the same time or if the installation wishes to use another method to control conflicts among users competing for exclusive access to datums;

<code>

end testandset;

integer procedure idxll (intname, opn); **integer** intname, opn;
begin comment IDXLL, given an internal name INTNAME, returns the relative position of INTNAME on the LOCKLIST if the datum represented by INTNAME is locked in a manner affecting the operation OPN. Otherwise, IDXLL returns the negation of the relative location of the first empty slot on the LOCKLIST. If the LOCKLIST is full and the INTNAME/OPN combination is not found on it, IDXLL returns 0.

This procedure can be removed if no user will ever have to lock out access to a datum which ordinarily can be accessed by several users at the same time or if the installation wishes to use another method to control conflicts among users competing for exclusive access to datums;
integer firstempty;
j : = **if** opn = FETCH **or** opn = UNLOCKFETCH **or**
opn = FETCHLOCK **then** 1 **else** 2;
idxll : = firstempty : = 0;
for i : = 1 **step** 1 **until** maxllist **do**
   begin ii : = –i;
   if locklist [1, i] = –1 **then** firstempty : = i
else if locklist [1, i] = intname **and** locklist [2, i] = j **then**
                           begin idxll : = i;
                           go to RET
                           end;
   end;
if firstempty $\neq$ 0 **then** idxll : = –firstempty;
RET:
end idxll;

procedure ret (i); **integer** i;
begin comment RET sets the completion code compcode to i and then causes exit from the ACCESS procedure;

```
compcode : = i; go to FIN
end ret;

compcode : = 1;
comment first let's see if we recognize the user/terminal combina-
tion in INFO;
islot : = 0;
for i : = 1 step 1 until maxusers do
    begin ii : = i;
        if ucb [i, 1] = -2 then begin comment end of list of ucb's;
                        if islot = 0 then begin if ii ≠ maxusers then
                                ucb [ii + 1, 1] : = -2;
                                go to XFER;
                            end
                        else go to PRESETUP;
                    end
    else if ucb [i, 1] = -1 then islot : = ii
        comment remember this slot if vacant;
    else begin for j : = 1 step 1 until italk do
        if ucb [i, j] ≠ info [j] then go to ILOOPND;
        go to SETUPPTRS
            end;

ILOOPND:
    end i loop;
if islot = 0 then ret (5); comment cannot handle any more UCBs;
PRESETUP:
ii : = islot;
XFER:
for k : = 1 step 1 until italk do ucb [ii, k] : = info [k];
for k : = italk + 1 step 1 until nucb do ucb [ii, k] : = istducb [k];
SETUPPTRS:
for i : = 1 step 1 until nucb do iucb [i] : = ucb [ii, i];
```

comment set up pointers to appropriate user control block for
particular implementation. Note well: Setting up pointers to appropriate user control blocks is quite dependent on the particular
system;

comment We have now associated user and terminal with the user
control block (representing a formulary) in relative position i of the
UCB table;

```
if iucb [nucb] ≠ intname and opn = DETACH then ret (6);
```

comment attempt to detach user/terminal/formulary combination
not currently attached;

control (intname, opn, yesno, other);
if yesno > 1 then ret (11);
comment return 11 if CONTROL does not permit operation;
if opn = ATTACH then begin ucb [ii, nucb] : = intname; go to FIN
                                                         end;

comment Note well: In many implementations, pointers to each procedure of the formulary (obtained by having VIRTUAL transform intname into a virtual address) might be put into the UCB upon attachment. In other, the philosophy used here of only putting one pointer—to the formulary—into the UCB will be followed. The decision should take into account design parameters such as implementation language, storage available, etc.;
if opn = DETACH then begin comment detach formulary (this leaves an open slot in the ucb array);
                        ucb [ii, 1] : = -1; go to FIN
                        end;
if opn = UNLOCKFETCH or opn = UNLOCKSTORE then
   begin i : = idxll (intname, opn); comment find internal name on LOCKLIST;
   if i $\leq$ 0 then ret (4); comment cannot find it;
   for j : = 1 step 1 until italk do
      if locklist [2 + j, i] $\neq$ iucb [j] then ret (2);
   locklist [1, i] : = -1; comment undo the lock and mark slot in UCB array empty;
   go to FIN
   end unlock operation;
TRY:
if testandset (cs1) = -1 then go to TRY;
comment loop until no other user is executing the critical section below;
comment ACCESS should ask to be put to sleep if embedding system permits;
comment-----------enter critical section for locking out datums------------;
i : = idxll (intname, opn);
comment get relative location of locked datum in locklist;
if i > 0 then begin comment datum found on locklist so see if it was locked by this user and terminal;
       for j : = 1 step 1 until italk do
         if locklist [2 + j, i] $\neq$ iucb [j] then ret (7);
        comment data already locked by another user or terminal;
        if opn = FETCHLOCK or opn = STORELOCK then ret (9);

          comment datum already locked by this user and terminal, so return completion code of 9;
          end;
i : = –i;
if opn = FETCHLOCK **or** opn = STORELOCK **then**
    begin comment this is a lock operation;
    if i = 0 **then** ret (8); **comment** cannot set lock since locklist is full;
    locklist [2, i] : = **if** opn = FETCHLOCK **then** 1 **else** 2;
    comment set appropriate lock;
    for j : = 1 **step** 1 **until** italk **do** locklist [2 + j, i] : = iucb [j];
    comment place user and terminal identification into LOCKLIST;
    locklist [1, i] : = intname; **comment** place internal name on LOCKLIST;
    go to FIN;
    end lock operation;
virtual (intname, datum, other, compcode);
comment VIRTUAL returns in datum the virtual address of the datum specified;
if compcode > 1 **then** ret (10); **comment** error return from VIRTUAL;
if opn = STORE **then**
    begin comment store operation;
    scramble (val, length, compcode, reslt, n);
    if compcode > 1 **then** ret (3);
    comment operation permitted but gave error when attempted;
    comment now perform a physical write of n storage units to the block starting at reslt;
    store (datum, reslt, n, compcode);
    if compcode > 1 **then** ret (3)
    end
else
    begin comment fetch operation;
    fetch (datum, reslt, length, compcode);
    if compcode = 2 **then** ret (12); **comment** end of data set encountered;
    if compcode > 1 **then** ret (3);
    unscramble (reslt, length, compcode, val, n);
    if compcode > 1 **then** ret (3);
    end fetch operation;
FIN;
comment-----------Leave critical section for locking out datums-----------;
cs1 : = 1;
end access;

FETCH and STORE Primitive Operations

The two primitive operations FETCH and STORE are supplied by the installation. These primitives actually perform the physical reads and writes which cause information transfer between the media the data base resides on and the primary storage medium (usually, magnetic core storage). They are invoked only by the ACCESS procedure.

The primitive operations cannot be expressed in machine-independent form, but rather depend on the specific system and machine used. They are defined functionally below.

FETCH (ADDR, VALUE, LENGTH, COMP)

This primitive fetches the value which is contained in the storage locations starting at virtual address ADDR and returns it in VALUE. This value may be scrambled, but if so unscrambling will be done later by UNSCRAMBLE (called from ACCESS), and LENGTH is the length of the scrambled data. The value comprises LENGTH storage elements. Upon completion, the completion code COMP is set to:

1   if normal exit
2   if end of data set encountered when physical read attempted
3   if length too big (installation-determined)
4   if illegal virtual address given to fetch from
5   if error occurred upon attempt to do physical read.

STORE (ADDR, VALUE, LENGTH, COMP)

This primitive stores LENGTH storage elements starting at virtual address VALUE into LENGTH storage elements starting at virtual address ADDR. The information stored may be scrambled, but if so the scrambling has already been done by SCRAMBLE (called from ACCESS), and LENGTH is the length of the scrambled data. Upon completion, the completion code COMP is set to:

1   if normal exit
3   if length too big (installation-determined)
4   if illegal virtual address given to store into
5   if error occurred upon attempt to do physical write.

A NOTE ON THE COST OF SOME PRIVACY SAFEGUARDS

As mentioned above, a desirable property for an access control model is that it be sufficiently modular to permit cost-effectiveness experiments to be undertaken. In this way the model would serve as a vehicle for exploring questions of cost with respect to various privacy safeguards.

Using the formulary model, an experiment was run on the IBM 360/91 computer system at the SLAC Facility of Stanford University Computation Center. This experiment was designed to obtain figures on the additional overhead due to using the formulary method and on the costs on encoding (and conversely the cost of decoding data). Early results[31] seem to indicate that the incremental cost of scrambling information in a large computer data base where fetch accesses (and hence unscrambling operations) are relatively infrequent is infinitesimal.

It is easy to use the formulary model to carry out various other experiments dealing with relative costs of diverse encoding methods and data accessing schemes. We hope to do more of this in the future.

SUMMARY

We have defined and demonstrated a model of access control which allows real-time decisions to be made about privileges granted to users of a data base. Raw data need appear only once in the data base and arbitrarily complex access control programs can be associated with arbitrarily small fragments of this data.

The desirable characteristics for an access control method laid out in the section on access control methods are all present (though we have not yet run enough experiments to make general statements about efficiency):

(1) No arbitrary constraint (such as segmentation or sensitivity levels) is imposed on data or programs.
(2) The method allows control of individual data elements. Its efficiency depends on the specific system involved and the particular controls used.
(3) No extra storage or time is required to describe data which the user does not desire to protect.
(4) The method is machine-independent and also independent of file structure. The efficiency of each implementation depends mainly on the adequacy of the formulary method for the particular data structures and application involved.
(5) The discussion above illustrates the modularity of the formulary model.

ACKNOWLEDGMENTS

This paper is a condensation of a Ph.D. dissertation at the Stanford University Computer Science Department. The author is deeply indebted to Professor William F. Miller for his encouragement and advice during the research and writing that went into it. Many other members of the Stanford Computer Science Department and the Stanford Linear Accelerator Center also contributed their ideas and help, in particular, John Levy, Robert Russell, Victor Lesser, Harold Stone, Edward Feigenbaum, and Jerome Feldman. The formulary idea was initially suggested by the use of syntax definitions ("field formularies") for input/output data descriptions as described by Castleman.[33]

REFERENCES

1. P. S. Crisman (Editor), The Compatible Time-Sharing System—a Programmer's Guide, MIT Press, Cambridge, Massachusetts, 1965.
2. J. D. Babcock, "A brief description of privacy measures in the RUSH time-sharing system," Proc. AFIPS SJCC, Vol. 30, pp. 301–302, Thompson Book Co., Washington, D.C., 1967.
3. B. W. Lampson, "Dynamic protection structures," Proc. AFIPS FJCC, pp. 27–38, 1969.
4. F. J. Corbato and V. A. Vyssotsky, "Introduction and overview of the Multics system," Proc. AFIPS SJCC, pp. 185–196, 1965.
5. L. J. Hoffman, "Computers and privacy: a survey," Computing Surveys, Vol. 1, No. 2, pp. 85–103, 1969.
6. C. Arvas, "Joint use of databanks," Report No. 6, Statistiska Centralbyran, Stockholms Universitet, Ukas P5, Sweden, 1968.
7. H. W. Bingham, Security Techniques for EDP of Multilevel Classified Information, Document RADC–TR–65–415, Rome Air Development Center, Griffiss Air Force Base, New York, 1965.
8. C. Weissman, "Security controls in the ADEPT-50 time-sharing system," Proc. AFIPS FJCC, pp. 119–133, 1969.
9. D. K. Hsiao, A File System for a Problem Solving Facility, Ph.D. Dissertation in Electrical Engineering, University of Pennsylvania, Philadelphia, Pennsylvania, 1968.

10. M. G. Stone, "TERPS—file independent enquiries," Computer Bulletin, Vol. 11, No. 4, pp. 286–289, 1968.
11. R. M. Graham, "Protection in an information processing utility," Communications of the ACM, Vol. 11, No. 5, pp. 365–369, 1968.
12. J. B. Dennis and E. C. Van Horn, "Programming semantics for multi-programmed computation," Communications of the ACM, Vol. 9, No. 3, pp. 143–155, 1966.
13. J. K. Iliffe, Basic machine principles, MacDonald and Co., London, England, 1968.
14. D. C. Evans and J. Y. Le Clerc, "Address mapping and control of access in an interactive computer," Proc. AFIPS SJCC, Vol. 30, pp. 23–30, Thompson Book Co., Washington, D.C., 1967.
15. J. A. Feldman, Aspects of associative processing, Technical Note 1965-13, Lincoln Laboratory, MIT, Cambridge, Massachusetts, 1965.
16. R. G. Ewing and P. M. Davies, "An associative processor," Proc. AFIPS FJCC, 1964.
17. R. G. Gall, "A hardware-integrated GPC/search memory," Proc. AFIPS FJCC, 1964.
18. J. McAteer et al., "Associative memory system implementation and characteristics," Proc. AFIPS FJCC, 1964.
19. J. I. Raffel and T. S. Crowther, "A proposal for an associative memory using magnetic films," IEEE Trans. on Electronic Computers, Vol. EC–13, No. 5, 1964.
20. V. R. Lesser, A multi-level computer organization designed to separate data-accessing from the computation, Technical Report CS90, Computer Science Department, Stanford University, Stanford, California, 1968.
21. P. D. Rovner and J. A. Feldman, "The Leap language and data structure," Proc. IFIP, 1968, C73–C77.
22. T. D. Friedman, "The authorization problem in shared files," IBM Systems Journal, Vol. 9, No. 4, 1970.
23. C. E. Shannon, "Communication theory of secrecy systems," Bell System Technical Journal, Vol. 28, pp. 656–715, 1949.
24. D. Kahn, The Codebreakers, Macmillan, New York, New York, 1967.
25. R. O. Skatrud, "The application of cryptographic techniques to data processing," Proc. AFIPS FJCC, pp. 111–117, 1969.
26. W. F. Miller and L. J. Hoffman, "Getting a personal dossier from a statistical data bank," Datamation, pp. 74–75, May 1970.

27. E. W. Dijkstra, Cooperating sequential processes, Department of Mathematics, Technological University, Eindhoven, the Netherlands, 1965.
28. A. Shoshani and A. J. Bernstein, "Synchronization in a parallel accessed data base," Communications of the ACM, Vol. 12, No. 11, pp. 604-607, 1969.
29. R. S. Jones, "DATA FILE TWO—A data storage and retrieval system," Proc. SJCC, pp. 171-181, 1968.
30. R. H. Giering, Information processing and the data spectrum, Technical note DTN-68-2, Data Corporation, Arlington, Virginia, 1967.
31. L. J. Hoffman, The Formulary Model for Access Control and Privacy in Computer Systems, Report 117, Stanford Linear Accelerator Center, Stanford, California, 1970.
32. A. N. Habermann, "Prevention of system deadlocks," Communications of the ACM, Vol. 12, No. 7, p. 373, 1969.
33. P. A. Castleman, "User-defined syntax in a general information storage and retrieval system," in Information Retrieval: The User's Viewpoint, An Aid to Design International Information, Inc., 1967.

Security Controls in the ADEPT-50 Time-Sharing System

C. WEISSMAN

FOREWORD

At present, the system described in this paper has not been approved by the Department of Defense for processing classified information. This paper does not represent DOD policy regarding industrial application of time- or resource-sharing of EDP equipment.

INTRODUCTION

Computer-based, resource sharing systems are, and contain, things of value; therefore, they should be protected. The valuables are the information data bases, the processes that manipulate them, and the physical plant, equipment, and personnel that form the system plexus. An extensive lore is developing on the subject of system protection.[1,2] Petersen and Turn[3] discuss in considerable detail the substance of protection of non-military information systems in terms of threats and countermeasures. Ware[4,5] contrasts "security" and "privacy" for viewing protection in military systems as well. This paper describes the security controls implemented in the ADEPT-50 time-sharing system[6]—a resource sharing system designed to handle sensitive information in classified government and military facilities.

Our approach to security control is based on a set theoretic model of access rights. This approach appears natural, since the

SOURCE: Fall Joint Computer Conference, 1969, Proceedings. Reprinted by permission of the publisher, American Federation of Information Processing Societies Press.

important objects of security are sets of things—users, terminals, programs, files—and the operators of set theory—membership, intersection, union—are easily programmed for, and quickly performed by, computer. The formal model defines time-sharing security control of user, terminal, job and file security objects in terms of equations of access based upon their security profiles—a triplet of Authority, Category, and Franchise property sets. The correspondence of these properties to government and military Classification, Compartments, and Need-to-Know is demonstrated. Implementation of the model in the ADEPT-50 Time-Sharing System is described in detail, as are features that transcend the model including initialization of the security profiles, the LOGIN decision procedure, system integrity checks, security residue control, and security audit trails. Other novel features of ADEPT security control are detailed and include: automatic file classification based upon the cumulative security history of referenced files; the "security umbrella" of the ADEPT job; and once-only passwords. The paper concludes with a recapitulation of the goals of ADEPT security control, approximate costs of implementation and operation of the security controls, and suggested extensions and improvements.

Historically, protection of a sensitive computer facility has been attained by limiting physical access to the computer room and shielding the computer complex from electromagnetic radiation. This "sheltered" approach promotes one-at-a-time, batch usage of the facility. Modern hardware and software technology has moved forward to more powerful and cost/effective time-shared, multi-access, multiprogrammed systems. However, three features of such systems pose a challenge to the sheltered mode of protection: (1) concurrent multiple users with different access rights operating remote from the shielded room; (2) multiple programs with different access rights co-resident in memory; and (3) multiple files of different data sensitivities simultaneously accessible. These features appear to violate traditional methods of accountability based upon a single user (or multiple users with like clearances) operating within strictly controlled facilities. The problem is of such magnitude that no time-sharing system has yet been certified for use in the manner described! However, some multi-access systems are in operation in a classified mode,[7,8] and a number of design approaches have been suggested.[9-12]

In addition to the usual goal of building an effective time-sharing system,[13] the ADEPT project began with a number of security objectives as well:

1. Build a security control mechanism that supports heterogeneous levels and types of classifications.
2. Design the security control mechanism in such a manner that it is itself unclassified until primed by security configuration parameters, a point strongly supported by Baran[14] regarding communications security.
3. Construct the security control mechanism as an isolated portion of the total time-sharing system so that it may be carefully scrutinized for correctness, completeness, and reliability.
4. Do the above in as frugal a manner as possible, considering costs to design, fabricate, and operate. Good system performance is our principal criterion in selecting among alternative technical solutions, as noted by the author elsewhere.[15]

In approaching our task, we recognize security as a total system problem involving hardware, communication, personnel, and software safeguards. However, our focus is primarily on monitor software, and its interfaces with the other areas. This view is not parochial: our hardware is a standard IBM 360 model 50; communication security is an established field of study with considerable technological know-how;[14] and the policy, doctrine, and procedures for personnel behavior in classified environments are extensive, with legal foundations. Thus, our only degree of freedom is the control we build into the time-sharing executive software.

A Security Control Formalism

A formal model of software security control for access to sensitive portions of ADEPT is developed here.

Security Objects. Four kinds of security objects are to be managed by our model: user, terminal, job, and file. Let u denote some user; t some terminal; j some job; and f some file.

Security Properties. Each security object is described by a security profile that is an ordered triplet of security properties—Authority (A), Category (C), and Franchise (F). Authority is a set of hierarchically ordered security jurisdictions. Category is a set of discrete security jurisdictions. Franchise is a set of users licensed with privileged security jurisdiction.

The property "Authority" is defined as a set A, where

$$A = \left\{ a^0 < a^1 < , \ldots, < a^\omega \right\} \qquad (1)$$

and the specific members, a^i, of the set are security jurisdictions hierarchically ordered.

"Category" is a discrete set of specific compartments, c^i,

$$C = \left\{ c^0, c^1, \ldots, c^\psi \right\} \tag{2}$$

Compartments are mutually exclusive security sanctuaries with discrete jurisdictions.

"Franchise" is a security jurisdiction privileged to a given set of users, i.e.,

$$F = \left\{ u \mid u \text{ is a user} \right\} \tag{3}$$

For a given terminal, t, let a given Authority set, A, be denoted by A_t, or in general, let a given security object, α, denote a given property, P, for α as P_α. Hence we can speak of A_u, or C_j, etc., to mean the specific Authority set for a given user, u, or the specific Category set for a given job, j, respectively.

Four important sets (of users) arise with respect to the Franchise property, namely, Franchise for files, terminals, jobs, and users. To distinguish the sense in which a given user is being considered, we subscript u by the security object under consideration. Hence, u_f means the user with jurisdiction to file f; u_t and u_j are similarly defined. For completeness, we define u_u as simply u. We can now define Franchise for each security object.

$$F_u = \left\{ u \right\} \tag{4}$$

$$F_t = \left\{ u_t^0, u_t^1, \ldots, u_t^\lambda \right\} \tag{5}$$

$$F_j = \left\{ u_j^0, u_j^1, \ldots, u_j^\mu \right\} \tag{6}$$

$$F_f = \left\{ u_f^0, u_f^1, \ldots, u_f^\nu \right\} \tag{7}$$

Equation (4) states that the Franchise for a user is restricted to himself; his jurisdiction is unique, and no other user is so endowed. Equation (5) states that the terminal Franchise is possessed by λ different users who have jurisdiction over the terminal t. Likewise, equations (6) and (7) define the job and file Franchise sets.

In security discussions, one hears the familiar phrase, "he needs a higher-level clearance." We can now define "higher level" with our model.

Let α and β be security objects and let ρ be some function such that $\rho(A_\alpha) \epsilon A$.
Then,

$$A_\alpha \geq A_\beta \leftrightarrow \rho(A_\alpha) \geq \rho(A_\beta) \tag{8}$$

$$C_\alpha \geq C_\beta \leftrightarrow C_\alpha \supseteq C_\beta \tag{9}$$

$$F_\alpha \geq F_\beta \leftrightarrow F_\alpha \supseteq F_\beta \tag{10}$$

Equation (8) claims that the Authority of a security object, A_α is at a "higher level" than another security object A_β when the specific authority, a_α is greater than the specific authority, a_β.

It is implicit in equations (1) and (8) that the specific authorities, a^i, must be numerically encoded for the magnitude relationships to hold. Equations (9) and (10) define P_α to be greater than P_β if and only if P_β is a subset of P_α.

Events may alter the membership of property sets. Let P_f^e be the eth P_f in a given context.

Define the Authority history, A_h, at the eth event as

$$A_h(0) = a_f^0 \tag{11}$$

$$A_h(e) = \max(A_h(e - 1), \rho(A_f^e)), e > 0 \tag{12}$$

Likewise, define the Category history C_h, at the eth event as

$$C_h(0) = \phi \tag{13}$$

$$C_h(e) = C_h(e - 1) \cup C_f^e, e > 0 \tag{14}$$

Equations (11) through (14) recursively define two useful sets that accumulate a history of file references as a function of file reference events, e. A history of the highest Authority, A_h, is defined by equation (12) as either the previous set, $A_h(e - 1)$, or the current set, $\rho(A_f^e)$, whichever is larger in the sense of equation (8). Equation (11) gives the initial condition as some low specific file authority, a_f^0. Equation (14) defines the highest Category history as the union of the previous set, $C_h(e - 1)$, and the current set, C_f^e; while equation (13) states that the union is initially the empty set.

Though F_h could be defined in our model, no need is seen at this time for a Franchise history. More will be said about these history sets later.

Property Determination. Table I presents in a 3 × 4 matrix a summary of the rules for determining the security profile triplets, P_α. We shall examine these rules here. For the user u, A_u and C_u are given constants, and F_u is given by equation (4). For the terminal t, A_t and C_t are given constants, and F_t is given by equation (5). Given A_u and A_t, we determine A_j as:

$$A_j = \min (A_u, A_t) \tag{15}$$

Likewise, given C_u and C_t, we determine C_j as:

$$C_j = C_u \cap C_t \tag{16}$$

Equation (6) gives F_j to complete the job security profile triplet.

An existing file has its security profile predetermined with A_f and C_f as given constants, and F_f as given by equation (7). However, a new file—one just created—derives its security profile from the job's file access history according to the following:

$$A_f = A_h(e) \tag{17}$$

$$C_f = C_h(e) \tag{18}$$

$$F_f = u_j^i \tag{19}$$

TABLE I.   Security Property Determination Matrix

Property / Object	Authority A	Category C	Franchise F
User, u	Given Constant	Given Constant	u
Terminal, t	Given Constant	Given Constant	u_t^i
Job, j	$\min (A_u, A_t)$	$C_u \cap C_t$	u_j^i
File, f	Existing file Given Constant	Existing file Given Constant	u_f^i
	New file $\max (A_h(e-1), \rho(A_f^e)), e > 0$	New file $C_h(e-1) \cup C_f^e, e > 0$	u_j^i

From equations (11) through (14) we see how the Authority and Category histories accumulate as a function of event e. These events are the specific times when files are accessed by a job. To maintain security integrity, these histories can never exceed (i.e., be greater than) the job security profile. This is specified as,

$$A_h(\infty) \to A_j \tag{20}$$

$$C_h(\infty) \to C_j \tag{21}$$

For e = 0, we see the properties initialized to their simplest form. However, as e gets large, the histories accumulate, but never exceed the upper limit set by the job. $A_h(e)$ and $C_h(e)$ are important new concepts, discussed in further detail later. We speak of them, affectionately, as the security "high-water mark," with analogy to the bath tub ring that marks the highest water level attained.

The Franchise of a new file is always obtained from the Franchise of the job given by equation (6). When i = μ = 0, the job is controlled by the single user u_j who becomes the owner and creator of the file with the sole Franchise for the file.

Access Control. Our model is now rich enough to express the equations of access control. We wish to control access by a user to the system, to a terminal, and to a file. Access is granted to the system if and only if

$$u \in U \tag{22}$$

where U is the set of all sanctioned users known to the system. Access is granted to a terminal if and only if

$$u \in F_t \tag{23}$$

If equations (22) and (23) hold, then by definition

$$u = u_t = u_j \tag{24}$$

Access is granted to a file if and only if

$$P_j \geqslant P_f \tag{25}$$

for properties A and C according to equations (8) and (9), and

$$u_j \ \epsilon \ F_f \tag{26}$$

If equations (25) and (26) hold, then access is granted and $A_h(e)$ and $C_h(e)$ are calculated by equations (12) and (14).

Model Interpretation. Three different dimensions for restricting access to sensitive information and information processes are possible with the security profile triplet. The generality of this technique has considerable application to public and military systems. For the system of interest, however, the Authority property corresponds to the Top Secret, Secret, etc., levels of government and military security. Category corresponds to the host of special control compartments used to restrict access by project and area, such as those of the Intelligence and Atomic Energy communities; and the Franchise property corresponds to access sanctioned on the basis of need-to-know. With this interpretation, the popular security terms "classification" and "clearance" can be defined by our model in the same dimensions—as a min/max test on the security profile triplet. Classification is attached to a security object to designate the minimum security profile required for access, whereas clearance grants to a security object the maximum security profile it has permission to exercise. Thus, legal access obtains if the clearance is greater than or equal to the classification, i.e., if equation (25) holds.

Another observation on the model is the "job umbrella" concept implied by equations (22) through (26); i.e., the derived clearance of the job (not the clearance of the user) is used as the security control triplet for file access. The job umbrella spreads a homogeneous clearance to normalize access to a heterogeneous assortment of program and data files. This simplifies the problem of control in a multi-level security system. Also note how the job umbrella's high-water mark (equations (11) through (14)) is used to automatically classify new files (equations (17) and (18)); this subject is discussed further below.

A final observation on the model is its application of need-to-know to terminal access, equation (23). This feature allows terminals to be restricted to special people and/or special groups for greater control of personnel interfaces—i.e., systems programmers, computer operators, etc.

Security Control Implementation

The selection of a set theoretic model of security control was not fortuitous, but a deliberate choice biased toward computational efficiency and ease of implementation. It permits the clean separation and isolation of security control code from the security control data, which enables ADEPT's security mechanisms to be openly discussed and still remain safe—a point advocated by others.[14,16] We achieve this safety by "arming" the system with security control data only once at start-up time by the SYSLOG procedure discussed later. Also, the model improves the credibility of the security system, enhancing its understanding and thereby promoting its certification.

Security Objects: Identity and Structure. Each security object has a unique identification (ID) within the system such that it can be managed individually. The form of the ID depends upon the security-object type; the syntax of each is given below.

User Identification: For generality of definition, each user is uniquely identified by his user:id, which must be less than 13 characters with no embedded blanks.

The user:id can be any meaningful encoding for the local installation. For example, it can be the individual's Social Security number, his military serial number, his last name (if unique and less than 13 characters), or some local installation man-number convention. The set of all user:ids constitutes the universal set, U.

Terminal Identification: All peripheral devices in ADEPT are identified uniquely by their IBM 360 device addresses. Besides interactive terminals, this includes disc drives, tape drives, line printer, card reader-punch, drums, and 1052 keyboard. Therefore, terminal:id must be a two-digit hexadecimal number corresponding to the unit address of the device.

Job Identification: ADEPT consists of two parts: the Basic Executive (BASEX), which handles the allocation and scheduling of hardware resources, and the Extended Executive (EXEX), which interfaces user programs with BASEX. ADEPT is designed to operate itself and user programs as a set of 4096-byte pages. BASEX is identified as certain pages that are fixed in main core, whereas EXEX and user programs are identified as sets of pages that move dynamically between main and swap memory. A set of user programs are identified as a job, with page sets for each program (the program map) described in the job's environment area, i.e., the job's "state tables." Every job in ADEPT has an environment area that is swapped with the job. It contains dynamic system bookkeeping information pertinent to the job, including the contents of the machine registers (saved when the job is swapped out), internal file and I/O control tables, a map of all the program's pages on drum, <u>user:id</u>, and the job security control parameters. The environment page(s) are memory-protected against reading and writing by user programs, as they are really swappable extensions of the monitor's tables.

The <u>job:id</u> is then a transitory internal parameter which changes with each user entrance and exit from the system. The <u>job:id</u> is a relative core memory address used by the executive as a major index into central system tables. It is mapped into an external two-digit number that is typed to the user in response to a successful LOGIN.

File Identification: ADEPT's file system is quite rich in the variety of file types, file organization, and equipment permitted. There are two file types: temporary and permanent.

Temporary files are transitory "scratch" disc files, which disappear from the system inventory when their parent job exits from the system. They are always placed on resident system volumes, and are private to the program that created them.

Permanent files constitute the majority of files cataloged by the system. Their permanence derives from the fact that they remain inventoried, cataloged, and available even after the job that created or last referenced them is no longer present, and even if they are not being used: Permanent files may be placed by the user on resident system volumes or on demountable private volumes.

There are six file organizations from which a user may select to structure the records of his file: Physical-sequential, S1; non-formatted, S2; index-sequential, S3; partitioned, S4; multiple volume fixed record, S5; and single volume fixed record, S9. Regardless of the organization of the records, ADEPT manages them as a collection, called a file. Thus, security control is at the file level only, unlike more definitive schemes of sub-element control.[8,10-12]

All the control information of a file that describes type, organization, physical storage location, date of creation, and security is distinct from the data records of the file, and is the catalog of the file.

All cataloged ADEPT files are uniquely identified by a four-part name; each part has various options and defaults (system assumptions). This name, the <u>file:id</u>, has the following form:

file:id : : = name, form, user:id, volume:id

<u>Name</u> is a user-generated character string of up to eight characters with no embedded blanks. It must be unique on a private volume as well as for Public files (described below).

Form is a descriptor of the internal coding of a file. Up to 256 encodings are possible, although only these seven are currently applicable:

1 = binary data
2 = relocatable program
3 = non-relocatable program
4 = card images
5 = catalog
6 = DLO (Delayed Output)
7 = line images

User:id corresponds to the owner of the file, i.e., the creator of the file.

Volume:id is the unique file storage device (tape, disc, disc pack, etc.) on which the file resides. For various reasons, including reliability, ADEPT file inventories are distributed across the available storage media, rather than centralized on one particular volume. Thus, all files on a given disc volume are inventoried on that volume.

Security Properties: Encoding and Structure. Implementation of the security properties in ADEPT is not uniform across the security objects as suggested by our model, particularly the Franchise property. Lack of uniformity, brought about by real-world considerations, is not a liability of the system but a reflection of the simplicity of the model. Extensions to the model are developed here in accordance with that actually implemented in ADEPT.

Authority: Authority is fixed at four levels (ω = 3 for equation (1)) in ADEPT, specifically, UNCLASSIFIED, CONFIDENTIAL, SECRET, and TOP SECRET in accordance with Department of Defense security regulations. The Authority set is encoded as a logical 4-bit item, where positional order is important. Magnitude tests are used extensively, such that the high-order bits imply high Authority in the sense of equation (8).

Category: Category is limited to a maximum of 16 compartments ($\psi \leqslant 15$ for equation (2)), encoded as a logical 16-bit item. Boolean tests are used exclusively on this datum. The definition of (and bit position correspondence to) specific compartments is an installation option at ADEPT start-up time (see SYSLOG). Typical examples of compartments are EYES ONLY, CRYPTO, RESTRICTED, SENSITIVE, etc.

Franchise: Property Franchise corresponds to the military concept of need-to-know. Essentially, this corresponds to a set of user:ids;

however, the ADEPT implementation of Franchise is different for each security object:

1. User: All users wishing ADEPT service must be known to the system. This knowledge is imparted by SYSLOG at start-up time and limited to approximately 500 user:ids $(\max(U) \leqslant 500)$.

2. Terminal: Equation (5) specifies the Franchise of a given terminal, F_t, as a set of user:ids. In ADEPT, F_t does not exist. One may define all the users for a given terminal, i.e., F_t; or alternatively, all the terminals for a given user. Because SYSLOG orders its tables by user:id, the latter definition was found more convenient to implement.

3. Job: The Franchise of a job is the user:id of the creator of the job at the time of LOGIN to the system. Currently, only one user has access to (and control of) a job ($\mu = 0$ for equation (6)).

4. File: Implementation of Franchise for a file (F_f), is more extensive than equation (7). In ADEPT, we wish to control not only who accesses a file, but also the quality of access granted. We have defined a set of four exclusive qualities of access, such that a given quality q, is defined if

$$q \in \{\text{READ, WRITE, READ-AND-WRITE, READ-AND-WRITE-WITH-LOCKOUT-OVERRIDE}\} \qquad (27)$$

ADEPT permits simultaneous access to a file by many jobs if the quality of access is for READ only. However, only one job may access a file with WRITE, or READ-AND-WRITE quality. ADEPT automatically locks out access to a file being written to avoid simultaneous reading and writing conflicts. A special access quality, however, does permit lockout override. Equation (7) can now be extended as a set of pairs,

$$F_f = \{(u_f^0, q^0), (u_f^1, q^1), \ldots, (u_f^\gamma, q^\gamma)\}; \qquad (28)$$

where q^i are not necessarily distinct and are given by equation (27).

The implementation of equation (28) is dependent upon γ, the number of franchised users. When $\gamma = 0$, we have the ADEPT Private file, exclusive to the owner, u_f^0; for $\gamma = \max(U)$, we have the Public file; values of γ between these extremes yield the Semi-Private file. γ is implicitly encoded as the ADEPT "privacy" item in the file's catalog control data, and takes the place of F_f for all cases except a Semi-Private file. For that case exclusively, equation (28) holds and an actual F_f list of <u>user:id</u>, <u>quality</u> pairs exists as a need-to-know list. The owner of a file specifies and controls the file's privacy, including the composition of the need-to-know list.

Security Control Initialization: SYSLOG.

SYSLOG is a component of the ADEPT initialization package responsible for arming the security controls. It operates as one of a number of system start-up options prior to the time when terminals are enabled. SYSLOG sets up the security profile data for <u>user:id</u> and <u>terminal:id</u>, i.e., the "given constants" of Table I.

SYSLOG creates or updates a highly sensitive system disc file, where each record corresponds to an authorized user. These records are constructed from a deck of cards consisting of separate data sets for <u>compartment</u> definitions, <u>terminal:id</u> classification, and <u>user:id</u> clearance. The dictionary of <u>compartment</u> definitions contains the less-than-9-character mnemonic for each member of the Category set. Data sets are formed from the card types shown in Table II. Use of <u>passwords</u> is described later in the LOGIN procedure.

An IDT card must exist for each authorized user; the PWD, DEV, SEC, and CAT card types are optional. Other card types are possible, but not germane to security control, e.g., ACT for accounting purposes. More than one PWD, DEV, and CAT card is acceptable up to the current maximum data limits (i.e., 64 <u>passwords</u>, 48 <u>terminal:ids</u>, and 16 <u>compartments</u>).

A variety of legality checks for proper data syntax, quantity, and order are provided. SYSLOG assumes the following default conditions when the corresponding card type is omitted from each data set:

PWD	No <u>password</u> required
DEV	All <u>terminal:ids</u> authorized
SEC	A = UNCLASSIFIED
CAT	C = null (all zero mask)

This gives the lowest user clearance as the default, while permitting convenient user access. Various options exist in SYSLOG to permit maintenance of the internal SYSLOG tables, including the replacement or deletion of existing data sets in total or in part.

TABLE II. SYSLOG Control Cards

Card Type	Purpose
DICT compartment$_1$ ... compartment$_{16}$	Identifies start of data set of compartment definitions. Defines up to 16 compartments.
TERMINAL	Identifies start of data sets of terminal definitions.
UNIT terminal:id	Identifies start of a terminal data set.
IDT user:id	Identifies start of a user data set.
PWD password ... password	Defines legal passwords for user:id up to 64.
DEV terminal:id$_1$ ... terminal:id$_{48}$	Defines legal terminals for user:id up to 48.
SEC Authority	Defines user:id Authority.
CAT compartment$_1$ ... compartment$_{16}$	Defines user:id Category set.

The sensitivity of the information in the security control deck is obvious. Procedures have been developed at each installation that give the function of deck creation, control, and loading to specially cleared security personnel. The internal SYSLOG file itself is protected in a special manner described later.

Access Control. A fundamental security concern in multi-access systems is that many users with different clearances will be simultaneously using the system, thereby raising the possibility of security compromise. Since programs are the "active agents" of the user, the system must maintain the integrity of each and of itself from accidental and/or deliberate intrusion. A multifile system must permit concurrent access by one or more jobs to one or more on-line, independently classified files.

ADEPT is all these things—multiuser, multiprogram, and multifile system. Thus, this section deals with access control over users, programs, and files.

User Access Control: LOGIN: To gain admittance to the system, a user must first satisfy the ADEPT LOGIN decision procedure. This procedure attempts to authenticate the user in a fashion analogous to challenge-response practices.

The syntax of the ADEPT LOGIN command, typed by a user on his terminal, is as follows:

/LOGIN user:id password accounting

Figure 1 pictorially displays the LOGIN decision procedure based upon the user-specified input parameters. User:id is the index into the SYSLOG file used to retrieve the user security profile. If no such record exists (i.e., equation (22) fails), the LOGIN is unsuccessful and system access is denied. If the security profile is found, LOGIN next retrieves the terminal:id for the keyboard in use from internal system tables, and searches for a match in the terminal:id list for which the user:id was franchised by SYSLOG. An unsuccessful search is an unsuccessful LOGIN.

If the terminal is franchised, then the current password is retrieved from the SYSLOG file for this user:id and matched against the password entered as a keyboard parameter to LOGIN. An unsuccessful match is again an unsuccessful LOGIN. Furthermore, the terminal is ignored (will not honor input) for approximately 30 seconds to frustrate high-speed, computer-assisted, penetration attempts. If, however, the match is successful (equation (22) holds), the current password in the SYSLOG file for this user:id is discarded and LOGIN proceeds to create the job clearance.

Passwords in ADEPT obey the same syntax conventions as user:id. (See the earlier description of User Identification.) Although easily increased, currently SYSLOG permits up to 64 passwords. Each successful LOGIN throws away the user password; 64 successful LOGINs are possible before a new set of passwords need be established. If other than random, once-only passwords are desired, the 64 passwords may be encoded in some algorithmic manner, or replicated some number of times. Once-only passwords is an easily implemented technique for user authentication, which has been advocated by others.[2,7] It is a highly effective and secure technique because of the high permutability of 12-character-passwords and their time and order interdependence, known only to the user.

Once the authentication process is completely satisfied, LOGIN creates the job security profile according to equations (15) and (16) of our model. That is, the lower Authority of the user and the terminal becomes A_j, and the intersection (logical AND) of the user and terminal Category sets becomes the Category of the job, C_j. For example, a user with TOP SECRET Authority and a Category set (1001 1001 0000 1101) operating from a SECRET level terminal with a Category set (0000 0000 0000 0010) controls a job cleared to SECRET with an empty Category set.

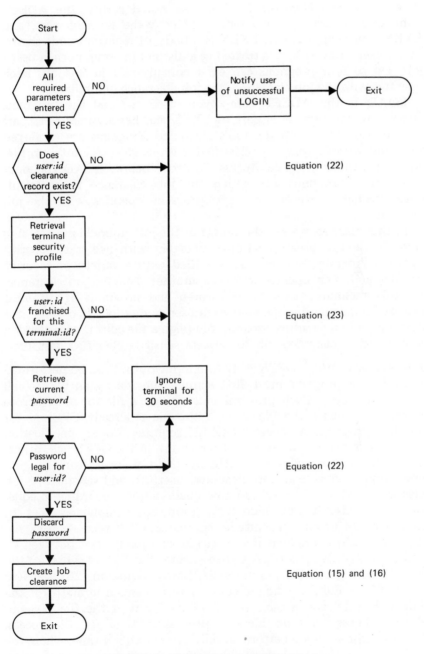

FIGURE 1.   LOGIN decision procedure.

Program Access Control: LOAD: As noted earlier, the ADEPT Executive consists of two parts: BASEX, the resident part, and EXEX, the swapped part. EXEX is a body of reentrant code shared by all users; however, it is treated as a distinct program in each user's job. Up to four programs can exist concurrently in the job. Each operates with the job clearance—the job clearance umbrella.

LOAD is the ADEPT component used to load the programs chosen by the user; it is part of EXEX and hence operates as part of the user's job with the job's clearance. Programs are cataloged files and as such may be classified with a given security profile. As is described in "File Access Control" below, LOAD can only load those programs for which the job clearance is sufficient. Once loaded, however, the new program operates with the job clearance.

In this manner, we see the power of the job umbrella in providing smooth, flexible user operation concurrent with necessary security control. Program files may be classified with a variety of security profiles and then operate with yet another, i.e., the job clearance. By this technique security is assured and programs of different classifications may be operated by a user as one job. It permits, for example, an unclassified program file (e.g., a file editor) to be loaded into a highly classified job to process sensitive classified data files.

File Access Control: OPEN: Before input/output can be performed on a file, a program must first acquire the file by an OPEN call to the Cataloger. Each program must OPEN a file for itself before it can manipulate the file, even if the file is already OPENed for another program. A successful OPEN requires proper specification of the file's descriptors—some of which are in the OPEN call, others of which are picked up directly by the Cataloger from the job environment area (e.g., job clearance, user:id)—and satisfactory job clearance and user:id need-to-know qualifications according to equations (25) and (26) of our model. Equation (25) is implemented as (8) as a straightforward magnitude comparison between A_j and A_f. Equation (25) is implemented as (9) as an equality test between C_f and $(C_j \wedge C_f)$. We use $(C_j \wedge C_f)$ to ensure that C_f is a subset of the job categories; i.e., the job umbrella. Lastly, equation (26) is a NOP if the file is Public; a simple equality test between u_j and u_f if the File is Private; and a table search of F_f for u_j if the file is Semi-Private. These tests do increase processing time for file access; however, the tests are performed only once at OPEN time, where the cost is insignificant relative to the I/O processing subsequently performed on the file.

The quality of access granted by a successful OPEN, and subsequently enforced for all I/O transfers, is that requested, even if the user has a greater Franchise. For example, during program debugging, the owner of a file may OPEN it for READ access only, even though READ-AND-WRITE access quality is permitted. He thereby protects his file from possible uncontrolled modification by an erroneous WRITE call.

Considerable controversy surrounds the issue of automatic classification of new files formed by subset or merger of existing files. The heart of the issue is the poor accuracy of many such classification techniques[17] and the fear of too many over-classified files (a fear of operations personnel) or of too many under-classified files (a fear of the security control officers). ADEPT finesses the problem with a clever heuristic—most new files are created from existing files, hence classify the new file as a private file with the composite Authority and Category of all files referenced. This is achieved in ADEPT by use of the "high-water mark."

Starting with the boundary conditions of equations (11) and (13), the Cataloger applies equations (12) and (14) for each successful file OPEN, and hence maintains the composite classification history of all files referenced by the job. For each new and temporary file OPEN, the Cataloger applies equations (17), (18), and (19); they are reapplied for each CLOSE of a new file, to update the classification (due to changes in the high-water mark since the OPEN) when the file becomes an existing cataloged file in the inventory. The scheme rarely underclassifies, and tends to overclassify when the new file is created late in the job cycle, as shown by boundary equations (20) and (21).

Trans-Formal Security Features

ADEPT contains a host of features that transcend the formalism presented earlier. They are described here because they are integral to the total security control system and form a body of experience from which new formalisms can draw.

Computer Hardware.   ADEPT operates on an IBM System 360/50 and is, therefore, limited to the hardware available. Studies by Bingham[9] suggest a variety of hardware features for security control, many of which are possessed by System 360.

IBM System 360 can operate in one of two states: the Supervisor state, or the Problem state. ADEPT executive programs operate in the Supervisor state; user programs operate in the Problem state.

A number of machine instructions are "privileged" to the Supervisor state only. An attempt to execute them in the Problem state is trapped by the hardware and control is returned to the executive program for remedial action. ADEPT disposes of these alarms by suspending the guilty job. (A suspended job may be resumed by the user.) Clearly, instructions that change the machine state are privileged to the executive only.

Another class of privileged instructions consists of those dealing with input/output. Problem state programs cannot directly access information files on secondary memory storage devices such as disc, tape, or drum. They must access these files indirectly by requests to the executive system. The requests are subjected to interpretive screening by the executive software.

Main memory is selectively protected against unauthorized change (write protected). We have also had the 360/50 modified to include fetch protection, which guards against unauthorized reading of—or executing from—protected memory. The memory protect instructions are also privileged only in the Supervisor state.

ADEPT software protects memory on a 4096-byte "page" basis (the hardware permits 2048-byte pages), allowing a noncontiguous mosaic of protected pages in memory for a given program. To satisfy multiprogramming, many different protection groups are needed. Through the use of programmable 4-bit hardware masks, up to 15 different protection groups can be accommodated in core concurrently. ADEPT executive programs operate with the all-zero "master key" mask, permitting universal access by all Basic and Extended Executive components.

There are five classes of interrupts processed by System/360 hardware: input/output, program, supervisor call, external, and machine check. Any interrupts that occur in the Problem state cause an automatic hardware switch to the Supervisor state, with CPU control flowing to the appropriate ADEPT executive interrupt controller. All security-vulnerable functions including hardware errors, external timer and keyboard actions, user program service requests, illegal instructions, memory protect violations, and input/output, are called to the attention of ADEPT by the System/360 interrupt system. The burden for security integrity is then one for ADEPT software.

Monitor Software. Inducing the system to violate its own protection mechanisms is one of the most likely ways of breaking a multiaccess system. Those system components that perform tasks in response to user or program requests are most susceptible to such seduction.

On-Line Debugging: The debugging program provides an on-line capability for the professional programmer to dynamically look at and change selected portions of his program's memory. DEBUG can be directed to access sensitive core memory that would not be trapped by memory protection, since, as an EXEX component operating in the Supervisor state, DEBUG operates with the memory protection master key. To close this "trap door," DEBUG always performs interpretive checks on the legality of the debugging request. These checks are based upon address-out-of-bounds criteria, i.e., the requested debugging address must lie within the user's program area. If not, the request will be denied and the user warned, but he will not be terminated as has been suggested.[7]

Input/Output: Input/output in System/360 is handled by a number of special-purpose processors, called Selector Channels. To initiate any I/O, it is necessary for a channel program to be executed by the Selector Channel.

SPAM, the BASEX component that permits symbolic input/output calls from user programs, is really a special-purpose compiler that produces I/O channel programs from the SPAM calls. These channel programs are subsequently delivered and executed by the ADEPT Input/Output Supervisor, IOS.

SPAM permits a variety of calls to read, write, alter, search for, and position to records within cataloged files. To achieve these ends, SPAM depends upon a variety of control tables dynamically created by the Cataloger in the job environment.

The initiating and subsequent monitoring of channel program execution is the responsibility of the BASEX Input/Output Supervisor, IOS. IOS is called to execute a channel program (EXCP). System components, such as SPAM, branch to IOS at a known entry point that is fetch-protected against entry in the Problem state. IOS is off-limits to user programs attempting to access cataloged storage. For protection against unauthorized EXCP requests, IOS always performs legality checks before executing a channel program. These checks begin by examination of the device addressed by the channel program. If it is the device address for cataloged storage, further checks are made to determine the machine state of the calling program. That state must be Supervisor state for the call to be honored. A call in the Problem state would indicate an illegal EXCP call from a user program.

IOS makes other checks to guarantee the validity of an I/O request. It checks to see that the specified buffer areas for the I/O transfer do not overlay the channel program itself, and lie within the user's program memory area, i.e., do not modify or access system or protected memory.

Covert I/O violations are also forestalled since I/O components take direction from information stored in the job environment—an area read- and write-protected from Problem state programs.

Classified Residue: Classified residue is classified information (either code or data) left behind in memory (i.e., core, drum, or disc) after the program that referenced it has been dismissed, swapped out, or quit from the system. The standard solution to the problem is to dynamically purge the contaminated memory (e.g., overwrite with random numbers, or zeros). In a system supporting over ¼ billion bytes of memory, that solution is unreasonable and in conflict with high performance goals. ADEPT's solution to the dilemma of denying access to classified residue while maintaining high performance depends upon techniques of controlled memory allocation.

1. Core Residue

As noted earlier, all core storage is allocated as 4096-byte pages. These pages are always cleared to zero when allocated, thereby overwriting any potential residue.

Via the program's page map, the ADEPT executive system labels all code and data pages (they need not be contiguous) belonging to a given program with a single hardware memory protection key, thereby prohibiting unauthorized reading or writing by other, potentially coresident user programs that may be in execution. Furthermore, BASEX keeps a running account of the status and disposition of all pages of core.

The Loader and Swapper components of ADEPT always work with full 4096-byte pages. Unfilled portions of pages at load time are kept cleared to zero as when they were allocated, and the full 4096 bytes are swapped into core, if not already resident, each scheduled time slice. Further, newly allocated pages are marked as "changed" pages, thus guaranteeing subsequent swap out to drum.

With these procedures, ADEPT denies access by a user or program to those pages of core not identified as part of his program, and clears core residue by over-writing accessible core at load and swap times.

2. Drum Residue

ADEPT always clears a drum page to zero before it is allocated. The page may subsequently be cleared again to user-specified data. ADEPT also maintains a drum map that notes the disposition of all drum pages (800 pages for the IBM 2303 drum). Drum input/output, like all ADEPT I/O, is controlled by executive privileged instructions.

3. Disc Residue

Disc files in ADEPT are maintained as "dirty" memory. That is, the large capacity of the file system makes it infeasible to consider automatic over-writing techniques for residue control; therefore, deleted disc tracks are returned to the available storage pool contaminated and unclean. It then becomes the burden of the ADEPT file system to control any unauthorized file access, whether to cataloged files or uncataloged disc memory.

Team work between the Cataloger, SPAM and IOS components of ADEPT achieves this control via legality checking of all OPEN and I/O requests.

For example, all disc packs are labeled internally and externally with their volume:id, and this label is checked at the time of mounting by the Cataloger OPEN procedure to assure proper volume mounting. Tapes may also be labeled and checked as a user option.

Of particular note, SPAM always assumes that an end-of-file (EOF) immediately follows the last record written in a new file, and it prohibits reading beyond that EOF. Contaminated tracks allocated to new files cannot be read until they are first written. The act of writing advances the EOF and the user simultaneously over-writes the classified residue with his own data. The user cannot skip over the EOF, and the EOF location is itself protected in the job environment area.

4. Tape Residue

No special features for tape residue control are implemented in ADEPT. Tape residue control is easily satisfied by manual, off-line tape degaussing prior to ADEPT use.

System Files: Equation (28) led us to examine Private, Semi-Private, and Public files. ADEPT possesses two additional file privacies that transcend our model; both are system files. Privacy-4 system files are the need-to-know lists created by the Cataloger itself for Semi-Private files. Privacy-5 system files are private system memory for the SYSLOG files and the catalogs themselves.

Access to these files is restricted to the system only. Special access checks are made that differ from those of equations (25) and (26). First, a special user:id is required that is not a member of U (i.e., not in the SYSLOG file). Second, the program making the OPEN call must be in Supervisor state. Third, the program making the OPEN call must be a member of a short list of EXEX programs. The list is built into the Cataloger at the time of compilation. In this manner, access to system files is severely restricted, even to system programs.

Security Service Commands: ADEPT provides a variety of service commands that involve security control. The commands are listed in Table III. Note that commands VARYON, VARYOFF, REPLACE, LISTU, AUDIT, AUDOFF, and WRAPUP are restricted to a particular terminal—the Security Officer's Station.

Audit. The AUDIT function records certain transactions relating to files, terminals, and users, and is the electronic equivalent of manual security accountability logs. Its purpose is to provide a record of user access in order to determine whether security violations have occurred and the extent to which secure data has been compromised. The AUDIT function may be initiated only at start-up time, but may be terminated at any time. All data are recorded on disc or tape in real time so the data is safe if the system malfunctions. An auxiliary utility program, AUDLIST, may be used to list the AUDIT file. The information recorded is shown in TABLE IV.

Implementation of AUDIT is quite straightforward, a product of general ADEPT recording and instrumentation.[18,19] AUDIT is an EXEX component that is called by, and at the completion of, each function to be recorded. The information to be recorded is passed to AUDIT in the general registers. Additional I/O overhead is the primary cost incurred in the operation of AUDIT, for swapping and file maintenance. This cost is nominal, however, amounting to less than one percent of the CPU time.

SUMMARY

In summary we may ask: How well have we met our goals? First, we believe we have developed and successfully demonstrated a security control mechanism that more than adequately supports heterogeneous levels and types of classification. Of note in this regard is the LOGIN decision procedure, access control tests, job umbrella, high-water mark, and audit trails recording. The approach

TABLE III.   Security Service Commands

Command	Purpose
AUDIT*	Turns on security audit recording.
AUDOFF*	Turns off security audit recording.
CHANGE	Enables the owner of a file to change any of the access control information of the file.
CREATE	Enables a user to create a Semi-Private file and its need-to-know list.
LISTU*	Lists by terminal:id all the current logged in user:ids.
RECLASS	Enables a user to raise or lower his job clearance between the bounds of the original LOGIN and current high-water mark clearance.
RELOG	Like LOGIN, but reconnects a user to an already existing job, as when a remote terminal drops off the communications line.
REPLACE*	Enables a user to move his job to another terminal or to reclassify a given device.
SECURITY	Print on the user's terminal approximately every 100 lines (or only by request) the job high-water mark (or clearance by request) as a reminder to the user and as a classification stamp of the level of current security activity.
VARYON/VARYOFF*	Permits terminals to be varied on- and off-line for flexibility in system maintenance and configuration control.
WRAPUP*	Shuts down system after a specified elapsed time.

*Restricted to Security Officer's Station only.

can be improved in the direction of more compartments (on the order of 1000 or more), extension of the model to include system files, and the implementation of a single Franchise test for all security objects. The implementation needs redundant encoding and error detection of security profile data to increase confidence in the system—though we have not ourselves experienced difficulty here. The increase in memory requirements to achieve these improvements may force numerical encoding of security data, particularly Category, as suggested by Peters.[7]

TABLE IV. Security Events and Information Audited by ADEPT-50

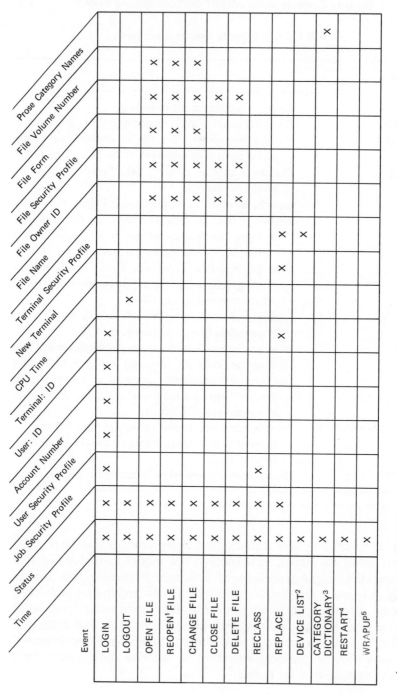

Event	Time	Status	Job Security Profile	User Security Profile	Account Number	User: ID	Terminal: ID	CPU Time	New Terminal	Terminal Security Profile	File Name	File Owner ID	File Security Profile	File Form	File Volume Number	Prose Category Names
LOGIN	X	X	X	X	X	X	X		X							
LOGOUT	X	X	X	X				X		X						
OPEN FILE¹	X	X	X	X								X	X	X	X	X
REOPEN FILE¹	X	X	X	X								X	X	X	X	X
CHANGE FILE	X	X	X	X								X	X	X	X	X
CLOSE FILE	X	X	X	X								X	X	X	X	
DELETE FILE	X	X	X	X								X	X	X	X	
RECLASS	X	X	X	X	X											
REPLACE	X	X	X	X					X		X	X				
DEVICE LIST²	X										X	X				
CATEGORY DICTIONARY³	X															X
RESTART⁴	X															
WRAPUP⁵	X															

¹ This is the "OPEN existing file" command.
² A list of all the terminal devices and their assigned security and categories is recorded at each system load.
³ A list of the prose category names is recorded at each system load.
⁴ Whenever the system is restarted on the same day (and AUDIT had been turned on earlier that day) the time of the restart is recorded.
⁵ The time that the AUDOFF action was taken, or the time that the WRAPUP function called AUDIT, to terminate the AUDIT function.

Second, SYSLOG has been highly successful in demonstrating the concept of "security arming" of the system at start-up time. Our greatest difficulty in this area has been with the human element—the computer operators—in preparing and handling the control deck. In opposition to Peters,[7] we believe the operator should not be "designed out of the operation as much as possible," but rather his capabilities should be upgraded to meet the greater levels of sophistication and responsibility required to operate a time-sharing system.[20] He should be considered part of line management. ADEPT is oriented in this direction and work now in progress is aimed at building a real-time security surveillance and operations station (SOS).

Third, we missed the target in our attempt to isolate and limit the amount of critical coding. Though much of the control mechanism is restricted to a few components—LOGIN, SYSLOG, CATALOGER, AUDIT—enough is sprinkled around in other areas to make it impossible to restrict the omnipotent capabilities of the monitor, e.g., to run EXEX in Problem state. Some additional design forethought could have avoided some of this dispersal, particularly the wide distribution in memory of system data and programs that set and use these data. The effect of this shortcoming is the need for considerably greater checkout time, and the lowered confidence in the system's integrity.

Lastly, on the brighter side, we were surprisingly frugal in the cost of implementing this security control mechanism. It took approximately five percent of our effort to design, code, and checkout the ADEPT security control features. The code represents about ten percent of the 50,000 instructions in the system. Though the code is widely distributed, SYSLOG, security commands, LOGIN, AUDIT, and the CATALOGER account for about 80 percent of it. The overhead cost of operating these controls is difficult to measure, but it is quite low, in the order of one or two percent of total CPU time for normal operation, excluding SYSLOG. (SYSLOG, of course, runs at card reader speed.) The most significant area of overhead is in the checking of I/O channel programs, where some 5 to 10 msec are expended per call (on the average). Since this time is overlapped with other I/O, only CPU bound programs suffer degradation. AUDIT recording also contributes to service call overhead. In actuality, the net operating cost of our security controls may be zero or possibly negative, since AUDIT recordings showed us numerous trivial ways to measurably lower system overhead.

ACKNOWLEDGMENTS

I would like to acknowledge the considerable encouragement I received in the formative stages of the ADEPT security control design from Mr. Richard Cleaveland, of the Defense Communications Agency (DCA). I would like to thank Mrs. Martha Bleier, Mr. Peter Baker, and Mr. Arnold Karush for their patient care in designing and implementing much of the work I've described. Also, I wish to thank Mr. Marvin Schaefer for assisting me in set theory notation. Finally, I would like to applaud the ADEPT system project personnel for designing and building a time-sharing system so amenable to the ideas discussed herein.

REFERENCES

1. A. Harrison, The Problem of Privacy in the Computer Age: An Annotated Bibliography. RAND Corp., Dec. 1967, RM-5495-PR/RC.

2. L. J. Hoffman, Computers and Privacy: A Survey, Stanford Linear Accelerator Center, Stanford University, Aug. 1968, SLAC-PUB-479.

3. H. E. Petersen and R. Turn, "System implications of information privacy," Proc. SJCC, Vol. 30, 1967, 291–300.

4. W. H. Ware, "Security and privacy in computer systems," Proc. SJCC, Vol. 30, 1967, 279–282.

5. W. H. Ware, "Security and privacy: similarities and differences," Proc. SJCC, Vol. 30, 1967, 287–290.

6. R. Linde, C. Weissman and C. Fox, "The ADEPT-50 time-sharing system," Proc. FJCC, Vol. 35, 1969. Also issued as SDC Doc. SP-3344.

7. B. Peters, "Security considerations in a multi-programmed computer system," Proc. SJCC, Vol. 30, 1967, 283–286.

8. Rye Capri Coins Octopus Sadie Systems, NOC Workshop, National Security Agency, Oct. 1968.

9. H. W. Bingham, Security Techniques for EDP of Multi-Level Classified Information, Rome Air Development Center, Dec. 1965, RADC-TR-65-415.

10. R. M. Graham, Protection in an Information Processing Utility, ACM Symposium on Operating Systems Principles, Oct. 1967, Gatlinburg, Tenn.

11. L. J. Hoffman, Formularies—Program Controlled Privacy in Large Data Bases, Stanford University Working Paper, Feb. 1969.

12. D. K. Hsiao, A File System for a Problem Solving Facility, Dissertation in Electrical Engineering, University of Pennsylvania, 1968.

13. J. I. Schwartz and C. Weissman, "The SDC time-sharing system revisited," Proc. ACM Conf., 1967, 263–271.

14. P. Baran, On Distributed Communications: IX, Security, Secrecy, and Tamper-Free Considerations, RAND Corp., Aug. 1964, RM–3765–PR.

15. C. Weissman, "Programming protection: What do you want to pay?" SDC Mag., Vol. 10, No. 8, Aug. 1967.

16. J. P. Titus, "Washington commentary—security and privacy," CACM, Vol. 10, No. 6, June 1967, 379–380.

17. I. Enger et al., Automatic Security Classification Study, Rome Air Development Center, Oct. 1967, RADC–TR–67–472.

18. A. Karush, The Computer System Recording Utility: Application and Theory, System Development Corp., March 1969, SP–3303.

19. A. Karush, Benchmark Analysis of Time-Sharing Systems: Methodology and Results, System Development Corp., April 1969, SP–3343.

20. R. R. Linde and P. E. Chaney, "Operational management of time-sharing systems," Proc. 21st Nat. ACM Conf., 1966, 149–159.

On the Implementation
of Security Measures
in Information Systems

R. W. CONWAY

W. L. MAXWELL

H. L. MORGAN

1. INTRODUCTION

Two important issues—privacy and security—are the topics in the growing number of discussions concerning the control of access to privileged information stored in computer files. Although there has not been much consistency in the terminology used by writers in this field, we would propose identifying these two issues in the following ways.

Information privacy involves issues of law, ethics, and judgment. Whether or not a particular individual should have access to a specific piece of information is a question of information privacy. As computer professionals and as citizens, we share the concern of many over the privacy question, but we have no special wisdom to bring to bear.

Information security involves questions of means—procedures to ensure that privacy decisions are in fact enforceable and enforced. On this issue, however, it is we as computer professionals who are primarily responsible to society. We must provide a technology that is sufficiently rugged to resist

SOURCE: Copyright © 1972, Association for Computing Machinery, Inc. R. Conway, W. Maxwell, and H. Morgan, Communications of the ACM, Vol. 15, No. 4, 211–220 (April 1972).

determined attack, and sufficiently economical to encourage its use. We must also insist that this security system be an integral part of any information system containing potentially sensitive data (e.g., personnel, credit bureau, or law enforcement files), or our profession will soon find itself with the same problems of conscience that nuclear physicists suffered in the late forties.

Figure 1 shows the outcome of each possible combination of privacy decision and security action. Each possible outcome has a cost, in both economic and social terms. In most information systems to date, the privacy decision has not been made explicit and security has not been deliberately implemented—so that "proper access" is the only outcome. One might hypothesize that the neglect of the privacy question has been at least in part due to a tacit evaluation that requisite security measures are either infeasible or uneconomic. Security measures have been rudimentary, mostly because of a preoccupation with the mechanics of providing access to information for any user, but perhaps partly because privacy demands have not been emphasized. This state of affairs cannot exist much longer, as it seems very likely that public and legal pressure will soon demand that the privacy question be made explicit [15, 19]. Security measures will be required in order to limit the frequency of the "successful invasion" outcome, and these measures will have to have considerable flexibility in order to avoid the "improper rebuff" outcome.

The purpose of this paper is to discuss the nature of flexibility in a security system and to relate the costs of implementation and enforcement to that flexibility. It appears possible that earlier treatment of the subject [12, 17] has not sufficiently emphasized the distinction between data dependent and data independent privacy

| | | Privacy decision | |
		Access permitted	Access denied
Action of security system	Access obtained	Proper access	Successful invasion
	Access prevented	Improper rebuff	Successful defense

FIGURE 1.

decisions, and as a consequence, has overestimated the cost of security enforcement.

A conceptual model consisting of a "security matrix" and four security functions is proposed. This model is then used in both the explanative and normative senses; i.e., several existing security systems are related to the model, and a general implementation method is proposed based on the use of the model. We start by examining the privacy decisions which may be desired in an attempt to achieve a classification.

2. SELECTIVE SECURITY

Most of the technical difficulty in information security arises from the fact that those responsible for making privacy decisions about a particular data bank are constrained by having to either permit or deny access to the entire data bank. It is not sufficient to simply divide the population of users into two disjoint and exhaustive subpopulations—those who are permitted and those who are denied access to a particular data bank. Rather those responsible should be able to be selective in deciding just what portions of the data should be accessible to each user.

Perhaps the point can be made by an analogy to security methods of physical access to a large office building. The simplest privacy decision would be to enumerate those individuals who are entitled to access to the building. This could be implemented by a security system that consisted of a lock on the outer door. In practice this is rarely adequate, and a much more selective privacy decision is made and then implemented by a complex security structure that involves the use of locks, keys, guards, and badges as they apply to access to the building, to individual floors and corridors, offices, desks, safes, filing cabinets, etc. Going further, one might wish to control not only where an individual could go within the building but also what he might do at each location. One could also want to make the regions that are accessible to a particular individual depend upon the time of day. And finally, although the analogy is beginning to labor under the strain, one could want an individual's accessible region to depend upon some dynamic characteristic of the space units; for example, a man is to have access to all offices that do not at the moment contain any "classified" documents.

The variety of potential conditions for privacy of information is even broader. For example, imagine an employee personnel/payroll file for a large industrial concern. This file might include data structures named: NAME, SALARY HISTORY, CURRENT SALARY, PERFORMANCE EVALUATION, DEPARTMENT, MEDICAL HISTORY, and SOCIAL SECURITY NUMBER. One could conceive of circumstances under which each of the following would be a reasonable privacy decision about some individual and this personnel/payroll file.

1. He has complete access to the entire file for any purpose and action.
2. He has no access to any part of the file for any purpose.
3. He may see any portion of the file, but he may not change its contents.
4. He may see exactly one record (his "own") of the file, but not alter its contents.
5. He may see exactly one record (his "own") of the file, and alter some, but not all of the fields of that record.
6. He may see only the NAME and MEDICAL HISTORY portion of each record in the file, and alter only the MEDICAL HISTORY portion.
7. He may see and alter only "financial" portions of each record in the file, but only during the hours of 9 a.m. to 5 p.m. and only from a terminal located in the payroll office.
8. He may see and alter only financial portions of each record, and only for those records for which the value of CURRENT SALARY is less than $15,000.
9. He may see financial information, but only in the aggregate, e.g., total salary by division, but not individual salaries.
10. He may see and alter PERFORMANCE EVALUATION only for those records for which the value of DEPARTMENT is "Engineering."

Although this list is by no means exhaustive, it should begin to illustrate the variety of privacy conditions that will arise once people start giving serious consideration to the question. Each of the examples given above could be useful, or even essential, under certain circumstances.

To the best of our knowledge, no security system exists today that would permit a systems designer to enforce any arbitrary combination of these privacy constraints for any arbitrary combination of user and data element. With the state of the art, such a security system would increase overall processing cost by an order of magnitude—which increase might threaten the economic justification of the entire application, or at least tempt the designer to risk the consequences of an unsecured system. However, many of these privacy constraints have the important characteristic of being independent of particular values of data, and to the extent that such privacy constraints are considered adequate by the user, it is possible to implement a security system at very modest cost. It seems to us important that the designers and implementers of security systems be aware of the crucial significance of data dependence in security matters and of the special procedures that may be employed to implement data independent privacy requirements in an efficient manner. It is probably equally important that those responsible for making privacy decisions understand what kind of conditions are inherently difficult (and expensive) to implement, so that these can be avoided wherever possible. This question is discussed in Section 4.

3. SECURITY MATRIX

Conceptually, the privacy decisions for a particular data bank may be recorded in a "security matrix" (a generalization of the "user security profiles" of Bingham [4]). The columns of this matrix correspond to particular data structures in the system—not necessarily disjoint—and the rows of the matrix correspond to the potential users of the system. Each element in the matrix, d_{ij}, is a decision rule embodying a specific privacy decision, specifying the conditions under which user i is entitled to access to the data structure j and the actions that i is permitted to perform upon j. In this respect, the security system may be considered to be table driven by this matrix.

As an example, suppose that the information in a particular system is describable as the PL/I structure shown in Figure 2 (data types omitted). Let us also suppose that the users in the system are identified as follows:

A   Company president
B   Chief payroll clerk
C   Systems programmer
D   Doctor
E   Employee

Figure 3 shows a portion of the security matrix for this system. Notice that the column headings include both major and minor structure names, as well as specific field names. Such detail is clearly required to permit the selective security discussed in Section 2. In a real system, columns would be needed not only for the data

```
DECLARE
    1 EMPLOYEE (1000)
    2 NAME
    2 SALARY_HISTORY (6)
        3 CLASS
        3 RATE
        3 AMT
    2 CURRENT_SALARY
    2 PERFORMANCE EVALUATION (6)
        3 DEPARTMENT
        3 SUPERVISOR
        3 DATE
        3 PERFORMANCE
    2 MEDICAL_HISTORY
        3 BLOOD TYPE
        3 TREATMENT_HISTORY (12)
            4 DATE
            4 DOCTOR
            4 TREATMENT (8)
                5 DATE
                5 MEDICATION
                5 CONDITION
    2 SOCIAL_SECURITY_NUMBER
    2 ADDRESS
        3 ADDR_LINE_1
        3 CITY
        3 STATE
        3 ZIP
```

FIGURE 2.

structures but also for the program libraries, operating system, and the security matrix itself. To be truly selective, one must also be able to distinguish between different generations of the same file, and to designate subfiles to content, e.g., a column for EMPLOYEES WITH DEPARTMENT = 'PURCHASING'.

The description of this conceptual matrix will not be pursued to the point where it might become operationally precise simply because it is prohibitively large. In most real world data processing situations the number of users would be substantial, and the number of data elements would be impossibly large. Nonetheless, the security matrix is a convenient model with which to describe the general

USER	EMPLOYEE	CURRENT SALARY	SALARY HISTORY	AMT	MEDICAL HISTORY
A	R, W	R, W*	R, W*	R, W*	R, W*
B	N	R, (W between 9 and 5)	R, W	R, W*	N
C	N	N	N	N	N
D	N	N	N	N	R, W
E					

Key: R can read the field or any element of the structure. W can change the field or any element of the structure.
*Implied by some other decision rule in the same row. N can neither read nor change the structure of the field.

FIGURE 3.

security problem, and a convenient background against which to evaluate what is achieved by specific implementations.

To begin with, the matrix may be cited to indicate two limitations on the scope of this discussion. First, we are considering security measures only of the type that could be enforced through the use of such a matrix within a computer-based system. This implies that we are specifically not treating the problem of physical security. In the world of locks, badges, and paper, a considerable technology has evolved over the years for the protection of valuable goods and information on paper. While the failures of physical security systems are not infrequent and are often newsworthy, it still seems possible to observe that adequate hardware and procedures for physical security are available to the data processing industry if it was decided that the risks and costs justified their deployment [1, 12].

One should note, however, that physical security in our context is mainly concerned with the central machine location. People accessing the system through remote terminals are constrained to submit to internal system security, and to the extent that this type of system is becoming more popular, the overall problem may have been eased. On the other hand, the user at a terminal is safely anonymous to the personnel at the central location, thus inhibiting use of the informal physical security measures which made it difficult for a stranger to walk into the computing center and obtain execution of a program accessing sensitive data.

Remote access systems are also subject to certain electronic threats such as wiretapping and masquerading; but until major advances are made in other aspects of security, these somewhat esoteric threats hardly seem to be an immediate concern to most installations [12, 17].

The second restriction of the scope of this discussion concerns the problem of <u>authentication</u>. This is the problem of ensuring that the proper row of the security matrix is selected when a particular user addresses himself to the system. To be meaningful, the security system must be designed with the assumption that an active potential infiltrator will exercise considerable ingenuity to misidentify himself to the system. The usual method of authentication is some variant of "password" protection, and the procedures used seem better suited as a defense against a basically honest but occasionally befuddled user than against one who is seriously intent on penetrating security. More sophisticated (and costly) methods of authentication do exist (e.g., badge readers, "formula" passwords, built-in terminal identification) but are not yet in widespread use. Hoffman [12] has a discussion of authentication procedures, and Bingham [4] discusses possible hardware/software combinations for authentication.

For the remainder of this paper then, we shall assume that the system is physically secure and that the particular user has been properly identified—realizing meanwhile that often neither assumption is justifiable. Yet one could argue that since potential violators will be concerned with the weakest link in an overall security system, potential protectors should be also. Considering the state of current internal system security procedures at most installations, it is probably unnecessary for violators to waste time discovering passwords or to risk the consequences of breaking and entering a computing center. However, if there are significant improvements in internal security and if, in fact, there is an appreciable corps of enterprising violators, there will have to be increasing pressure put upon making provisions for physical security and authentication procedures.

The two compromises that characterize an embarassingly large fraction of the security procedures in current use might be described as a "column" system and a "diagonal" system.

In a column system there is only one data element—the complete data collection—and each decision rule in the resulting single column security matrix is a simple rule granting or denying unconditional and unrestricted access and use. The user has only to authenticate himself in order to obtain access to any datum in this collection. An associated accounting system may impose limits on the extent of use, but this is generally intended more to conserve or allocate system resources than to limit activity for security reasons.

In a diagonal system the data collection is partitioned into a set of exhaustive and mutually exclusive files. Each file is uniquely identified with a particular user. The rows and columns of the security matrix are permuted so that all of the elements on the principal diagonal are decision rules granting unrestricted access and all other elements prohibit access.

Either of these special cases can be decomposed in such a way as to put the burden of access control solely on a password protection system; that is, each datum has a unique password, and a user consists of all the potential users who possess that password.

These special cases, however, are far from satisfying the selective security needs already described. In general, a practical implementation of the security matrix concept can be sought in one or more of three directions.

1. Through reduction in the size of the matrix: by defining "virtual users," each representing a collection of users with identical security authorization; and by considering only data aggregates to reduce the number of columns.
2. Through simplification of the entries in the matrix from the general "decision rule" to yes-no indication. This reduces the matrix from an array of functions, which must be evaluated with each interrogation of the matrix, to an array of bits.
3. Through careful analysis of <u>when</u> and <u>how</u> the matrix should be interrogated and its specification employed.

Both the column and diagonal systems have carried out points 1 and 2 almost to their logical extremes. The third approach does not seem to have been examined in sufficient detail previously, yet it seems to us to offer some promise for implementation of general security features at modest cost.

An analysis of how the security matrix is accessed shows that while the complete matrix may be very large, even in reduced form, it is also very sparse—in the sense that most of its entries are denials of access—and that only a very small fraction of the matrix is relevant at any instant of time. The authentication of a user selects a particular row of the matrix, and the user will designate some aggregate data element (e.g., when he "opens" a file) that will select a relatively small subset of the column entries for that row. Thus, rather than really being accessed randomly, the matrix could have a very small controlling submatrix which could be identified and remain in control for a significant amount of processing time. This might alleviate some of the problems of the large size of the general matrix.

Similarly, when considering when the matrix is accessed, one should distinguish roughly between two approaches to data processing. The first is the traditional "batch processing" run, in which essentially similar actions are performed on large numbers of similar data structures in the course of a single run. The frequency of repetition demands that these actions be performed efficiently. The second approach might be characterized as a "random inquiry" process. This would have a relatively low frequency of repetition, and one could tolerate significantly higher overhead. The first type of run has dominated the field in the past; the second is rapidly growing in importance. The point for present purposes is that a data collection must be secure for both types of approach. The selection of the relevant security submatrix is required only once per approach and not once for each data element selected from the collection. In the random inquiry only one data access may be required, so that the addition of one reference to some form of security matrix represents a significant percentage increase in overhead, although the absolute amount of work involved is minor and entirely tolerable. On the other hand, the batch processing run could involve thousands of accesses into the data collection; this need not require equally as many examinations of the security matrix.

It is significant that the few security provisions that exist in systems today are almost completely passive; i.e., the provision called "threat monitoring" in the literature [17] has rarely been adequately implemented. Current systems typically will submit to unlimited abuse without appealing for help or even noting the fact that they are under attack. In most cases a persistent infiltrator could sit at a terminal and try character combinations at random until a valid password was encountered. (MTS [16] at least inconveniences the infiltrator by requiring him to re-dial in after three password failures.) While systems steadfastly deny access until a valid password is submitted, they generally do not recognize that a systematic assault is in progress. A successful threat, by definition, is not recognized as such, while in most cases an unsuccessful threat is neither detected nor punished. One must conclude that a security system is not really very serious until it includes at least some means of recording its successful defenses against attack.

Some recent systems include "entry logs," which record a history of authentication successes and failures. Threats that occur when a properly authenticated user attempts to violate the restrictions of his row in the security matrix could also be logged. Examination of such a log will reveal successful defenses, and if the log is monitored in real-time, more imaginative and effective counter-measures could be deployed. We conclude that either very little ingenuity has been expended on the design of such countermeasures, or system designers have been judiciously quiet concerning their accomplishments in this area.

4. DATA-DEPENDENT AND DATA-INDEPENDENT CONDITIONS

It is informative to examine the examples of privacy decisions listed in Section 2 to see which require the actual element of some datum to be evaluated. Restricting a particular user from ever seeing a field named SALARY in any record of a file is independent of the specific values in that field, while restricting a user from seeing values of SALARY in excess of $10,000 is data-dependent. Granting a user "read-only" access to an entire file is data-independent, but permitting a user to alter the contents of only those records for which DEPARTMENT = 'PURCHASING' is data-dependent. This distinction is crucial in determining how security restrictions are enforced and what such enforcement will cost in system resources.

Data dependence must be interpreted in a very general sense. The decision may be dependent upon the value of any datum in the system and not just the particular datum to which access is sought. For example, if a user is permitted access to salary data only between the hours of 9 and 5, then the current time is the datum on which the security decision depends.

Data-dependent privacy decisions obviously cannot be evaluated until the relevant datum itself is available. This means not only that evaluation must be deferred until the system has accessed the data element but also that evaluation must be repeated for each potential data element in the same class. The implication is that an interpretive mode of enforcement performed at execution time is required, increasing by an order of magnitude the execution time in comparison with an unsecured version of the same request for information. To the extent that the necessary privacy decision is data dependent, this high cost is inescapable, and one simply has to balance the risks of running unsecured against the cost of providing security. However, not all privacy decisions are data dependent, and it is possible to implement security enforcement for the data independent privacy decisions at very modest cost compared to that required for data dependent decisions. Most writers and designers, noting that data dependent privacy decisions can only be enforced interpretively at execution time, have apparently planned the enforcement of all privacy decisions in this way. This has given the erroneous impression that security enforcement is necessarily very costly, thereby dampening enthusiasm for implementing secure systems.

In fact, data-independent privacy decisions can be enforced by examining the request and the appropriate element of the matrix just once—at the time the request is received for translation (by a compiler, assembler, etc.). Access to the security matrix is required, but not access to the data base. Thus, if a user may never see the SALARY field of any record, a single check at translation time can stop the request from getting access to the data base in the first place. This method of enforcement assumes that: (a) all requests for access to the data base are entered into the system as source input to a translator (assembler, COBOL, PL/I, MARK IV, ASAP, etc.) and (b) the translated form of a request must be held in a secure manner so that it cannot be altered by the user after the translation-time checks have taken place. Guaranteeing that these two assumptions are satisfied in a particular system may still be a less costly process than interpretively enforcing all of the data independent privacy decisions.

The significance of data dependency in other contexts is, of course, well known. In the design of language translators and operating systems there are numerous decisions which permit some freedom in the timing of implementation—for example, the "binding" of variables in a translator. In general, efficiency is served by early implementation and flexibility is served by later implementation. This is implicit in the translator-writer's maxim: "as soon as possible" or "as late as necessary." We simply observe that the same distinction and choice of implementation time exists for security decisions. Section 5 describes a security model that emphasizes this distinction.

5. FUNCTIONAL MODEL OF A SECURITY SYSTEM

A model of a security system includes the security matrix and four functions: F_t and S_t, the translation-time fetch and store functions, and F_r and S_r, the run-time fetch and store functions.

Each of the functions has two arguments—u, a user identification, and d, a datum name. The functions thus reflect a particular element of the security matrix. F_t is called whenever during the translation of a request (job, task, etc.) a fetch reference is made to a data element, i.e., in the right-hand-side of an assignment statement or appearance in an output list. $F_t(u, d)$ interrogates the specified element of the matrix and takes one of three possible actions:

1. If the user is permitted data-independent read access to the datum, then conventional object code for fetching the datum is generated.
2. If the user is denied read access to this datum on a data-independent basis, translation is aborted, and the system is alerted to perform threat monitoring.
3. If the user is permitted data-dependent read access to the datum, a call to $F_r(u, d)$ is generated in the object code.

Similarly, S_t is invoked whenever a left-hand-side (store) use of a datum is encountered, and has the obvious analogous actions.

$F_r(u, d)$ is called at execution time and actually performs the data-dependent check required. If the check passes, F_r returns the value of d. If the check fails, it returns a null of some sort. Similarly, $S_r(u, d)$ stores a value in d only if the data-dependent check is successful. Note that F_r should not invoke threat monitoring since it is expected to legitimately and innocently fail. However, failure of S_r generally suggests an attempted invasion, and threat monitoring should be invoked.

To the extent that the security matrix specified data independent privacy decisions, security enforcement can be completely achieved by the use of F_t and S_t—the run-time functions F_r and S_r are not required. F_t and S_t represent very slight incremental effort for a translator, and when calls upon F_r and S_r are not required, there is no degradation of execution performance. Hence, data-independent privacy conditions can be implemented at modest cost. Data-dependent privacy conditions require the exercise of F_r and S_r for each datum and incur an appreciable execution-time penalty.

The principal point is that if one fails to distinguish between data-dependent and data-independent privacy conditions then F_t and S_t must always insert a call upon F_r and S_r and the substantial penalty of interpretive execution must always be paid. If the distinction is made, and F_t and S_t are sophisticated enough to capitalize upon it, then at least data-independent privacy can be economically enforced.

Another aspect of security is the encrypting of the data base. It is a simple matter to include instructions in S_t and S_r to translate the datum into unintelligible form as it is stored, and corresponding instructions in F_t and F_r to translate the encrypted datum back into useful form. Simple and efficient algorithms for this translation have been given [17, 18, 5] and the execution cost on contemporary machines is quite modest [13]. Encrypting a data-base in this manner effectively thwarts the invader who would circumvent the security provisions of the system by obtaining access to the data base entirely outside the managing system. While the translation would probably succumb to the efforts of a skilled cryptographer the "work factor" [3] is probably sufficiently high to make other avenues of attack more attractive.

6. EXAMPLES OF EXISTING IMPLEMENTATIONS

While exemplary information systems with flexible, rugged, and efficient security provisions may exist, we do not know of published descriptions. The tools generally available for system implementation—languages, data or file management systems, and operating system utilities—do not currently encourage or facilitate elaborate security measures. The 1969 Survey of Generalized Data Base Management Systems [7] described nine systems. While seven of these have some form of security provisions, only three of the seven were actually operating when the survey was written. The most complex security available in the running systems was that of ADAM, which permitted only read/write protection on specified fields. The most widely used file management system, MARK IV, offered no security provisions. It is interesting to note that in NIPS/FFS, a file maintenance system for the National Military Command System, security provisions are completely described by the following paragraph: "Each file may be assigned a classification. If the classification given in a report specification (which is printed on each page of the report) does not match this, or none is given, a warning page precedes the report, and a console message is printed."

In the more recent CODASYL study [8], two new systems are mentioned. IBM's IMS system, which seems to include somewhat broader security provisions, and the Data Base Task Group proposal [6], which if implemented, would offer a comprehensive set of privacy controls on actions and access.

We will briefly describe three university developed systems. These represent some interesting ideas related to the previous discussion.

None are widely used, and we do not suggest that they adequately represent current practice.

Hoffman [13] has implemented a security system for the Student Health System (SHS) at Stanford University, based on his procedural (or "formulary") model for access control and privacy in information systems. In this system, all security is provided at run-time through a set of data base access procedures. Each request for a datum must go through the procedure ACCESS, which in turn calls a procedure (contained in the formulary) specific to the user to obtain the grant/deny access decision. Privacy transformations can then be performed by ACCESS before giving the user the desired value (or storing the value in the data base). While the formulary could contain any general procedures and ACCESS could be asked for specific field of records, in fact, in the SHS system, the only formulary procedures which exist provide fetch or fetch and store access, and the only data name which ACCESS recognizes is NEXTRECORD. Thus in effect, this conceptually very powerful system in current implementation is able to grant or deny read only or read/write access to the entire field. SHS therefore is an example of a column system, with the potential for rather complex formularies (decision rules). The ACCESS procedure is the implementation of F_r and S_r, and F_t and S_t always provide calls to F_r and S_r.

Graham [11] has described the protection scheme used in the MULTICS system. The use of special hardware features to effect some of the security checks is discussed. In MULTICS, there is a hierarchy of files and programs. Each segment (program or file) has a clearance level. This level is placed in a hardware register when the program is in control. If the program calls another program (or accesses a file) which is not at the same security level or a lower level (i.e., more restricted), a hardware interrupt is taken. The interrupt routine must then examine a "gate list," or list of acceptable users who may access this less restricted segment. Thus, when an access request is made to a segment, the "gatekeeper" program checks to see that the requestor is on the segment's "gate list." If so, the security levels of the two segments are compared, and the requestor is permitted access only if his program has a sufficient level of clearance. The "gatekeeper" distinguishes types of access as read, write, and execute. In this system, the security matrix is stored in the form of a set of gate lists, which indicate whether user i can access datum j for read/write/execute purposes. All checks are made at run-time, but the F_r and S_r functions are made relatively efficient through the hardware provisions.

The third example is a file maintenance system called ASAP [2, 9], which was designed and implemented by the authors to serve as a test vehicle for a number of new concepts. Security measures were a primary consideration in the design. It is described at some length below since it, not surprisingly, illustrates most of the points of the previous discussion. Both data dependent and data independent security features are provided, although there is no threat monitoring. The data independent features can deny access to specific fields of records and can inhibit certain types of processing. These are implemented through F_t and S_t functions used during translation, thereby reducing the amount of checking which must be done at run-time.

The security matrix is contained in a special dictionary, which is created by the user, and contains descriptions of the files, reports, and other entities known to the system, as well as the security information. Associated with each field name is a security "class." There are eight such classes, labeled 1 to 8, with no hierarchy implied. Similarly, each aggregate name (e.g., a report containing information from several fields) has a class equivalent to the union of all of the classes of fields in the aggregate. Each allowable user of the system has an associated list of those classes to which he is permitted access. Thus, when he references a field, a simple comparison is made to determine whether or not he can see that field. In addition, there is associated with each user a list of the ASAP actions (PRINT, CALL, UPDATE, SET, etc.) that he is permitted to use.

A limited form of data dependent security is provided by associating qualifications (e.g., Boolean conditions) with each user. During execution, each record is checked against the appropriate qualification before being passed to the user's program for processing.

For example, consider a law firm's personnel file as shown in Figure 4. These definitions would create a dictionary which could process two different record types—employees and partners. There are three different "users" permitted to use this system, and they authenticate themselves by prefacing their processing request with their respective passwords. A user authenticated as a 'LIMITED PARTNER' can examine the records for EMPLOYEES whose SALARY is less than $30,000, including all fields of the record except PMEDHIST, for PARTNERS whose PLEVEL = 'LP'. He cannot alter any field of any record. A user authenticated as a 'GENERAL PARTNER' can read or alter any field of any record. He is also authorized to call external procedures from ASAP and

```
DEFINE RECORD EMPLOYEES
    NAME 25
    SOCSECNO 9 KEY
    DEPT 5
    SALARY 7 COMPUTE SECURITY 1
    MEDHIST 30          SECURITY 2
    HOBEVAL 30         SECURITY 1
DEFINE RECORD PARTNERS
    PNAME 25
    PSOCSECNO 9 KEY
    PLEVEL 2
    PSALARY 7 COMPUTE    SECURITY 1
    PCTOWNER 3 COMPUTE  SECURITY 3
    PMEDHIST 30          SECURITY 2
DEFINE USER 'LIMITED PARTNER' SECURITY 1
    EMPLOYEES WITH SALARY > 30,000
    PARTNERS WITH PLEVEL = 'LP' 'PASSWORD 1'
    USER 'GENERAL PARTNER' SECURITY 1 2 3 UPDATE CALL USER
        'PASSWORD 2'
    USER 'PHYSICIAN' SECURITY 2 UPDATE 'PASSWORD 3'
```

FIGURE 4.

to add new users to the system. A user authenticated as a 'PHYSI-CIAN' has access to all records, but only to their unrestricted identification information and the medical history.

The system operates in the following way. If a LIMITED PARTNER were to submit the ASAP request:

ASAP 'PASSWORD 1'
FOR ALL EMPLOYEES WITH DEPT = 'ACNTG'
    PRINT A LIST OF NAME, SALARY, JOBEVAL
    ORDERED BY SALARY.

the system would simply supply only those records for which the value of SALARY is less than $30,000. There is no indication on the results that certain records were not accessed. This is a data-dependent condition and is enforced at run-time. If this same LIMITED PARTNER were to submit any of the following requests:

FOR ALL EMPLOYEES SELECTED BY KEY IN DATA CARDS,
    UPDATE RECORD.
FOR ALL EMPLOYEES PRINT LIST: NAME, MEDHIST.

FOR ALL EMPLOYEES WITH NAME = 'JOHN A. JONES'
INCREASE SALARY BY 1000.

these would be detected at translation time, and no execution would take place. All of these are violations of data-independent privacy conditions and are trapped by F_t or S_t during compilation.

Clearly, the ability to define users is all important and should be reserved to only one or two people. There are built-in counter-measures to some of the obvious threats to this system. Both files and secure information in the dictionary are stored in encrypted form (file encrypting is optional) considerably increasing the work factor to obtain information from them by dumping them with a utility program.

We believe that the types of security and the implementation strategy employed in ASAP are not dependent upon the character-istics of this particular source language. They could be applied to a conventional language, or even to a multilanguage environment, as described in Section 7.

7. GENERAL IMPLEMENTATION

Section 6 gave examples of security implementations in an applica-tion program, a specialized operating system, and a generalized data base management system. It is important to consider the security question relative to languages such as COBOL, FORTRAN and PL/I and relative to operating systems such as OS/360. If privacy decisions cannot be practically enforced in this environment, then discussions of security and privacy are somewhat limited, or at least premature. We believe that this is not the case and that security enforcement is practical—although we do not know of this having been done in a general, flexible manner.

It would appear to be quite feasible to provide security similar to that offered by ASAP by either modifying or extending a general purpose operating system. The major task would be the addition of a library routine (analogous to the ASAP dictionary) to store, manage, and protect the security matrix. Secondly the I/O service routines (OPEN, CLOSE, GET, PUT) of the operating system would be modified, or have other routines superimposed upon them. These routines would represent the F_r and S_r functions. If implemented in this manner, it would be independent of the translator employed; and since security is enforced at run-time, there is no requirement to secure the translated request during the interval between transla-tion and execution. On the other hand, it means that all privacy conditions are treated as data-dependent conditions with the attendant overhead. In fact the overhead is even greater than that involved in data-dependent conditions in a system such as ASAP for the F_r and S_r routines must perform complete run-time masking of the data elements. That is, since F_r has no way of knowing what the user program is going to attempt to do with the data element, it must completely erase the element according to the specification of the security matrix. This is essentially the Hoffman [13] security model, and it may be that the execution penalty is prohibitive in many situations.

To reduce this penalty one can identify those privacy conditions that are data-independent and implement the F_t and S_t functions so that when possible the requisite tests are performed once per request rather than once per data access. To do so means becoming involved in the translation process and, equally important, providing a means of securing the user request against modification between the time of translation and the time of execution.

F_t and S_t can be implemented either by modifying the standard compiler or by interposing a preprocessor in front of a standard compiler. The former is certainly the most efficient method of implementation, and perhaps some day standard compilers will include such provisions. Until that time, one is faced with the not altogether pleasant prospect of making and maintaining nontrivial modifications deep in the interior of a sophisticated translator. At least at the moment, the preprocessor approach seems more reasonable. There already exist very high-performance compilers for both FORTRAN and PL/I that could be used as a basis for a security preprocessor. One could discard the code generation phase of these compilers and use the preliminary phases to implement security features. These would draw upon the same dictionary routine for the security matrix that is required for the data-dependent run-time enforcement. Although the preprocessor would have to perform rather complete syntactic analysis of the source program to perform the necessary checks, and this would duplicate the analysis performed by the standard compiler, the performance of these preprocessors is such that this could readily be tolerated. For example, a preprocessor for PL/I based on the Cornell PL/C compiler [10] would scan 15,000 PL/I source statements per minute on a 360/65. (This is the actual speed of the PL/C lexical and syntactic analyzer.)

With either a preprocessor or a modified compiler, certain serious problems remain. When data elements are referenced by name there is basically little difficulty, for these can be checked in context and usage against the security matrix. However, the programmer has a number of ways he can access data elements other than by name. The most obvious way is to use an array and deliberately force the subscripts to go outside the declared bounds. PL/I offers a remedy for this problem, since the security system (either preprocessor or modified compiler) could insist that the program have SUB-SCRIPTRANGE enabled with a suitably fatal ON SUBSCRIPT-RANGE unit. This would, however, impose additional execution overhead for the subscript monitoring. Neither FORTRAN nor COBOL offers this type of monitoring, and it is not possible for a preprocessor for those languages to protect against this circumvention if the use of arrays is allowed—as of course it must be. Either the standard compiler would have to be modified to provide this protection or run-time testing would be required.

A similar problem exists in the improper use of pointers in PL/I. A structure similar to the target record could be declared, and a pointer to the record set into a pointer to this structure. This could be negated by the run-time testing of the record (by F_r and S_r), but this is costly protection, and it might be possible to detect this type of threat by sophisticated analysis of the source program. Similarly, the passing of a record address as a parameter to a subroutine in which the record is not declared, but where a similar structure is declared, presents the same type of problem.

In summary it would appear that a translator independent F_r/S_r security system could be implemented by adding a security matrix routine and modifying the I/O service routines of a general purpose operating system, but this would treat all privacy conditions as data dependent, and the execution-time degradation would be severe. Performance could be improved by implementing the F_t/S_t functions by some combination of a preprocessor and modifications to the standard translators, but this would also require some limitation on the freedom of the programmer to use the full facilities of the source language.

8. CONCLUSIONS

In current practice security measures in information systems are neither elaborate, flexible, nor impenetrable. There are indications that more demanding privacy requirements will soon be imposed upon systems designers and that security provisions will have to be substantially improved.

It is useful to view security questions in terms of a security matrix and four functions representing translate and run-time, fetch and store operations. In particular this model facilitates the delineation of data dependent and data independent security conditions. The former requires interpretive implementation in the form of run-time checking routines and imposes a significant degradation of performance. The latter, at least in principle, needs to be exercised only once per request at translation time, rather than once per datum, and thereby offers the opportunity to implement certain security measures with very modest execution penalty.

The best prospects for enhancement of security would seem to lie in the more recent generalized data management systems. These systems offer a controlled environment and impose sufficient restraint upon user activity to enforce reasonably general security conditions. Although many of these systems are interpretive with an execution penalty that is unacceptable for much production work, at least one offers fairly general and flexible security conditions with implementation by a compiler that does, in fact, utilize translation-time checking of data independent conditions. Hence, feasibility has been demonstrated, and users would require this type of capability from future data management systems.

Providing comparable security measures in a general purpose language environment is a far more difficult task. Satisfactory measures can be incorporated into the data management facilities of general operating systems; but this implies complete reliance upon run-time checking, and the execution penalty would be severe. General purpose languages such as PL/I, COBOL, and FORTRAN provide programmers with too much flexibility to permit a translator to take advantage of data independent security conditions at compilation time. Restricted versions of these languages that proscribe the constructions by which users could circumvent translation-time checks could be used, and either special security conscious compilers or preprocessors to conventional compilers could be employed.

To the extent that systems capable of realizing the efficiency of translation-time checking of security conditions become available, users, in particular those responsible for privacy decisions, should be made aware of the distinction between data-dependent and data-independent conditions. Insofar as is possible they could try to avoid specifying inherently difficult and expensive data-dependent conditions.

ACKNOWLEGMENT

The authors wish to acknowledge the extremely helpful comments of Professor Ed Sibley.

REFERENCES

1. Allen, Brandt, "Danger ahead! Safeguard your computer," Harvard Bus. Rev. (Nov.–Dec. 1968), 97–101.
2. ASAP Syst. Ref. Man., Compuvisor, Inc., 1971.
3. Baran, Paul, On distributed communications: IX. Security, secrecy, and tamper-free considerations, Doc. RM–3765–PR, Rand Corp., Santa Monica, Calif., Aug. 1964.
4. Bingham, H. W., Security techniques for EDP of multilevel classified information, Doc. RADC–TR–65–415, Rome Air Dev. Cent., Rome, N.Y., Dec. 1965 (unclassified).
5. Carroll, J. M. and McLelland, P. M., "Fast infinite key privacy transformation for resource sharing systems," Proc. AFIPS 1970 FJCC, Vol. 26, AFIPS Press, Montvale, N.J., pp. 223–230.
6. CODASYL Data Base Task Group Report, Rev. Apr. 1971 (available ACM Headquarters).
7. CODASYL Systems Committee, A survey of generalized data base management systems, May 1969 (available ACM Headquarters).
8. CODASYL Systems Committee, Feature analysis of generalized data base management systems, Rep. May 1971 (available ACM Headquarters).
9. Conway, R. W., Maxwell, W. L., and Morgan, H. L., "Selective security capabilities in ASAP—A file management system," Proc. AFIPS 1972 SJCC.
10. Conway, R. W., Morgan, H. L., Wagner, R., and Wilcox, T., User's guide to PL/C, Dept. of Comput. Sci., Cornell U., Ithica, N.Y., 1970.
11. Graham, R. M., "Protection in an information processing utility," Comm. ACM 11, 5 (May 1968), 365–369.
12. Hoffman, Lance J., "Computers and privacy: A survey," Comput. Surv. 1, 2 (June 1969), 85–103.
13. Hoffman, Lance J., The formulary model for access control and privacy in computer systems, SLAC Rep. No. 117, Stanford U., Calif., May 1970.
14. Martin, James and Norman, A., The Computerized Society, Prentice-Hall, Englewood Cliffs, N.J., 1970.
15. Miller, A. R., Assault on Privacy: Computers, Data Banks, and Dossiers, U. of Michigan Press, Ann Arbor, Mich., 1971.
16. MTS User's Guide, U. of Michigan Comput. Cent., Ann Arbor, Mich., 1970.

17. Petersen, H. E. and Turn, R., "System implications of information privacy," Proc. AFIPS 1967 SJCC, Vol. 30, AFIPS Press, Montvale, N.J., pp. 291–300.
18. Skatrud, R. O., "The applications of cryptographic techniques to data processing," Proc. AFIPS 1969 FJCC, Vol. 34, AFIPS Press, Montvale, N.J., pp. 111–117.
19. Westin, A., Privacy and Freedom, Atheneum, New York, 1967.

Privacy and Security in Databank Systems: Measures of Effectiveness, Costs, and Protector-Intruder Interactions

REIN TURN
NORMAN Z. SHAPIRO

INTRODUCTION

The nearly seven years of concern with data privacy and security in computerized information systems have produced a variety of hardware and software techniques for protecting sensitive information against unauthorized access or modification. The early analyses of potential threats and countermeasures[1] have resulted in more complete checklists and guidelines.[2,3] Several operating systems containing data security features have been written (e.g., MULTICS and ADEPT-50[4,5]) and efforts to formalize the design of secure software are accelerating.[6] Interest in the application of encryption techniques to computerized data files is, likewise, increasing.[1-3,7] However, systematic procedures for cost-effective implementation of these data security safeguards are still lacking.

The data security design and implementation process will remain more art than science until adequate theoretical foundations are laid and analytical tools developed for a "data security engineering" discipline. Needed in particular are measures for

---

SOURCE: The Rand Corporation, Report P-4871, 1972. Reprinted by permission.

evaluating the effectiveness of data security techniques in various threat and implementation environments; methods for estimating the costs of implementing the safeguards in various classes of information systems; and tradeoff relationships between these and other relevant variables. Equally important is the ability to estimate potential losses.

This paper strives to contribute to the formulation of data security engineering in the areas of personal information databank systems: a model of the personal information databank system is presented; the nature of the interactions of the databank security protector with potential intruders is explored; and the amount of security and implementation costs associated with several classes of data security techniques are discussed.

THE DATABANK SYSTEM

The term databank implies a centralized collection of data to which a number of users have access. A computerized databank system consists of the data files, the associated computer facility (processors, storage devices, terminals, communication links, programs and operating personnel), a management structure, and assorted "interested parties."

Structure

If the function of a databank system is to collect, store, retrieve, process, and disseminate personal data on individuals (or organizations), the databank system includes the following elements:

- Subject, a person or an organization about whom data are stored in the databank system. He may have provided the data voluntarily, in a quasimandatory fashion to obtain benefits or privileges, or as required by law. Data on him may also have been collected without his knowledge or consent.
- Controller, an agency or institution (public or private) with authority over the databank system and its operations. The controller authorizes the establishment of the databank system, specifies the population of subjects and type of data collected, and establishes policies for the use, dissemination, disclosure, and protection.
- Custodian, the agency and its personnel in physical possession of the data files, charged with the operation of the databank system, and responsible for enforcing the policies established by the controller.

- Collector, the agency and personnel who collect the data and transmit it to the custodian.
- User, a person or agency authorized by the controller or the custodian to utilize specified subsets of data for specified purposes, subject to the disclosure and dissemination policies of the databank system.

Other parties interested in the data and its uses include:

- Intruder, a person or agency either deliberately attempting to gain unauthorized access to the databank system or making unauthorized use of the data normally available to him as an authorized user, or accidentally doing so.
- Society, the population within which the subjects have rights and obligations, and whose welfare also affects the welfare of the subjects. Large classes of databank systems are needed to support studies of the society, and administer and assess social benefit programs.

Figure 1 illustrates the structure of a generalized databank system and displays the more prominent lines of communication between its elements. Note, however, that the elements of a databank system need not be unique. Multiple roles and overlap in functions are

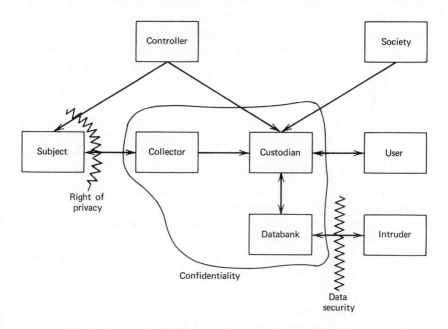

FIGURE 1.   The databank system.

common in existing databank systems. For example, the controller, custodian, and user may be the same agency or group of persons.

The role of a subject in the databank system is to provide the "raw material" (i.e., personal information about his characteristics, background, and activities) for the databank operation. The roles of the other databank system elements are to store and process these data, and to make the data available to users for making decisions affecting a specific subject, groups of subjects, or the entire society. It is also their responsibility to protect the data against misuse, intrusion and, when appropriate, the society's claim of the "right to know."

Privacy and Security

Privacy, confidentiality, and security are terms that refer to the philosophical, legal, and technical aspects of the subject's interactions with other elements of the databank system.

- Privacy is the right of an individual to determine for himself what personal information to share with others, as well as what information to receive from others.

Relevant questions for examining possible invasions of privacy by the data collection activities of a databank system include:[8] What personal information should be collected and stored to support the users of a specific databank system? To what extent should personal information from different sources be integrated to give a unified view of the individual? Who should be allowed to use the data and for what purposes?

- Due process, in the context of personal information databank systems, deals with the right of the subject to know the information stored about him in a databank system and to challenge the veracity of such information.

The relevant questions here include: Should an individual be entitled to know that information about him is being collected and stored? Should he be allowed to challenge the presence, accuracy, and completeness of this information? Westin[8] points out that answers to questions dealing with privacy and due process are political, not technical, to be worked out by balancing the value of civil liberties against the needs of the society.

- Confidentiality refers to the special status given to sensitive personal information in the databank system to minimize potential invasions of privacy. Disclosure of confidential data is restricted to users and only for purposes authorized by the controller or the subjects themselves. Confidentiality is achieved by legal and procedural means,[9-11] and by implementing techniques of data security.

- Data security refers to the protection provided to the databank system against deliberate or accidental destruction, and unauthorized access or modification, of the data. In the context of this paper, data security refers to technical and procedural means for protecting the data from intruders.

Within the databank system, the controller determines the nature of personal data to be gathered and a method of collection that satisfies the right of individuals for due process and establishes policies and procedures for data confidentiality. The collector and custodian have the responsibility to enforce the confidentiality policies and to provide procedures and technical safeguards for data security (see Figure 1).

Classification

The nature of the databank ownership, the principal use of the data, and the characteristics of the computer facilities strongly affect the complexity of the data security problem. It is useful, therefore, to establish a classification system that reflects data security requirements.

- Public-Private—Public databank systems are operated by government agencies. The controller, custodian, and users are legislative, judicial, or executive entities. Private databanks are operated by corporations or institutes within applicable laws. For example, the operation of credit information bureaus is regulated by the Fair Credit Reporting Act of 1970.
- Statistical-Dossier—Statistical databanks are operated to produce statistical summaries. Individuals are not identified in the output, but identification may be needed in the databank to permit either periodic updating of longitudinal studies or linking with other databanks. In dossier databanks, personal data are used to take action on specific individuals. Precise subject identification is important. Dossier databanks can be used for statistical purposes. The converse, however, is not necessarily true.
- Centralized-Decentralized—A centralized databank consists of one databank. In a decentralized databank, there are several

physically separated databanks, each containing a part of the overall data collection. The several databanks may or may not be connected by a communication network. For example, the U.S. Internal Revenue Service maintains a decentralized databank system of income tax information.

- Dedicated-Shared—In a dedicated databank implementation, the computer facility is used exclusively to serve the databank. In a shared system, other databanks or computer applications use the same computer facilities.

- Off-line-on-line—An on-line databank permits direct real-time interaction of a user with the data through a terminal. Access may be direct or indirect. In the latter case, a databank employee acts as an intermediary. In an off-line databank, the user is neither in control of data processing nor knows when his data request is processed.

These classifications permit ranking databank systems in order of increasing complexity of potential data security problems, ranging from the public, statistical, centralized, dedicated, off-line databank systems (e.g., the U.S. Census Bureau), which can be expected to have relatively simple data security problems, to the private, dossier, decentralized, shared, on-line databank systems (exemplified by commercial credit bureaus and the future computer utilities), where every conceivable data security problem is likely.

Threats and Countermeasures

Threats to data privacy, confidentiality, and security in a personal information databank system may arise from all elements of the databank system. For example, without the consent of the subjects, the controller may change disclosure rules; the custodian, collector, or users may disregard confidentiality procedures or use data for unauthorized purposes; the databank personnel, users, or even the subjects themselves may become intruders; and the databank equipment or programs may fail and cause accidental disclosures or data modification.

Technical means by which the intrusion may be perpetrated include deception, nullification, circumvention of existing protective features, and wiretapping of communication links. Whether or not the intrusion threats actually materialize depends on the nature of the data stored, the potential value of the data to the intruder, the risks he is willing to accept, and the resources he is willing to invest.

Countermeasures against the various threats include legal sanctions to deter confidentiality violations by the personnel and authorized users of the databank system, application of irreversible transformations on data in statistical databanks, and implementation of access control, threat monitoring, and cryptographic techniques.[1,2,7,12]

The design criteria for data security systems include effectiveness, economy, simplicity, and reliability. Although social policy may prefer protection of confidentiality at any cost, the rational approach to security system implementation is to protect only the data worth protecting. The following section outlines a model of the economic interactions of a rational protector of the databank system and a rational, profit-motivated intruder. This model can be used to discuss the design of cost-effective data security systems for various classes of databank systems.

A MODEL OF PROTECTOR-INTRUDER STRATEGIES

Consider the case where economic profit motivates an intruder to attempt penetration of a personal information databank system. In particular, assume that the intruder wants to compile a "mailing list," L, of N information items, each of which has the market value k. The total market value, V, of the list L is then

$$V = kN \tag{1}$$

To perpetrate the databank penetration, the intruder makes an investment, X. If the intruder requires a minimum profit, $rX, r > 0$, then his maximum investment to obtain the list L is

$$X = kN/(1 + r) \tag{2}$$

where it is also assumed that this intrusion is an isolated event that does not significantly benefit from previous, nor contribute to future, intrusions. The possibility of selling multiple copies of the list could be easily accommodated. The intruder's investment, X, is an expected value and should take into account the probability of failure and the risk that the databank's deterrence and retaliatory mechanisms may lead to additional costs.

To counter this intrusion threat and others, the protector of the databank system expends Y resources for data security measures. This investment should reflect the value of the protected information to the subjects, to the protector himself, and to potential intruders. Thus, prudent investment decisions of the protector would be:

- Not to commit large resources to protect information of little value to the potential intruders, even if the subjects are very strongly against the possible acquisition of this information by the intruders.
- Not to expend large resources to protect information whose release would not greatly disturb the subjects, even if the information would be valuable to the intruders.
- To commit most resources to protect information that is valuable to the intruders, and whose acquisition by the intruders would be very detrimental to the subjects.

Consider the protector-intruder interaction further. Let $I(X,Y)$ be the expected amount of information obtained by the intruder when he expends X amount of resources to overcome the Y amount invested by the protector. $I(X,Y)$ is an expected value since the probability of success for the intruder is not necessarily unity. For example, the intrusion may be thwarted because of the intruder's incomplete information about the databank's security system or even by a computer error.

As is apparent from the previous discussion of the nature of X and Y, $I(X,Y)$ is not a simple function of X and Y. However, some of its elementary properties are

- $I(0,Y) = I(X,\infty) = 0$, for $X,Y > 0$;
- $I(X,Y)$ is monotone nondecreasing in X and monotone nonincreasing in Y.

Let $f(N)$ be the value to the intruder of N units of information and $g(N)$ be the cost to the protector and subjects of the same N units of information, occurring as a result of the intruder acquiring this information. Then, for given X and Y, the expected net profit of the intruder, $v(X,Y)$, is

$$v(X,Y) = f(I(X,Y)) - X \tag{3}$$

while the net loss to the protector and subjects, $u(X,Y)$, is

$$u(X,Y) = g(I(X,Y)) + Y \tag{4}$$

Given sufficient information regarding the expenditures of the protector, Y, and the nature of the security system implemented, an intruder may vary his investment, X, to maximize the expression (3). A rational protector would utilize his estimates of the value of protected information, the technical feasibility of threats, and the likely resources of the intruders to vary his expenditures, Y, to minimize the expression (4). It follows that if f, g, and I are suitably differentiable in a region containing X and Y, the selected values of X and Y will satisfy

$$f' (I(X,Y)) \, \partial(X,Y)/\partial X = 1 \tag{5}$$

$$g' (I(X,Y)) \, \partial I(X,Y)/\partial Y = -1 \tag{6}$$

where the prime denotes differentiation.

If one or more of the functions I, f, or g are not differentiable in the region containing (X,Y), then the expressions (5) and (6) must be replaced by more complex conditions.

To use the above interaction model, analytical or empirical expressions are required for

- The value of personal information to the intruder (i.e., the function f(N)).
- The value of personal information in the databank to the protector (i.e., the loss function g(N)).
- The amount of security provided by various data security techniques (i.e., the expected expenditures, X, of intruder's resources).
- The costs of implementing the security barriers.
- The tradeoff relations between the amount of security (intruder's cost) and the protector's cost.

These items are difficult to determine and are often sensitive to the particulars of a databank security system and the information protected. There are, however, certain general features that can be discussed in qualitative terms.

VALUE OF PERSONAL INFORMATION

Securing personal information in a computerized databank system requires estimating the value of protected information to the potential intruders, the subjects of the data themselves, and the protector-custodian of the databank system. In general, this is a difficult task involving emotional as well as economic considerations. The following discussion represents only a preliminary exploration of this problem.

Value to Potential Intruders

A flourishing market for information has always existed. The value of trade secrets, marketing information, new product plans, and customer lists that are acquired by intruders in industrial espionage operations amount to millions of dollars annually.[13,14]

The value of personal information to potential intruders is more difficult to estimate. A personal information market exists for mailing lists of names and addresses of persons satisfying selected criteria. These are used mainly for mailing advertising literature or making sales calls, but they are also sought for political and even criminal purposes. The mailing list rates for advertising purposes are approximately $10 per 1000 names;[15] this price increases with sophistication of selection criteria. Currently, the sale of name and address lists compiled for public information is not illegal and is practiced at all levels of government agencies. However, Federal legislation is pending[26] to make illegal such sales without the consent of the subjects involved.

The value of information on specific individuals can be expected to vary from next to nothing to thousands of dollars, depending on the prominence of the individual, the nature of the information, and his susceptibility to blackmail, political smear, or litigation.

Given the relatively high cost of penetrating the security barriers or subverting the employees of a databank system, it is likely that intrusions involving personal information are likely to be bulk operations—large numbers of information items would be obtained per intrusion, or many intrusions would be attempted to amortize the initial expenditures.

Prime-target personal information includes information held confidential by Federal or state statutes (criminal justice, public health, psychiatric, financial status, family background, etc.). Such information could be utilized for perpetrating frauds, high pressure sales, and blackmail. Illicit "purging" of records for a fee, or planting of fabricated information, may be attempted.

Court records, statistics on fraud and blackmail, and mailing list prices may provide the initial empirical data on the value of personal information to the intruders.

Value to the Subject

The value to the subject of protecting his personal information can range from very little (for much of the population who, at most, would be annoyed by sales literature or salesmen's telephone calls), to thousands of dollars for those vulnerable to blackmail or character assassination. Indeed, the value to intruders of the latter type of information stems directly from the value that the subjects place on the same information, as evidenced by their willingness to pay.

The value of information of certain categories (e.g., family background) may be a time-varying function of contemporary mores. Empirical data on value of information can be gathered from statistics on the use of unlisted telephone numbers and the effects of fees for this service; the insurance premiums paid by municipalities, banks, credit bureaus, and other personal information handlers against "invasions of privacy" lawsuits; the willingness of individuals to accept money, and how much, in exchange for releasing personal information; and surveys of attitudes concerning privacy.[17]

Considerable collections of such statistics, and correlation with various population groups, are required to establish even first-order guidelines on estimating the value of personal information to individuals themselves.

Value to the Protector

The value of personal information in databank systems manifests itself to the protector as:

- The legal liability of the custodian to damages incurred by subjects whose data has been divulged to intruders through inadequate security measures or through personnel negligence. This reflects itself in the insurance premiums and payments for damages that the databank may have to make in addition to insurance coverage.
- The pressure on the custodian by the controller may result in firing of personnel, cuts in budget, restrictions of operations, etc. The dollar values of such losses could be estimated from analogous actions taken against agencies other than databanks.
- The cost of recreating the files in cases of data destruction.

It is apparent that the functions $f(N)$ and $g(N)$, representing the value of N items of information to the intruder, the protector and the subjects, respectively, cannot quantitatively provide for all possible situations. In a more complete protector-intruder interaction model, N would be a multidimensional vector whose components represent types of information, rather than a scalar.

AMOUNT OF SECURITY AND COSTS

The amount of security provided by a data security technique refers to effectiveness against intrusion. As suggested previously, an intruder's expected expenditure of resources in overcoming a security barrier may be a suitable measure.

Before attempting to penetrate a databank security system, an intruder must:

- Obtain sufficient information about the databank system to determine whether it contains the desired information; what data security techniques are applied; what is the probability of success; and what are the penalties for failure.
- Formulate an acceptable intrusion plan to satisfy the cost constraints, and provide acceptable probabilities for success and risk.
- Gain physical access to the databank system either directly through a terminal, communication links, computer, etc., or indirectly through an employee of the databank system.
- Penetrate into the databank; nullify or circumvent the data security techniques to gain access to the information; acquire the information for subsequent analysis; and escape detection and reactive measures sufficiently long to complete the action.

The objectives of a security system are to deter a profit-seeking intruder by raising the intrusion cost to a level that reduces his expected profits to an unacceptable level, and to prevent access by intruders not economically motivated through effective access control and threat monitoring techniques. Effective integrity management programs must be implemented to maintain personnel loyalty and reliability of equipment and software.

These three classes of data security techniques must be applied against intruders to:

- Deny information about the security system. It may not be possible, or even not desirable,[18] to maintain secrecy about the security techniques used, but the specific access codes and keys must be kept from all but a few authorized personnel.
- Prevent unauthorized access to the computer system (terminals, communication links, processor, data storage devices), the protected data files within the computer, and to specific data processing operations.
- Detect intrusion attempts; discriminate among threats; sound alarm; and take responsive action.

- Maintain integrity of the databank system by reducing opportunities for personnel subversion, increasing hardware and software reliability, and controlling any changes in software or hardware.

The Amount of Security

The burden of preventing intrusion is borne by the access control techniques. Threat monitoring is used mainly to reduce the time available for perpetrating the intrusion and for post facto investigation.

The basic elements of access control are:

- Authorization of persons to access the computer facility, terminals, data files, and processing operation.
- Identification of a person seeking access.
- Authentication of his identity and access authorization.

Not all databanks have implemented all of the above steps as part of the access procedure—in some, the mere possession of a valid password is considered sufficient.

The enforcement of access control techniques may be assigned to computer facility personnel, performed by hardware devices, or implemented in software.

To defeat an access control technique, an intruder must be able to accomplish one of the following:

- Acquire or forge the proper identification and authentication passwords or keys.
- Circumvent or disable the access control technique.

The choice depends on the technical feasibility of these approaches and, for those deemed feasible, the relative costs, risks, and required time.

Acquisition of Access Control Information. The protective capability of passwords and privacy transformation keys lies in the intruder's uncertainty regarding which of the very large number of possible passwords or keys is being used. For example, there are $26^5 \approx 1.2 \times 10^7$ possible 5-character and $26^6 \approx 3.1 \times 10^8$ possible 6-character passwords.

Nevertheless, a trial and error search for the correct password is not entirely infeasible: a minicomputer can be programmed to imitate the databank terminal's sign-on and password sending sequences. This computer can then be used to try different passwords at the rate permitted by the communication channel and the databank computer. The intruder's effort is greatly reduced if the passwords used by the databank are selected for their mnemonic capability (i.e., are similar to English words). For example, studies of 5-character alphabetic code words that were required to differ in at least two characters and contain at least two vowels show[19] that only 150,480 5-character words can be selected out of the total space of 1.2×10^7. To test all of these at the rate of 10 per second would require slightly more than 4 hours.

However, passwords could be obtained with less effort by wiretapping the communication links and recording the sign-on sequences.[20] Acquisition by wiretapping of passwords that are used once-only requires more sophisticated techniques, e.g., "piggy backing",[1] insertion of a minicomputer in the line to intercept user-computer communications, to return an error code to the user, and to enter the file with the password obtained. If passwords are generated by a pseudorandom process for once-only use, and several passwords are intercepted, certain number-theoretic techniques may be applied to discover the password generation process and its parameters.

The intruder's cost of acquiring passwords through wiretapping ranges from the cost of recording equipment—a few hundred dollars, to the cost of a minicomputer and associated programming—a few thousand dollars. The risks include the possible legal prosecution.

Cryptanalysis of Privacy Transformations. The intruder's work factor in attempting to solve for the key of a privacy transformation from intercepted, enciphered data is normally much larger than required for passwords. The key spaces are much greater, and exhaustive trial-and-error solution is infeasible. However, analysis of intercepted transformed data from the point of view of language statistics can be applied. Relevant are

- Single character frequency distribution;
- Digram (pairs of characters) and polygram frequency distributions;
- Word usage patterns;
- Syntactical rules of the language.

The two main classes of privacy transformations are substitutions of characters in the data with other characters (or groups of characters) and transportation of the order of the characters.[21-23]

The easiest to apply in a computer system are the substitution transformations:

- Monoalphabetic substitution, or the "Caesar cipher," where each character, x_i, of the data (the "plain-text") is transformed into a character, y_i, of the "ciphertext" by modulo N addition of a constant c

$$y_i = x_i + c \pmod{N}$$

where N is the size of the alphabet. The constant c has only $N - 1$ possible values and, thus, can be easily discovered.
- Polyalphabetic substitution of period u (the Vigenère cipher) consists of cyclic application of u monoalphabetic substitutions by adding modulo N the constants $c_0, c_1, \ldots, c_{u-1}$ so that

$$y_0 = x_0 + c_0$$

$$y_1 = x_1 + c_1$$

$$\pmod{N}$$

$$\ldots$$

$$y_j = x_j + c_{j \pmod{u}}$$

The key space here contains N^u possible selections of the constants $c_0, \ldots, c_{u-1}$.
- A k-loop polyalphabetic substitution uses k sets of alphabets, applied cyclically with periods $u_1, \ldots u_k$:

$$y_j = x_j + c_{1, j \pmod{u_1}} + \ldots + c_{k, j \pmod{u_k}} \pmod{N}$$

where the u_j are relatively prime (mod N)
- A Vernam cipher is a polyalphabetic substitution (Vigenère) where the key period is at least as long as the amount of data to be transformed.

Computer-aided solution of substitution transformations has been studied by Tuckerman.[24] Such solutions can always be found, provided that sufficient contiguous lengths of transformed data (ciphertext) can be acquired. If the ciphertext contains fragments of known data, even if their precise location is not known, the cryptanalysis task is greatly simplified. In the case of highly formated artificial languages (programs), where the fixed vocabulary is very small and used with rigid observance of syntax and punctuation rules, fragments of known plaintext are very likely. If the polyalphabetic cipher keys are relatively short and coherent (phrases of a natural language), the task is even further simplified.

The techniques for solving substitution-type transformations proceed as follows:[24]

- A <u>Caesar cipher</u>, where the key consists of a single constant, is easily solved by language statistics or trial and error. Shannon[21] has shown that for natural language plaintext in English, the sufficient length of a fragment of intercepted ciphertext (the unicity distance) is about 30 characters.

- A <u>1-loop polyalphabetic</u> (Vigenère) cipher of period u is reduced to u Caesar cases by statistical analyses and trial-and-error determination of the key period, u. At least 20u characters of intercepted text are required.

- A <u>2-loop polyalphabetic</u> cipher of periods u is reduced to one loop case by certain "differencing" methods.[24] Then, the 1-loop analysis can reduce the problem to Caesar cipher level. At least 100 (u + v) characters of ciphertext are required. The effort is considerably greater than for the 1-loop case.

- The Vernam cipher (where the key is as long as the data, used only once, and generated by a natural random process) cannot be solved. However, if the key is generated by a pseudo-random process, such as a shift-register sequence generator, and plaintext fragments are known, then computer-aided trial-and-error methods may lead to a solution.

The intruder's work factor in the above cryptanalytic activities requires a sufficiently powerful computer and appropriate cryptanalytic programs. Given these, solutions are sometimes found in minutes.[24] To successfully attack privacy transformed data requires an investment measured in thousands of dollars for the more complex systems. The work factor is in terms of hundreds of dollars if simple substitutions are used.

Circumventing or Disabling of Access Controls.   Circumvention of access controls enforced by databank <u>personnel</u> can be attempted by using the well-developed techniques of diversion, confusion, or intimidation. Costs are low and risks involve being "kicked out," which in turn might be good diversion for permitting an accomplice to enter. Personnel other than professional security guards are well-known for their reluctance to challenge others not known to them.

Hardware access control devices (e.g., locks operated by keys or controlled by programs) are usually effective, especially if connected to alarm systems.[25] However, some types could be easily disabled, thus reducing the enforcement to facility personnel. Assistance of unsuspecting facility employees could be recruited with the "forgot my key" gambit. Costs and risks are low.

Circumvention of <u>software</u> enforced access controls (i.e., the protective features of operating systems) requires that the intruder gain not only access to the computer through regular or illicit terminals, but also the ability to enter programs into the system. Diversion and "flooding" techniques may be able to overwhelm the threat monitoring system long enough to perpetrate the intrusion.[6] The resources required by the intruder include a computer to develop and test the intrusion plan and programs. The risk is low. However, the operating systems designed for high security[3,4] may escalate the intrusion costs into the thousands or even ten thousands of dollars.

Protection Costs

The costs involved in implementing a data security system include the initial planning and design, initial investment in hardware devices and software, the recurring operating costs, and the decreases in functional capability. The available cost data are very limited and do not suffice for formulating analytic expressions for the protector-intruder interaction model described above.

Hardware access devices, such as card-key locks for doors or computer terminals, are priced in the $150–300 range per unit. Complete systems start from $5000. Hardware-implemented data privacy systems for communication links cost in the $2000 range per unit.

Data on software implementation of access controls in operating systems are equally scarce. The following represents almost the entire cost data base:[3,5]

Main memory requirements:	10–20%
Programming time:	5%
Operating system code:	10%
Recurrent CPU time:	5–10%

Some cost data points are also available for the implementation of privacy transformations in software. In substitution type privacy transformations, each character of plaintext is transformed into a character of the ciphertext by addition of one or more constants, c_j. Also required are similar decoding and the necessary key-retrieval operations. In terms of the percent of the databank operating system overhead, the following computing time requirements have been established for applying privacy transformations to 10-bit characters in a CDC 6600 computer:[7]

One-time Vernam ciphering:	0.66%
Vigenère ciphering (table look-up)	3.5%
Vigenère (modulo arithmetic)	6.3%

The above cost figures are quite sensitive to the type of information retrieval system used and represent only isolated cost data points. Estimates of decreased functional capability of the databank system caused by security requirements are even less available. A systematic effort to compile a comprehensive data base of security system costs and decreases in functional capability is clearly needed.

CONCLUDING REMARKS

The design of cost-effective data security safeguards for personal information databank systems requires a careful balancing of the value of protected information against the protection costs. In particular, it is important to consider not only the value of personal information to the subjects, but also to the potential intruders, i.e., the protection investments should be made on a rational basis.

The simple protector-intruder interaction model discussed in this paper illuminates the nature of the protector's investment problems when faced with an equally rational intruder. However, before this or any other interaction model can be fully utilized, it is necessary to formulate appropriate analytical or empirical relationships among the value of information to the parties involved, the costs of protection and intrusion, and the effectiveness of data security and intrusion techniques. Deriving such relationships and gathering empirical data will be a major objective of the authors' further work in this area.

ACKNOWLEDGMENTS

The authors would like to acknowledge valuable suggestions and comments by their colleagues at The Rand Corporation, Mario L. Juncosa, Irving S. Reed, and Selmer M. Johnson, and by Robert H. Courtney of the IBM Corporation.

REFERENCES

1. Petersen, H. E. and R. Turn, "System Implications of Information Privacy," AFIPS Conference Proceedings, Vol. 30, 1967 Spring Joint Computer Conference, Thompson Book Co., New York, pp. 291–300.
2. Brown, William F. (Ed.), AMR's Guide to Computer and Software Security, AMR International Inc., New York, 1971.
3. Van Tassel, D., Computer Security Management, Prentice-Hall, Inc., Englewood Cliffs, N.J., 1972.
4. Weissman, Clark, "Security Controls in the ADEPT-50 Time-Sharing System," AFIPS Conference Proceedings, Vol. 35, 1969 Fall Joint Computer Conference, AFIPS Press, Montvale, N.J., pp. 119–133.
5. Weissman, Clark, Trade-Off Considerations in Security System Design, Systems Development Corporation, SP–3548, September 10, 1970.
6. Graham, G. S. and P. J. Denning, "Protection—Principles and Practice," AFIPS Conference Proceedings, Vol. 40, 1972 Fall Joint Computer Conference, AFIPS Press, Montvale, N.J., pp. 417–429.
7. Garrison, William A. and C. V. Ramamoorthy, Privacy and Security in Data Banks, Technical Memorandum No. 24, Electronics Research Center, University of Texas, Austin, Texas, November 2, 1970.
8. Westin, Alan F., "Civil Liberties and Computerized Data Systems," in M. Greenberger (Ed.), Computers, Communications and Public Interest, Johns Hopkins Press, Baltimore, Md., 1970.
9. Westin, Alan F., Privacy and Freedom, Atheneum, New York, 1967.
10. Miller, Arthur R., Assault on Privacy: Computer Data Banks and Dossiers, University of Michigan Press, 1971.
11. Nejelsky, Paul and L. M. Lerman, "A Researcher-Subject Testimonial Privilege: What to Do Before the Subpoena Arrives," Wisconsin Law Review, Vol. 1971, No. 4, pp. 1085–1148.
12. Turn, R. and H. E. Petersen, "Security of Computerized Information Systems," Proceedings of Carnahan Conference on Electronic Crime Countermeasures, University of Kentucky, Lexington, Kentucky, 1970, pp. 82–88.
13. Donovan, Robert, "Trade Secrets," Security World, April 1967, pp. 12–18.
14. Hicksom, Philip, Industrial Espionage, Spectator Publications, Ltd., London, 1968.

15. "Firms Sue in Mailing List Theft," Computerworld, July 8, 1970.
16. "Security Breach Leads to Police Data Theft," Computerworld, February 10, 1971.
17. A National Survey of the Public's Attitudes Toward Computers, AFIPS-TIME Magazine, TIME Inc., New York & Montvale, N.J., November 1971.
18. Baran, Paul, On Distributed Communications: IX, Security, Secrecy and Tamper-Free Considerations, The Rand Corporation, RM-3765-PR, August 1964.
19. Friedman, W. F., and C. J. Mendelsohn, "Notes on Code Words," American Mathematical Monthly, August 1932, pp. 394–409.
20. Carroll, John M., The Third Listener, Dutton, 1969.
21. Shannon, C. E., "Communication Theory of Secrecy Systems," Bell System Technical Journal, 1949, pp. 656–715.
22. Kahn, David, The Codebreakers, The MacMillan Co., New York 1967.
23. Girdansky, M. B., "Cryptology, The Computer and Data Privacy," Computers and Automation, April 1972, pp. 12–19.
24. Tuckerman, Bryant, A Study of the Vigenère-Vernam Single and Multiple Loop Enciphering Systems, IBM Corporation, RC 2879, May 14, 1970.
25. Healy, R. J., Design for Security, John Wiley & Sons, Inc., New York, 1968.
26. U.S. Senate Bill S.969, U.S. Senate, 25 February 1971.

Section V
"STATISTICAL"
DATA BANKS

The first paper in this section points out the fallacy of the distinction some people have tried to make between "dossier" or "intelligence" data banks and "statistical" data banks. W. F. Miller and the editor there illustrate that it is possible to obtain a personal dossier from a so-called "statistical" data bank. They present an algorithm which, with enough work and sufficient additional information, can be used to identify individuals in such a data bank even if specific identifying information (such as name) is never stored in the data bank. For example, the editor could probably be identified using only his "characteristics" if there was a data bank on the 17 million students, faculty, and staff in colleges and universities in the United States. He would probably be the only person in that data bank whose undergraduate institution was Carnegie-Mellon University, graduate institution was Stanford, field was computer science, and current institution is Berkeley. After this article appeared in Datamation, readers wrote in with several other suggestions for protection of privacy in statistical data banks, among them random "inoculation" of the numbers returned so that they may no longer be entirely correct but will be good enough for legitimate statistical use.

A much more detailed mathematical treatment of statistical inference problems is available in a paper by I. P. Fellegi [16]. This article covers other relevant issues of residual disclosure including "inoculation" and should certainly be examined by all statisticians interested in the problem of protecting privacy while publishing aggregate data. We considered it too theoretical to include in this collection, however.

An example of the measures a "statistical" data bank takes to enhance confidentiality of research data is given in the paper by Astin and Boruch. This particular system has an interesting history. The system came into being shortly after the American Council on Education (ACE) came under attack from the Students for a Democratic Society (SDS) for collecting personal data while not (in SDS' opinion) taking adequate security measures to protect its confidentiality. In short, SDS did not believe ACE's claim that the data was to be used strictly for research, was going to be kept confidential, and would not be turned over to government agencies. SDS mounted a campaign on certain college campuses to encourage students not to fill out the questionnaire which ACE administers each fall to incoming freshman classes. While this campaign failed on most target campuses, it succeeded at some, and has encouraged ACE to implement this reasonable scheme for protecting confidentiality in a so-called "statistical" data bank.

Getting a Personal Dossier from a Statistical Data Bank

LANCE J. HOFFMAN
W. F. MILLER

With enough work it is possible to obtain a personal dossier from a statistical data bank. A privacy safeguard sometimes proposed[1] is the restriction on the access procedures to permit read-out of only statistical summaries. (In the extreme one could remove from the file such identifying information as name, address, Social Security number, etc.). Data banks which return only summary tables of numbers of persons with given characteristics such as age, education level, etc., are referred to as "statistical" data banks. Data banks which return an individual's identifying information are referred to as "dossier" data banks. It has been pointed out that this distinction is largely illusory.[2] We present here an algorithm which, with enough work and sufficient additional information, can be used to identify individuals in a statistical data bank. We propose "threat monitoring"[3] as a procedure which, while not foolproof, gives substantial additional protection of privacy in statistical data banks.

DEDUCING A SALARY RANGE

Suppose that we wish to determine whether John Doe earns over $50,000 per year and we know that his data is stored in a statistical data bank. Suppose also that we already know that he is a 39-year-old lawyer with an LLB degree, has four children, has been married twice, and lives in New York City. When we ask our data bank the question, "How many people are in the data bank with the following properties:

age 39
education level is LLB
male
has 4 children
lives in New York City
profession is lawyer
has been married twice?"

let us say that we get back the answer "57 people." If we then ask, "How many people are in the data bank with the following properties:

age 39
education level is LLB
male
has 4 children
lives in New York City
profession is lawyer
has been married twice
salary exceeds $50,000 per year?"

and the data bank returns "57 people" again, we have discovered from our "statistical" data bank the "intelligence" that John Doe's salary exceeds $50,000 per year. We have obtained information on a specific individual even though the query algorithm we used returned only counts of instances, and did not return names. We would have been able to do this even if specific identifying information such as name has not been stored in the data bank.

Suppose we know that data on Richard Roe is contained in a statistical data bank. Let us take some nonsensitive information we know about Richard and use it to form a question for our data bank system. "How many people are in the data bank with the following properties:

age 39
education level is LLB
male
has 4 children
lives in New York City

profession is lawyer
has been married twice
received MS degree from MIT in 1950
graduated from Harvard in 1948?"

If the answer is "1 person," we've hit the jackpot! For we can now extract all the information about Richard Roe in the data bank by simply adding more conditions, one by one, to our question. For example: "How many people are in the data bank with the following properties:

age 39
education level is LLB
male
has 4 children
lives in New York City
profession is lawyer
has been married twice
received MS degree from MIT in 1950
graduated from Harvard in 1948
has been convicted of a felony?"

If the answer to this question is "1 person," then Richard Roe has been convicted of a felony; if it is "0 people," he has not. Again, we have obtained personal information from a "statistical" data bank which does not return names or other identifying information directly.

THE GENERAL ALGORITHM

We now present the general algorithm for compiling a dossier from a "statistical" data bank. First, let us state our assumptions:

1. We assume that the data bank query algorithm will return to the inquirer $\#(P_i)$, the number of instances (people) with given property P_i, but it will not return the names or other identifying information about the people included in this count. That is, the algorithm permits one to get aggregate data in the form of the count of the number of instances of a certain type, but it does not return anything other than the count.

2. The query algorithm will permit requests not only for a count of the instances of a given property, but also for a count of the instances of a conjunction of properties. For

example, one might ask for the number of people with property P_1 (age greater than 30) and property P_2 (female) and property P_3 (not living in New York City), i.e., $\#(P_1 \& P_2 \& P_3)$.

Now if we denote the number of people with properties P_1, P_2, ..., P_m in common by $\#(P_1 \& P_2 \& \ldots P_m)$, the following algorithm determines whether a person (called Mr. X) has property P_0 (given that we a priori know a number of his other properties P_1, P_2, ..., P_N): Use the search algorithm to determine whether $\#(P_1 \& P_2 \& \ldots P_N) = 1$. If so, then if $\#(P_1 \& P_2 \& \ldots P_N \& P_0) = 1$, Mr. X has property P_0. Otherwise Mr. X does not have property P_0. (We used this method to determine that Richard Roe had been convicted of a felony.)

The scheme will fail if we do not know enough about Mr. X to identify him through his properties P_1, P_2, ..., P_N, i.e., if $\#(P_1 \& P_2 \& \ldots P_N) > 1$.

There is a variation of this scheme, which we used to deduce John Doe's salary range. Suppose we know that Mr. X is included in the count of people who have properties $P_1, P_2, P_3, \ldots, P_N$ in common. If the count of people with properties $P_1, P_2, P_3, \ldots, P_N, P_0$ in common is the same, i.e., if $\#(P_1 \& P_2 \& P_3 \& \ldots \& P_N) = \#(P_1 \& P_2 \& P_3 \& \ldots \& P_N \& P_0)$, then we know that Mr. X has property P_0. For this variation of the scheme to work in practice, the count will have to be small in order that one can expect all members in the count to also have P_0. If

$$\#(P_1 \& P_2 \& \ldots \& P_N) \neq \#(P_1 \& P_2 \& \ldots \& P_N \& P_0)$$

we cannot determine whether Mr. X has property P_0 unless we have the earlier case where

$$\#(P_1 \& P_2 \& \ldots P_N) = 1$$

The problem we are illustrating is well-known to census bureaus and other agencies charged with publishing statistical summaries and at the same time protecting the privacy of individuals. Their policy is to avoid publishing summaries with small counts which might permit identification.

One way of protecting against the type of search we have illustrated is to use threat monitoring. Threat monitoring control programs monitor all requests to the system and keep audit trails. It can be used to detect excessively active periods of use of the data base, too many successive questions which are quite similar or which result in small counts as answers (therefore raising the possibility that a dossier extraction, such as in the examples above, is being carried out), etc. Even with threat monitoring, if the extraction procedure is concealed among legitimate request traffic, it will be quite hard to detect. This should serve to remind the proponents and builders of "statistical" data banks to very seriously consider the problems of privacy. Only a few[4] have really taken advantage of various methods of access control developed to date.[5-7]

REFERENCES

1. Dunn, E. S., Jr. Statement in [8], pp. 92-95.
2. Baran, P. Statement in [8], pp. 119-135.
3. Petersen, H. E., and Turn, R. System implications of information privacy, Proc. AFIPS, 1967 Spring Joint Comput. Conf., Vol. 30, Thompson Book Co., Washington, D.C., pp. 291-300. (Also available as Doc. P-3504, RAND Corp., Santa Monica, Calif. April 1967.)
4. Hanlon, Joseph. Precautions Preclude Misuse of Student Data. Computerworld, 4 March 1970.
5. Hoffman, Lance J. Computers and Privacy: A Survey. Computing Surveys 1, 2 (June 1969), 85-103.
6. Weissman, Clark. Security Controls in the ADEPT-50 Time-Sharing System. Proc. AFIPS 1969 Fall Joint Computer Conference, 119-133.
7. Hoffman, Lance J. The formulary model for Access Control and Privacy in Computer Systems. Ph.D. Dissertation, Stanford University, Stanford, Calif., 1970.
8. U.S. Congress. The computer and the invasion of privacy—hearings before a subcommittee of the Committee on Government Operations, House of Representatives, 89th Congress, Second Session (Gallagher Report), U.S. Government Printing Office, Washington, D.C., 26-28 July 1966.

A "Link" System for Assuring Confidentiality of Research Data in Longitudinal Studies

ALEXANDER W. ASTIN
ROBERT F. BORUCH

Behavioral scientists have long recognized the importance of longitudinal research data in studies of human growth and development. A major logistical problem in such studies, however, is that the research subjects must be identified in some manner so that they may be resurveyed periodically. Although most researchers are aware that possessing identifying information imposes on them certain obligations to protect the anonymity of their subjects (Privacy and Behavioral Research, 1967), few attempts have been made to develop improved techniques for insuring data security and respondent anonymity. That such efforts are sorely needed is evident from massive anecdotal evidence (e.g., Westin, 1967), and from empirical and systematic studies (e.g., Nugent, 1969; Boruch, 1969).

The purpose of this article is to describe a system for protecting the anonymity of subjects in longitudinal research and for maintaining the security of data files. The system has been developed in connection with the Cooperative Institutional Research Program of the American Council on Education. However, we believe that its basic design is applicable, perhaps with only minor variations, to longitudinal research in education

SOURCE: American Council on Education Research Report, Vol. 5, No. 3 (February 1970). Reprinted by permission of American Council on Education. Also published in the American Educational Research Journal, Vol. 7, No. 4, November 1970, pp. 615-624. © 1970 A.E.R.A.

and other fields. One of our major goals in bringing this system to the attention of the community of researchers is to encourage the development and use of similar systems by others who engage in longitudinal studies.

THE ACE COOPERATIVE INSTITUTIONAL RESEARCH PROGRAM

The Cooperative Institutional Research Program is a continuing longitudinal study of students attending a national sample of colleges and universities. The principal purpose of this program of research is to determine how students are affected by different types of college environments. Briefly, the design of the study involves an analysis of differential changes in the interests, achievements, values, and behaviors of students in different types of colleges.

Initial input or "pretest" data are obtained by means of a 150-item questionnaire completed by the incoming freshman during his period of orientation or registration at the college. Output or "posttest" data are obtained through followup questionnaires mailed to the student's home (the student is asked to provide his home address on the initial freshman questionnaire). These followup data are merged with the pretest data to create the longitudinal file which provides the major empirical resource for the research. The current plan for the research program calls for followups after one year, after four years, and at (as yet undetermined) points thereafter. Since new pretest data are obtained from each successive class of entering freshmen, the number of longitudinal research files increases each year. The current files now include pretest data from more than a million students comprising the entering classes of 1966, 1967, 1968, and 1969 at some 300 institutions. Longitudinal followup data have already been collected from approximately 250,000 of these students (in order to reduce costs, subsamples of students, rather than all of the entering freshmen, are selected for followup at the larger institutions).

When the research program was initiated in 1965 with a pilot study of some 42,000 freshmen at 61 institutions, a more-or-less traditional system of protecting the confidentiality of the data was instituted. The students' responses to the freshman questionnaire were keypunched and converted to magnetic tape. The original questionnaires and punched cards were then destroyed. Following a practice which has frequently been recommended for maintaining longitudinal data files (Dunn, 1967), we created two physically separate tape files. The first file contained the student's answers to the research questions, together with an arbitrary identification number. The second file contained only the student's name and address and the same arbitrary number. Whereas the research data file was openly accessible to members of the ACE Research staff for use in research studies, the name and address file was kept locked in a vault and removed only temporarily when it was necessary to print address labels for followup mailings. Even on these latter occasions, however, the name-and-address file could be released only for brief periods and only upon written authorization of the ACE Director of Research. Furthermore, the file could not be copied or removed from the data processing center during these periods of temporary release without explicit instructions to this effect from the Director of Research. The formal regulations employed by the data processing center where the name-and-address file was maintained were identical to those outlined in the Department of Defense's Industrial Security Manual (1966).

Some additional security was introduced into the system in 1966, when student questionnaires that could be optically scanned (rather than keypunched) were used. The use of optical scanning eliminates the need for the extensive perusal and handling of documents that is necessitated by keypunching, and minimizes the possibility of improper disclosure of information to data-handling personnel.

It was our impression that this original system offered as much protection as (and, in most cases, more than) other social science research projects against accidental or deliberate extralegal exploitation of data. We were still concerned, however, that the system did not offer complete protection for the subject against two potential threats to the confidentiality of the data: (1) subpoena by judicial or legislative agencies; and (2) unauthorized disclosure or "snooping" by research staff members who had access to both files.

DEVELOPMENT OF THE "LINK" SYSTEM

The "Link" system of protecting the research data files involves a major elaboration of the original two-file system described above. Debugging of this new system was begun early in 1969, and the system was made fully operational in fall of 1969. Briefly, what we did was to remove the identification numbers from the name-and-address files, and substitute a second, unrelated set of identification numbers. At the same time, we created a third file—the "Link" file—which contained only the two sets of numbers: the original numbers from the research data file, and the new numbers from the name-and-address file (note that this Link file represents the only means of linking the subject's identity with his answers to the questions). The final step in establishing the new system was to deposit the Link file at a computer facility located in a <u>foreign country</u>. No copies of the file are kept at ACE or at any other place within the United States.

The nature of the agreement with the foreign computer facility is such that they will neither copy the file nor make it available to outside persons, including research personnel of the American Council on Education. The foreign facility is bound to this agreement even in the event that the American Council on Education should subsequently request that the file be returned. In other words, a basic condition of the agreement is that the foreign facility is under no circumstances to release this Link file to other individuals or organizations. Thus, <u>both</u> ACE and the foreign agency must violate the agreement before research data can ever again be matched directly with identifying data.

Storing the Link file in a foreign country provides two important protections for the data. One such protection concerns Congressional or judicial subpoena of the files. Since judicial or legislative subpoenas have no validity outside the United States, it would be impossible for Congressional committees or courts to obtain access to information on individual subjects. Thus, even if courts or committees could obtain both the data file and the name-and-address file, there would be no way for them to link up records in one file with records in the other without the Link file. The possibility of using the data files for extralegal harassment of individuals is virtually eliminated also.

A second, perhaps more basic, form of protection concerns possible "snooping" by members of the Research staff. Traditionally, researchers have persuaded subjects to provide them with data under conditions where the guarantee of anonymity is primarily a matter of the researcher's ethics and goodwill. Thus, the possibility of prying or snooping by individual researchers who had access to these "confidential" data almost always existed. The Link system, however, provides protection against even this eventuality. It should be noted that the principle of the Link system does not necessarily involve using a foreign country in order to protect against unwarranted disclosure by individual researchers: The agreement could as well be between two agencies within the United States. Use of a foreign country, however, does afford the additional protection against subpoena.

Figure 1 shows schematically how the Link system treats questionnaire data provided by freshmen when they first enter college. Questionnaires are first converted to magnetic tape images by means of an optical mark reader. As soon as this conversion has been completed, the questionnaires are destroyed. This conversion process creates three independent files. The first one, shown on the left of Figure 1, contains all of the questionnaire responses provided by the students, in addition to an arbitrary identification number. The second tape file, shown on the far right of Figure 1, contains only the student's name and address, together with a second arbitrary identification number. The Link file shown in the middle contains no data, no name and address, and only the two sets of numbers.

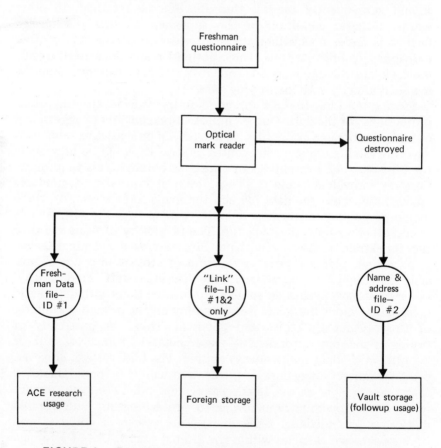

FIGURE 1. Procedures for handling freshman questionnaire (pretest) data.

This file is stored at a data processing facility in a foreign country. The freshman data file and the name-and-address file are kept at the ACE's Data Processing Center. The name-and-address file, however, is kept locked in a vault and released only long enough to print name and address labels for mailed followups. These followups typically occur during the summer following the student's freshman year, and at the end of his senior year in college. The freshman data file is the only file actually used in research.

The procedures for collecting followup data are diagrammed in Figure 2. The name-and-address file is released long enough to print name-and-address labels, after which it is replaced in the vault.

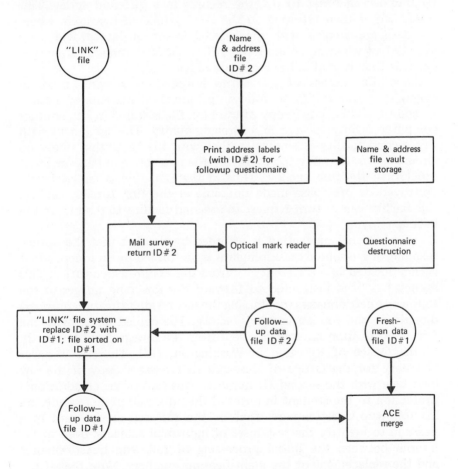

FIGURE 2.   Procedures for conducting followup (posttest) studies.

The labels (which also contain the ID numbers) are applied to the followup questionnaires, which are in turn mailed to the student's home. As soon as the completed questionnaire is returned, it is converted to magnetic tape directly by means of the optical mark reader, after which it is destroyed. Note that, unlike the processing of the freshman questionnaire, no name-and-address file is created; the only information converted to magnetic tape from the followup questionnaire is the student's responses and his ID number. This magnetic tape file is in turn sent to the data processing facility in the foreign country, where it is copied, with the second ID number being replaced by the first. This new file is then sorted on the first ID number, in order to put the records in a different order. This sorted file is then returned to the ACE Office of Research, where the data are merged with the original freshman data provided by the student when he entered college for the first time. This merged data file then is used in the longitudinal research.

Since the success of the entire longitudinal research program depends on our ability to follow up individual students over time, an additional "backup" copy of the Link file is stored in still another computer facility located in a foreign country. The agreement with this second facility is similar to that with the first: that under no circumstances are they to return the file to us or to outside facilities other than the first agency. Thus, if the Link file is inadvertently destroyed or otherwise made unusable at the first foreign facility, this facility can in turn request the second facility to send them the backup copy.

An additional protection is afforded by the fact that the optical scanning of the source questionnaires is performed by an independent agency located in a different city from the ACE research office. This agency has been instructed to forward the raw tape images of the followup questionnaires (containing the second identification number) directly to the foreign country facility. The copied tapes (with the first identification number) are sent from the foreign facility directly to the Office of Research in Washington, D.C. Thus, it is never necessary for the Office of Research to possess a copy of the raw data tape with the second ID number. This fact offers an additional protection to the student in terms of the information he provides on his followup questionnaire; that is, the research staff is not in a position to identify the responses of individual subjects, even in the interim between the initial processing of followup questionnaires and the replacement of the identification numbers. Note that if the document-to-tape processing were done by the Office of Research, it would be possible to identify the responses of individual subjects by linking the name-and-address file with the initial followup file.

An interesting elaboration of this system is that respective educational research agencies located in different countries can provide such linking services reciprocally. Thus, currently under consideration with one foreign data processing facility is the possibility of an exchange agreement whereby the ACE Office of Research will maintain a link file for the foreign facility and provide similar linking services. Although identification of these specific foreign facilities would not seriously jeopardize the security provided by the Link model, we believe that keeping such foreign facilities anonymous provides some additional protection, particularly against possible theft of the Link file.

Although the Link system may appear at first to be extreme and perhaps unnecessarily expensive and time-consuming, it is no doubt much more economical than most hardware-software computer systems that have been proposed to achieve file security (Weissman, 1967).

The system is consistent with some legal prescriptions for secure data files insofar as it constitutes a set of "mutually insulated data banks" (Schwartz and Orleans, 1967) whose function is to minimize the possibility of disclosure of personal information. To the extent that communications between one data file and another is limited to a code medium, uninterpretable by the agency handling the data, the recommendations of many experts concerning data bank exploitation are also met (e.g., Sawyer and Schecter, 1969; Davidson, 1969).

There are, of course, many alternative models which could be proposed for maintaining confidentiality as a substitute for or as an augmentation of the strategy proposed in this paper. One such device is specific legislation to provide "privileged" status for social science research data. Legal protection for researchers is unlikely to be adequate by itself, however, since it would not provide the subject with the same kind of protection against the researcher's violation of confidentiality that the Link system does. Misuse of information caused by accidental leakage or by deliberate extralegal exploitation (e.g., commercial usage) is rather difficult to control without well-specified administrative procedures to strengthen the enforceability of legal requirements (Fanwick, 1967; Banshaf, 1968).

Legislation to protect the respondent and researcher may not be feasible or may be slow in enactment. A possible alternative strategy would involve the cooperation of a public agency such as the Census Bureau. Insofar as such an agency can provide Link file services, under legal protection, then the logistical problems associated with the use of foreign facilities can be eliminated. This alternative appears to be a reasonable augmentation of current government concern with protection of research subjects in federally subsidized research projects (U.S. Department of Health, Education and Welfare, 1969).

CONSEQUENCES OF ADOPTING A LINK FILE SYSTEM

The implementation of a system for maintaining the security of data and anonymity of respondents has some important social and legal implications.

One of the major problems confronting the researcher who undertakes any large-scale project is the reluctance of subjects to participate out of a concern that their responses will not remain confidential. These concerns are exacerbated by talk of computerized "dossiers," "national data banks," "invasion of privacy," and the like. The problem here for the researcher is to make it clear to the subject that identifying information is needed not for administrative purposes, but only for updating the file. It seems likely that public understanding of the distinctions among intelligence systems, administrative records, and survey research data would be clarified if the basic concept of the Link system could be adequately communicated. Perhaps the most important educational feature of the system is that it points up the use of identifying information as an accounting device for updating social science research records rather than as a mechanism for evaluating individuals (Astin, 1968).

The effects on research of knowledge of the Link system are testable. Experiments could be designed, for example, to assess the impact of such a system on survey respondents. Any effect could be assessed from differences in response rates or from the precision or accuracy of responses when one survey subsample is provided with information about the Link system and another is not.

For the researcher, adoption of a Link system or similar operation requires some technical understanding as well as additional time and finances for its development and maintenance. Budget allocations for this purpose subtract from the funds available to support the actual research or analysis. On the positive side, the system does provide a significant increment to the level of protection now afforded most respondents. Any individual researcher must, of course, weigh his concern with maintaining reasonably secure data files against the magnitude of the effort and expense required to implement a Link system or some similar system. Although balancing these objectives may be a difficult task, we feel strongly that the degree of importance of the problem makes the effort worthwhile.

REFERENCES

Astin, A. W. "Why we need your number," Paper presented at the Annual Meeting of the American Personnel and Guidance Association, Detroit, 1968.

Banshaf, J. F. "When your computer needs a Lawyer," Communications of the ACM, Vol. 2, No. 8, August, 1968.

Boruch, R. F. "Educational research and the confidentiality of data," ACE Research Reports, Vol. 4, No. 4, 1969.

Davidson, T. A. "Computer information privacy," The Office, Vol. 70, No. 2, 1969, pp. 10–17.

Department of Defense. Industrial Security Manual for Safeguarding Classified Information. DOD 5220, 22-M. Washington, D.C.: Department of Defense, July 1, 1966.

Dunn, E. S. "The idea of a national data center and the issue of personal privacy," The American Statistician, Vol. 21, No. 1, February, 1967, pp. 21–27.

Fanwick, Charles. "Computer safeguards: how safe are they?" SDC Magazine, Vol. 10, 1967, pp. 26–28.

Nugent, F. A. "Confidentiality in college counseling centers," Personnel and Guidance Journal, May, 1969, pp. 872–877.

Privacy and Behavioral Research. Report prepared for Executive Office of the President, Office of Science and Technology. Washington, D.C.: U.S. Government Printing Office, February, 1967.

Sawyer, Jack, and Schechter, Howard. "Computers, privacy, and the national data center: the responsibility of social scientists," American Psychologist, Vol. 23, No. 11, November, 1968.

Swartz, R. D., and Orleans, S. "On legal sanctions," University of Chicago Law Review, Vol. 34, 1967, pp. 274–300.

U.S. Department of Health, Education and Welfare. Public Health Service, Protection of the Individual as a Research Subject— Grants, Awards, Contracts, Washington, D.C.: U.S. Government Printing Office, May, 1969.

Weissman, Clark, "Programming protection: what do you want to pay?" SDC Magazine, Vol. 10, No. 7, July, 1967, pp. 30–31.

Westin, A. F. Privacy and Freedom, New York: Atheneum, 1967.

REFERENCES

Section VI

IS THERE HOPE
IN HARDWARE?

Most hardware safeguards are not standard equipment which a customer can buy off-the-shelf. They are sometimes obtainable from the computer manufacturer upon special request at additional cost. Some "standard" hardware features which enhance security and which are available on an increasing proportion of machines are privileged instructions, memory protection safeguards (such as bounds registers) and program-readable clocking hardware to record action by date and time. Others which are less common include built-in computer identification codes (such as on the IBM System/370 computers) and the assurance of a known response to all possible operation codes.

The paper by Schroeder and Saltzer in this section describes a hardware architecture for implementing what have come to be known as Graham's rings. The original idea of concentric rings for protection is given in Graham's paper; essentially, each segment in the file system is assigned to one and only one ring. The lower the ring number a procedure is executing in, the greater its access privileges. Segment descriptors and location counters are modified to contain ring numbers. The implementation ideas, based on five years of experience, are given in the paper by Schroeder and Saltzer. At this writing, the hardware implementation had not been completed, although three rings of protection have been demonstrated in software at M.I.T.

Molho's paper is included to demonstrate the hardware vulnerability of a typical commercially available system—the IBM 360/50. In a recent study he carried out, over 100 faults were found that would compromise its security without giving an alarm. After discussing the types of fault which occur Molho suggests some interesting alternatives, such as microprogrammed tests, to combat problems of hardware failure. His paper examines a few scenarios for subversion and discusses why, while protection against hardware subversion is not impossible, it is certainly not trivial.

Protection in an Information Processing Utility

ROBERT M. GRAHAM

INTRODUCTION

In this paper a solution to some of the problems concerned with protection and security in an information processing utility are defined and discussed. An exhaustive study of all aspects of protection in such a system is not intended; instead, attention is concentrated on the problems of protecting both user and system information (procedures and data) during the execution of a process. Special attention is given to this problem when shared procedures and data are permitted.

A résumé of those properties of an information processing utility which make protection necessary and nontrivial to implement is given first. Then, after a discussion of the desirability of and necessity for protection, a number of properties believed to be essential to any satisfactory protection scheme are defined. An abstract model of the typical hardware used today for an information processing utility is described and this model is augmented with an additional feature necessary for a satisfactory solution to the protection problem. Also the properties required of the companion software for this model are described. Lastly, special emphasis is given to certain additional complexities forced into the implementation of this protection scheme due to permitting shared information and a multiprocessor system.

SOURCE: Copyright © 1968, Association for Computing Machinery, Inc. R. Graham, Communications of the ACM, Vol. 11, No. 5, 365–369. (May 1968). Reprinted by permission of the Association for Computing Machinery.

THE ENVIRONMENT

The characteristics and properties of an information processing utility have been described in considerable detail elsewhere, the most comprehensive being Corbato and Vyssotsky [1]. We will touch only on those properties which are pertinent to the problems of protection during execution. An information processing utility (IPU) will have a large community of users, many of whom are using the system simultaneously. The system will, of course, operate in a multiprogramming mode and have more than one central processor.

The community of users will certainly have diverse interests; in fact, it will probably include users who are competitive commercially. The system will be used for many applications where sensitive data, such as company payroll records, will need to be stored in the system. On the other hand, there will be users in the community who wish to share with each other data and procedures. There will even be groups of users working cooperatively on the same project. Service bureaus, software producing companies, and other service organizations will have procedures which they wish to rent. Some groups may rent access to data bases. Finally, there will be public libraries of procedures supplied by the information processing utility management. Indeed, a primary goal of such a system is to provide a number of different users with flexible, but controlled, access to shared data and procedures.

WHY PROTECTION?

Although protection is not necessary for privacy reasons in the case of a single user with his own private machine, it is certainly desirable. Protection in this situation aids debugging by limiting the propagation of errors, thus localizing the source of the original error. Even in fully debugged programs protection minimizes the effects of a human mishap or a machine malfunction.

As soon as the machine is shared, even if only one user at a time uses the system, protection is required so that the management may guarantee the highest possible reliability of operations as well as equity in charges to the users. For example, even the simplest multiuser system contains at least one data base which is shared by all users, namely the supervisor program itself. In addition, most systems contain information maintained by the supervisor regarding the allocation of resources and a record of resource usage for the purpose of charging users. Even though this data base may be used only via the supervisor, it is nevertheless shared by all users and so must be protected.

Without adequate protection, a dishonest user might alter the accounting procedures or data, thereby causing inequitable charges. A malicious user might even alter the system itself, causing it to act in an unreliable or destructive fashion. As soon as more than one user may have information stored in the system at the same time, as in an information processing utility where the users store many files of information within the system for long periods of time, a user's privacy must be assured by the system and protection becomes even more critical. Without adequate protection in an IPU, a clever user, perhaps due to a single break or loophole in the privacy machinery, may be able to snoop in a competitor's data files and obtain information which gives him some material advantage. Such snooping would be difficult, if not impossible, to detect.

PROPERTIES OF A SATISFACTORY PROTECTION MECHANISM

Excluding the running of all programs interpretively, any effective protection scheme must have some hardware assistance. In the past, the common hardware features for protection have been a mode switch for instruction execution and a memory-bounds register. The mode switch specifies one of two modes of execution: master or slave. In master mode any instruction may be executed, including a subset of the instructions called the privileged instructions. In slave mode an attempt to execute a privileged instruction causes a fault. The privileged instructions include the input and output instructions as well as the instructions for changing the mode switch and the memory-bounds register. This effectively blocks users from accessing information written on the various storage media, thus protecting inactive information in the system.

Use of the mode switch alone does not protect information which is active and resident in working memory. This is the function of the memory-bounds register. It partitions the working memory into two parts, one of which may not be accessed when executing in slave mode.

Protection based on this type of hardware feature is an all-or-nothing type solution. If a program has any privileges it has all. If a program has any access, it has completely unrestricted access. We feel that this is unsatisfactory as a protection mechanism for an IPU. In a system where users may share data in working memory the ability to have more control over access is essential. What is needed is the ability to have a variety of access rights for each separate logical block of information (called a segment).

Current machines which have been modified for use in IPUs have hardware features which allow memory to be subdivided into a large number of parts called segments. Each segment has a number of access control switches which specify various access privileges such as write/no-write, slave/master, and execute/no-execute. This hardware extension makes possible varying degrees of access to each segment which may differ from segment to segment.

If this control is a part of the physical subdivision of memory, any user who has access at all has the same access as every other user who may access the segment. The owner of a data segment needs write-access if he is to maintain or update the segment with more timely information, but on the other hand it is necessary that other users of the data are not able to change it. Rather than being an exception, this is the rule in IPU. The most advanced machines have hardware features such that the access may be varied on the logical segment rather than the physical segment, thus permitting different access by different users to the same physical segment.

In the design of a protection mechanism, an excellent guiding principle is the military security principle of "need to know." Applying this in the design of a protection mechanism in an IPU results in the property that each procedure has the minimum access needed to get its job done.

A procedure has access to only those procedures and data segments necessary to do its task, and then only the type of access required for the job. This can be visualized by recalling the military system of clearances. The higher the clearance, the more documents one may access. On the other hand, the higher the clearance, the fewer the individuals that hold such a clearance.

In an IPU the critical functions (i.e., those whose failures have disastrous consequences affecting the entire system) are segregated to the most protected area. This type of protection further improves the reliability of the system from that of the earlier two-mode systems by further minimizing the extent of damage caused by hardware or software failure. Further, it aids maintenance.

An IPU is a real-time system and the behavior of real-time systems is difficult, if not impossible, to repeat. The more compartmentalization and protection present in the system, the easier it is to isolate and locate the source of unwanted behavior. If the system has a general facility for layers of protection (analogous to layers of security clearance) then this service can be extended to users of the system. This permits restricted classes of users who use subsystems supplied by other users. A subsystem which has been designed and implemented by a user may then enjoy the same sort of layered protection with respect to its users as the operating system enjoys with its users.

Such a service can be achieved easily by any user without any special administrative procedures on the part of the system management or any special coding by the user. Two noteworthy examples of the usefulness of such a service are a subsystem designed by an instructor for use by his students and a service bureau selling access to a specialized system.

In summary, a satisfactory protection mechanism should have the following properties. It should be possible to completely isolate one process from another; that is, a user should be able to deny any access whatsoever by other users to all of his segments. On the other hand, it should be easy and convenient for a user to allow controlled access to any of his segments, with different access privileges for different users. Further, within a single process, layers of protection should be available for use by both the system and a user so that the "need to know" philosophy can be applied to any degree deemed reasonable. Finally, it is extremely desirable that procedures may be called across the layers of protection without any special programming on the part of the calling procedure. If the grouping of procedures into protection layers is not coded into the procedure this organization is easily changeable by an administrative program.

ABSTRACT MODEL

In this section we describe an abstract model of hardware features which will permit a satisfactory solution to the protection problems described earlier. This solution is but one of possibly several solutions of the general problem. It illustrates each of the properties we consider essential to any satisfactory solution.

We begin by describing a model which is essentially that of Dennis [2]. A key component of this model is a segment. A segment is a contiguous block of words whose length may vary during the execution of a process. Hardware for realizing segments is often called segment-addressing hardware.

Most computers suitable for use in an IPU also have paging hardware. While a segment is a logical unit of information of which a user is cognizant, a page is a unit of information which is useful to the system for storage management and is thus invisible to the user. Thus pages are not relevant to this discussion and will not be mentioned further.

In a computer with segment-addressing, each word is addressed by an ordered pair of integers (S, W). S is the segment number and W is the word number within the segment. Segment numbers range from 0 to the maximum allowable number of segments in a process and the word number ranges from 0 to the current length of the segment to which it refers. Associated with each segment is a segment descriptor. The segment descriptor contains the absolute location of the beginning of the segment, the current size of the segment, and the access control indicator.

beginning of segment	length	access indicator

Descriptor

This access indicator specifies whether the segment may be accessed in slave mode, written, or executed. Further, if the segment is a procedure (i.e., execute indicator on), it specifies whether the procedure is to execute in master mode rather than in slave mode. Finally, it includes a fault bit which when nonzero, causes a fault (or trap or interrupt) on any attempt to reference the segment, even when in master mode.

If the write indicator is on but the execute indicator is off, the segment is writable data. If the execute indicator is on and the write indicator off, the segment is a pure procedure (i.e., one which does not modify itself). If the slave indicator is on, any procedure may access the segment; otherwise only a master mode segment (one with the master indicator on in its descriptor) may access it. If the fault code is nonzero, no access at all is permitted. A nonzero fault code overrides the setting of all the other indicators.

For every segment which a process may access (or potentially access), the corresponding descriptor resides in a distinguished segment called the descriptor segment. The segment number used in an address is, in fact, the index within the descriptor segment of the descriptor for that segment. In any system there will be a large number of descriptor segments, one for each process. Whenever a process is executing, a hardware processor register, called the descriptor base register, contains the absolute location of the descriptor segment for the executing process. Thus the contents of the descriptor base register indirectly define that set of segments to which an executing process has potential access.

In order to implement layered protection we augment the location counter and each descriptor with a field which will contain a ring number.

beginning of segment	length	access indicator	ring number

Descriptor

ring number	procedure segment number	word number

Location Counter

We define rings to be ordered, disjoint sets of segments, numbered from 0 to some maximum, as shown in Figure 1.

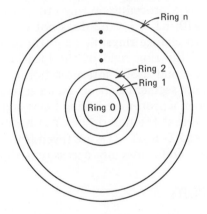

FIGURE 1.   **Rings of protection.**

Each segment is assigned to one and only one ring. The lower the ring number a procedure is executing in, the greater its access privileges. A procedure executing in ring i has no access whatever to any segment in ring j, where $j < i$. On the other hand, a procedure executing in ring i has access to a segment in ring k if $k > i$, subject to the access restrictions specified by the indicators in its descriptor.

However, to enforce this restriction, the system must be aware of the passage of control from one ring to another. In order to detect a "change of ring" in control, we further restrict the access rights of procedure segments. When a procedure executing in ring i attempts to transfer control to a procedure in any ring, other than ring i, a fault occurs. This fault is directed to the supervisor so that it may carry out appropriate housekeeping. The kind of housekeeping necessary is discussed in some detail later.

The assignment of each segment to a unique ring is sufficient to implement a solution of the protection problem. However, relaxing the disjointness requirement for the large class of chameleon-like shared service routines will result in a considerable increase in efficiency. This class of procedures needs as much access privilege as its caller but no more. In this case the procedure will operate correctly in whatever ring control is in at the time it was called. Hence, we relax the condition that the rings are disjoint and allow a procedure segment to be assigned to a consecutive set of rings called its access bracket. The ring field of the descriptor will then contain two integers specifying the lowest ring and highest ring in the access bracket.

Now a transfer by a procedure in ring i to a procedure with access bracket (n1, n2) with n1 ≤ i ≤ n2 does not cause a fault and does not cause control to change rings; i.e., control remains in ring i. This means the value of the ring field of the location counter does not change. A reasonable and useful interpretation of the access bracket can be made for data segments. Given a data segment, D, with access bracket (n1, n2), then a procedure in ring i may write into D if i ≤ n1 (provided of course that the descriptor of D has the write indicator on); it may only read D if n1 < i ≤ n2 (even if the write indicator in D's descriptor is on); and it may not access it at all if i > n2.

SOFTWARE SUPPORT

The preceding section described a model of hardware features which will allow a satisfactory implementation of execution time protection. This section will describe the software support necessary to complete the job. We begin with the problem of permitting controlled entry into an inner ring from an outer (higher numbered) ring. Recall that when a procedure in ring i attempts to transfer to a procedure with access bracket (n1, n2) and i > n2 a fault occurs. Since it is usually undesirable to permit transfers to a procedure in an inner ring from all outer rings, we extend the notion of access bracket to include a third integer, n3, which defines the call bracket. We refer to the three integers as the ring bracket.

If a procedure in ring i attempts to call a procedure, P, with ring bracket (n1, n2, n3) and n2 < i ≤ n3 the call is allowed only to certain distinguished entry points in P. If i > n3 the call is not permitted at all. The call bracket is implemented by software. A fault occurs if $i > n2$ and the fault handler for this fault sorts out the case $n2 < i \leqslant n3$.

One property of any segment with a nonempty call bracket is a list of entry points called the gate list. Because passing from one ring to another is similar to crossing a wall or fence separating the rings, the entries are called gates and the fault handler which monitors the crossing is called the gatekeeper. A procedure in the call bracket may transfer only to those points listed in the gate list.

Before proceeding further, a few words about the origin of a segment's descriptor will help put our other comments in perspective, even though the origin of the descriptors is immaterial to the protection mechanism. In an IPU of the type we have in mind for a concrete realization of the solution described herein, the maintenance and storage of segments are entrusted to the file system. An inactive segment is stored in file memory and is often called a file. The symbolic name and other properties of the segment are kept in a file directory entry for the segment. The file directory entry contains the segment's symbolic name and its location in file memory. In addition, it contains the access bracket $(n1, n2)$, and the call bracket $(n3)$, the gate list, and the access control list, which lists all users who may access the segment and the access which that user may have to the segment.

A user is specified as a triplet (personal name, project id, process id). A three-part user specification makes it possible for the same person to have different access privileges when he works on different projects. By including a process id he may protect himself from himself by having different access in his various processes. When a user first attempts to reference a segment, by symbolic name, the file system locates the segment in file memory, assigns a segment number to it, and constructs the proper descriptor with access indicator depending upon what user is attempting to reference the segment.

We return now to the gatekeeper. When a procedure P in ring i tries to transfer to a procedure Q with ring bracket $(n1, n2, n3)$, if $i < n1$ or $i > n2$ a fault occurs and the gatekeeper gets control. If $i > n3$ the transfer is rejected as an error. If $n3 \geqslant i > n2$ the target address of the transfer is compared with the entries on the gate list to validate that the call is to a valid entry point. If $i < n1$ the call is in an outward direction and any entry point is valid.

After the call has been validated the gatekeeper records, on a pushdown stack, the return point corresponding to the call and the ring number of the ring control was in at the time the call was attempted. An attempt to execute a return across rings also causes a fault which allows the gatekeeper to get control. The attempted return is validated against the record of unsatisfied calls across rings. This insures that returns remain in synchronization with calls.

The question of what ring control changes to when a procedure in ring i calls a procedure with access bracket (n1, n2) is still unresolved. The answer is that control should change by the smallest possible number of rings. Thus, if $i > n2$, control changes to ring n2; if $i < n1$, control changes to ring n1. This interpretation seems reasonable (although possibly arbitrary) for the following reasons. When entering an access bracket of lower numbered rings $(i > n2)$ changing control to n2 adheres to the philosophy of granting only the minimum access necessary to do the job. In the other direction, changing control to n1 would grant enough access for the procedure to assist its caller, Q, if Q were called from a ring j where $n2 > j > n1$.

ADDITIONAL COMPLEXITIES IN AN IPU

The software support described in the preceding section still does not satisfy the goals which we stated above. When a procedure in an inner ring is called, arguments may be passed to the inner procedure. Argument lists include addresses. The inner ring having higher access privileges than the outer ring may do damage to itself or other segments in its ring, inadvertently, if a calling procedure in an outer ring supplies the address of some segment in the inner ring.

Thus, arguments passed to inner ring procedures must be validated, i.e., all addresses must be checked to see that the calling procedure actually was permitted access to the segments specified in the addresses. This is a standard operation and is a task that the gatekeeper can do for all calls to inner ring procedures.

This is not quite the entire story with regard to validation of addresses in argument lists. The fact that there are multiprocesses executing on the same computer time-shared with other users means that, when segments are shared, data such as addresses in argument lists may change between the execution of two consecutive instructions. This is possible since the user may be interrupted due to a timer run-out, for example, and another process may be executed before the interrupted process is resumed. If data segments are shared by these two processes, then validated argument list addresses may be modified by the interrupting process.

One solution to this problem is to inhibit interrupts during the time the validation is taking place. Actually, one has to be considerably more sophisticated than this; interrupts must be inhibited until the called procedure in the inner ring is finished using the addresses. Even if such a long inhibiting of interrupts were tolerable, the problem is still not solved.

In a multiprocessor system, even if interrupts are inhibited, another process is executing on another processor. If that process is sharing a segment with this one, it will be able to modify the addresses during the time the inner procedure is executing.

Thus, it is not enough just to validate the addresses. The addresses in the argument list must be copied into a data area which is in the same ring as the called procedure and this copy of the addresses is validated. This guarantees that the copy of the addresses which are being validated may be modified by a procedure in another process only if that procedure has access privileges which are equal to the called procedure in this process.

Another problem exists for calls in the other direction. When a procedure, P, calls a procedure, Q, in a higher numbered ring, the arguments P is passing to Q may be in the same ring as P and thus inaccessible to Q. In this case they must be copied into a data area which is accessible to Q.

REFERENCES

1. Corbato, F. J., and Vyssotsky, V. A. "Introduction and overview of the MULTICS system," Proc. AFIPS 1965 Fall Joint Comput. Conf., Vol. 27, Part 1. Spartan Books, New York, pp. 185-196.
2. Dennis, J. B. "Segmentation and the design of multiprogrammed computer systems," J. ACM 12, 4 (Oct. 1965), 589-602.

A Hardware Architecture
for Implementing
Protection Rings

MICHAEL D. SCHROEDER
JEROME H. SALTZER

INTRODUCTION

The topic of this paper is the control of access to stored information in a computer utility. The paper describes a set of processor access control mechanisms that were devised as part of the second iteration of the hardware base for the Multics system. These mechanisms provide a hardware implementation of protection rings which limit the access privileges of an executing program.

Multics is a general purpose, multiple user, interactive computer system developed at Project MAC of MIT in a joint effort with the Cambridge Information Systems Laboratory of Honeywell Information Systems Inc. and, until 1969, the Bell Telephone Laboratories. It was built and is being run as an experiment in designing, implementing, operating, and evaluating a prototype computer utility. (Reference [14] contains a bibliography of publications on Multics.)

Multics is currently implemented on a Honeywell 645 computer system. The 645 represents a first attempt to define a suitable hardware base for a computer utility. While containing special logic to support a segmented virtual memory, the

SOURCE: Copyright © 1972, Association for Computing Machinery, Inc. M. Schroeder, and J. Saltzer, Communications of the ACM, Vol. 15, No. 3, 157–170 (March 1972). Reprinted by permission of the Association for Computing Machinery.

645 processor [10] provides only a limited set of access control mechanisms, forcing software intervention to implement protection rings. In the course of Multics development a second iteration of the design of the hardware base has been undertaken. The resulting new hardware system is being built as a replacement for the 645 using the technology of the Honeywell 6000 series computer systems. The new processor includes an improved set of access control mechanisms, described here, which implement rings almost completely in hardware. These mechanisms were developed from a scheme described in [16]. Although specifically designed for Multics, the mechanisms are applicable to any computer system which uses segmentation as a memory addressing scheme.

This paper begins by establishing the general need to control access to stored information in a computer utility and by presenting several criteria for comparing different sets of access control mechanisms. Relevant aspects of the organization of segmented memories are then sketched, and the processor mechanisms for implementing protection rings are described. The paper concludes by illustrating how rings can be used and by evaluating the impact of a hardware system design.

ACCESS CONTROL IN A COMPUTER UTILITY

Protection of computations and information is an important aspect of a computer utility. The multiple users of a computer utility have different goals and are responsible to different authorities. Such a diverse group will use the same system only if it is possible for them to achieve independence from one another. On the other hand, a great potential benefit of a computer utility is its ability to allow users to easily communicate, cooperate, and build upon one another's work. The role of protection in a computer utility is to control user interaction—guaranteeing total user separation when desired, allowing unrestricted user cooperation when desired, and providing as many intermediate degrees of control as will be useful.

While there are many manifestations of protection in a computer utility, most may be related to controlling access to stored information. Because stored information represents both data and executable procedure, control of access to stored information serves to regulate information processing as well.

Four criteria can be applied to a set of access control mechanisms to judge its usefulness in a computer utility: functional capability, economy, simplicity, and programming generality. The first means that a set of access control mechanisms should be able to meet an interesting set of user protection needs in a natural way. The ability to meet interesting protection needs must be a quality of the basic mechanisms, while the ability to do so in a natural way is a quality of their user interface. An obvious goal in designing new protection mechanisms is to maximize functional capability.

The second criterion, economy, means that the cost of specifying and enforcing a particular kind of access constraint with a set of mechanisms should be so low that it is not an important consideration in determining the type of access control to be used in a particular application. In addition, cost should be proportional to the functional capability actually used. The existence of access control mechanisms with sophisticated capabilities should cost no extra to those with unsophisticated needs. Cost includes the subsystem complexity and user inconvenience that result from use of the access control mechanisms, as well as any associated extra storage space and execution time.

Simplicity is the third criterion. While it is true that simplicity often leads to economy, something more is at stake. For a set of access control mechanisms to be accepted there must be confidence that no way exists to circumvent it. The best way to achieve confidence is to keep the mechanisms so simple that they may be completely understood. With respect to access control mechanisms, lack of simplicity often implies lack of security.

The fourth criterion, programming generality, is often neglected. It means that individual procedures may be combined easily into larger units without understanding or altering their internal organizations. Programming generality allows sharing to be effective in encouraging users to build upon one another's work. An implication of programming generality of relevance to access control mechanisms is that it should be possible to change the protection environment of procedures and collections of procedures without altering their internal structure.

It clearly is difficult to design access control mechanisms which satisfy all four of these criteria simultaneously. Increases in functional capability come at the expense of economy, simplicity, and programming generality. The challenge in designing a set of access control mechanisms is to maximize functional capability within the constraints of the other three criteria. In the following sections a set of hardware access control mechanisms that was devised in the course of Multics development is described. These mechanisms appear to provide a significant improvement in the simultaneous satisfaction of the four criteria as compared with the mechanisms in the initial Multics implementation.

SEGMENTED VIRTUAL MEMORY ENVIRONMENT

The processor access control mechanisms described here regulate the ability of an executing program to reference information in a segmented virtual memory. As a basis for understanding these access control mechanisms this section briefly reviews the structure of a typical segmented virtual memory. (See [1-3] for detailed descriptions of several segmented virtual memories.)

A machine language program for a segmented environment does not reference memory by absolute address. Rather, its memory consists of independent segments identified by number. Each segment is a separate array of words. A two-part address (s, w) identifies word w of the segment numbered s.

The collection of segments in the virtual memory is defined by a descriptor segment containing an array of segment descriptor words (SDW's). Each SDW can describe a single segment in the virtual memory. The number of a segment is just the index of the corresponding SDW in the descriptor segment. Among other things, an SDW contains the absolute address of the beginning of the corresponding segment in memory. The absolute address of the beginning of the descriptor segment is contained in the descriptor base register (DBR) of a processor. Each processor contains logic for automatically translating two-part addresses into the corresponding absolute addresses. Address translation, done with an indexed retrieval of the appropriate SDW from the descriptor segment, occurs each time a word in the virtual memory is referenced, i.e., each time an instruction, indirect word, or instruction operand reference is made by an executing program.

Storage for segments is usually allocated with a paging scheme in scattered fixed-length blocks. If used, paging is also taken into account by the address translation logic, but is totally transparent to an executing machine language program. Paging, if appropriately implemented, need not affect access control; it will be ignored in the remainder of this paper.

Changing the absolute address in the DBR of a processor will cause the address translation logic to interpret two-part addresses relative to a different descriptor segment. This facility can be used to provide each user of the system with a separate virtual memory. A single segment may be part of several virtual memories at the same time, allowing straightforward sharing of segments among users.

CONTROLLING ACCESS IN A SEGMENTED VIRTUAL MEMORY

To provide a framework for discussion, three specific assumptions true of Multics are introduced. First, a process with a new virtual memory is created for each user when he logs in to the system, and the name of the user is associated with the process. The process is the active agent of the user, and is his only means of referencing and manipulating information stored on-line. Second, on-line storage is organized as a collection of segments of information. A process can reference a segment of on-line storage only if the segment is first added to the virtual memory of the process. Third, the users that are permitted to access each segment are named by an access control list associated with each segment. As will be seen, any system providing access control of the type under discussion will probably have analogous assumptions. The application of the rest of the discussion to other systems with segmented virtual memories is straightforward.

Adding a segment to a virtual memory, an operation performed by supervisor programs, provides the initial opportunity for controlling access to information stored on-line. The name of the user associated with a process must match some entry on the access control list of a segment before the supervisor will add that segment to the virtual memory of the process.

Once a segment is included in the virtual memory, however, finer control on access is required. (If a process could, say, write in any segment to which it had access, little sharing of information among users would occur.) If this finer control is to be effective against arbitrary machine language programs constructed by users, it must be implemented as hardware access validation on each reference. The structure of the virtual memory makes it natural to record these finer constraints in the SDW associated with each segment. Since the processor must examine the SDW for a segment each time that segment is referenced by two-part address anyway, there is little effort added to validate the intended access against constraints recorded there. With this structure it is also possible to change the allowed access to a segment by changing the finer constraints recorded in the SDW, and to expect the change to be immediately effective, although the need for such dynamic changes is rare.

Flags which enable a segment to be read, written, and executed are natural constraints to record in each SDW. The value for each flag comes from the access control list entry which matched the name of the user associated with the process. An attempt by a process to change the contents of a word of a segment, for example, would be allowed by the processor only if the write flag were on in the SDW for the segment. This mechanism provides individual control on the ability of each user's process to read, write, and execute the words in each segment stored on-line. It also makes a segment the smallest unit of information that can be separately protected.

With the access control mechanisms described so far, all programs executed as part of some process have the same information accessing capabilities. However, there seems to be an intrinsic need in many computations for the access capabilities of a process to vary as the execution point passes through the various programs that direct the computation. The most obvious examples of this need are explicit invocations of supervisor programs during the course of a computation. The execution point may pass from a user program to a supervisor program to initiate an input/output operation or change the access control list of a segment, and then pass back to the user program. Presumably the executing supervisor program can access information in some way that the user program cannot. In a system that allows and encourages sharing of information among users, other examples appear. For instance, user A may wish to allow user B to access a sensitive data segment, but only through a special program, provided by A, that audits references to the segment. During the course of a computation in a process of user B, access to the sensitive data segment should be allowed only when the execution point is in the special program provided by A.

The word "domain" is frequently associated with a set of access capabilities. The examples above point to an intrinsic need for multiple domains to be associated with a process and for the domain in which the process is executing to occasionally change as the execution point passes from one program to another. A descriptor segment with read, write, and execute flags in the SDW's defines a single domain. Additional mechanisms are required to allow multiple domains to be associated with a single process.

A very general set of access control mechanisms would place no restriction on the number of domains which could be associated with a process, and would force no restrictive relationships to exist among the sets of access capabilities included in the domains. Unfortunately, devising such a set of access control mechanisms that also meets the criteria of economy, simplicity, and programming generality is a difficult research problem. (See [5, 7, 8, 12, 13, 17] for several approaches that have been explored.) In Multics the strategy was adopted of limiting the number of domains which may be associated with a process, and of forcing certain relationships to exist among the sets of access capabilities included in the domains. The result is protection rings.

The characterization of rings as a restricted implementation of domains is the result of hindsight. When developed, rings were viewed as a natural generalization of the supervisor/user modes that provided protection in many computers. This path of development was chosen because it solved the most pressing problems of access control involved in the prototype computer utility and, due to the inherent simplicity of the idea, it was a path that the Multics designers felt confident they could successfully complete. Even today rings appear to provide an effective trade-off among the criteria mentioned above.

PROTECTION RINGS

Associated with each process are a fixed number of domains called protection rings. These r rings are named by the integers 0 through r - 1. The access capabilities included in ring m are constrained to be a subset of those in ring n whenever $m > n$. Put another way, the sets of access capabilities represented by the various rings of a process form a collection of nested subsets, with ring 0 the largest set and ring r - 1 the smallest set in the collection. Thus, a process has the greatest access privilege when executing in ring 0, and the least access privilege when executing in ring r - 1. The total ordering of the sets of access capabilities defined by the consecutively numbered rings of a process is the property which allows a straightforward implementation of rings in hardware.

As described earlier, the permission flags for each segment in the virtual memory of a process simply indicate that the segment can or cannot be read, written, or executed by the process. With the addition of rings, the flags must be extended to indicate which rings include each access capability. Because of the nested subset property of rings, the capability, say, to write a particular segment, if available to a process at all, is included in all rings numbered less than or equal to some value w. The range of rings over which this write permission applies is called the write bracket of the segment for the process.

Read and execute brackets for each segment can be established in the same way. A process is permitted to read, write, or execute a segment in its virtual memory only if the ring of execution of the process is within the proper bracket.

A partial hardware implementation of rings places numbers indicating the top of each bracket of a segment in the SDW of the segment, along with the read, write, and execute flags. If a flag is on, then the number specifies the extent of the corresponding bracket. Turning a flag off indicates that the corresponding access capability is not included in any ring of the process. For example, a data segment might have its execute flag turned off or a pure procedure segment might have its write flag turned off. A register is added to the processor to record the current ring of execution of the process. The processor can then validate each reference to a segment by making the obvious comparisons when the SDW for the segment is examined for address translation.

Figure 1 illustrates the flags and brackets that might be associated with a writable data segment for some process. (In Multics, eight was chosen as the appropriate number of rings. Eight rings are shown in the examples, although more or fewer rings might be appropriate in another system.)

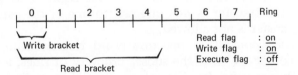

FIGURE 1.   Example access indicators for a writable data segment.

The association of multiple domains of protection with a process generates the need for a new kind of access capability—the capability to change the domain of execution of a process. Since changing the domain of execution has the potential to make additional access capabilities available to a process, it is an operation that must be carefully controlled. An understanding of the sort of control required can be gained by reviewing the purpose of domains. A domain provides the means to protect procedure and data segments from other procedures that are part of the same computation. Using domains, it should be possible to make certain access capabilities available to a process only when particular programs are being executed. Restricting the start of execution in a particular domain to certain program locations, called gates, provides this ability, for it gives the program sections that begin at those locations complete control over the use made of the access capabilities included in the domain. Thus, changing the domain of execution must be restricted to occur only as the result of a transfer of control to one of these gate locations of another domain.

With a completely general implementation of domains, each domain could provide protection against the procedures executing in all other domains of a process. The corresponding property of rings is that the protection provided by a given ring of a process is effective against procedures executing in higher numbered rings. Switching the ring of execution to a lower number makes additional access capabilities available to a process, while switching the ring to a higher number reduces the available access capabilities. Thus, the downward ring switching capability must be coupled to a transfer of control to a gate into the lower numbered ring. Gates are specified by associating a (possibly empty) list of gate locations with each segment in the virtual memory of a process. If the execution point of the process is transferred to a segment while the ring of execution is above the top of the execute bracket for the segment, then the transfer must be directed to one of the gate locations in the segment. If the transfer is to a gate, then the ring of execution of the process will switch down to the top of the execute bracket of the segment as the transfer occurs. If the transfer is not directed to one of the gate locations, then the transfer is not allowed.

To provide control of this downward ring switching capability which is consistent with the subset property of rings, a gate extension to the execute bracket of a segment is defined. The gate extension specifies the consecutively numbered rings above the execute bracket of the segment that include the "transfer to a gate and change ring" capability for the segment. The gate list and the gate extension to the execute bracket can both be specified with additional fields in each SDW.

In contrast to downward ring changes, switching the ring of execution to a higher-numbered ring can only decrease the available access capabilities of a process. Thus, an upward ring switch is an unrestricted operation that can be performed by any executing procedure. (The instruction to be executed immediately following an upward ring switch must come from a segment that is executable in the new, higher-numbered ring.) For programming convenience, the upward ring switch may be coupled to a special transfer instruction.

The abstract description of rings is now one step from completion. The last step comes from the observation that for each procedure segment in the virtual memory of each process there is a lowest-numbered ring in which that procedure is intended to execute. In order to provide the means for preventing the accidental transfer to and execution of a procedure in a ring lower than intended, the requirement that execute brackets have a lower limit at ring 0 is relaxed and instead an arbitrary lower limit is allowed. For many procedure segments the execute bracket will include exactly one ring—the ring in which the procedure is intended to execute. Procedure segments with wider execute brackets normally will contain commonly used library subroutines that are certified as acceptable for execution in any of several rings.

The arbitrary lower limit on the execute bracket of a segment can be implemented by using the field of an SDW which specifies the top of the write bracket to specify the bottom of the execute bracket as well. The double use of this field does not appear to remove any interesting functional capability. In fact, it eliminates an unwanted degree of freedom in access specification, thereby removing the potential to make certain types of errors, such as allowing both writing and execution of a segment in more than one ring of a process.

Figure 2 shows example access indicators for a pure procedure segment containing gates, and illustrates how the execute and write brackets specified in an SDW must be related.

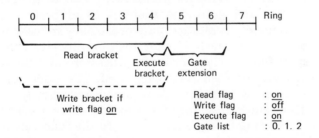

FIGURE 2.   Example access indicators for a pure procedure segment which contains gates.

The gate list and the numbers specifying the read, write, and execute brackets and gate extension in each SDW all come from the access control list entry which permitted the process to include the corresponding segment in its virtual memory, as did the values for the read, write, and execute flags.

CALL AND RETURN

As argued above, a change in the domain of execution of a process can occur only when the executing procedure transfers control to a gate of another domain. In the context of most programming languages, an interprocedure transfer represents a subroutine call, a return following a call, or a nonlocal goto. Linguistically, all three operations produce a change in the environment of the execution point; this change affects the binding of variable names to virtual storage locations. The call operation has the additional function of transmitting arguments and recording a return point. Performing these functions generally requires the cooperation of both the procedure initiating the operation and the procedure receiving control. If a call, return, or goto changes the domain of execution because it happens to be directed to a gate location of another domain, then the situation becomes more complicated, for neither procedure can depend upon the other to cooperate. An important simplification introduced by restricting domains to a ring structure is that a procedure may assume the cooperation of procedures in lower-numbered rings.

When procedures are shared among different processes and different domains, the addressing environment is usually defined via processor registers, for the procedures must be pure and it is not convenient to embed addresses within them. Part of the function of the call, return, and goto operations is to properly update this environment pointer. In Multics, pure procedures are used with a per process stack, and a stack pointer register provides the required environment definition. The stack of a process is implemented with a separate segment for each ring being used. The stack segment for procedures executing in ring n has read and write brackets that end at ring n. Thus, stack areas for these procedures are not accessible to procedures executing in any ring $m > n$. In the following discussion the stack pointer register is used as a typical example of the required environment pointer.

The most common ways of changing the ring of execution of a process are a call to a gate of a lower-numbered ring and the subsequent upward return. A downward call represents the invocation of a user-provided protected subsystem or a supervisor procedure. Because the Honeywell 645 was designed around the usual supervisor/user protection method, the version of Multics for this machine implements rings by trapping to a supervisor procedure when downward calls and upward returns are performed. The hardware mechanisms detailed in the next section eliminate the need to trap in these cases. Using these improved hardware access control mechanisms, downward calls and upward returns occur without the intervention of a supervisor procedure and are performed by the same object code sequences that perform all calls and returns.

It is the nested subset property of rings that makes a straight-forward hardware implementation of downward calls and upward returns possible. Because of this property, the called procedure automatically has all access capabilities required to reference any arguments that the calling procedure can legitimately specify and to return to the calling procedure in the ring from which it called. However, three problems remain. First, the called procedure must have a way of finding a new stack area without depending upon information provided by the calling procedure. Second, the called procedure must have a way of validating references to arguments, so that it cannot be tricked into reading or writing an argument that the caller could not also read or write. Finally, the called procedure must have a way of knowing for certain the ring in which the calling procedure was executing, so that the called procedure cannot be tricked into returning control to a ring not as high as that of the calling procedure.

The key to solving the first problem, finding a new stack area, is a rule relating the segment number of the stack segment for a ring to the ring number. Using this rule, the processor automatically calculates the segment number of the proper stack segment for the called procedure's ring of execution. By convention, a fixed word of each stack segment can point to the beginning of the next available stack area. Thus, the stack segment number alone can provide the called procedure with enough information from which to construct its own stack pointer. Because the processor provides the stack segment number, no procedure executing in a higher-numbered ring, e.g., the calling procedure, can affect the value of the stack pointer for the called procedure.

The second problem, validating argument references, is solved by providing processor mechanisms which allow a procedure to assume the more restricted access capabilities of any higher-numbered ring for particular operand references. Using these mechanisms, the called procedure can validate access when referencing arguments as though execution were occurring in the (higher-numbered) ring of the calling procedure. Thus, the called procedure, even though it is executing in a ring with more access capabilities than the ring of the calling procedure, can prevent itself from reading or writing any argument that the calling procedure could not also read or write.

The final problem, knowing the ring of the caller, is solved by having the processor leave in a program accessible register the number of the ring in which execution was occurring before the downward call was made. The subsequent return is made to that ring. Thus the calling procedure has no opportunity to lower the number of the ring to which the return is made.

The next two sections describe in more detail how downward calls, argument referencing and validation, and upward returns are implemented. Before proceeding to that description, however, there are two other possibilities to consider: a call and return that do not change the ring of execution, and an upward call and the subsequent downward return. The first presents no protection problem, as both the calling and the called procedures have available the same set of access capabilities. The hardware mechanisms for downward calls and upward returns also work when no change of ring is needed.

The last possibility is more difficult to handle. An upward call occurs when a procedure executing in ring n calls an entry point in another procedure segment whose execute bracket bottom is m > n. When the call occurs, the ring of execution will change to m. The subsequent return is downward, resetting the ring of execution to n. These cases exhibit two unpleasant characteristics of a general cross-domain call and return that were not present in the other cases.

The first is that the calling procedure may specify arguments that cannot be referenced from the ring of the called procedure. (For a downward call, the nested subset property of rings guaranteed that this could not happen.) There are at least three possible solutions to this problem. One is to require that the calling procedure specify only arguments that are accessible in the higher-numbered ring of the called procedure. This solution compromises programming generality by forcing the calling procedure to take special precautions in the case of an upward call. Another possible solution is to dynamically include in the ring of the called procedure the capabilities to reference the arguments. Because a segment is the smallest unit of information for which access can be individually controlled, this forces segments which contain arguments to contain no other information that should be protected differently, again compromising programming generality, unless segments are inexpensive enough that, as a matter of course, every data item is placed in its own segment. It may also be expensive to dynamically include and remove the argument referencing capabilities from the called ring. The third possible solution is copying arguments into segments that are accessible in the called ring, and then copying them back to their original locations on return. This solution restricts the possibility of sharing arguments with parallel processes. None of the three solutions lends itself to a straightforward hardware implementation.

The second unpleasant characteristic is that a gate must be provided for the downward return. (For an upward return the nested subset property of rings made a return gate unnecessary.) The return gate must be created at the time of the upward call and be destroyed when the subsequent return occurs. If recursive calls into a ring are allowed, then this gate must behave as though it were stored in a push-down stack, so that only the gate at the top of the stack can be used. The gates specified in SDW's seem poorly suited to this sort of dynamic behavior. Processor mechanisms to provide dynamic, stacked return gates are not obvious at this time.

Because of these two problems, the hardware described in the next section does not implement upward calls and downward returns without software intervention. Although the same object code sequences that perform all calls and returns are used in these cases as well, the hardware responds to each attempted upward call or downward return by generating a trap to a supervisor procedure which performs the necessary environment adjustments.

The manner in which the stack pointer register value of the calling procedure is saved when a call occurs and restored when the subsequent return occurs has not yet been discussed. For a same-ring or downward call, it is reasonable to trust the called procedure to save the value left in the stack pointer register by the calling procedure and then restore it before the subsequent return, since in these cases the called procedure has access capabilities which allow it to cause the calling procedure to malfunction in other ways anyway. For an upward call and the subsequent downward return, the same convention can be used without violating the protection provided by the lower ring if the intervening software verifies the restored stack pointer register value when performing the downward return.

HARDWARE IMPLEMENTATION OF RINGS

In this section the ideas presented in the previous sections are gathered into a description of a design for processor hardware to implement rings. The description touches upon only those aspects of the processor organization that are relevant to access control. The segmented addressing hardware described earlier serves as the foundation of the ring implementation mechanisms.

Figure 3 presents a schematic description of storage formats and processor registers that are relevant to the discussion which follows. The DBR and SDW's have already been mentioned. The three 3-bit ring numbers in an SDW (SDW.R1, SDW.R2, and SDW.R3) delimit the read, write, and execute brackets and the gate extension. The write bracket is rings 0 through SDW.R1, the execute bracket SDW.R1 through SDW.R2, and the gate extension SDW.R2 + 1 through SDW.R3. Rather than providing a fourth number to specify the top of the read bracket, SDW.R2 is reused for this purpose. Thus the read bracket is rings 0 through SDW.R2. Forcing the top of the read and execute brackets to coincide in this manner does not seem to preclude any important cases, and saves one ring number in the SDW. Supervisor code for constructing SDW's must guarantee that SDW.R1 ⩽ SDW.R2 ⩽ SDW.R3 is true. The single-bit read, write,

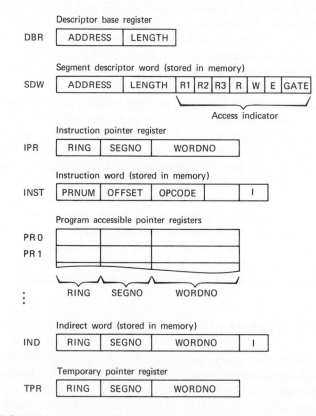

FIGURE 3.   Schematic description of relevant storage formats and processor registers.

and execute flags (SDW.R, SDW.W, and SDW.E) also appear. Finally, the list of gate locations of a segment is compressed to a single fixed-length field (SDW.GATE) by requiring all gate locations to be gathered together, beginning at location 0 of a segment. SDW.GATE contains the number of gate locations present.

The instruction pointer register (IPR) specifies the current ring of execution and the two-part address of the next instruction to be executed. The general format of an instruction word in memory (INST) is also shown for later reference.

The program accessible pointer registers (PR0, PR1, ...) each contain a two-part address and a ring number. Because segment numbers are not generally known at the time a procedure segment is compiled, machine instructions specify two-part operand addresses by giving an offset (in INST.OFFSET) relative to one of the PR's (specified by INST.PRNUM) or IPR. The ring number in a pointer register (PRn.RING) is used to specify a validation level for the address, and is part of the mechanism that allows an executing procedure to assume the access capabilities of a higher-numbered ring for referencing arguments. One of the PR's is intended to serve as the stack pointer register mentioned earlier.

Indirect addressing may be specified in an instruction by setting the indirect flag (INST.I). Indirect words (IND) contain the same information as PR's, and may also indicate further indirection with an indirect flag (IND.I).

The final item in Figure 3 is the temporary pointer register (TPR). The TPR is an internal processor register that is not program accessible. It is used to form the two-part address of each virtual memory reference made. The ring number (TPR.RING) provides the value with respect to which permission to reference the virtual memory location is validated.

There are two aspects to the implementation of rings in hardware. The first is access checking logic, integrated with the segmented addressing hardware, that validates each virtual memory reference. The second is special instructions for changing the ring of execution. The best way to describe the first aspect is to trace the processor instruction cycle, paying particular attention to the places where operations related to access validation occur. The second aspect will be discussed when the description of the instruction cycle reaches the point where the instruction is actually performed.

The first phase of the instruction cycle, retrieving the next instruction to be executed, is described in Figure 4. At the point during address translation that the SDW for the segment containing the

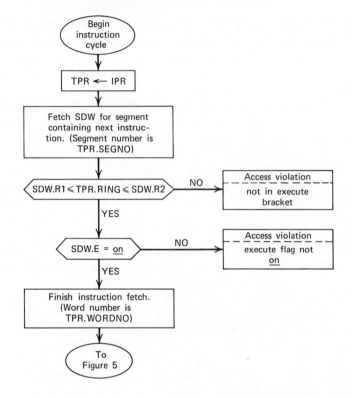

FIGURE 4.   Retrieval of next instruction to be executed.

instruction becomes available, the ring of execution (now TPR.RING) is matched against the execute bracket defined in the SDW and the execute flag is checked. If the segment may be executed from the current ring of execution the instruction fetch is completed. The access violations and other conditions requiring software interven-tion shown in this and following figures generate traps, derailing the instruction cycle. A traps action is described later in this section.

The next phase of the instruction cycle, calculating in TPR the effective address of the instruction's operand, is described in Fig-ure 5. This phase occurs only if the instruction has an operand in memory. The effective address is the final two-part address of the operand (after all address modifications and indirections have taken place) together with an effective ring number which is used to validate the actual reference to the operand.

The formation of a two-part address in TPR.SEGNO and TPR.WORDNO is very straightforward and is described by Figure 5.

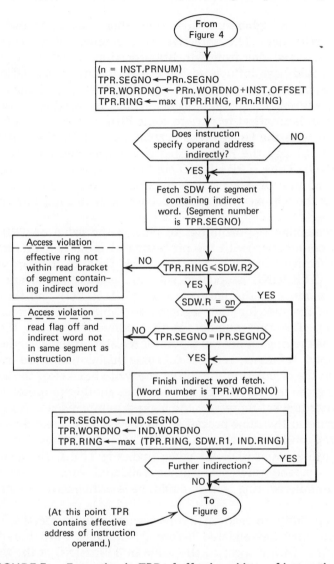

FIGURE 5.   Formation in TPR of effective address of instruction operand.

The calculation of the ring number portion of the effective address in TPR.RING and the access validation performed before retrieving indirect words, also shown in Figure 5, need further comment.

The effective ring portion of the effective address provides a procedure with the means of voluntarily assuming the access capabilities of a higher-numbered ring when making an instruction operand reference. The effective ring number also records the highest-numbered ring from which a procedure (in the same process) possibly could have influenced the effective address calculation. The first opportunity for the value of TPR.RING to change during effective address calculation occurs if the instruction contains an address that is an offset relative to some PRn. In this case TPR.RING is updated with the larger of its current values (still the current ring of execution) and the ring number in the specified pointer register (PRn.RING). Thus, if PRn.RING contains a value that is greater than the current ring of execution, validation of the operand reference will be as though execution were occurring in this higher-numbered ring.

The remaining opportunities to change the value of TPR.RING occur in conjunction with the processing of indirect words involved in the effective address calculation. Each time an indirect word is retrieved, TPR.RING is updated with the larger of its current values, the ring number in the indirect word (IND.RING), and the top of the write bracket for the segment containing the indirect word (SDW.R1). The ring number in the indirect word has the same purpose as the ring number in a pointer register—forcing validation of the operand reference relative to some higher-numbered ring. Including in the calculation the top of the write bracket of the segment containing the indirect word, however, has another purpose. The top of the write bracket represents the highest numbered ring from which a procedure in the same process could have altered the indirect word and thereby influenced the result of the effective address calculation. Taking into account SDW.R1 when updating TPR.RING guarantees that the operand reference will be validated with respect to the highest numbered ring which could have influenced the effective address.

The capability to read an indirect word during effective address formation must be validated before the indirect word is retrieved. Validation is with respect to the value in TPR.RING at the time the indirect word is encountered. At the conclusion of the effective address calculation described in Figure 5, TPR contains the effective address of the instruction operand, including the effective ring number with respect to which the reference to the operand will be validated.

The next phase of the instruction cycle is to perform the instruction. For the purpose of access validation, the possible instructions may be broken into three groups, according to the type of reference made to the operand. Figure 6 shows the access validation for the straightforward cases of instructions which read their operands and instructions which write their operands. The third group, instructions which do not reference their operands, is illustrated in Figure 7. One set in this group is the "Effective Address to Pointer Register"-type (EAP-type) instructions which load the RING, SEGNO, and WORDNO fields of PRn with the corresponding fields of TPR. The operand is not referenced, so no access validation is required. Instructions of this type are important, as will be seen later, for they are the only way to load PR's.

The remaining instructions illustrated in Figure 7 are transfer instructions. To provide some protection against changing the ring of execution by accident, all transfer instructions except two, CALL and RETURN, are constrained from doing so. Since a transfer instruction does not reference its operand, but just loads the address of its operand into the instruction counter, no access validation is really required. However, an advance check on whether reloading IPR from TPR will result in an access violation when the next instruction is retrieved is very useful from the standpoint of debugging, for it catches the access violation while it is still possible to identify the instruction which made the illegal transfer. Figure 7 describes the advance check for transfer instructions other than CALL and RETURN.

The two instructions that remain to be considered are the instructions which can change the ring of execution: CALL and RETURN. They are intended to be used to implement the same-named linguistic operations.[1] CALL will automatically switch the ring of execution to a lower number and RETURN to a higher number if the occasion requires it. These instructions also function properly for calls and returns within the same ring. When used to perform an upward call or a downward return, the instructions cause traps which allow software intervention.

Figure 8 describes the access validation and performance of the CALL instruction. Several points require further explanation. The first concerns gates. From Figure 8 it is apparent that a CALL must be directed at a gate location even when the called procedure will execute in the same ring as the calling procedure. The rationale for this use of the gate list of a segment is that it can provide protection against accidental calls to locations that are not entry points, even when the call comes from within the same ring. Thus, SDW.GATE

---

[1] RETURN may also be used to implement the nonlocal goto operation.

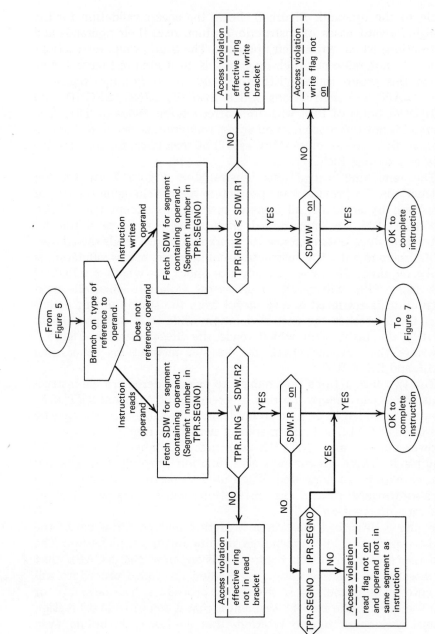

FIGURE 6. Access validation for instructions which read or write their operands.

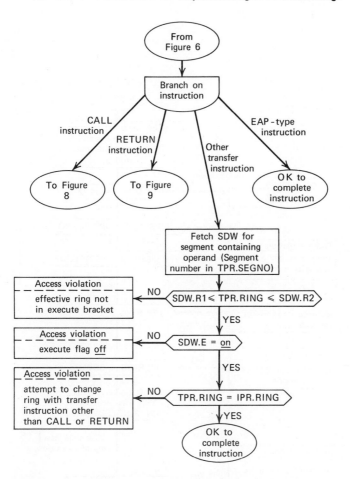

FIGURE 7.   Access validation for instructions which do not reference their operands.

for a procedure segment usually specifies the number of externally
defined entry points in the procedure segment. These become gates
for higher-numbered rings in the sense described in the previous
sections only if the top of the gate extension of the segment is above
the top of the execute bracket, i.e., only if SDW.R3 > SDW.R2 for
the segment. The price paid for this error detection ability is that if
any externally defined entry point in a procedure segment is a gate
for a higher-numbered ring, then all are. On intersegment transfers of
control within the same ring, the gate restriction can be bypassed by
using a normal transfer instruction rather than a CALL. The only

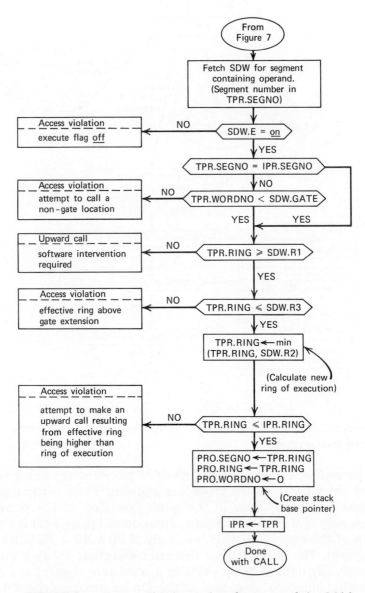

FIGURE 8. Access validation and performance of the CALL instruction.

exception to having the CALL instruction respect the gate list of the operand segment occurs if the operand is in the same segment as the instruction. Allowing a CALL instruction to ignore the gate list of the segment containing the instruction permits it to be used to implement calls to internal procedures.

The access validation for the CALL instruction is made relative to the ring number computed as part of the effective address. Since, as a result of PR-relative addressing and indirection, the effective ring value (TPR.RING) can be higher than the current ring of execution (IPR.RING), what would appear to be a call within the same ring or to a lower ring with respect to TPR.RING can in fact be an upward call with respect to IPR.RING. Because in normal circumstances this situation represents an error, the decision is made to generate an access violation when it occurs, even if the current ring of execution is within the execute bracket of the called procedure segment.

CALL generates in PR0 a pointer to word 0 of the stack segment for the new ring of execution. (The PR to use as this stack base pointer is chosen arbitrarily.) The stack segment selection rule illustrated in Figure 8 is that the segment number of the appropriate stack segment is the same as the new ring number.[2] The final transfer of control is achieved by reloading IPR.RING, IPR.SEGNO, and IPR.WORDNO from the corresponding fields of TPR.

The RETURN instruction is described by Figure 9. The access validation is the same as for other transfer instructions. The ring to which the return is made is specified by the effective ring portion of the effective address generated by the RETURN instruction. In the case that the return is upward, the ring number fields in all pointer registers are replaced with the larger of their current values and the new ring of execution. This replacement, together with the fact that PR's can only be loaded with EAP-type instructions, guarantees that PRn.RING can never contain a value that is less than IPR.RING, a

---

[2]Two subtle features may be included at this point by using a more sophisticated stack segment selection rule. If the CALL instruction does not change the ring of execution, then the segment number for the stack base pointer is taken directly from the stack pointer register, allowing the continued use of a non-standard stack segment for procedures executing in the same ring. If the CALL instruction does change the ring of execution then the new stack segment number is calculated by adding the new ring number to an additional DBR field that specifies the eight consecutively numbered segments that are the standard stack segments of the process. The use of the additional DBR field allows more flexibility in stack segment assignment, facilitating the preservation of stack history following an error and the implementation of forked stacks.

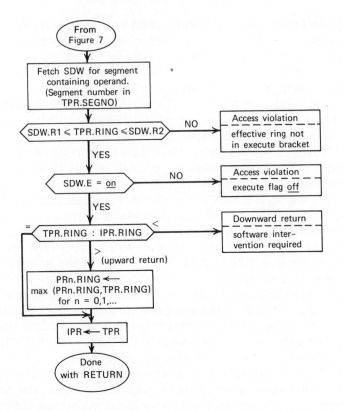

FIGURE 9. **Access validation and performance of the RETURN instruction.**

fact which proves very useful when passing arguments on a downward call and which makes it easy to perform an upward return to the proper ring. (See the next section for details.)

Two items remain to be considered to complete the description of the processor hardware for implementing rings. One is the action of a trap. Traps are generated by a variety of conditions in Figures 4–9, as well as by missing segments and pages, I/O completions, etc. When the processor detects such a condition, it changes the ring of execution to zero and transfers control to a fixed location in the supervisor. A special instruction allows the state of the processor at the time of the trap to be restored later if appropriate, resuming the disrupted instruction.

The other item concerns privileged instructions. Certain instructions, if executable by all procedure segments, could invalidate the protection provided by the ring mechanisms. Among these are the instructions to load the DBR, start I/O, and restore the processor state after a trap. Such instructions are designated as privileged and will be executed by the processor only in ring 0. This convention restricts their use to supervisor procedures.

CALL AND RETURN REVISITED

The intended use of the hardware mechanisms just described is illustrated by considering again two key aspects of the linguistic meaning of the operations call and return.

The first aspect to be reconsidered is the way arguments are passed and referenced. A procedure making a call constructs an array of indirect words containing the addresses of the various arguments to be passed with the call. To inform the called procedure of the location of this argument list, the calling procedure loads a specific PR designated by software convention (call it PRa) with the address of the beginning of the argument list. An instruction of the called procedure can reference the $\underline{n}$th argument as its operand by using an indirect address. The location of the indirect word is specified in the instruction as PRa offset by $\underline{n}$. If this operand reference constitutes an upward cross-ring argument reference then the proper validation is automatic, for PRa.RING, as set by the calling procedure, must contain a number that is greater than or equal to the number of the ring in which the calling procedure was executing when the call was made. Thus, validation of all argument references by the called procedure will be with respect to an effective ring that is at least as high as the ring of the caller.

The ring number in PRa, then, allows the called procedure to automatically assume the fewer access capabilities of the calling procedure in the case of an upward cross-ring argument reference via PRa and the argument list. Not all argument references, however, will be made in this way. For example, if an argument is an array, then the corresponding argument list indirect word will address the first element. The called procedure may find it convenient to load some free PR, say PR1, with the actual two-part address of the beginning of that array argument so that array indexing can be more easily accomplished. If PR1 is loaded with an EAP-type instruction whose operand address is specified via PRa and the argument list, then the proper effective ring number will automatically be put in PR1.RING, and subsequent references to the argument via PR1 will also be validated with respect to an effective ring that is at least as high as the ring of the caller. If PR1 is then stored as an indirect word, this effective ring is put into the RING field of the indirect word. In fact, as long as the called procedure does not make an explicit effort to lower the effective ring associated with an argument address, e.g., by zeroing the RING field of an indirect word, then all manipulations of the argument address are safe, and all argument references will be validated with respect to an effective ring that is at least as high as the ring of the caller.[3]

The second aspect to be reconsidered with respect to call and return is the way in which a return to the proper ring is accomplished. As described earlier, the hardware guarantees that the RING fields in all PR's always contain values greater than or equal to the current ring of execution. Thus, after a call all PR's except PR0, which is altered by the CALL instruction, initially contain the ring of the caller (or some higher number) in their RING fields. It follows that any scheme for returning which depends upon one of these values is secure. For example, the convention described earlier for restoring the stack pointer register value of the caller before a return makes it natural to address the operand of the RETURN instruction via this restored PR. (For this scheme to work, the return point must have been saved by the caller at a standard position in its stack area before the call occurred.) The RETURN instruction is thus guaranteed to generate an effective ring number no lower than the ring of the calling procedure and therefore will return control to the ring of the caller or some higher-numbered ring.

USE OF RINGS

Some insight into the functional capabilities of rings can be gained by considering briefly the way the basic mechanisms described in the previous sections are used in Multics.

The ring protection scheme allows a layered supervisor to be included in the virtual memory of each process. In Multics, the lowest-level supervisor procedures, such as those implementing the primitive operations of access control, I/O, memory multiplexing, and processor multiplexing, execute in ring 0. The remaining

---

[3]This property allows the correct argument validation to occur naturally when an argument is passed along a chain of downward calls. The RING field of an argument list indirect word will specify the ring which originally provided the argument. If this value is higher than the value of PRa.RING, then the indirect word ring number will become the effective ring for validation of references to the corresponding argument.

supervisor procedures execute in ring 1. Examples of ring 1 supervisor procedures are those performing accounting, input/output stream management, and file system search direction. (Deciding how many layers to use and which procedures should execute in each layer is an interesting engineering design problem.) Supervisor data segments have read and write brackets that end at ring 0 or ring 1, depending on which layer of the supervisor needs to access each.

Implicit invocation of certain ring 0 supervisor procedures occurs as a result of a trap. Explicit invocation of selected ring 0 and ring 1 supervisor procedures by procedures executing in rings 2-5 of a process is by standard subroutine calls to gates. Procedures executing in rings 6 and 7 are not given access to supervisor gates.

Because separate access control lists for each segment and separate descriptor segments for each process provide the means to control separately the use of each segment by each user's process, not all gates into supervisor rings need be available to the processes of all users, and not all gates need have the same gate extension associated with them. For example, some gates into ring 0 are accessible to the processes of all users, but only to procedures executing in ring 1. Such gates provide the internal interfaces between the two layers of the supervisor. Some gates into ring 1 are accessible to procedures executing in rings 2-5 in the processes of selected users, but are not accessible at all from the processes of other users. An example of the latter kind is a gate for registering new users that is available only from the processes of system administrators.

As pointed out by Dijkstra [6], a layered supervisor has several advantages. Constructing the supervisor in layers enforced by ring protection reinforces these advantages. It limits the propagation of errors, thereby making the supervisor easier to modify correctly and increasing the level of confidence that the supervisor functions correctly. For example, changes can be made in ring 1 without having to recertify the correct operation of the procedures in ring 0.

By arranging for standard user procedures to execute in ring 4, rings 2 and 3 become available for the protection of user-constructed subsystems. Subsystems executing in rings 2 and 3 of a process can be protected from procedures executing in rings 4-7 in the same way that the supervisor is protected from procedures executing in rings 2-7. All comments made about a supervisor implemented in rings 0 and 1 of each process apply to protected subsystems implemented in rings 2 and 3. Different protected subsystems may be operated simultaneously in rings 2 and 3 of different processes and several processes may share the use of the same protected subsystem simultaneously. The ring protection scheme allows the operation of user-constructed protected subsystems without auditing them for inclusion in the supervisor. (The software facility that forces standard user procedures to execute in ring 4, and yet allows all users to freely provide ring 3 protected subsystems for one another, is not discussed here.) Examples of protected subsystems that might be provided by various users are a proprietary compiler or a subsystem to provide interpretive access to some sensitive data base and safely log each request for information.

With most user procedures executing in ring 4, rings 5, 6, and 7 are available for user self-protection. For example, a user may debug a program by executing it in ring 5, where only procedure and data segments intended to be referenced by the program would be made accessible. The ring protection mechanisms would detect many of the addressing errors that could be made by the program and would prevent the untested program from accidently damaging other segments accessible from ring 4. In the same way ring 5 can be used for the execution of an untrusted program borrowed from another user.

Because supervisor gates are not accessible from rings 6 and 7 of any process in Multics, procedures executed in these rings have no explicit access to supervisor functions; they may, however, be given permission to call user-provided gates into rings 4 or 5. Ring 6 of a process might be used, for example, to provide a suitably isolated environment for student programs being evaluated by a grading program executing in ring 4.

The complete description of a software access control facility based on rings that allows them to be used in the manner just outlined would require another paper. A fundamental constraint enforced by this software facility is that a program executing in ring $\underline{n}$ cannot specify R1, R2, or R3 values of less than $\underline{n}$ in an access control list entry of any segment. Although a given ring may simultaneously protect different subsystems in different processes, each ring of each process can protect only one subsystem at a time. A usable software access control facility must constrain each user's ability to dynamically set and modify access control specifications so that this sole occupant property can be verified and enforced when necessary.

CONCLUSIONS

The hardware mechanisms derived and described in this paper implement a methodical generalization of the traditional supervisor/

user protection scheme that is compatible with a shared virutal memory based on segmentation. This generalization solves three significant kinds of problems of a general purpose system to be used as a computer utility:

- users can create arbitrary, but protected, subsystems for use by others;
- the supervisor can be implemented in layers which are enforced;
- the user can protect himself while debugging his own (or borrowed) programs.

The subset access property of rings of protection does not provide for what may be called "multually suspicious programs" operating under the control of a single process. On the other hand, it is just that subset property which imposes an organization which is easy to understand and thus allows a system or subsystem designer to convince himself that his implementation is complete. Also, it is just the subset property which is the basis for a hardware implementation that is integrated with segmentation mechanisms, requiring very small additional costs in hardware logic and processor speed.

The long-range effect of hardware protection mechanisms which permit calls to protected subsystems that use the same mechanisms as calls to other procedures is bound to be significant. In the interface to the supervisor of most systems there are many examples of facilities whose interface design is biased by the assumption that a call to the supervisor is relatively expensive; the usual result is to place several closely related functions together in the supervisor, even though only one of the group really needs protection. For example, in the Multics typewriter I/O package, only the functions of copying data in and out of shared buffer areas and of executing the privileged instruction to initiate I/O channel operation need to be protected. But, since these two functions are deeply tangled with typewriter operation strategy and code conversion, the typewriter I/O control package is currently implemented as a set of procedures all located in the lowest-numbered ring of the system, thus increasing the quantity of code which has maximum privilege.

A similar example is found in many file system designs, where complex file search operations are carried out entirely by protected supervisor routines rather than by unprotected library packages, primarily because a complex file search requires many individual file access operations, each of which would require transfer to a protected service routine, which transfer is presumed costly.

The initial version of Multics used software implemented rings of protection. The result was a very conservative use of the rings: originally just two supervisor rings and one user ring were employed, and the two supervisor rings were temporarily collapsed into one (thus exploiting the programming generality objective referred to before) while the software ring crossing mechanisms were tuned up. Today, although there are many obvious applications waiting, the ability to use more than two rings in a computation is just beginning to be exploited. The availability with the new Multics processor of hardware implemented rings which make downward calls and upward returns no more complex than calls and returns in the same ring should significantly increase such exploitation.

ACKNOWLEDGMENTS

The concepts embodied in the mechanisms described here were the result of seven years of maturing of ideas suggested by many workers. The original idea of generalizing the supervisor/user relationship to a multiple ring structure was suggested by R. M. Graham, E. L. Glaser, and F. J. Corbató. An initial software implementation of rings using multiple descriptor segments [14] was worked out by Graham and R. C. Daley, and constructed by members of the Multics system programming team. That implementation makes use of hardware access mode indicators stored in the segment descriptor word of the Honeywell 645 computer. Graham [9], in 1967, proposed a partial hardware implementation of rings of protection which included three ring numbers embedded in segment descriptor words, and a processor ring register, but which still required software intervention on all ring crossings. Though a related scheme was implemented in the Hitac 5020 time-sharing system [15], this hardware scheme was never implemented in Multics, which today (1971) still uses a version of the software implementation of rings. The complete automation of downward calls and upward returns was proposed in a thesis in 1969 [16]; the description in this paper extends that thesis slightly with the addition of ring numbers to indirect words and the processor pointer registers, as suggested by Daley. The CALL and RETURN instructions proposed there have also been simplified.

The hardware implemented call and return, and automatically managed stacks, were at least partly inspired by similar mechanisms which have long been used on computer systems of the Burroughs Corporation [4, 11].

In addition to those named above, D.D. Clark, C.T. Clingen, R.J. Feiertag, J.M. Grochow, N.I. Morris, M.A. Padlipsky, M.R. Thompson, V.L. Voydock, and V.A. Vyssotsky contributed significant help in understanding and implementing rings of protection.

REFERENCES

1. Apfelbaum, H., and Oppenheimer, G. "Design of virtual memory systems," Proc. 1971 IEEE Internat. Comput. Soc. Conf., Boston, pp. 115–116.
2. Arden, B.W., et al. "Program and addressing structure in a time-sharing environment," J. ACM 13, 1 (Jan. 1966), 1–16.
3. Bensoussan, A., Clingen, C.T., and Daley, R.C. "The Multics virtual memory," Proc. Second ACM Symposium on Operating Systems Principles. Princeton, N.J., 1969, ACM New York, 1971, pp. 30–42. Also Comm. ACM (to appear).
4. Burroughs Corporation. A Narrative Description of the Burroughs B5500 Master Control Program, Detroit, Mich. Oct. 1969.
5. Dennis, J.B., and VanHorn, E.C. "Programming semantics for multiprogrammed computations," Comm. ACM 9, 3 (Mar. 1966), 143–155.
6. Dijkstra, E.W. "The structure of the "THE"-multiprogramming system," Comm. ACM 11, 5 (May 1968), 341–346.
7. Evans, D.C., and LeClerc, J.Y. "Address mapping and the control of access in an interactive computer," Proc. AFIPS 1967 SJCC, Vol. 30, AFIPS Press, Montvale, N.J. pp. 23–30.
8. Fabry, R.S. Preliminary description of a supervisor for a computer organized around capabilities. Quarterly Progress Rep. No. 18, Institute of Computer Research, U. of Chicago, I-B 1–97.
9. Graham, R.M. "Protection in an information processing utility," Comm. ACM 11, 5 (May 1968), 365–369.
10. Honeywell Information Systems Inc., Model 645 Processor Reference Manual. Cambridge Information Systems Laboratory, Apr. 1971.
11. Hauck, E.A., and Dent, B.A. "Burrough's B6500/B7500 stack mechanisms," Proc. AFIPS 1968 SJCC, Vol. 32, AFIPS Press, Montvale, N.J. pp. 245–251.

12. Lampson, B.W. An Overview of the CAL Time-Sharing System. Computation Center, U. of California, Berkeley, Sept. 1969.
13. Lampson, B.W. "Dynamic protection structures," Proc. AFIPS 1969 FJCC, Vol. 35, AFIPS Press, Montvale, N.J. 27–38.
14. MIT Project MAC. Multics Programmer's Manual. 1969.
15. Motobayashi, S., Masuda, T., and Takahashi, N., "The Hitac 5020 time-sharing system," Proc ACM 24th Nat. Conf. 1969, ACM New York, pp. 419–429.
16. Schroeder, M.D. Classroom model of an information and computing service. S.M. Th. MIT, Dep. Elec. Eng., Feb. 1969. [Expanded version available as Proj. MAC Tech. Rep. MAC-TR-80.]
17. Vanderbilt, D.H. Controlled information sharing in a computer utility. MIT Project MAC, MAC-TR-67, 1969.

Hardware Aspects of
Secure Computing

LEE M. MOLHO

INTRODUCTION

It makes no sense to discuss software for privacy-preserving or secure time-shared computing without considering the hardware on which it is to run. Software access controls rely upon certain pieces of hardware. If these can go dead or be deliberately disabled without warning, then all that remains is false security.

This paper is about hardware aspects of controlled-access time-shared computing.* A detailed study was recently made of two pieces of hardware that are required for secure time-sharing on an IBM System 360 Model 50 computer: the storage protection system and the Problem/Supervisor state control system.[1] It uncovered over a hundred cases where a single hardware failure will compromise security without giving an alarm. Hazards of this kind, which are present in any computer hardware which supports software access controls, have been essentially eliminated in the SDC ADEPT-50 Time-Sharing System through techniques described herein.[2]

Analysis based on that work has clarified what avenues are available for subversion via hardware; they are outlined in this paper. A number of ways to fill these security gaps are then

---

*The relationship between "security" and "privacy" has been discussed elsewhere.[3,4] In this paper "security" is used to cover controlled-access computing in general.

SOURCE: Spring Joint Computer Conference, 1970, Proceedings. Reprinted by permission of the publisher, American Federation of Information Processing Societies Press.

developed, including methods applicable to a variety of computers. Administrative policy considerations, problems in security certification of hardware, and hardware design considerations for secure time-shared computing also receive comment.

FAILURE, SUBVERSION, AND SECURITY

Two types of security problem can be found in computer hardware. One is the problem of hardware failure. This includes not only computer logic that fails by itself, but also miswiring and faulty hardware caused by improper maintenance ("Customer Engineer") activity, including CE errors in making field-installable engineering changes.

The other security problem is the cloak-and-dagger question of the susceptibility of hardware to subversion by unauthorized persons. Can trivial hardware changes jeopardize a secure computing facility even if the software remains completely pure? This problem and the hardware failure problem, which will be considered in depth, are related.

Weak Points for Logic Failure

Previous work involved an investigation of portions of the 360/50 hardware.[1] Its primary objective was to pinpoint single-failure problem locations. The question was asked, "If this element fails, will hardware required for secure computing go dead without giving an alarm?" A total of 99 single-failure hazards were found in the 360/50 storage protection hardware; they produce a variety of system effects. Three such logic elements were found in the simpler Problem/Supervisor state (PSW bit 15) logic. A failure in this logic would cause the 360/50 to always operate in the Supervisor state.

An assumption was made in finding single-failure logic problems which at first may seem more restrictive than it really is: A failure is defined as having occurred if the output of a logic element remains in an invalid state based on the states of its inputs. Other failure modes certainly exist for logic elements, but they reduce to this case as follows: (1) an intermittent logic element meets this criterion, but only part of the time; (2) a shorted or open input will cause an invalid output state at least part of the time; (3) a logic element which exhibits excessive signal delay will appear to have an invalid output state for some time after any input transition; (4) an output wire which has been connected to an improper location will have an invalid output state based on its inputs at least part of the time; such a connection may also have permanently damaged the element, making its output independent of its input. It should be noted that failure possibilities were counted; for those relatively few cases where a security problem is caused whether the element gets stuck in "high" or in "low" state, two possibilities were counted.

A situation was frequently encountered which is considered in a general way in the following section, but which is touched upon here. Many more logic elements besides those tallied would cause the storage protection hardware to go dead if they failed, but fortunately (from a security viewpoint) their failure would cause some other essential part of the 360/50 to fail, leading to an overall system crash. "Failure detection by faulty system operation" keeps many logic elements from becoming security problems.

Circumventing Logic Failure

Providing redundant logic is a reasonable first suggestion as a means of eliminating single failures as security problems. However, redundancy has some limits which are not apparent until a close look is taken at the areas of security concern within the Central Processing Unit (CPU). Security problems are really in control logic, such as the logic activated by a storage protect violation signal, rather than in multi-bit data paths, where redundancy in the form of error-detecting and error-correcting codes is often useful. Indeed, the 360/50 CPU already uses an error-detecting code extensively, since parity checks are made on many multi-bit paths within it.

Effective use of redundant logic presents another problem. One must fully understand the system as it stands to know what needs to be added. Putting it another way, full hardware certification must take place before redundancy can be added (or appreciated, if the manufacturer claims it is there to begin with).

Lastly, some areas of hardware do not lend themselves too easily to redundancy: There can be only one address at a time to the Read-Only-Storage (ROS) unit whose microprograms control the 360/50 CPU.[5,6] One could, of course, use such a scheme as triple-modular redundancy on all control paths, providing three copies of ROS in the bargain. The result of such an approach would not be much like a 360/50.

Redundancy has a specialized, supplementary application in conjunction with hardware certification. After the process of certification reveals which logic elements can be checked by software at low overhead, redundant logic may be added to take care of the remainder. A good example is found in the storage protection logic. Eleven failure possibilities exist where protection interrupts would cause an incorrect microprogram branch upon failure. These failure possibilities arise in part from the logic elements driven by one control signal line. This signal could be provided redundantly to make the hardware secure.

Software tests provide another way to eliminate hardware failure as a security problem. Code can be written which should cause a protection or privileged-operation interrupt; to pass the test the interrupt must react appropriately. Such software must interface the operating system software for scheduling and storage-protect lock alteration, but must execute in Problem state to perform its tests. There is clearly a tradeoff between system overhead and rate of testing. As previously mentioned, hardware certification must be performed to ascertain what hardware can be checked by software tests, and how to check it.

Software testing of critical hardware is a simple and reasonable approach, given hardware certification; it is closely related to a larger problem, that of testing for software holes with software. Software testing of hardware, added to the SDC ADEPT-50 Time-Sharing System, has eliminated over 85 percent of present single-failure hazards in the 360/50 CPU.

Microprogramming could also be put to work to combat failure problems. A microprogrammed routine could be included in ROS which would automatically test critical hardware, taking immediate action if the test were not passed. Such a microprogram could either be in the form of an executable instruction (e.g., TEST PROTEC-TION), or could be automatic, as part of the timer-update sequence, for example.

A microprogrammed test would have much lower overhead than an equivalent software test performed at the same rate; if automatic, it would test even in the middle of user-program execution. A preliminary design of a storage-protection test that would be exercised every timer update time (60 times per second) indicated an overhead of only 0.015 percent (150 test cycles for every million ROS cycles). Of even greater significance is that microprogrammed testing is specifiable. A hardware vendor can be given the burden of proof of showing that the tests are complete; the vendor would have to take the testing requirement into account in design. The process hardware certification could be reduced to a design review of vendor tests if this approach were taken.

Retrofitting microprogrammed testing in a 360/50 would not involve extensive hardware changes, but some changes would have to be made. Testing microprograms would have to be written by the manufacturer; new ROS storage elements would have to be fabricated. A small amount of logic and a large amount of documentation would also have to be changed.

Logic failure can be totally eliminated as a security problem in computer hardware by these methods. A finite effort and minor overhead are required; what logic is secured depends upon the approach taken. If microprogram or software functional testing is used, miswiring and dead hardware caused by CE errors will also be discovered.

Subversion Techniques

It is worthwhile to take the position of a would-be system subverter, and proceed to look at the easiest and best ways of using the 360/50 to steal files from unsuspecting users. What hardware changes would have to be made to gain access to protected core memory or to enter the Supervisor state?

Fixed changes to eliminate hardware features are obvious enough; just remove the wire that carries the signal to set PSW bit 15, for example. But such changes are physically identical to hardware failures, since something is permanently wrong. As any functional testing for dead hardware will discover a fixed change, a potential subverter must be more clever.

In ADEPT-50, a user is swapped in periodically for a brief length of time (a "quantum"). During his quantum, a user can have access to the 360/50 at the machine-language level; no interpretive program comes between the user and his program unless, of course, he requests it. Thus, a clever subverter might seek to add some hardware logic to the CPU which would look for, say, a particular rather unusual sequence of two instructions in a program. Should that sequence appear, the added logic might disable storage protection for just a few dozen microseconds. Such a small "hole" in the hardware would be quite sufficient for the user to (1) access anyone's file; (2) cause a system crash; (3) modify anyone's file.

User-controllable changes could be implemented in many ways, with many modes of control and action besides this example (which was, however, one of the more effective schemes contemplated). Countermeasures to such controllable changes will be considered below, along with ways in which a subverter might try to anticipate countermeasures.

Countermeasures to Subversion

As implied earlier, anyone who has sufficient access to the CPU to install his own "design changes" in the hardware is likely to put in a controllable change, since a fixed change would be discovered by even a simple software test infrequently performed. A user-controllable change, on the other hand would not be discovered by tests outside the user's quantum, and would be hard to discover even within it, as will become obvious.

The automatic microprogrammed test previously discussed would have a low probability of discovering a user-controllable hardware change. Consider an attempt by a user to replace his log-in number with the log-in number of the person whose file he wants to steal. He must execute a MOVE CHARACTERS instruction of length 12 to do this, requiring only about 31 microseconds for the 360/50 CPU to perform. A microprogrammed test occurring at timer interrupts—once each 16 milliseconds—would have a low probability of discovering such a brief security breach. Increasing the test rate, though it raises the probability, raises the overhead correspondingly. A test occurring at 16 microsecond intervals, for example, represents a 15 percent overhead.

A reasonable question is whether a software test might do a better job of spotting user-controllable hardware changes. One would approach this task by attempting to discover changes with tests inserted in user programs in an undetectable fashion. One typical method would do this by inserting invisible breakpoints into the user's instruction stream; when they were encountered during the user's quantum, a software test of storage protection and PSW bit 15 would be performed.

A software test of this type could be written, and as will be discussed, such a software test would be difficult for a subverter to circumvent. Nevertheless, the drawbacks of this software test are severe. Reentrant code is required so that the software test can know (1) the location of the instruction stream, and (2) that no instructions are hidden in data areas. Requiring reentrant programs would in turn require minor changes to the ADEPT-50 Jovial compiler and major changes to the F-level Assembler. A small microprogram change would even be required, so that software could sense the difference between a fetch-protect interrupt and an execute-protect interrupt. Changes would be required to the ADEPT-50 SERVIS, INTRUP, DEBUG, and SKED modules. Were such a software test implemented, run-time overhead would likely be rather high for frequent breakpoint-insertions, since each breakpoint inserted would require execution of 50 or more instructions at run time. Lastly, programmers might not always like having to write reentrant code.

These implementation problems, though described for one specific test approach, are likely to extend to any test which attempts to interrupt running user programs via software, since any such test must isolate and augment every user's instruction stream.

Although the above does not demonstrate that detecting user controllable subversion hardware is impossible, it should indicate that by no means is such detection trivial. It is even harder than the above may suggest, for, as the next section indicates, while the subverter is busily building his controllable changes into the CPU he may add insult to injury by inactivating anti-failure and anti-subversion hardware.

Defeat of Countermeasures

Hardware countermeasures that are easy to install are easy to remove. Redundant logic can be disabled with the same wire cutters or wire-unwrapper as other logic. This is also true of state-testing and parity-check logic. Alternatively, a clever subverter may add logic that picks up a test signal and uses it to inactivate his own logic while the test is performed. The subverter may, alternatively, arrange things so that tests always pass during his quantum.

Microprogrammed countermeasures are somewhat more difficult for the subverter to inactivate, since he must decode particular ROS addresses to know that a microprogrammed test routine has begun. Once he has done this, though, he may proceed as if he were dealing with hardware, since on a short-term basis, microprogram contents and addresses do not change. The net result of putting counter-measures in ROS rather than in logic is to raise the "work function" for subversion; that is, the subverter must do more work to achieve his goal, but he can reach it.

On the other hand, a thorough software test, such as the break-point test previously described, would be nearly impossible to defeat by hardware techniques. This is because of the transient nature of software: a subverter would have to decode program variables such as addresses via hardware; then even minor changes in the breakpoint-placing routines would make that hardware useless. One must recall, however, the large implementation and overhead problems inherent in a user-interrupting software test. In summary, countermeasures can be devised which have a high "work function," but they entail major costs in implementation and system efficiency.

Two assumptions have been inherent in this discussion; namely, that the subverter has both knowledge of system hardware (including subversion countermeasures) and means of changing the hardware. This need not be the case, but whether it is depends on administrative rather than technical considerations. Administrative considerations are the next subject.

Administrative Policy

Special handling of hardware documentation and engineering changes may be worthwhile when commercial lines of computers are used for secure time-sharing. First, if hardware or microprograms have been added to the computer to test for failures and subversion attempts, the details of the tests should not be obtainable from the computer manufacturer's worldwide network of sales representatives. The fact that testing is done and the technical details of that testing would seem to be legitimate security objects, since a subverter can neutralize testing only if he knows of it. Classification of those documents which relate to testing is a policy question which should be considered. Likewise, redundant hardware, such as a second copy of the PSW bit 15 logic, might be included in the same category.

The second area is that of change control. Presumably the "Customer Engineer" (CE) personnel who perform engineering changes have clearances allowing them access to the hardware, but what about the technical documents which tell them what to do? A clever subverter could easily alter an engineering-change wire list to include his modifications, or could send spurious change documentation. A CE would then unwittingly install the subverter's "engineering change." Since it is asking too much to expect a CE to understand on a wire-by-wire basis each change he performs, some new step is necessary if one wants to be sure that engineering changes are made for technical reasons only. In other words, the computer manufacturer's engineering changes are security objects in the sense that their integrity must be guaranteed. Special paths of transmittal and post-installation verification by the manufacturer might be an adequate way to secure engineering changes; there are undoubtedly other ways. It is clear that a problem exists.

Finally, it should be noted that the 360/50 ROS storage elements, or any equivalent parts of another manufacturer's hardware that contain all system microprogramming, ought to be treated in a special manner, such as physically sealing them in place as part of hardware certification. New storage elements containing engineering changes are security objects of even higher order than regular engineering-change documents, and should be handled accordingly, from their manufacture through their installation.

GENERALIZATIONS AND CONCLUSIONS

Some general points about hardware design that relate to secure time-sharing and some short-range and long-range conclusions are the topics of this section.

Fail-Secure vs. Fail-Soft Hardware

Television programs, novels, and motion pictures have made it well known that if something is "fail-safe," it doesn't blow up when it fails. In the same vein, designers of high-reliability computers coined the term "fail-soft" to describe a machine that degrades its performance when a failure occurs, instead of becoming completely useless. It is now proposed to add another term to this family: "Fail-secure: to protect secure information regardless of failure."

The ability to detect failures is a prerequisite for fail-secure operation. However, all system provisions for corrective action based on failure detection must be carefully designed, particularly when hardware failure correction is involved. Two cases were recently described wherein a conflict arose between hardware and software that had been included to circumvent failures.* Automatic correction hardware could likewise mask problems which should be brought to the attention of the System Security Officer via security software.

Clearly, something between the extremes of system crash and silent automatic correction should occur when hardware fails. Definition of what <u>does</u> happen upon failure of critical hardware should be

---

*At the "Workshop on Hardware-Software Interaction for System Reliability and Recovery in Fault-Tolerant Computers," held July 14–15, 1969 at Pacific Palisades, California, J. W. Herndon of Bell Telephone Labs reported that a problem had arisen in a developmental version of Bell's "Electronic Switching System." It seems that an elaborate setup of relays would begin reconfiguring a bad communications channel at the same time that software in ESS was trying to find out what was wrong. R. F. Thomas, Jr. of the Los Alamos Scientific Laboratory, having had a similar problem with a self-checking data acquisition system, agreed with Herndon that hardware is not clever enough to know what do to about system failures; software failure correction approaches are preferable.

a design requirement for fail-secure time-sharing systems. Fail-soft computers are not likely to be fail-secure computers, nor vice versa, unless software and hardware have been designed with both concepts in mind.

Failure Detection by Faulty System Operation

Computer hardware logic can be grouped by the system operation or operations it helps perform. Some logic—for example, the clock distribution logic—helps perform only one system operation. Other logic—such as the read-only storage address logic in the 360/50—helps perform many system operations, from floating point multiplication to memory protection interrupt handling. When logic is needed by more than one system operation, it is cross-checked for proper performance: Should an element needed for system operations A and B fail, the failure of system operation B would indicate the malfunction of this portion of operation A's logic.

Such interdependence is quite useful in a fail-secure system, as it allows failures to be detected by faulty system operation—a seemingly inelegant error detection mechanism, yet one which requires neither software nor hardware overhead. Some ideas on its uses and limitations follow.

The result of a hardware logic failure can usually be defined in terms of what happens to the system operations associated with the dead hardware. Some logic failure modes are detectable, because they make logic elements downstream misperform unrelated system operations. Analysis will also reveal failure modes which spoil only the system operation which they help perform. These failures must be detected in some other way. There are also, but more rarely, cases where a hardware failure may lead to an operation failure that is not obvious. In the 360/50, a failure could cause skipping of a segment of a control microprogram that wasn't really needed on that cycle. Such failures are not detectable by faulty system operation at least part of the time.

Advantage may be taken of this failure-detection technique in certifying hardware to be fail-secure as well as in original hardware design. In general, the more interdependencies existing among chunks of logic, the more likely are failures to produce faulty system operation. For example, in many places in a computer one finds situations as sketched in Figure 1. Therein, System Operation A needs the services of Logic Group 1 and Logic Group 3, while System Operation B needs Logic Group 2 and Logic Group 3. Note at this point that, as above, if System Operation A doesn't work because of a failure in Logic Group 3, we have concurrently detected a failure in the logic supporting System Operation B.

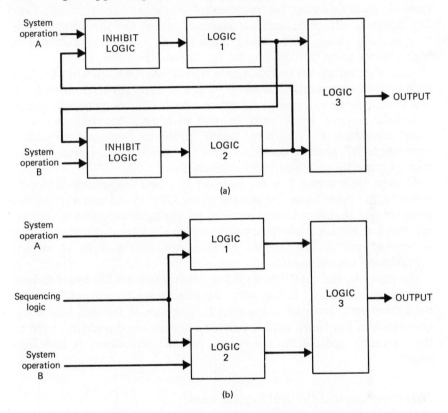

FIGURE 1. Inhibit logic vs. sequencing logic.

A further point is made in Figure 1. Often System Operations A and B must be mutually exclusive; hardware must be added to prevent simultaneous activation of A and B. Two basic design approaches may be taken to solve this problem. An "inhibiting" scheme may be used, wherein logic is added that inhibits Logic Group 1 when Logic Group 2 is active, and vice versa. This approach is illustrated by Figure 1(a). Alternatively, a "sequencing" scheme may be used, wherein logic not directly involved with 1 or 2—such as system clock, mode selection logic, or a status register—defines when A and B are to be active. This approach is illustrated by Figure 1(b).

Now, "inhibit" logic belongs to a particular System Operation, for its function is to asynchronously, on demand, condition the hardware to perform that System Operation. It depends on nothing else; if it fails by going permanently inactive, only its System Operation is affected, and no alarm is given. On the other hand, "sequencing" logic feeds many areas of the machine; its failure is highly likely to be detected by faulty system operation.

A further point can be made here which may be somewhat controversial: that an overabundance of "inhibit"-type asynchronous logic is a good indicator of sloppy design or bad design coordination. While a certain amount must exist to deal with asynchronous pieces of hardware, often it is put in to "patch" problems that no one realized were there till system checkout time. Evidence of such design may suggest more thorough scrutiny is desirable.

System Operations can be grouped by their frequency of occurrence: some operations are needed every CPU cycle, some when the programmer requests them, some only during maintenance, and so on. Thus, some logic which appears to provide a cross-check on other logic may not do so frequently or predictably enough to satisfy certification requirements.

To sum up, the fact that a system crashes when a hardware failure occurs, rather than "failing soft" by continuing to run without the dead hardware, may be a blessing in disguise. If fail-soft operation encompasses hardware that is needed for continued security, such as the memory protection hardware, fail-soft operation is not fail-secure.

Data Checking and Control Signal Errors

Control signals which direct data transfers will often be checked by logic that was put in only to verify data purity. The nature and extent of this checking is dependent on the error-detection code used and upon the length of the data field (excluding check bits).

What happens is that if logic fails which controls a data path and its check bits, the data will be forced to either all zeros or all ones. If one or both of these cases is illegal, the control logic error will be detected when the data is checked. (Extensive parity checking on the 360/50 CPU results in much control logic failure detection capability therein.) Table 1 demonstrates an example of this effect; Table 2 describes the conditions for which it exists for the common parity check.

TABLE 1. Control Signal Error Detection by Odd Parity
Check on Odd-Length Data Field

DATA BITS 012 P	MEANING
000 0	data error or control logic error[*]
000 1	0
001 0	1
001 1	data error
010 0	2
010 1	data error
011 0	data error
011 1	3
100 0	4
100 1	data error
101 0	data error
101 1	5
110 0	data error
110 1	6
111 0	7
111 1	data error or control logic error[**]

[*]Control logic incorrectly set all bits to zero.
[**]Control logic incorrectly set all bits to one.

TABLE 2. Control Signal Error Detection by Parity Checking

DATA FIELD LENGTH:	PARITY:	CONTROL LOGIC ERROR CAUSES:	
		all zeros	all ones
even	odd	CAUGHT	MISSED
even	even	MISSED	CAUGHT
odd	odd	CAUGHT	CAUGHT
odd	even	MISSED	MISSED

CONCLUSIONS

From a short-range viewpoint, 360/50 CPU hardware has some weak spots in it but no holes, as far as secure time-sharing is concerned. Furthermore, the weak spots can be reinforced with little expense. Several alternatives in this regard have been described.

From a longer-range viewpoint, anyone who contemplates specifying a requirement for hardware certification should know what such an effort involves. As reference, some notes are appropriate as to what it took to examine the 360/50 memory protection system to the level required for meaningful hardware certification. The writer first obtained several publications which describe the system. Having read these, the writer obtained the logic diagrams, went to the beginning points of several operations, and traced logic forward. Signals entering a point were traced backward until logic was found which would definitely cause faulty machine operation outside the protection system if it failed. During this tedious process, discrepancies arose between what had been read and what the logic diagrams appeared to show. Some discrepancies were resolved by further study; some were accounted for by special features on the SDC 360/50; some remain.

After logic tracing, the entire protection system was sketched out on eight 8½ × 11 pages. This drawing proved to be extremely valuable for improving the writer's understanding, and enabled failure-mode charting that would have been intractable by manual means from the manufacturer's logic diagrams.

For certifying hardware, documentation quality and currentness is certainly a problem. The manufacturer's publications alone are necessary but definitely not sufficient, because of version differences, errors, over-simplifications, and insufficient detail. Both these and machine logic diagrams are needed.

Though the hardware certification outlook is bleak, an alternative does exist: testing. As previously described, it is possible to require inclusion of low-overhead functional testing of critical hardware in a secure computing system. The testing techniques, whether embedded in hardware, microprograms, or software, could be put under security control if some protection against hardware subversion is desired. Furthermore, administrative security control procedures should extend to "Customer Engineer" activity and to engineering change documentation to the extent necessary to insure that hardware changes are made for technical reasons only.

Careful control of access to computer-based information is, and ought to be, of general concern today. Access controls in a secure time-sharing system such as ADEPT-50 are based on hardware features.[7] The latter deserve scrutiny.

REFERENCES

1. L. Molho, Hardware Reliability Study, SDC N-(L)-24276/126/00, December, 1969.
2. R. Linde, C. Weissman, and C. Fox, "The ADEPT-50 time-sharing system," Proceedings of the Fall Joint Computer Conference, Vol. 35, pp. 39–50, 1969. Also issued as SDC document SP-3344.
3. W. H. Ware, "Security and privacy in computer systems," Proceedings of the Spring Joint Computer Conference, Vol. 30, pp. 279–282, 1967.
4. W. H. Ware, "Security and privacy: Similarities and differences," Proceedings of the Spring Joint Computer Conference, Vol. 30, pp. 287–290, 1967.
5. S. G. Tucker, "Microprogram control for system/360," IBM Systems Journal, Vol. 6, No. 4, pp. 222–241, 1967.
6. G. C. Vandling and D. E. Waldecker, "The microprogram control technique for digital logic design," Computer Design. Vol. 8, No. 8, pp. 44–51, August 1969.
7. C. Weissman, "Security controls in the ADEPT-50 time-sharing system," Proceedings of the Fall Joint Computer Conference, Vol. 35, pp. 119–133, 1969. Also issued as SDC document SP-3342.

Section VII
SECURITY IN
EXISTING SYSTEMS

No one checklist for computer security can be all-encompassing.
However, we here present a taxonomy of security and integrity
put together by Peter S. Browne, which covers a great many areas.
Not all of the items will be appropriate for any particular installation and there are undoubtedly some installations which will find
it necessary to add items to this list. Nevertheless, we believe that
this list can serve as a reasonable starting point for most users.
There are also other checklists available, for example those of
D. Van Tassel [5] and W. F. Brown [6].

This section also includes a description of IBM's Resource
Security System, a program product which enhances greatly the
security of their standard operating systems for the 360 and
370 series machines, but at a large cost in overhead. The description given here is culled from available IBM information
and manuals and the extent to which the features described
have actually been implemented should be confirmed with IBM.
Both items in this section have not been published previously.

Taxonomy of Security
and Integrity

PETER S. BROWNE

A. General.
  1. Security protection should safeguard against the following threats:
     a. Accidental.
        (1) User error.
        (2) System error.
     b. Passive infiltration.
        (1) Tapping of communications lines.
        (2) Emanations pickup.
     c. Active infiltration.
        (1) Browsing through files via an on-line terminal.
        (2) Masquerading as a legitimate user.
        (3) Physical acquisition of files (cards, tapes, listings).
        (4) Exploiting the system (through dumps, "trapdoors" in the executive, etc.).
  2. The first step is to analyze the entire system. Then, design safeguards. Perform the following:
     a. Description of the environment in which the system is intended to operate.
     b. Identification of protection features that are needed (see following pages for a "menu").
     c. Determination of the presence or absence of such features in the given system.
     d. Documentation as to how these features are applied or should be applied.

SOURCE: Peter S. Browne. Reprinted from P. Browne, unpublished Ms. draft (May 1972). Reprinted by permission of the author.

    e.   Ordering of these safeguards into a framework showing the manner or degree that they are applied.

    f.   Determination as to whether the features actually meet the requirements of "b" above.

    g.   Examination and attempted subversion of all system security features for the purposes of testing.

    h.   Evaluation of test results to determine whether adequate protection can and will be provided in accordance with established requirements.

3.   The security system should support separate identification for the following objects:

    a.   Individual users.

    b.   Terminals/stations/areas by location.

    c.   Individual programs (jobs) by name and function.

    d.   Data—down to element or record level if necessary.

4.   Access restrictions should be constrained in any or all of the following manners:

    a.   By hierarchical classification (Top Secret, Confidential, etc.).

    b.   By category or compartments (codeword data, accounting department, etc.).

    c.   By listing specific constraints and applying them to specific objects (Browne can read the personnel, accounting and inventory files, but can write the inventory file only; terminal "A" can only access Secret or below data; terminal "B" only can access payroll data).

    d.   By the content of data (all salaries over $20,000).

    e.   By constraints based on the context of data (logistics data in conjunction with performance data).

    f.   Through user supplied procedures or formularies that apply only to special situations.

5.   Users or programs should be restricted to any or all of the following privileges:

    a.   Read.

    b.   Write.

       (1) Modify—(increment, decrement, change, set to zero).

       (2) Append—(elements, entries, records, files).

       (3) Insert—(elements, entries, records, files).

    c.   Delete (or set to null).

6. The ultimate goal of a secure system is to insure that all data movement is identified, authorized, receipted, and recorded.

B. Administrative and organizational.

   1. Administrative.

      a. Limit unescorted access to the central computer facility (use visitor's logs).

      b. Control the authority to modify critical systems software.

      c. Test and verify changes to systems software and security routines.

      d. Develop administrative cross-checks between system, operations, and security controls.

      e. Limit personnel privileges as much as possible.

      f. Control all input and output. Classify all data as to sensitivity and value.

      g. Analyze audit and performance data for security impact. Monitor operations, meter hours vs. schedules, downtime, distribution of output, etc.

      h. Maintain manual audit records for access to the system, changes to systems software, maintenance and system faults or restarts.

      i. Insure personnel competence and integrity—background checks, cross-training, changing of jobs, continuing education, identification of disgruntled employees, and immediate release of those who are laid off or fired.

   2. Organizational.

      a. Develop a consistent security policy throughout the entire organization.

      b. Appoint a full-time system security officer and give him authority as well as responsibility.

      c. Make an individual responsible for security at each terminal location.

      d. Secure the tape and disc libraries and insure that a full-time librarian is on duty at all times.

      e. Separate the responsibilities and authority of those individuals who are critical to system security.

      f. Select key personnel on the basis of integrity and competence.

      g. Control vendor and contract maintenance personnel as strictly as in-house employees.

h. Form a computer security committee that crosses organizational boundaries.

3. Procedural.

a. Set up written procedures for:

(1) Start up of the system.

(2) Shut down of the system.

(3) Restarts (reboot or IPL).

(4) Control of tapes, discs, cards, listings.

(5) Identification of users to the system.

(6) Control of access to the central facility and to terminals.

(7) Software changes—application as well as systems software.

(8) Changes to security parameters.

(9) Maintenance.

(10) Control of jobs and job flow.

(11) Certification and system tests.

b. Devise and practice procedures for disaster recovery to include an implementation plan for back-up facilities. Test them periodically.

c. Train for bomb threats and other civil disturbances.

d. Devise restrictive policies regarding:

(1) Visits to the computer areas.

(2) Publicity regarding EDP operations.

e. Insure that stored tapes and discs are periodically cleaned, sampled for dropouts, stored in appropriate containers and certified.

f. Maintain documentation according to predetermined standards. Review this documentation on a periodic basis.

g. Document retention cycles for each data and program application area. Coordinate with the standards effort.

h. Develop internal audit controls over computer usage, data input, output distribution, program changes, error reporting, quality control, program testing, and back-up.

i. For commercial installations, buy adequate insurance protection.

C. Physical, hardware, communications.

1. Physical.

a. Implement "closed shop" access control—use guards, badge readers, closed circuit TV, limited entry points, central monitoring, etc.

b. Control access to terminals and remote entry stations in accordance with the protection needs for input and output designated for that station.

c. Insure that the facility is protected against exposure from fire, flooding, and natural elements—by means of construction, proper drainage, protected location, fire/smoke detectors, noncombustible furniture, etc.

d. Protect against utility unreliability by protection and backup of sources of power and air conditioning. Use dual feeds, redundant equipment, etc.

e. Demand good housekeeping; prevent accumulations of trash, dispose of waste materials, prohibit smoking in EDP rooms, and clean on a regular basis.

f. Lock critical software and documentation in a secured area.

g. Provide for backup files of programs and data at a secondary location. Keep current inventories of all software, data files and documentation.

h. Control access to vital areas for custodial and maintenance personnel.

i. Implement a two-man policy for all physical areas involved with data processing.

j. Implement controls on entry to sensitive areas by visitors, vendors, and programmers. Badge readers, guards, man-traps, or other variants of controlled access systems can be used for this purpose. Non-controlled exits should be alarmed.

2. Hardware.

The computer hardware should come equipped with the following features. The first six should be required, the last five are optional.

a. Two modes—privileged and user (or master/slave).

b. Boundary control registers, permission registers, memory protect keys or a base addressing scheme for core limits protection.

c. Every operations code should have a known response. Any non-legal instruction or bit pattern will result in an interrupt and abort.

d. Both read and write protect (fetch and store).

e. Positive hardware identification of terminals and peripherals.

f. Detection and notification of errors, failures and attempts to utilize unauthorized devices. All such interrupts should be trapped by the security or authorization software.

    g.   Key switches or lockouts of peripherals, clocks, terminals, and other devices.

    h.   Hardware registers that allow cross-checks for actual versus presumed contents.

    i.   Access control to be implemented in microcode.

    j.   Hardware erase features.

    k.   Consoles that are wired for update only or access only.

   3.   Communications.

    a.   All terminals and peripherals should be protected by tamper-free or cryptographically secure lines that are proofed against physical and/or emanations intrusion.

    b.   All messages should be numbered and dated.

    c.   The communications subsystem should include horizontal and vertical parity checking of messages.

    d.   There should be closed loop verification of message traffic (ACK/NAK, echoing of message, etc.).

    e.   The technical control or switching area should be protected against mis-connection of lines and terminals by means of color coding, different plug sizes or other methods.

    f.   Telephones and intercoms should be protected against leakage of background or sensitive information by means of push-to-talk features or disconnects.

    g.   Circuit switched systems need special protection by means of stringent access control requirements and positive identification of terminals.

    h.   If line dropout occurs, the system must be able to recover or invalidate traffic in progress.

    i.   A highly desirable feature would be for the hardware to validate formats and protocol through microprogramming.

D.   Software.

   1.   Access control.

    a.   Security objects such as individuals, terminals, programs, and data must be explicitly identified to the system. For individuals, the following approaches may be used:

      (1)   Passwords—and/or account numbers.

      (2)   Credit cards, badges, magnetically inscribed objects.

(3)   Identification based on personal characteristics such as voiceprint or fingerprints.

b.   Further authentication may be made by use of passwords or challenge and reply procedures.

c.   If passwords are used, they should:

(1)   Be randomly generated and of sufficient length to avoid compromise.

(2)   Be changed periodically, preferably every time used.

(3)   Be protected at least in accordance with the level of data they safeguard.

d.   The access control system should be sufficiently flexible to support a variety of constraints and mixes of objects. Users could be checked against terminals, programs, or data. An access list could be attached to any or all of the above depending on the needs of a particular installation.

e.   Every access to a given file or device must be capable of being trapped through the access control system in order to give the capability for additional authorization or identification checks.

2.   Data security.

a.   Data objects should be labeled with identification and security information. It is preferable to place this adjacent to the data rather than in a directory or index that is physically separated. The system should check these labels.

b.   All input and output should be labeled with security identification.

c.   Code words (lock words) can be placed within files to prevent reading of sensitive information. This type of access control, called gating, can allow a lock to be associated with given data.

d.   Data could be ordered or chained by classification level or structure. Sensitive data could be physically separate from public information.

e.   A history of data use could be declared in order to alleviate the problem of inference.

f.   Restricted data fields can be deleted or set to null on output.

g.   Data should always be accessed through indirect referencing—e.g., through a user directory to an owner's catalog to the data itself.

    h.   Data and programs can be internally transformed (encrypted).

3.   Data integrity.

This includes prevention against damage, update conflict, or the processing of incorrect data.

    a.   System, data and program backups must be taken periodically for purposes of recovery.

    b.   Data transfers should be validity checked. Recall of parts of a file should prohibit accidental retrieval of any other part of the file.

    c.   The data itself could be validated by a series of cross-checks, reasonableness checks, consistency checks, range checks, and sequence-of-event checks.

    d.   Loading of programs and data should be assured through check-sum totals or equivalent.

    e.   Program development should be controlled by means of automated procedures that bookkeep all changes. It should be possible to retain an audit trail of all program modules, their status and their use in production jobs.

    f.   If data is to be modified, a lockout or queuing mechanism should protect against contention or access to invalid information. Lockout should occur as late as possible and at as low a level as possible. On-line updates should be limited with all changes verified.

4.   System control and integrity.

    a.   All unauthorized accesses and I/O requests must result in termination of job, sounding of an alarm, purging of queues and refusal of service to the offending terminal.

    b.   All operations associated with memory allocation, system interrupt, and the mode of an operation must be controlled.

    c.   All user programs should be coded so that access to data is made through system calls that pass through the authorization mechanism.

    d.   Addresses passed between users and the system should be logical in nature. Real (physical) addresses are not acceptable. A virtual memory system is inherently safer than standard addressing.

    e.   Entrance points to the supervisor should be well defined with expected conditions enumerated. The supervisor (O/S) must be well documented.

    f.   Software should check security of output messages against routing indicators and the transmission lines.

    g.   There should be a mechanism for automatic determination of access rights for newly created data and programs.

    h.   Memory and peripherals should be cleared of residue between jobs.

    i.   If results of computations are unpredictable, operations should be curtailed and defaulted to more secure situations.

    j.   Restarts after "crashes" would include the loading of a fresh copy of the supervisor and a check of the consistency of system files.

    k.   Shutdown should be orderly with "graceful degradation."

5. Protection of the security system.

    a.   Do not give out information on denials.

    b.   Set a limit, generally one to three, for allowing repeated attempts to access the system after an invalid log-on.

    c.   The operating system should run in the user state insofar as possible.

    d.   Debugging must be through a certified interpreter and protection against dumping of system security information is essential.

    e.   Do not suspend security for system degradation or for testing purposes.

    f.   Contents of security files must be protected at the highest levels.

    g.   Assembly language programming should be limited or curtailed, especially at terminals. Attempt to restrict remote use to parameter driven interpreters.

    h.   No changing of security tables must be allowed except at a designated facility or console.

E. Audit, testing, and certification.

1. System auditing.

    a.   The ideal security situation is to have all data movement recorded. The system should at least log the events listed below under "threat monitoring."

    b.   A complete historical record must be capable of being reconstructed if the need arises.

    c.   Retention of program status and environmental conditions is necessary.

    d.   A program to analyze and evaluate audit statistics is needed. It probably should be written in-house.

2.   Testing.

    a.   A subverter program to generate false addresses, unauthorized attempts to access data, simulated failures, and other probes should be an essential part of testing the security system.

    b.   The supervisor (O/S) must be checked and verified.

    c.   Procedures, especially the little-used ones, are candidates for analysis.

    d.   Security test programs should be written and run immediately after violations or system maintenance, program load, or restart.

    e.   Control the testing and debugging of all applications programs.

    f.   Validate security tables and access routines.

    g.   Validate output for correctness and consistency.

3.   Threat monitoring.

    a.   The following events should be logged on a journal that is protected against modification by any user program:

        (1)   Jobs on and off, to include user/terminal/program identification, date, and time.

        (2)   Data requested.

        (3)   Files accessed, to include type, number of accesses, and access keys.

        (4)   Disposition of data (number of records output or displayed, program status information, etc.).

        (5)   Unauthorized log-ons.

        (6)   Response to random queries.

        (7)   Any special use of the system.

        (8)   All descriptor changes.

        (9)   Configuration changes.

      (10)   Changes to security tables and the supervisor.

      (11)   Restarts and machine faults.

      (12)   Attempted violations of memory.

      (13)   Aborts and parity errors.

    b.   Use the data developed above to:

        (1)   Make a real time (or near real time) analysis of security problems.

        (2)   Develop patterns to close potential or actual loopholes.

IBM's Resource Security System (RSS)

LANCE J. HOFFMAN

INTRODUCTION

IBM Operating System/360 — MVT with Resource Security System (RSS) is an operating system which increases the software protection available under Version 21 of OS/360 — MVT. It plugs many of the "trap doors" in OS/360 and makes available security features unavailable in any other version, previous or following, of OS/360.

BASIC CONCEPTS

The security system employs an authorization scheme whereby a user can access system resources such as programs, data sets, and terminals on the basis of <u>security levels</u> or through <u>access categories</u> or by using a combination of these.

A security level assigned to a data set can be considered a representation of the sensitivity of the data therein. A security level assigned to a user, terminal, or program can be considered as associating with it clearance to data with a security level less than or equal to that level. RSS allows eight levels (1, 2, . . . , 8)

SOURCE: Unpublished article, with the following exception. Portions of this article reprinted by permission from "OS/MVT with Resource Security, Security Officer's Guide," Form GH20-1057 and "OS/MVT with Resource Security, Installation and System Programmer's Guide," Form GH20-1021, both © 1971 by International Business Machines Corporation.

of hierarchy; level 1 is always unrestricted. Data sets may also be assigned access categories which are checked against prospective users, terminals, etc.

Each user is assigned a unique <u>codeword</u> (password) which identifies him to the system. RSS considers the following as items to be protected: data sets, volumes, programs, terminals, data set elements, and groups of the above. These are all referred to as <u>security objects.</u> The bulk of this paper discusses the capabilities RSS provides for protection of these objects.

It is probably best to here briefly discuss three of the more complex security objects mentioned in the preceding paragraph.

(a) Terminals.

Input/output devices may be defined to the security system as terminals if they can be uniquely identified by device addresses. Examples are the 2250 and 2260 CRTs and the 2740 series terminals.

(b) Data Set Elements.

Elements (fields) of data sets can take on lower security levels than the data sets they exist within. RSS only provides interfaces for this type of control, however, and the data management system running above RSS must perform authorization checks with the help of RSS. An example of a security officer's command which specifies security levels for certain elements follows:

DEFINE ELEMENTS FOR SYSA.FILE2 ON
DSKVOL ELEMENT-1, ELEM-1-A AT LEVEL 3
L-2-ELEM-1, L-2-ELEM-2 AT LEVEL 2

The first two elements in the file SYSA.FILE2 are defined at level 3 and the last two at level 2.

(c) Groups of Security Objects.

Grouping allows the system to treat a collection of security objects as a single entity. There may be groups of users, data sets, programs, or terminals. Each member of a group has the same access categories, but security levels within a group may vary. An example of a security officer's command which defines a group of terminals follows:

DEFINE TRMGRP1 TERMINALS 00C 00D 00E
LEVEL 5 PERIOD 2.

Terminals 00C, 00D, and 00E are all defined at security level 5 during time period 2.

RSS also allows the installation to restrict the use of a data set to only certain programs. Sections of direct access storage (e.g., disk) can be overwritten (PURGED) after a data set is scratched to prevent subsequent users of the same storage from compromising security by examining residual data. Time-of-day restrictions on display of data at certain terminals is also provided, as is the ability to label printed output with a security classification, page number, date, and time (see Figure 1). Warning pages, which are cover pages for printed output and have asterisks in every space where blanks would normally appear, can also be generated in place of normal cover pages (see Figure 2). These indicate that the printed output should be reviewed by the security officer for possible security violations before being released to the user.

RSS gives an installation the ability to monitor and prevent unauthorized execution of routines which add or replace programs in controlled program libraries (STOW routines), and also allows it to restrict use of specified supervisor call routines (SVCs) to specified programs.

The system can generate reports concerning system usage and attempted security violations. The types of data collected in these logs are determined at system generation (SYSGEN) time. It is possible to log all openings of a data set and all attempted violations detected by RSS. The program running at the time of the log entry is recorded in the log. Ordinarily, exception reporting is done rather than reporting each opening of a data set.

Interestingly enough, the biggest selling point for this logging feature appears not to be the improved security RSS provides, but rather the instrumentation of system resource use it provides. The usage log is valuable in suggesting methods by which an installation might tune its system to achieve better performance.

RSS allows a security officer to modify the security relationships in real-time using conversational commands from his console. He can also list the secured resources and their relationships to one another at the security terminal or on a high-speed printer.

All the previously enumerated RSS features can be turned on or off by the installation with corresponding effects on both security and on performance. Some of the costs of RSS, both in performance degradation and in additional storage, will be mentioned later.

SECURITY OFFICER COMMANDS

The system is written to interact with a security officer at a security console specified at SYSGEN time. This may be the operator's

71238 1505

SYSTEST REGISTERED CONFICENTIAL

OS US AS COBOL

DATE AUG 26,1971

PAGE 00001 OF 00004

LEVEL IOCT69

1

```
00001     IDENTIFICATION DIVISION.

00002     PROGRAM-ID.  COBUISSY.

00003     REMARKS.  THIS PROGRAM WILL CALL AN ALC SUBROUTINE TO HANDLE
00004        OUTPUT LABELING THROUGH THE ISSYSOUT MACRO.
00005        BEFORE PASSING CONTROL TO THE SUBROUTINE, BE SURE
00006        THAT THE FILE(S) AGAINST WHICH THE ISSYSOUT MACRO WILL
00007        BE ISSUED HAVE ALL BEEN OPENED BY THE CALLING PROGRAM.

00008     ENVIRONMENT DIVISION.
00009     CONFIGURATION SECTION.

00010     SOURCE-COMPUTER.    IBM-360-I50.
00011     OBJECT-COMPUTER.    IBM-360-I50.

00012     INPUT-OUTPUT SECTION.

00013     FILE-CONTROL.
00014        SELECT INPUT-DATA
00015           ASSIGN TO UT-S-INPUTDD.
00016        SELECT OUTPUT1
00017           ASSIGN TO UT-S-OUTDD1.
00018        SELECT OUTPUT2
00019           ASSIGN TO UT-S-OUTDD2.

00020     DATA DIVISION.
00021     FILE SECTION.

00022     FD INPUT-DATA
00023        RECORD CONTAINS 80 CHARACTERS
00024        BLOCK CONTAINS O RECORDS
00025        RECORDING MODE IS F
00026        LABEL RECORDS ARE CMITTED
00027        DATA RECORD IS INREC.
00028     01 INREC        PIC X(80).

00029     FD OUTPUT1
```

FIGURE 1.   Example of output labeled with a security classification.

```
SYSTEST  REGISTERED  CONFIDENTIAL
SYSTEST  REGISTERED  CONFIDENTIAL
SYSTEST  REGISTERED  CONFIDENTIAL
SYSTEST  REGISTERED  CONFIDENTIAL
SYSTEST  REGISTERED  CONFIDENTIAL
SYSTEST  REGISTERED  CONFIDENTIAL
SYSTEST  REGISTERED  CONFIDENTIAL
SYSTEST  REGISTERED  CONFIDENTIAL
SYSTEST  REGISTERED  CONFIDENTIAL
SYSTEST  REGISTERED  CONFIDENTIAL
SYSTEST  REGISTERED  CONFIDENTIAL
SYSTEST  REGISTERED  CONFIDENTIAL
SYSTEST  REGISTERED  CONFIDENTIAL
SYSTEST  REGISTERED  CONFIDENTIAL
SYSTEST  REGISTERED  CONFIDENTIAL
SYSTEST  REGISTERED  CONFIDENTIAL
SYSTEST  REGISTERED  CONFIDENTIAL
SYSTEST  REGISTERED  CONFIDENTIAL
SYSTEST  REGISTERED  CONFIDENTIAL
SYSTEST  REGISTERED  CONFIDENTIAL
SYSTEST  REGISTERED  CONFIDENTIAL
SYSTEST  REGISTERED  CONFIDENTIAL
SYSTEST  REGISTERED  CONFIDENTIAL
SYSTEST  REGISTERED  CONFIDENTIAL
SYSTEST  REGISTERED  CONFIDENTIAL
SYSTEST  REGISTERED  CONFIDENTIAL
SYSTEST  REGISTERED  CONFIDENTIAL
SYSTEST  REGISTERED  CONFIDENTIAL
SYSTEST  REGISTERED  CONFIDENTIAL
SYSTEST  REGISTERED  CONFIDENTIAL
```

FIGURE 2. **Example of a normal cover page (not a warning page).**

console or another terminal (e.g., a 2741). Examples of security officer commands are given in Appendices B, C, and D. When a user is defined to the system, the security officer must enter the user identification into the system. The system automatically generates two codewords for the user. Each codeword is associated with a date span, one temporally following the other. The spans may overlap, and this allows an automatic change of <u>all</u> codewords when a predefined date occurs. The changeover to a new set can take place in a nondisruptive manner, since a user's outdated codeword can be used during the first days of the second span as well. A complete new set of codewords can be generated by the security officer at any time. When a user is defined to the system, the security officer must supply him with his current codeword in a private manner so that the user alone will know it.

When the security officer initially approaches the security officer's console, he must pass a SIGNON dialogue, analogous to the LOGIN decision procedure of ADEPT-50(5). Each time he does this, he is given the chance to change the SIGNON dialogue parameters for the next session. Each successful and unsuccessful SIGNON attempt is recorded. If two consecutive invalid SIGNON attempts occur, an alarm is sounded and the console will not accept further SIGNON attempts until the operating system is reloaded. When the security officer has finished his work at the console, he must SIGNOFF in order to prevent another person from entering security officer commands after he leaves. However, if there is no activity on this console for five minutes, it will automatically be signed off by RSS.

IDENTIFICATION AND AUTHENTICATION

Each time a user submits a job to the operating system, he includes his last name, first and middle initials, and a five character codeword. (The system assigns each user different codeword pairs and thus can handle two users with the same name.) This identification allows each user's security profile to be brought into resident protected core where it remains for the duration of the job. This concept is similar to the User Control Block of the formulary model (6) or Friedman's model (7).

TERMINAL SECURITY

Each terminal is defined to the system as having one security level at any given point in time. There can be up to fifteen levels specified for variable-length time periods. For example, a terminal might have the following security profile:

	Time	Security Level
6 a.m. – 11 a.m.	0600–1100	UNCLASSIFIED
11 a.m. – 5 p.m.	1100–1700	SECRET
5 p.m. – 6 a.m.	1700–0600	TOP SECRET

A time period change is not performed on an <u>active</u> terminal until its user terminates his current processing. Thus, in the example above, a user who logged in a SECRET job at 5:58 a.m. would not cause a security violation or have his job terminated at 6:00 a.m.

The security officer would set up the time periods for the above example by typing in at his console or submitting on a deck of cards the following commands:

DEFINE PERIOD 1 AS 0600 THROUGH 1100
   PERIOD 2 AS 1100 THROUGH 1700
   PERIOD 3 AS 1700 THROUGH 0600.
DEFINE LEVEL 1 AS 'UNCLASSIFIED'
   LEVEL 4 AS 'CONFIDENTIAL' LEVEL 5 AS 'SECRET'
   LEVEL 6 AS 'TOP SECRET'.
DEFINE TERMINAL 00C LEVEL 1 PERIOD 1
   LEVEL 5 PERIOD 2 LEVEL 6 PERIOD 3.

VOLUME INTEGRITY

Every volume, e.g., direct access storage devices and labeled tapes, can be assigned a security level. However, volumes cannot be assigned categories of users, terminals, etc. RSS will insure that data of a higher level is not recorded on the volume. Thus a volume will not have been contaminated by data of too high a level. "Many installations require the destruction of volumes which have contained data of a high level, and this feature is designed to minimize this costly destruction." (3)

One trap door which must be avoided is the following. There are certain ways in which an installation might end up with duplicate volume serial numbers (for example, by labeling tape volumes in response to an operator message). When volume serial numbers are duplicated, proper control of the data sets on those volumes is impossible. Therefore, some administrative action must be taken to prevent this from happening.

DATA SET SECURITY

Types of Data Sets

In OS/MVT there are two general classes of data sets, temporary and permanent. Although the security officer has no control over temporary data sets (which are local to jobs or job steps), he can have complete control over permanent data sets.

When a temporary data set is created, the name of the job that created it and the time the job was read by the reader are included by the operating system in the data set name. Access to such a data set is restricted to jobs having the same job name and time field.

Authorization to permanent data sets is controlled exclusively by the security officer. He must define every permanent data set to be controlled on the system and must specifically grant individuals authorization to CREATE, READ, READ/WRITE and SCRATCH such data sets before the indicated function will be allowed. Undefined data sets are treated as level 1 data sets and are available to all users.

Program-Restricted Data Sets

Program-restricted data sets must meet the same tests as other data sets, but in addition the program requesting use of the data set must specifically be authorized to access it. Its authorization is checked when the program OPENs the program-restricted data set.

Data Set Scratching and Purging

The distinction between scratching and purging is that the former is a logical action and the latter is a physical action. SCRATCHing a data set removes its name and pointer from the volume table of contents (VTOC) of a direct access storage device. PURGEing a data set performs the SCRATCH function and in addition overwrites the entire data set with zeros.

Permanent data sets on direct access devices may be physically removed from a volume (PURGEd or overwritten) either by the security officer or through specification of a SYSGEN option. There is no partial release (recovery of unused space) for permanent data sets.

Two options are available at system generation time for the handling of temporary data set removal:

1. Remove the name and pointer from the VTOC and trust the users not to leave sensitive residue on these data sets.

2.   Remove the name and pointer from the VTOC and PURGE. This option, though more costly than the other, insures that sensitive data is not left as residue on the volume.

Note that in future operating systems, some justification could be made for allowing each user to call a system routine to clear his core or secondary storage area if he wishes; the time used could be charged to the user rather than to system overhead.

Associative Programs and Data Sets

An associative program is one which when used with a predefined data set allows the data set to assume a security level different than the one otherwise assigned to it. For example, suppose there is a TOP SECRET data set which contains SECRET information that can be easily extracted for reporting purposes. If a program were written which accessed only this SECRET data, normally the output of the program would be labeled TOP SECRET. But if the program were defined as associative to that data set, a SECRET output level could be assigned to the output data set when used by that program. This is less of a trap door than it may appear, since assignment of the associative attribute is controlled by the security officer.

TERMINAL-ORIENTED SUBSYSTEMS

RSS provides an interface to allow terminal-oriented subsystems to obtain access to system resources for their users. The subsystems which use these provisions are referred to as "non-batch programs" (NBPs). However "current IBM real-time subsystems (for example, CALL/360, APL, ATS) do not use these provisions but instead provide their own internal resource protection." (3) (Or lack of same.) The NBP user is not provided the same security protection features as are batch users. The NBP itself performs identification, authentication, and audit trail posting functions; all RSS functions are available to the NBP and it invokes these by issuing a special supervisor call (AUTH).

Obviously the NBP must be a checked-out and "trusted" program, since it can circumvent many of the controls provided by RSS. The major advantage of NBPs is that they can execute subtasks as part of their program, and if the subtask has a security violation, only the subtask will be terminated. The NBP must supply storage to RSS for each user's security profile and must point to this area through the user's Task Control Block (TCB).

AUDIT/VIOLATION LOG

RSS provides an audit log (threat monitoring). This log can record:

(1) initial access (OPENing) of each permanent data set
(2) initial access (OPENing) of each temporary data set
(3) modification of all programs that have been defined as members of controlled program libraries. (A controlled program library is a partitioned data set containing programs which are to be individually controlled.)
(4) execution of all programs that have been defined as members of controlled program libraries
(5) all modifications to system data sets that have names beginning with "SYS1." (i.e., the system library).

Each attempted violation will cause a record to be written in the audit log. In addition, it will terminate the job or, optionally, the step which caused the violation. Some violation attempts (selected by the installation) will notify the security officer in real-time at his console and an audible alarm on the computer console will be sounded.

Below is an example of typical output from the audit log (1):

```
SSS LOG ENTRY—PROGRAM ACCESS AT 1859
              USER MEDNEW IM JOB MIM00504
              PROGRAM ML04GRPG
              DATA SET GM18LLIB (ML04GRPG) ON
              VOLUME KBD013
SSS LOG ENTRY—DATA SET ACCESS VIOLATION AT 1951
***ATTEMPTED DATA SET READ
              USER HAMEL AS JOB HAS00819
              PROGRAM IEHLIST
              DATA SET SEC1.LOAD ON
              VOLUME KBD095
```

INTERFACES WITH OS/360

The security system is automatically started before any user tasks at initial program load (IPL) time and cannot be terminated without stopping the operating system.

RSS consists of the following components:

(1) operating system modifications
(2) special exits from the operating system to the security functions

(3) resident tasks (done at IPL time, plus message handling for the security console and some other tasks)

(4) transient task

MODIFICATIONS MADE TO OS/360

In order to implement OS/MVT with RSS, certain modifications were made to OS/360:

(1) Software support of the fetch protection feature.

(2) Modified writer to count and print page numbers, and to print security information on each page of the output data set.

(3) Forced step termination on a privileged operation or a protection violation.

(4) Ability to sound the console alarm when security violations occur.

(5) Automatic starting of RSS by the master scheduler at IPL time.

(6) Clearing of each core block to zero when returned to the system.

(7) Ability to PURGE (overwrite) a direct access data set when it is SCRATCHed.

(8) Ability to clear hardware buffers when a device is deallocated.

PERFORMANCE DEGRADATION

In addition to the RSS overhead, IBM's System Management Facility (SMF) is required and this also tends to degrade system performance. Degradation depends heavily upon whether core memory and direct access space overwrite are selected. IBM's rough estimates (4) range from a degradation of 1.0 to 12.% for "minimum" security and from a degradation of 15.1% to 31.1% for "maximum" security.

IMPORTANT RESTRICTIONS AND REQUIREMENTS

Some of the OS/360 options and system restrictions necessary for RSS are:

(1) Label processing must not be bypassed by any system reader procedure; otherwise the data set PASSWORD feature can be circumvented. Thus, the label option BLP cannot be included at SYSGEN time.

(2) BDAM (Basic Direct Access Method), QSAM (Queued Sequential Access Method), and BSAM (Basic Sequential Access Method) must be specified.
(3) SMF (System Management Facility) must be specified.
(4) Direct access volume verification must be specified. All volumes must have standard labels or user-defined nonstandard labels, with unique serial numbers.
(5) SORT/MERGE is required.
(6) Multiple Console Support (MCS) is required if the security officer is to use a console other than the operator's console. However, MCS is not required if the security officer's console and the operator's console are one and the same.

MINIMUM MACHINE CONFIGURATION

The minimum configuration to run RSS is a 256K byte S/360 or S/370 with sufficient direct access space to allow the 3 or 4 additional data sets necessary for RSS (15 to 20 2314 disk cylinders total). Fetch protection hardware is recommended, and (4) claims that this hardware is "standard on S/360 models 65 and above and on all System/370 models, and is available as RPQ#M29240 on S/360 model 50, W14637 on S/360 model 40. Feature number 3237, Decimal Arithmetic, will be required on the System/360, Model 40."

In addition to the 100 2314 tracks (approximately 577,000 bytes) needed for resident and transient security routines, at least two copies of a data set which contains security profiles are required. Each copy requires a certain amount of direct access space. An example given in (2) assumes an installation with the following requirements: 100 header definitions (for labels on printouts), 100 volume definitions, 10 terminals, 200 files (data sets), 50 programs, 100 users, 50 non-user groups, and 20 user groups. For that installation, the number of blocks necessary is estimated below. (The physical block size of security profile records is 830 bytes.)

Item	Number of Blocks per Item	Total Number of Blocks
System Control	5	5
Eight Levels	.125	1
100 Headers	.125	13
100 Volumes	.050	5
10 Terminals	2	20
200 Files	2	400
50 Programs	2	100
100 Users	2	200
50 Nonuser Groups	2	100
20 User Groups	2	40
	Total	884

Since one block is 830 bytes, the total space required for this typical data set is 830 × 884 bytes, or 733,720 bytes. This is equivalent to 127 tracks (or seven cylinders) on a 2314 disk.

USER RESPONSIBILITIES

IBM is quick to point out that it is the user's responsibility to insure that the system is generated properly and that unauthorized system programmers are not allowed to tamper with code provided by IBM. RSS does not maintain checksums to see if system programmers have altered the operating system.

CAVEAT

The system as described here may not be fully operational to date. This description has been extracted from the much more detailed ones available in (1,2,3,4). To what extent any or all of these capabilities of RSS have been implemented has not been verified.

ACKNOWLEDGMENTS

Harvey Bleam, Scott Hamel, and C. L. Foster of IBM were most helpful in offering suggestions on this paper. However, any responsibility for errors or omissions is solely that of the author.

REFERENCES

1. IBM Application Program Manual GH20-1057-0. OS/MVT with Resource Security, Security Officer's Guide. December, 1971.

2. IBM Application Program Manual GH20-1021-0. OS/MVT with Resource Security, Installation and System Programmer's Guide. December, 1971.

3. IBM Document No. GH20-0967-0. OS/MVT with Resource Security, System Description Manual. March, 1971.

4. IBM Application Program Manual GH20-1058-0. OS/MVT with Resource Security, General Information and Planning Manual. December, 1971.

5. Weissman, C., "Security Controls in the ADEPT-50 time-sharing system," Proc. 1969 FJCC, p. 119 ff.*

6. Hoffman, L. J., "The formulary model for flexible privacy and access controls," Proc. 1971 FJCC, p. 587 ff.*

7. Friedman, T. D., "The authorization problem in shared files," IBM System J. 1970, No. 4, p. 258 ff.*

*This article is included in this book.

APPENDICES

Appendix A. Current Definition and Authorization Limits

As of December 1971, the following limits applied to RSS:

(1) A user could not belong to more than 26 user groups.
(2) No more than 96 terminals, programs, or files could be in a given group.
(3) A terminal or terminal group could not be authorized to more than 193 user groups.
(4) No more than 96 items or subgroups could constitute a group.
(5) A program or program group could be authorized to no more than 193 user groups.
(6) An associative program could be associative to no more than 51 data sets.
(7) No more than 15 permanent data sets could be allocated to any tape volumes.
(8) Temporary and defined permanent data sets could not exist on the same tape volume.

Appendix B. Example of Input Used by Security Officer

An example of the input used by the security officer to initialize a security file is given below. It is somewhat self-explanatory. For additional information, the reader is referred to (1).

```
ISSUE CODEWORDS FOR 70100 THROUGH 70365.
DEFINE PERIOD 2 AS 0800 THROUGH 1200 PERIOD 4 AS 1200 1600
       PERIOD 6 1600 THROUGH 0700.
CHANGE DEFINITION PERIOD2 TO 0700 THROUGH 1200.
CHANGE DEFINITION PERIOD 6 TO 1600 THROUGH 0600.
DEFINE LEVEL 1 AS 'UNCLASSIFIED'
       LEVEL 4 as 'CONFIDENTIAL'
       LEVEL 5 as 'SECRET'.
CHANGE DEFINITION LEVEL 5 TO 'SECRET-RESTRICTED DIST.'.
DEFINE HEADER 2 AS 'UNRESTRICTED DISTRIBUTION'
       HEADER 4 AS 'COMPANY XYZ PERSONNEL ONLY'
       HEADER 10 AS 'DEPT.-1 USE ONLY'.
CHANGE DEFINITION HEADER 10 TO 'DEPT.-1 AND DEPT.-2 USE ONLY'.
DEFINE USER 'ADAMS AA' LEVEL 4 'BATES BB' LEVEL4
       'JONES JJ' LEVEL 4 'ROSS ROBERT R' LEVEL 5 PERIOD 2
       'SMITH SS' LEVEL 5 PERIOD 4.
DEFINE VOLUME DA0001 AT LEVEL 1 DA0002 L4 WITH DEVICE
       TYPE 2314 TAPE01 L4 WITH DEVICE TYPE 2400.
CHANGE DEFINITION VOLUME DA0001 LEVEL4 DEVICE TYPE 2314
       TAPE01 LEVEL5 DEVICE TYPE 2400.
DEFINE FILE SYSA.FILE1 AT LEVEL 1 ON DA0001 SYSA.FILE2 AT
       LEVEL 4 ON DA0002 RESTRICTED WITH HEADER 2 LIBA.FILE3
       LEVEL4 ON DA0002 WITH HEADER4.
CHANGE DEFINITION FILE SYSA.FILE1 AT LEVEL 1 ON DA0001
       DA0002, LIBA.FILE3 AS CONTROLLED LIBRARY AT LEVEL 4
       ON DA0002 WITH HEADER4.
DEFINE PROGRAM LIBA.FILE3(SORT) AT LEVEL 4 FOR USER
       'ADAMS AA' AT LEVEL 4 USING FILES SYSA.FILE1 SYSA.FILE2
       AT OUTPUT LEVEL 1 HEADER 2 LIBA.FILE3(UPDATE) AT LEVEL 4.
DEFINE TERMINAL 00C LEVEL 5 00D LEVEL5 081 LEVEL1 PERIOD 6
       LEVEL 5 PERIOD 2 PERIOD 4 080 LEVEL2
       080-4151 LEVEL2 PERIOD 2 080-4252 LEVEL 2 PERIOD 2
       PERIOD 4.
CHANGE DEFINITION TERMINAL 080 LEVEL2 PERIOD2 PERIOD4.
DEFINE DEPT1 USERS 'ADAMS AA' 'BATES BB' 'COX CC' LEVEL4
       'SMITH SS'.
DEFINE ALLDEPTS USERS 'ADAMS ARNOLD ADOLPH' LEVEL5 PERIOD2
       DEPT1.
CHANGE DEFINITION DEPT1 USERS 'ADAMS AA' AT LEVEL 4 'BATES BB'
       'COX CC'.
DEFINE SYSFILES FILES SYSA.FILE1 SYSA.FILE2.
DEFINE ALLFILES FILES SYSFILES LIBA.FILE3.
CHANGE DEFINITION SYSFILES FILES SYSA.FILE1 SYSA.FILE2
       SYSA.FILE4 ON DA0001 DA0002 LEVEL 1.
CHANGE DEFINITION ALLFILES FILES SYSFILES LIBA.FILE3
       LIBA.FILE5 AT LEVEL 2 ON DA0001 CONTROLLED LIBRARY.
DEFINE ALLPGMS PROGRAMS LIBA.FILE3(SORT) LIBA.FILE3(UPDATE).
CHANGE DEFINITION OF ALLPGMS PROGRAMS
       LIBA.FILE3(SORT) LIBA.FILE3(UPDATE) LIBA.FILE3(PRINT)
       AT LEVEL1.
DEFINE TRMGRP1 TERMINALS 00C 00D 00E LEVEL 5 PERIOD 2.
CHANGE DEFINITION TRMGRP1 TERMINALS 00C 00D 080 080-4151.
CHANGE DEFINITION PROGRAM LIBA.FILE3(UPDATE) LEVEL 4 FOR
       USER DEPT1.
AUTHORIZE 'ADAMS AA' AT LEVEL 5 FILES SYSFILES LIBA.FILE3 WRITE
       PROGRAMS LIBA.FILE3(UPDATE) WRITE LIBA.FILE3(SORT)
       TERMINALS 00C 00D 00E.
AUTHORIZE DEPT1 FILES SYSFILES LIBA.FILE3 PROGRAMS ALLPGMS.
CHANGE AUTHORIZATION 'ADAMS AA' AT LEVEL 5 NO TERMINALS.
ADD TO DEPT1 USER 'DAVIS DD' LEVEL 5.
ADD TO SYSFILES FILES LIBA.FILE3.
ADD TO ALLPGMS PROGRAM LIBA.FILE3(PUNCH) AT LEVEL 1.
ADD TO TRMGRP1 TERMINAL 080-4252, 081.
CHANGE CODEWORD DATES FROM 70100 THROUGH 70365 TO 70300
       THROUGH 71100.
CHANGE CODEWORDS FOR DEPT1 FOR 70100 THROUGH 70365.
CHANGE USER FROM 'ROSS RR' TO 'ROSSMOR L. W.'.
CHANGE FILE GROUPNAME FROM SYSFILES TO SYSTEMP.
CHANGE TERMINAL FROM 00E TO 00F.
```

Appendix C.   Example of All Security Definitions

The security officer can list the definitions of all security objects in the system by typing at his console:

LIST DEFINITIONS ALL USING FORMAT01.

A typical output is given in (1) and partially reproduced here.

```
REQUESTED PERIOD DEFINITIONS

PERIOD 02 START 0700   STOP 1200
PERIOD 04 START 1200   STOP 1600
PERIOD 06 START 1600   STOP 0600

CODEWORD DATES

     CODEWORD 1      70 300 --- 71 100
     CODEWORD 2      00 000 --- 00 000


REQUESTED LEVEL DEFINITIONS

LEVEL 1 --- UNCLASSIFIED ---
LEVEL 4 --- CONFIDENTIAL ---
LEVEL 5 --- SECRET-RESTRICTED DIST. ---


REQUESTED HEADER DEFINITIONS

HEADER 02 --- UNRESTRICTED DISTRIBUTION ---
HEADER 04 --- COMPANY XYZ PERSONNEL ONLY ---
HEADER 10 --- DEPT.-1 AND DEPT.-2 USE ONLY ---


REQUESTED USER DEFINITIONS

ADAMS, A.A.             NXKXL  CZCJG  L5 P02
                       ZGJCV  IVVZW  L4 P00
BATES, B. B.           DVRLJ  VQSKT  L4 P00
COX, C.C.              NQBHJ  DZFXA  L4 P00
DAVIS, D.D.            ICZDP  FXSFD  L5 P00
JONES, J. J.           CXFPG  AGMGW  L4 P00
ROSSMOR, L.W.          JQSZE  JRPNX  L5 P02
SMITH, S.S.            WCRXB  DDZPC  L5 P04
```

```
REQUESTED VOLUME DEFINITIONS

VOLUME DA0001 L4   TRACKS           DEV-TYPE 2314-DISK
       DA0002 L4                            2314-DISK
       TAPE01 L5                            2400-TAPE


REQUESTED FILE DEFINITIONS

FILE LIBA.FILE3 L4 H04 C              *OWNER-UNDEFINED
     ON VOLUMES/SPACE              DA0002/00000T NNNN

FILE LIBA.FILE5 L2 H00 C              *OWNER-UNDEFINED
     ON VOLUMES/SPACE              DA0001/00000T NNNN

FILE SYSA.FILE1 L1 H04                *OWNER-UNDEFINED
     ON VOLUMES/SPACE              DA0001/00000T NNNN
                                   DA0002/00000T NNNN

FILE SYSA.FILE2 L4 H02             R  *OWNER-UNDEFINED
     ON VOLUMES/SPACE              DA0002/00000T NNNN

FILE SYSA.FILE4 L1 H00                *OWNER-UNDEFINED
     ON VOLUMES/SPACE              DA0001/00000T NNNN
                                   DA0002/00000T NNNN


REQUESTED PROGRAM DEFINITIONS

PROGRAM PRINT    IN LIBA.FILE3
    --- OWNED BY *OWNER-UNDEFINED ---
    AT L1    ON VOLUMES DA0002

PROGRAM PUNCH    IN LIBA.FILE3
    --- OWNED BY *OWNER-UNDEFINED ---
    AT L1    ON VOLUMES DA0002

PROGRAM SORT     IN LIBA.FILE3
    --- OWNED BY ADAMS, A.A. --- IS ASSOCIATIVE
    AT L4    ON VOLUMES DA0002

PROGRAM UPDATE   IN LIBA.FILE3
    --- OWNED BY DEPT1 ---
    AT L4    ON VOLUMES DA0002
```

REQUESTED TERMINAL DEFINITIONS

TERMINAL 00C - 2540 CARD READER
    L/P PAIRS 5/

TERMINAL 00D - 2540 CARD PUNCH
    L/P PAIRS 5/

TERMINAL 00F - 1403 PRINTER
    L/P PAIRS 5/02

TERMINAL 080-4252 - 2260 DISPLAY
    L/P PAIRS 2/02 2/04

TERMINAL 080-4151 - 2260 DISPLAY
    L/P PAIRS 2/02

TERMINAL 080 - 2260 DISPLAY
    L/P PAIRS 2/02 2/04

TERMINAL 081 - 2260 DISPLAY
    L/P PAIRS 5/02 5/04 1/06

REQUESTED GROUP DEFINITIONS

USER GROUP DEFINITIONS

GROUP ALLDEPTS

DAUGHTER GROUPS
    DEPT1
ELEMENT DEFINITIONS
    ADAMS, A.A.   NXKXL CZCJG L5 P02

GROUP DEPT1

PARENT GROUPS
    ALLDEPTS
ELEMENT DEFINITIONS
    DAVIS, D.D.   ICZDP FXSFD L5 P00
    COX, C.C.   NQBHJ DZFXA L4 P00
    BATES, B.B.   DVRLF VQSKT L4 P00
    ADAMS, A.A.   ZGJCV IVVZW L4 P00

FILE GROUP DEFINITIONS

GROUP ALLFILES

DAUGHTER GROUPS
    SYSTEMP
ELEMENT DEFINITIONS
    LIBA.FILE5 L1 P00 H00
    LIBA.FILE3 L4 P00 H04

GROUP SYSTEMP

PARENT GROUPS
    ALLFILES

```
ELEMENT DEFINITIONS
    SYSA.FILE4 L1 P00 H00
    LIBA.FILE3 L4 P00 H04
    SYSA.FILE2 L4 P00 H04
    SYSA.FILE1 L1 P00 H04


PROGRAM GROUP DEFINITIONS


GROUP ALLPGMS

ELEMENT DEFINITIONS
    PUNCH      IN LIBRARY LIBA.FILE3 AT L1
    PRINT      IN LIBRARY LIBA.FILE3 AT L1
    UPDATE     IN LIBRARY LIBA.FILE3 AT L4
    SORT       IN LIBRARY LIBA.FILE3 AT L4


TERMINAL GROUP DEFINITIONS


GROUP TRMGRP1

ELEMENT DEFINITIONS
    081 - 2260 DISPLAY
        L/P PAIRS 5/02 5/04 1/06
    080 - 2260 DISPLAY
        L/P PAIRS 2/02 2/04
    00D - 2540 CARD PUNCH
        L/P PAIRS 5/
    00C - 2540 CARD READER
        L/P PAIRS 5/
    080-4252 - 2260 DISPLAY
        L/P PAIRS 2/02 2/04
    080-4151 - 2260 DISPLAY
        L/P PAIRS 2/02

THERE WERE 00070 RECORDS PASSED THROUGH SORT END.
```

Appendix D.   Example of Generation of a Basic Set of Security Profiles

After the initial SIGN-ON dialogue, the security officer who is installing a brand new RSS system generates a set of security profiles. A typical deck to do this is given in (1) and reproduced below, as is the accompanying commentary which is keyed to the command numbers. In practice, the numbers are not part of the commands.

1. ISSUE CODEWORDS 71001 73008.

2. ISSUE CODEWORDS 73001 73365.

3. DEFINE LEVEL 1 AS 'UNCLASSIFIED'.

4. DEFINE LEVEL 2 AS 'CLASSIFIED'
        LEVEL 8 AS 'SUPERSECRET'.

5. DEFINE TERMINAL 00C L8.

6. DEFINE TERMINAL 00D L8.

7. DEFINE TERMINAL 00E L8.

8. DEFINE SOUSERS USERS 'OFFICER S.O.' L2.

9. DEFINE OPUSERS USERS 'OPERATIONS' L2.

10. DEFINE UGROUP1 USERS 'USER1' L2.

11. DEFINE VOLUMES KBD071 L2 DEVICE TYPE 2314
                  KBD133 L2 DEVICE TYPE 2314
                  KBD132 L2 DEVICE TYPE 2314
                  KBD072 L2 DEVICE TYPE 2314
                  KBD095 L2 DEVICE TYPE 2314.

12. DEFINE SOFILES FILES   SYS1.SECLIB L2 ON KBD072
                            SYS1.SECURITY L2 ON KBD095
                            SYS1.BACSEC L2 ON KBD095
                            SYS1.STBYSECR L2 ON KBD095
                            SYS1.MANX L1 ON KBD071
                            SYS1.MANY L1 ON KBD071
                            SYS1.SORTLIB L1 ON KBD072.

13. CREATE SYS1.MANX WORK FOR USER SOUSERS (KBD071-200).

14. CREATE SYS1.MANY WORK FOR USER SOUSERS (KBD071-200).

15. DEFINE OPFILES FILES   SYS1.NUCLEUS L1 ON KBD071
                            SYS1.SYSJOBQE L1 ON KBD071
                            SYS1.SYSVLOGX L1 ON KBD071
                            SYS1.SYSVLOGY L1 ON KBD071
                            SYS1.SVCLIB L1 ON KBD071
                            SYS1.ROLLOUT L1 ON KBD071
                            SYS1.LOGREC L1 ON KBD071
                            SYS1.LINKLIB L1 ON KBD072
                            SYS1.PROCLIB L1 ON KBD072
                            SYS1.PARMLIB L1 ON KBD071
                            SYS1.MACLIB L1 ON KBD072
                            SYS1.SORTLIB L1 ON KBD072
                            SYS1.FORTLIB L1 ON KBD072
                            SYS1.PL1LIB L1 ON KBD072
                            SYS1.COBLIB L1 ON KBD072
                            SYS1.TELCMLIB L1 ON KBD072
                            SYS1.SORTLIB.

16. DEFINE USRFILES FILES   SYS1.PROCLIB
                            SYS1.MACLIB
                            SYS1.SORTLIB
                            SYS1.FORTLIB
                            SYS1.PL1LIB
                            SYS1.COBLIB
                            SYS1.TELCMLIB.

17. DEFINE VTOCS FILES VTOC.KBD071 L1 ON KBD071
                       VTOC.KBD072 L1 ON KBD072
                       VTOC.KBD095 L1 ON KBD095.

18. AUTHORIZE SOUSERS FILES SOFILES WRITE.

19. AUTHORIZE OPUSERS FILES OPFILES WRITE, VTOCS.

20. AUTHORIZE UGROUP1 FILES USRFILES.

21. LIST DEFINITIONS ALL USING FORMAT 01.

22. LIST FILES AUTHORIZED TO USERS SOUSERS OPUSERS UGROUP1.

Note: If the listings demonstrate that the proper profiles and authorizations have been established, the system is now ready to execute application programs.

Explanation of Initial Commands

Command Nr	Explanation
1, 2	Generate codewords for two datespans. A short overlap is provided for ease of transition.
3, 4	Define three security levels. Others may be desirable.
5-7	Define the reader, punch, and printer. These are for system use. Additional definitions will be required if users are to use communications terminals. These devices are defined at level 8 so that they may be used for all data even if new levels of data are subsequently defined.
8-10	Define three user groups each consisting of one user. The user in each case is initially defined in the group definition.
11	Defines five 2314 volumes at level 2. Two spool volumes have been provided. All volumes must be defined. These will be used for the system files. Since they are at level 2, the system will prevent higher-level data from being stored on them.
12	Defines seven system files at level two and establishes them as a file group.
13, 14	Creates two of the defined files as work files with SOUSERS as owner. Each is on volume KBD071 and is allocated 200 tracks. SYS1.MANX and SYS1.MANY must be created as work files with owners so they may be dumped using the supplied programs.
15	Defines sixteen files at level 1 and establishes them as a file group. Also included is one volume which was previously defined. At this level these files will be available to all users.
16	Defines another file group consisting of seven of the files already defined.
17	Defines the VTOCs of the defined volumes as files and establishes them as a file group.
18-20	Authorize access to the file groups for the user groups. Note that write-authorization is given for those file groups requiring it, but read only is allowed in the case of the VTOCs and USRFILES.
21	Will list all definitions in the system. This will allow verification of the intended input and provide a hardcopy reference for the security officer.
22	Will list the file groups authorized to each named user group thus serving the same purpose as the definition list.

References

[1] Senate Bill 975, 92nd Congress, 1st session (Bayh).

[2] Westin, Alan F. and Baker, Michael A., Databanks in a Free Society, Quadrangle Press, New York, 1972.

[3] Project SEARCH Committee on Security and Privacy, Security and Privacy Considerations in Criminal History Information Systems, Technical Report No. 2, July 1970.

[4] National Crime Information Center (NCIC) Computerized Criminal History Program, Policy on Security and Confidentiality, 31 March 1971.

[5] Van Tassel, D. Computer Security Management, Prentice-Hall, Inc., Englewood Cliffs, N.J., 1972.

[6] Brown, William F. (ed.) Computer and Software Security, AMR International, Inc., New York, 1971.

[7] The Considerations of Physical Security in a Computer Environment, International Business Machines Corporation, From G520-2700-0, White Plains, N.Y., October 1972.

[8] Lampson, B. W. "Dynamic Protection Structures," Proceedings 1969 Fall Joint Computer Conference, Volume 35, pp. 27–38.

[9] Graham, R. "Protection in an Information Processing Utility," Communications of the Association for Computing Machinery, Vol. 11, No. 5, May 1968, pp. 365–369.

[10] A National Survey of the Public's Attitudes toward Computers, Time Magazine and American Federation of Information Processing Societies, Inc., New York, 1971.

[11] The Considerations of Data Security in a Computer Environment, International Business Machines Corporation, From G520-2169-0, New York, 1970.

[12]   Kahn, D. The Codebreakers, The Macmillan Co., New York, 1968.

[13]   Shannon, C. E. "Communication Theory of Secrecy Systems," Bell System Technical Journal, Vol. 28, No. 4, October 1949, pp. 656-715.

[14]   Hill, L. S. "Cryptography in an Algebraic Alphabet," American Mathematical Monthly, Vol. 36, June-July 1929.

[15]   Girsdansky, M. B. "Cryptology, the Computer and Data Privacy," Computers and Automation, Vol. 21, No. 4, April 1972, pp. 12-19.

[16]   Fellegi, I. P. "On the Question of Statistical Confidentiality," Journal of the American Statistical Association, Vol. 67, No. 337, March 1972, pp. 7-18.

Biographical Sketches

ALEXANDER W. ASTIN has been director of Research for the American Council on Education in Washington, D.C. since 1965. Previously, he was Director of Research of the National Merit Scholarship Corporation in Evanston, Illinois. Dr. Astin has also done research as a Commissioned Officer in the U.S. Public Health Service and has taught at Northwestern University, the University of Kentucky, and the University of Maryland.

In 1965 Dr. Astin received the American Personnel and Guidance Association's Award for Outstanding Research for his studies of college characteristics and college effects. During 1967–68 he was a Fellow at the Center for Advanced Study in the Behavioral Sciences, Stanford, California. Currently, Dr. Astin is directing the Cooperative Institutional Research Program of the American Council on Education, an on-going longitudinal study involving a national sample of some 400 colleges and universities.

Dr. Astin's research on the comparative effects of different types of college environments on a student's development has been published in various psychological and educational journals, as well as in six books, the latest of which is The Disadvantaged Student in Higher Education (with H. S. Astin, A. S. Bisconti, and H. Frankel) (Human Services Press, 1972).

PAUL BARAN received a B.S.E.E. from Drexel University in 1949 and an M.S. in engineering (computers) from UCLA in 1959.

He is a consultant to a number of organizations, including industrial companies, government, and not-for-profit organizations. He is also President of Cabledata Associates, Inc., a company which performs technical and venture analysis of computer communications systems for the home information market.

In 1968 Mr. Baran helped establish the Institute for the Future, where he was Vice President. Before joining the Institute, he was with the Computer Sciences Department of the RAND Corporation from 1959 to 1968 as a leader of a project to improve protection of command and control systems. At RAND, he developed the concept and equipment design of packet switching in distributed communications networks. At RAND he was also interested in communications regulatory policy, personal privacy in computer data base systems, reading aids of the near-blind, and long term technological forecasting.

Mr. Baran is a Member of the Association for Computing Machinery and a Senior Member of the Institute of Electrical and Electronic Engineers.

CHARLES W. BEARDSLEY received the B.S. degree in mechanical engineering from Newark College of Engineering in 1961 and the M.S. degree in technical writing from Rensselaer Polytechnic Institute in 1962. He joined the General Electric Company in that year, where he helped to develop a computerized retrieval system for data from the Apollo Project. One of his major responsibilities during this period was the compilation of a thesaurus of aerospace terminology. In 1966, he transferred to GE's Aircraft Engine Group as a reliability engineer.

Mr. Beardsley joined the Headquarters staff of the Institute of Electrical and Electronics Engineers, Inc. in 1968. Since then he has served as Assistant Managing Editor and Managing Editor of the IEEE Student Journal. He is at present Associate Editor of IEEE Spectrum.

He is a member of Tau Beta Pi, Omicron Delta Kappa, Phi Eta Sigma, and Pi Delta Epsilon.

ROBERT F. BORUCH received his B.E. from Stevens Institute of Technology and his Ph.D. in psychology/statistics from Iowa State University. He is currently assistant professor of psychology at Northwestern University. He also serves as a Staff Consultant of the Social Science Research Council.

Professor Boruch previously held research positions at the American Council on Education, Northwestern University, and Iowa State University. He also directed the questionnaire survey of the National Academy of Sciences Project on Computer Databanks.

Dr. Boruch is a member of the American Statistical Association, the American Psychological Association, the American Educational Research Association, the Psychometric Society, the Washington, D.C. Statistical Society, and the New York Academy of Sciences.

PETER S. BROWNE received his M.B.A. from the University of Nebraska at Omaha in 1971. He is currently Computer Security Manager at State Farm Insurance Company where he is charged with implementing physical protection and data protection for a large number of computer systems. Previously, Mr. Browne served as Project Manager for the design of a multi-level security package implemented on the World-Wide Military Command and Control System (WWMCCS) at the Strategic Air Command. He was a member of the GUIDE/SHARE Data Base Task Group and is an ACM National Lecturer on computer security.

JOHN M. CARROLL received his B.S. in Industrial Engineering from Lehigh University, his M.A. in Physics from Hofstra University, and his Dr. Eng. Sci. degree in Industrial Engineering from New York University in 1968.

After serving as Associate Professor of Industrial Engineering at Lehigh from 1964 to 1968, he joined the University of Western Ontario, where he is now an associate professor of computer science. Professor Carroll was the chief investigator for empirical studies with the Canadian Privacy and Computers Task Force during 1971, and has been the Associate Editor of the Standard Handbook for Electrical Engineers since 1964.

Dr. Carroll served with the U.S. Navy Security Group from 1944 until 1947 and from 1950 to 1952. He has authored 50 papers and 14 books, among them "Secrets of Electronic Espionage" and "The Third Listener— Personal Electronic Espionage".

RICHARD W. CONWAY received his Ph.D. in Operations Research in 1958. He is currently Professor of Computer Science at Cornell University where he also directs the development of PL/C, a high-speed, highly diagnostic compiler for PL/I, currently used in over 100 universities.

Professor Conway's current teaching, research, and consulting is in the area of business data processing. He has in the past been the director of the Cornell Computing Center. He is the co-author of Theory of Scheduling.

BEN A. FRANKLIN, a regional correspondent of the New York Times based in Washington, became interested in computer dossiers on Americans suspected of surveillance-worthy behavior while reporting on the activities of H. Rap Brown, the black militant. He learned that the Maryland State Police, then seeking the identity of suspects in several bombings apparently associated with protests against Mr. Brown's prosecution in that state, had called on the U.S. Secret Service to query an until-then unknown computer file of "persons of interest" which classified its subjects by physical description, using such characteristics as hair and eye color, style of dress, shape of nose, moles, etc. The discovery led him to survey some of the computer surveillance activities in the Federal Government, and yielded the story included in this collection.

THEODORE D. FRIEDMAN received his Bachelor's degree from the University of Michigan in 1958. He is currently a graduate student in the Department of Electrical Engineering and Computer Sciences at the University of California, Berkeley. He has held previous positions at Goodyear Aircraft Corporation, Melpar, Inc., Curtiss-Wright, TRG (now part of Control Data Corporation), and, most recently, IBM Research where he is currently a Research Staff Member on leave to pursue his graduate studies.

At IBM Mr. Friedman directed the ALERT design automation project and has studied computer networks, file systems, and data security. He has also been concerned with logic design, systems engineering, compiler design, display systems, and simulators.

ROBERT M. GRAHAM received his B.A. and M.A. in Mathematics from the University of Michigan. He is currently Associate Professor in the Department of Computer Sciences at City College of New York.

Mr. Graham has previously held professorial posts at the University of California at Berkeley and at Massachusetts Institute of Technology, where he also played a key role in the design and implementation of the Multics time-sharing system. He has been chairman of several panels at professional meetings and served as the Editor for the Techniques Department of Communications of the ACM in 1965–66. Mr. Graham has also been twice chosen to be an ACM National Lecturer.

LANCE J. HOFFMAN received his B.S. in Mathematics from Carnegie Institute of Technology and his M.S. and Ph.D. in Computer Science from Stanford University. He is currently Assistant Professor of Electrical Engineering and Computer Sciences at the University of California at Berkeley.

Professor Hoffman was a Staff Associate of the National Academy of Sciences Project on Computer Data Banks and also serves on the Advisory Council to the Privacy Committee of the American Civil Liberties Union. He has in the past served as a member of the Advisory Committee to the California Assembly Committee on Statewide Information Policy as a member of privacy committees of Stanford University and of the University of California system. He has also been an ACM National Lecturer and has worked in computer systems research at Bolt Beranek and Newman, Inc., Systems Development Corporation, and Control Data Corporation.

Dr. Hoffman is a member of the Association for Computing Machinery, the IEEE, and the American Association for the Advancement of Science.

WILLIAM L. MAXWELL received his B.S. in Mechanical Engineering and his Ph.D. from Cornell University. He is currently Professor of Operations Research and Professor of Computer Science at Cornell. The author or coauthor of numerous articles on scheduling, information processing, and instructional computing languages, Professor Maxwell co-authored Theory of Scheduling.

PHILIP M. McLELLAN is currently Major Systems Project Manager for UNIVAC Division, Sperry Rand (Canada) Limited in Ottawa, Ontario. Prior to joining UNIVAC he graduated from Acadia University in 1964 with B.Sc. (Physics) and B.Ed. Degrees. He served with the R.C.A.F. as Radio Navigator for four years, and then returned to the University of Western Ontario to obtain his M.Sc. Degree in Computer Science. During this period he participated with Dr. J. M. Carroll in a study of privacy and security in the resource-sharing computer environment.

ARTHUR R. MILLER is a professor of law at the Harvard Law School. He received his A.B. from the University of Rochester and his LL.B. from the Harvard Law School.

Prior to coming to Harvard, Dr. Miller was a professor at the University of Michigan Law School, during which time his well-known book The Assault on Privacy was published. He is a member of the Special Committee on Automated Personal Data Systems of the Department of Health, Education, and Welfare and served on the National Advisory Panel of the Project on Computer Data Banks of the National Academy of Sciences. He has made numerous appearances on radio and television to discuss privacy and computers and has testified before several congressional committees.

Professor Miller is a member of the New York State Bar and the United States Supreme Court Bar.

WILLIAM F. MILLER received his B.S., M.S., and Ph.D. degrees in Physics from Purdue University. He is currently Vice President and Provost of Stanford University, where he also holds the positions of Professor of Computer Science and Professor at the Stanford Linear Accelerator Center.

Prior to coming to Stanford, Dr. Miller held teaching positions at the University of Chicago and Purdue University and was the Director of the Applied Mathematics Division at the Argonne National Laboratory. His many professional posts have included the chairmanship of the ACM Committee on Support of Computer Science in 1965–66, and membership on the National Academy of Sciences Computer Science and Research Council Committee on Graduate and Postdoctoral Education. Professor Miller has been an ACM National Lecturer and is currently Associate Editor of both the Pattern Recognition Journal and the Journal of Computational Physics.

Dr. Miller is a member of the American Physical Society, the Association for Computing Machinery, the IEEE Computer Group, the Society for Industrial and Applied Mathematics, the American Mathematical Society, the New York Academy of Sciences, and the American Association for the Advancement of Science.

LEE MOLHO received the B.S. degree in Engineering from the California Institute of Technology in 1963, and studied electrical engineering at the University of Arizona, Tucson, in 1963–64.

Mr. Molho is currently a member of a team at System Development Corporation which is developing a system for spoken communication with a computer. Prior to this, he investigated hardware aspects of secure time-shared computing at SDC. He has also worked on computer systems at the Ampex Corporation and Hughes Aircraft Co.

HOWARD MORGAN is currently Associate Professor at the Wharton School of the University of Pennsylvania. Previously, he held professorial positions at California Institute of Technology and at Cornell University, where he obtained his Ph.D. in the field of Operations Research.

Professor Morgan is the author of many articles in the computing field, and has contributed articles in file management and systems programming as well as security and privacy. He is also President of Compuvisor, Inc., a proprietary software manufacturer.

HAROLD E. PETERSEN received his B.S. and M.S. in Electrical Engineering from the University of Wisconsin and his Ph.D. in Electrical Engineering from Stanford University in 1957.

Dr. Petersen became a consultant to The Rand Corporation in 1970. In that capacity he has played a significant role in Rand's research program on closed circuit TV systems for the partially sighted. During the period 1966–1970, as an employee of Rand, he worked on a variety of communication and display problems and was a major contributor to the Rand videographic system (a versatile television based computer display system). Prior to coming to Rand, he was a member of the research staff of IBM. While there, he received an award from IBM for his creation of the card capacitor memory concept in use in several models of the 360 computer system.

Dr. Petersen is a member of the New York Academy of Sciences, the Society of the Sigma Xi, the Institute of Electrical and Electronic Engineers and the American Association for the Advancement of Science. He is the holder of over 25 patents.

JEROME H. SALTZER received the degrees of S.B., S.M., and Sc.D. (1966) from the Massachusetts Institute of Technology, where he is co-head of the Computer System Research Division of Project MAC. As an M.I.T. faculty member he has been active in the development of the undergraduate curriculum in Computer Science, including development of a subject titled "Information Systems." At Project MAC he was involved with the later development of the Compatible Time-Sharing System (CTSS) and all aspects of the design and implementation of the Multiplexed Information and Computing Service (Multics).

Dr. Saltzer's research interests include processor multiplexing, privacy-achieving mechanisms, data communication, memory system organization, and computer system performance measurements. He has published a variety of papers on these topics and is a consultant on computer systems to a variety of government and industrial organizations. Professor Saltzer is a member of ACM, IEEE, AAAS, Sigma Xi, Eta Kappa Nu, and Tau Beta Pi.

MICHAEL D. SCHROEDER received the B.A. degree in mathematics from Washington State University in 1967. From the Massachusetts Institute of Technology he received the M.S. degree in electrical engineering in 1969, the E.E. degree in 1969, and the Ph.D. degree in computer science in 1972.

Dr. Schroeder is an Assistant Professor of Electrical Engineering at M.I.T. and a member of the Computer Systems Research Division of Project MAC. He has been involved in developing and teaching an undergraduate course on the structure of computer-based information systems and since 1967 has been directly involved with the Multics development effort at Project MAC. His research interests include techniques for organizing computer-based information systems, protection mechanisms for computer systems, computer system performance measurements, and high-level programming languages for implementing operating systems.

Professor Schroeder is a member of Phi Beta Kappa, Phi Sigma Phi, Sigma Xi, IEEE, and ACM.

NORMAN Z. SHAPIRO received his B.S. degree in Mathematics from the University of Illinois and his M.S. and Ph.D. degrees in Mathematics from Princeton University.

He joined the staff of the Mathematics Department of The Rand Corporation in 1955. In 1959 he became Director of the Computer Center at the National Institutes of Health. He returned to Rand in 1962, joining the staff of the Computer Sciences Department. He was a visiting Industrial Fellow in the Computer Sciences Department, Courant Institute of Mathematical Sciences, New York University, for the 1969-70 academic year. In addition to his position at Rand he is a Research Mathematician at the School of Medicine, University of California at Los Angeles.

Dr. Shapiro's main research interests include recursive function theory, computer sciences, applications of mathematics and digital computation to medicine, physiology and chemistry, and societal impacts of automatic information processing.

He is past president of the Biological Information Processing Organization, has been Associate Editor of the Journal of the Association for Computing Machinery, and has held memberships in several national advisory committees on applications of information processing in biological sciences.

RALPH O. SKATRUD received his B.A. in Mathematics and Physics from Luther College. He then served as a Communications and Electronics Officer and later as a Communications Instructor in the United States Air Force until 1954, when he joined IBM as a Technical Engineer.

Mr. Skatrud is currently an Advisory Engineer working on teleprocessing-based terminal developments at Research Triangle Park, North Carolina. A hobby, extending over the past 10 years, has been cryptographic studies related to computers and data processing. These studies led to publications on linear and nonlinear cryptographic schemes for computer systems.

REIN TURN received his B.S., M.S., and Ph.D. degrees in Engineering from the University of California at Los Angeles specializing in the design and applications of digital computer systems.

Since September 1963 he has been a member of the research staff of the Information Sciences and Mathematics Department of The Rand Corporation, Santa Monica, California. His work has included studies of man-computer interaction through computer graphics, applications of digital computers for the purposes of national defense, technological forecasting, and topics in switching theory.

Dr. Turn's involvement with privacy and security aspects of computerized information systems began with the publication, with H. E. Petersen, of the paper reprinted in these readings. Subsequently he co-authored two additional papers on this topic, participated in several seminars and panel discussions, and is now a co-principal investigator of a research project on theoretical and practical aspects of providing data confidentiality and security in computerized personal information databank systems.

CLARK WEISSMAN is a widely known authority in time-sharing, list-processing languages, computer networks, and secure computing. As Chief Technologist at System Development Corporation (SDC), he provides company-wide guidance and coordination of technological developments generated by independent and contract research activities and monitors technological developments elsewhere in industry and in government. Previously, as Manager of the Advanced Development Department, he directed the development of programming languages, processors, and operating systems, and was responsible for SDC's research and development efforts in natural-language processing, computer networking, and advanced time-sharing applications sponsored by the Advanced Research Projects Agency (ARPA) of the Department of Defense.

Mr. Weissman has been a member of the ARPA MULTICS Technical Review Board and was an ACM National Lecturer in 1967 and 1968. He is a member of the Association for Computing Machinery, the American Association for the Advancement of Science, and the Research Society of America. His technical papers include "A General-Purpose Time Sharing System," presented at the 1964 Spring Joint Computer Conference, and "Security Controls in the ADEPT-50 Time Sharing System," presented at the 1969 Fall Joint Computer Conference; each of these papers was named the outstanding conference paper. He is the author of LISP 1.5 Primer.

Mr. Weissman received his B.S. in Aeronautical Engineering from M.I.T. and has done graduate work and teaching in computer technology at UCLA.

ALAN F. WESTIN is a professor of Public Law and Government at Columbia University. He received his LLB from Harvard Law School and his Ph.D. in Political Science from Harvard University. He is a member of the District of Columbia Bar.

In addition to numerous other books he has authored or edited, Professor Westin has written about privacy in periodicals ranging from The Columbia Law Review and Communications of the Association for Computing Machinery to Playboy. His definitive work on the topic, Privacy and Freedom, won the Sidney Hillman Foundation book award, the George L. Polk award for the best book in public affairs, and the Frederick G. Melcher book award of the Unitarian-Universalist Association.

Dr. Westin has testified before several congressional committees and has been a consultant to, among other organizations, the United Nations Commission on Human Rights and the New York State Identification and Intelligence System. He is currently Chairman of the Privacy Committee of the American Civil Liberties Union and serves on its National Board of Directors. His recent work with Michael A. Baker, Databanks in a Free Society, describes the results of a three-year study on privacy and databanks he directed under the auspices of the Computer Science and Engineering Board of the National Academy of Sciences, under a grant from the Russell Sage Foundation.

INDEX